George Mercer Dawson, Alexander Sutherland

Elementary Geography of the British Colonies

George Mercer Dawson, Alexander Sutherland

Elementary Geography of the British Colonies

ISBN/EAN: 9783743347458

Manufactured in Europe, USA, Canada, Australia, Japa

Cover: Foto ©ninafisch / pixelio.de

Manufactured and distributed by brebook publishing software (www.brebook.com)

George Mercer Dawson, Alexander Sutherland

Elementary Geography of the British Colonies

PREFACE

THE portion of the present volume contributed by Dr. Dawson includes the British possessions in North America, the West Indies, and the southern part of the South Atlantic Ocean. It extends from the beginning to the end of the account of the Falkland Islands on p. 185. The remainder of the work, descriptive of the British colonies, dependencies, and protectorates in the northern part of the South Atlantic, Mediterranean Sea, Africa, Asia (exclusive of India and Ceylon, which are described in a separate volume of this Geographical Series, by Mr. H. F. Blanford), Australasia, and Oceania, has been written by Mr. Sutherland.

Illustrations for his part of the book have been supplied by Dr. Dawson, including some photographs taken by himself in the West. Another series of photographs has been furnished by Mr. Sutherland of characteristic scenes in Australia and New

Zealand. Six original drawings have been contributed by Mr. Pritchett (Figs. 21-26). These various illustrations have been engraved by Mr. J. D. Cooper. A few additional woodcuts have been supplied by the publishers from publications of which they have the copyright—viz. Figs. 20 and 29 from *The Cruise of H.M.S. Bacchante*, 1879-1882, compiled from the Private Journals, Letters, and Note-Books of Prince Albert Victor and Prince George of Wales, with additions by John N. Dalton; Figs. 27 and 28 from *The Straits Settlements and British Malaya*, by Sir Frederick Dickson, K.C.M.G. (*English Illustrated Magazine*); and Figs. 41-44 from *In New Guinea*, by Hume Nisbet (*English Illustrated Magazine*).

February 1892.

CONTENTS

	PAGE
I.—BRITISH NORTH AMERICA—	
Physical Geography and General Characteristics	1
II.—DOMINION OF CANADA AND NEWFOUNDLAND—	
Newfoundland	60
Dominion of Canada—	
(A.) Acadian Provinces	68
Nova Scotia	69
New Brunswick	78
Prince Edward Island	86
(B.) St. Lawrence Provinces	89
Quebec	90
Ontario	110
Manitoba	125
North-West Territory	131
North-East Territory	141
British Columbia	141
III.—THE WEST INDIAN COLONIES	159
The Bahamas	164
Jamaica	165

	PAGE
III.—THE WEST INDIAN COLONIES (*continued*)—	
Leeward Islands	169
The Windward Islands	172
Barbados	174
Trinidad	175
IV.—CENTRAL AMERICAN COLONY—	
British Honduras	178
V.—SOUTH AMERICAN COLONY—	
British Guiana	180
VI.—ATLANTIC ISLANDS—	
Bermuda	183
Falkland Islands	184
St. Helena, Ascension, Tristan d'Acunha	185
VII.—MEDITERRANEAN POSSESSIONS	187
VIII.—THE SOUTH AFRICAN COLONIES	191
Cape Colony	206
Natal	215
IX.—BRITISH WEST AFRICA	219
X.—BRITISH EAST AFRICA	224
XI.—POSSESSIONS IN THE RED AND ARABIAN SEAS AND INDIAN OCEAN	230
XII.—POSSESSIONS IN THE SOUTH-EAST OF ASIA	235

CONTENTS

		PAGE
XIII.—AUSTRALIA	.	243
New South Wales	.	277
Victoria	.	283
South Australia	.	289
Queensland	.	292
Western Australia	.	297
Tasmania	.	298
XIV.—NEW ZEALAND	.	301
XV.—PACIFIC ISLANDS	.	323

ILLUSTRATIONS

FIG.		PAGE
1.	SUMMER VIEW ON THE LEWES, A TRIBUTARY OF THE YUKON RIVER (LAT. 62°). From a Photograph by the Author	16
2.	SUMMER VIEW IN HUDSON STRAIT (LAT. 62°) WITH ESKIMO. From a Photograph by Dr. R. Bell	21
3.	BLACKFOOT INDIAN OF THE GREAT PLAINS. From a Photograph by Ross	37
4.	AHT INDIAN WOMAN OF THE COAST OF BRITISH COLUMBIA. From a Photograph	39
5.	SEALING STEAMERS IN THE ICE, HARBOUR GRACE, NEWFOUNDLAND. From the "Dominion Illustrated"	66
6.	HALIFAX, NOVA SCOTIA. From a Photograph by Notman	76
7.	ST. JOHN, NEW BRUNSWICK. From a Photograph by Notman	85
8.	MARGUERITE RIVER, A TRIBUTARY OF THE SAGUENAY, WITH BIRCH-BARK CANOE. From a Photograph by Topley	100
9.	CITY OF QUEBEC. From a Photograph by Topley	106
10.	MONTREAL, WINTER VIEW. From a Photograph by Notman	108
11.	MAP OF A SMALL PIECE OF THE LAURENTIAN PLATEAU-COUNTRY TO THE NORTH OF RAINY RIVER, ONTARIO	117

FIG.		PAGE
12.	KING STREET, TORONTO. From a Photograph by Notman	120
13.	PARLIAMENTARY BUILDINGS, OTTAWA, WITH RAFTS OF TIMBER ON THE RIVER. From a Photograph by Topley	122
14.	WHEAT FIELD ON THE MANITOBA PRAIRIE. From a Photograph	129
15.	VIEW ON THE GREAT PLAINS, WITH INDIAN ENCAMPMENT, WESTERN ASSINIBOIA. From a Photograph by the Author	137
16.	VIEW IN THE SELKIRK RANGE, BRITISH COLUMBIA, WHERE CROSSED BY THE CANADIAN PACIFIC RAILWAY. From a Photograph by Notman	145
17.	CAÑON OF THE FRASER RIVER WHERE IT BREAKS THROUGH THE COAST RANGE OF BRITISH COLUMBIA. From a Photograph by Notman	147
18.	FOREST OF DOUGLAS FIRS, VANCOUVER ISLAND. From a Photograph	155
19.	PART OF THE CITY OF VICTORIA, VANCOUVER ISLAND. From a Photograph by Notman	157
20.	JAMAICAN CACTUS AND PINGUIN HEDGES	162
21.	PORT ROYAL, JAMAICA	166
22.	PITCH LAKE, LA BREA, TRINIDAD	176
23.	GIBRALTAR	188
24.	TABLE MOUNTAIN AND DEVIL'S PEAK, CAPE OF GOOD HOPE	208
25.	ZANZIBAR	225
26.	MOMBASA—ENGLISH POINT	227
27.	SINGAPORE FROM THE EAST	236
28.	THE FISH MARKET, SINGAPORE	238

ILLUSTRATIONS

FIG.		PAGE
29.	Hong-Kong Locomotion	241
30.	South Head, and Entrance to Port Jackson	250
31.	Bridge over the Hawkesbury River, 3000 feet long	262
32.	Pitt Street, Sydney	278
33.	Bark Hut in Australia, with Aboriginals	282
34.	Collins Street, Melbourne	285
35.	King William Street, Adelaide	291
36.	Queensland—Prospectors' Camp	296
37.	Pembroke Mountains, Milford Sound, New Zealand	302
38.	Hall's Arm, Smith Sound, New Zealand	303
39.	A Maori	311
40.	Portobello, Otago Harbour	319
41.	Group of Fiji Men	325
42.	Peace Ornaments of New Guinea	326
43.	Weapons of New Guinea	327
44.	A Look into the Interior of New Guinea	329

I.—BRITISH NORTH AMERICA

PHYSICAL GEOGRAPHY AND GENERAL CHARACTERISTICS

a. **Geographical Position.**—The North American Continent is roughly triangular in **form, with** one angle pointing southward, where it is united **by a** narrow land connection with South America. **The base of** the triangle lies along the Arctic Circle, and the two remaining sides face **the Atlantic and** Pacific oceans respectively. **British North America** comprises the whole northern and wider half **of** this continent, with the exception of that part of its extreme north-western angle which is included in the Territory of Alaska. The various separate colonies and territories into which this part of the British Empire was formerly subdivided (except the Island of Newfoundland, which still remains a distinct colony) are now all politically united as the Dominion of Canada, **so** that the **name Canada**[1] **may be considered for** most general purposes **as** synonymous with British North America.

Though the area of British North America is nearly equal to that of Europe, more than one **half** of it **is** not suited

---

[1] The origin of the word **Canada** has long been a subject of discussion, but it **is** generally supposed **to** be **derived from an** Indian word meaning "a village." Cartier uses this **name for the** country of which Stadacona (Quebec) was the chief place.

to be the permanent habitation of civilised communities by reason of its northern position and rigorous climate. The fertile and habitable region of country has an average width of about 500 miles from south to north, but even of this but a small part is at all thickly peopled, and the entire number of inhabitants is thus yet insignificant as compared with the size and natural resources of the country. It results from this that the special consequences dependent on its geographical position, as a whole, have so far been only in part recognised or utilised.

While the 50th degree of north latitude passes through the extreme southern part of England, it will be found on tracing out that line on the map, that the whole southern border of British North America lies to the south of it. One projecting portion of Canada extends southward as far as latitude 42°, which parallel of latitude in Europe touches the southern extreme of France and passes near Rome. To the west, the same parallel nearly coincides with the position of Vladavostock at the southern limit of Russian territory on the Pacific. The 45th degree of latitude being that which is midway between the equator and the pole, it may thus be stated that nearly the entire area of British North America is comprised between this middle line and the polar regions.

A comparison such as has just been drawn between places in North America and Europe assists in fixing our ideas respecting position on the globe. But while identity in latitude implies a correspondence in length of day and night and other such astronomical conditions, it does not in itself lead to any accurate knowledge of the relative utility to man of places on the opposite sides of the Atlantic. This depends largely upon climate, which is a complex phenomenon, and in regard to which the British Islands and western part of the continent of Europe, in the exceptionally favourable climatic conditions which they enjoy, present a striking contrast to the eastern and inland portions of British North America in corresponding latitudes.

Because of the great width of the northern portion of North America, and the grouping together of the principal land-masses of the world about the Arctic region, the eastern end of British North America is much nearer to Europe than the rest of the continent, and the habitable portion on the west is similarly nearer on that side to the thickly-peopled regions of the east coast of Asia. Compared with other parts of the east coast of North America, the eastern extremity of British North America actually extends about one-third way across the Atlantic Ocean. It should further be noticed, however, in order to understand the relative positions of different portions of the American continents, that the line of longitude which touches the eastern extreme of British North America, in its southern prolongation, nearly bisects South America, while two-thirds of the western extent of British North America lies farther to the west than any portion of the Southern continent.

In common with other parts of the continent, British North America first became known and was peopled by civilised man on the Atlantic side, and the larger interests and trade of the continent have, since the earliest times, tended to unite it more and more closely with the older seats of commerce and population on the western seaboard of Europe. This depends also in part on the fact that the Atlantic is a much narrower ocean than the Pacific, and on the circumstances that most of the larger rivers of both continents flow into the Atlantic, while the long easy slopes and wide cultivable lands face toward that ocean on both sides. In British North America this is especially evidenced in the case of the great St. Lawrence river with its adjacent plains, which became the scene of the earliest settlements, and are still the seat of the chief centres of commerce and of manufactures.

Thus, while British North America may be described as practically closed toward the north by the rigorous conditions of the Arctic climate, it is open to the east, west, and south. The natural advantages of its geographical position were, in the earliest period of its history, utilised chiefly on its eastern side. At a later date commercial relations to the southward grew into importance, with that part of the continent now included in the United States, in which the first colonies soon reached an influential position; while on the Pacific coast population and trade began to plant themselves at a much later date, and can even at present be considered as only in their first growth.

With the aid of a globe, it will be clearly apparent that the shortest line between the commercial centres of Europe and those of the eastern part of Asia crosses the polar regions, but as these present a practically impassable barrier to commerce, the shortest practicable line lies across the Dominion of Canada. Within the last few years, by means of the construction of a transcontinental railway, a route available for purposes of communication has been opened across Canada, and the fact that the geographical position of that country enables it to be made an avenue of commerce between Europe and Asia, and to become a portion of the great east and west channel of trade around the world, has thus only begun to be appreciated or realised.

It is difficult to understand from a map alone, the advantage gained in distances by following, between two widely separated places on the globe, the line known as a great circle, instead of any other. In the particular case here under consideration, the distance from Liverpool to Yokahama in Japan by the Canadian route, *via* Quebec and Vancouver is 925 miles shorter than that *via* New York and San Francisco, the whole distance being 9946 miles by the first route, 10,871 miles by the second. This difference is accounted for by the approximate coincidence of the first route with a great circle, and the wider departure of the second from such a line.

Estimating the rate of travel by sea at 15 knots an hour only, and that by land at 35 miles an hour, the entire time required by the Canadian route would be $21\frac{1}{2}$ days as against 24 days by way of the United States, a saving of $2\frac{1}{2}$ days.

b. **Outer Form and Size.**—British North America is included between the 53d and 141st degrees of longitude west from Greenwich, being bounded on the east by the Atlantic and Davis Strait, on the west in part by the Pacific and in part by Alaska. Its southern boundary, separating it from the United States, follows a rather sinuous line between the 42d and 49th degrees of latitude, while it extends indefinitely northward, including the scarcely-known archipelago of the Polar Sea.

The total area of British North America, including Newfoundland and the barren Arctic Islands to the north of the continent, is 3,616,970 square miles. That of the Dominion of Canada proper, excluding the Colony of Newfoundland (42,000 square miles) and part of Labrador which is under the jurisdiction of that colony (estimated at 119,000 square miles) is 3,455,980 square miles, of which the Arctic Islands constitute 300,000 square miles.

Estimating the area of the entire British Empire, including the newly-acquired territories in Africa, at 11,355,057 square miles, it will be found that it comprises about one-fifth of the land surface of the globe. British North America constitutes one-third of the Empire by area; it is about 32,000 square miles larger than the United States, including Alaska, 200,000 square miles less in size than the whole of Europe, and nearly 445,000 square miles greater than Australasia, including New Zealand, part of New Guinea, and Fiji.

The greatest length of British North America is on a line drawn from the eastern point of Newfoundland in a west-north-westward direction to the Alaskan boundary, a distance of 3400 miles. A like distance, measured in an eastward direction from the same initial point in Newfoundland, would reach to beyond St. Petersburg.

The outline of the coast, which is everywhere much broken and indented, will best be understood by tracing it upon a map. It will be observed that from the eastern point of Newfoundland, the general trend of the coast is north-westward as far as the entrance to Hudson Bay, and south-westward to Nova Scotia and beyond. To the west of Hudson Bay the northern continental coast runs nearly west, approximately on the 70th degree of latitude; but as the channels which separate the closely-grouped Arctic Islands from the mainland are relatively narrow and not deep, these islands may be considered as in reality forming an extension of the continent, with which they have doubtless formed a single great land-mass at more than one former period of geological history.

The Pacific coast-line, beginning at the Strait of Fuca, runs north-north-westward to the southern extremity of Alaska on Dixon Entrance, a distance of 530 miles. It is characterised by extreme complexity in outline, resembling in this respect the west coasts of Greenland and Scandinavia, and has probably, following all its sinuosities, and including the coast-lines of its adjacent islands, a length of not less than 7000 miles. To the north of Dixon Entrance, for a farther distance of about 500 miles, the mainland coast belongs to Alaska, the boundary between the "coast-strip" of Alaska and the inland region which forms part of Canada, being drawn at a distance from the ocean never greater than 30 miles. The explanation of this peculiar boundary is found in the circumstance that it approximately marks the limit of trade as between the British and Russian Fur Companies in the early years of the century, at which time the line was determined by treaty, between Alaska (then Russian America) and the territory controlled by the Hudson's Bay Company. Farther north, the boundary between Canada and Alaska lies on the 141st degree of longitude, and bears no relation to natural features.

Hudson Bay and the Gulf of St. Lawrence are the most notable extensions of the Atlantic into the North American continent, and of these Hudson Bay is much the larger. Its size and position have suggested the application to it of the name of the "Mediterranean of North America." Notwithstanding its great area, however, and the extent of its penetration into the heart of Canada, its importance in connection with the history and development of the country has so far been small. This depends in part on the fact that its approaches are not only closed by ice in winter, but are likewise obstructed to a considerable degree, even in summer, by the icebergs and floe-ice of Davis Strait, in part on the circumstance that the shores of the Bay itself are generally unattractive and barren. But for these unfavourable conditions, the geographical position of this inland sea might have enabled it to become the main avenue of approach to the northern part of the continent, as the ports on the western side of the Bay, though so nearly in the centre of the land-mass, are actually about 100 miles nearer to Liverpool in sailing distance than New York on the eastern coast of the United States. Of late years it has been proposed to utilise this northern route, and, as the population of the west increases, it will doubtless become important notwithstanding the shortness of the season of navigation.

The Gulf of St. Lawrence, with the inland water communication of which it is the entrance, has, on the contrary, formed the most important line of approach to the interior of Canada since the earliest period of its history, and it will be found that the events of this history may be explained in great part as consequences of this geographical feature. But even the river St. Lawrence is entirely closed to navigation during the winter months, the only eastern ports of Canada which are continuously open to shipping being those of the south coast of Nova Scotia and of New Brunswick.

The existence of the great inland sea named Hudson Bay constitutes the most marked difference in respect to form between Canada and the United States, the territory included by the last-named country being an almost unbroken land area. The greatest area of unbroken continental land in Canada lies to the west of the middle line of the country, between Hudson Bay and the Pacific Coast. The Saskatchewan plains occupy the centre of this area, no part of which is distant more than 700 miles from some sea-coast.

Following the line of boundary by which Canada is separated from the United States, it will be observed that the eastern part of this line, from the Lake of the Woods, nearly in the centre of the continent, to the Atlantic, is very irregular; while the western part is perfectly straight, and lies upon the 49th degree of latitude all the way from the Lake of the Woods to the Pacific. The explanation of this difference is found in the circumstance that at the time the line was agreed upon, the eastern portion of the continent was already pretty well known and partly settled, while the western was almost unknown. The whole length of the southern boundary is about 3260 miles, and the difference just referred to will be rendered clearly apparent when it is stated that of the line to the east of the Lake of the Woods, 2000 miles in length, all but 200 miles coincides with natural features such as lakes, rivers, and watersheds. It so happens, however, that though the part of this boundary to the west of the Lake of the Woods was arbitrarily fixed, it was found, on the subsequent exploration of the country, to agree very nearly for a great portion of its length with the position of the watershed between the rivers flowing to Hudson Bay on the north, and those tributary to the Mississippi on the south.

c. **Configuration.**—As compared with the general surface features of Europe and Asia, those of North America are simple and broad. This is most clearly shown in the contrast presented by the mountain systems in the two cases, these representing geological lines of disturbance and uplift of the earth's crust, and being the governing features of the configuration of the land. In Europe and Asia the mountain systems are numerous and varied in trend, in North America few and direct. The convergence toward the south of the two sides of the North American land has already been noted, and the inspection of any good map will at once show that two principal mountain systems give form to the opposite coasts. Each of these mountain systems is composed of several more or less distinct ranges, which are known in different parts of their length by many different names. The general name for the mountains bordering the eastern coast is, however, the Appalachian system, while those which form a belt along the west coast are often collectively known as the Rocky Mountains, but are more correctly termed the Cordilleran system.

Of these two dominant mountain systems, that of the western side of the continent is much the more important, being, in fact, one of the principal mountain systems of the world. The Appalachians, indeed, when compared with the Cordillera, seem scarcely to deserve to be ranked as a mountain system, but they are nevertheless notable

as contrasted with the lowlands in **their vicinity, and
because of their effect not only** on the outer form **of the
continent, but also on** its drainage system, **and on the
history** of its occupation and settlement by civilised man.
The great influence of the Appalachian system **on the
surface** features is largely explained by the fact **that the
date** of its origin lies far back in geological **time.** The
crumpling and fracture of the earth's crust, **which** produced its ranges, had for a long **time been** practically completed before the similar disturbances which gave **form to**
most of the present bold features of the western Cordillera
had begun. In consequence of the **great age of the**
Appalachian **ranges** their original height has been very
much reduced by rain, rivers, and other natural agents of
waste, so that they are now but remnants of their former
selves.

The **Appalachian** system may be traced from **a point
not** far to the north of the Gulf of Mexico, in a northeasterly bearing, parallel to the shore of the United **States,**
and thence through parts of the Provinces of **Quebec, New
Brunswick, and, in a much reduced form, on to Newfoundland.** The peninsula of Nova Scotia is regarded as representing part of an elevation parallel to the **main ridges of**
the Appalachians and belonging to the **same system.** The
Cordilleran system forms a wide belt of strictly mountainous
country, which constitutes the entire high western border
of the continent.

In the southern half of the continent the region between
these two great mountain systems may be described as a
vast inland plain, broken by but a few irregular mountain
ranges, and sloping gradually up toward the higher plateaux
which join the base of the Cordillera on the west. In
tracing this plain to the northward, however, **we find that
its eastern part extends** no farther than to the **Great Lakes,**
while its western portion stretches on continuously, **though**
with decreasing width, to **the Arctic Ocean.** The partial
interruption of the great **interior plain** in Canada is due
to the existence and position of **the Laurentian** plateau,
which, as a physical feature, is scarcely second in importance to the Cordillera itself. The name of this plateau is

derived from that given to the old crystalline rocks of which it is chiefly composed, these, in turn, having been named from the St. Lawrence river, in the vicinity of which they were first recognised by geologists.

The Laurentian plateau, in certain places rugged and irregular, and sometimes incorrectly spoken of as a mountain range, has an average elevation of about 1500 feet only, and is several hundred miles in width. There is, however, every reason to believe that though now reduced to the condition of an irregular plateau of moderate elevation, this region holds the position of a former very ancient mountain system, much older even than the Appalachian system, which has gradually been worn down and has been the source of the material of a large part of the newer rocks of the continent. It represents the largest remaining portion of the oldest known beginning of the North American land-mass.

This plateau presents some peculiar physical characteristics, which are referred to elsewhere (see p. 94). Here it is necessary only to note its extent and form with its relation to the other main features of Canada. This is most easily done by examining a geological map of the continent, on which the colour representing the oldest rocks may be taken as defining in a general way the limits of the Laurentian plateau. It will be observed that the region thus marked out has a horse-shoe-like form surrounding the great central depression of Hudson Bay, and running from the Labrador Peninsula at one end to the Arctic Ocean at the other. The southern edge of the plateau forms the north side of the Gulf and River St. Lawrence nearly as far up as the city of Quebec, beyond which its main outline runs to the north shore of Lake Huron, and thence along the north side of Lake Superior to the Lake of the Woods and Lake Winnipeg, whence it continues in a north-westward direction to within the Arctic circle. It will further be remarked that all the great lakes of Canada lie on or near the southern or south-western margin of this plateau.

Having thus traced out the dominant physical features of the northern part of the continent, we are in a position

to understand the principal characteristics of the surface
of Canada. No classification of these can be complete or
correct in every particular, but as an aid to the compre-
hension of the broader aspects of the country it may be
divided as follows: (1) Eastern lowlands and hills, including the entire region to the south of the Laurentian
plateau east of Lake Huron. This is almost entirely
based on old and hard rocks included in the Palæozoic
division of geologists. (2) The Laurentian plateau, with
the limits above given, and consisting of still older and
harder crystalline rocks. (3) The inland plains, comprised
between the western part of the Laurentian plateau and
the Cordillera, and principally based on the comparatively
soft rocks of the Mesozoic or middle period of geological
history, which still lie nearly as flat as when they were
originally deposited. (4) The Cordilleran or western
mountain region.

Lying open as the region of the eastern lowlands and
hills does to communication with the Old World, it was
the first to be occupied by colonists, and is still more
thickly peopled than other parts of the country. In
consequence of the rough and rocky character of much of
the Laurentian plateau it has been only in small part,
and by slow degrees, penetrated by settlement, while it
forms an almost complete barrier to the connected spread
of agriculture where it borders on the Great Lakes. It is
thus only of late years that the fertile region of the inland
plain of Canada has been reached by any considerable
number of settlers, and the population to be found there
is still very scanty in comparison to the area and to the
extent of arable and pasture land. The distance separating
the western mountain region from the earlier settlements
of the eastern part of the continent is so great that, like
the inland plain, it long remained practically unknown
except to the fur trader. But the discovery of gold in
British Columbia initiated a flow of adventurers and
miners to this region, which they were enabled to reach
by sea from the west.

d. **Drainage System.**—In order to complete a general
survey of the surface features of Canada it will now be

necessary to note the principal elements of **the drainage system.** Further details are given in connection with the various **provinces, but** several of the larger rivers extend through more than one of these. **There is** perhaps no single feature more characteristic of Canadian topography **than** the length and magnitude of the rivers, and the **manner** in which these, with thousands of smaller tributary **streams fed by** countless lakes, penetrate **the** country in **all** its parts.

There are in North America three great hydrographic basins corresponding to the **three sides** of the triangular land-mass—the Atlantic, **Pacific,** and Arctic. Of these the Atlantic basin is further subdivided into that of the Atlantic proper, and that of the Gulf of Mexico; the Arctic into that of the Arctic proper, and that of Hudson Bay. Rivers belonging **to** all these **systems** with their subdivisions **are found within** the **limits of** Canada, but those flowing **to the Gulf of** Mexico **merely enter the southern border of the country, while those of both sub-**divisions of the Arctic basin are almost wholly **included in** it. The slope of the continent towards the **Pacific is** short and steep, and its rivers are consequently, as a rule, comparatively small and rapid, and only occasionally, and for short distances, suited to navigation. Much the **greater** part of Canada drains toward the Arctic or Atlantic, and on both these slopes we find very large **rivers with relatively moderate** currents and long unbroken **navigable stretches.**

Beginning on **the** Atlantic side, and again referring to the map, it will be observed that in the United States the inland slopes of the Appalachians are drained by tributaries of the Mississippi, while on the Atlantic slope proper, all the way from Florida to the **Gulf of St.** Lawrence, there are numerous short and small **rivers draining a** belt of **country,** which has **a width of 50 to 200 miles** only. **Coming** to the St. Lawrence, however, we **find** a river of **the first** magnitude, which rises almost **in the** centre of **the** continent, and is the outlet of the greatest system **of lakes in the** world. **The whole** history of Canada is intimately connected with this great river, by means of which pioneers starting from Quebec or Montreal had overrun a great part of the interior of the continent before the settlers of the Atlantic coast had crossed the Appalachians. The length of the St. Lawrence measuring from the lower end of the Island of Anticosti to its farthest source is 2100 miles, and the area drained by it 530,000 square miles (see p. 89).

To the north of the St. Lawrence basin the Labrador peninsula is drained by a number of large rivers, some of which are as much as 400 miles in length. Most of these flow westward and form part of a converging series of rivers which tend toward Hudson Bay from all sides. The most important of the rivers entering Hudson Bay is, however, the Nelson. This great river is the outlet of Lake Winnipeg and other large neighbouring lakes which receive the waters of the Saskatchewan, Red, and Winnipeg rivers, besides many smaller streams. While the Nelson itself runs across the Laurentian plateau, and the Winnipeg and some smaller tributaries rise within the area of this plateau, its larger feeders come from the west, the Saskatchewan drawing its waters even from the Cordillera. These western tributaries drain almost the whole southern portion of the Canadian part of the interior plain. This great river system was at one time the principal route for the fur trade of the Hudson's Bay Company. The length of the Nelson and Saskatchewan rivers is together about 1250 miles, the entire area of the drainage basin of the Nelson within the boundaries of Canada being 367,000 square miles.

The Mackenzie river flows directly to the Arctic Ocean, and with the Nelson and Mississippi shares in draining the interior plain of the continent. Its drainage basin is not, however, confined to this plain, but overlaps the Laurentian plateau on the east, and the Cordillera on the west, the manner in which some of its tributaries rise far back in the Cordillera belt being particularly remarkable. Its principal affluents are the Peace (length 730 miles), Athabasca[1] (length 600 miles), Liard[2] (length 470 miles),

[1] An Indian name meaning a grassy swamp, and probably referring to the marshes at the mouth of the river.
[2] French, *Rivière au Liard*, "Cottonwood river."

Great Bear and Peel. All these are themselves large rivers, and the main stream carries an enormous volume of water to the north. Athabasca and Great Slave Lakes, two of the largest of those previously noted as lying on the western margin of the Laurentian plateau, are on the main stream of the Mackenzie, and a third, Great Bear Lake, discharges into it by a short river. The Mackenzie constitutes the chief means of communication in the country through which it flows, but has never served as a route from the sea, because of the quantity of Arctic ice which blocks its mouth. The length of the Mackenzie is about 1800 miles, the area of its drainage basin 677,000 square miles.

The last of the great rivers which requires special mention in connection with the general surface features of Canada is the Yukon. This drains the greater portion of the northern part of the Cordillera belt. Its drainage basin slopes northward for the upper half of its length, and in reality belongs to the Arctic slope of the continent; but in the lower portion of its course the river makes an abrupt bend to the west, and flowing across the entire breadth of Alaska, eventually reaches the Pacific instead of the Arctic Ocean. The country drained by this great river is yet almost uninhabited, except by a scanty native population and a few roaming gold miners and traders. The river has therefore never assumed any importance as a means of communication, though much of it is navigable. The length of the Yukon is about 1450 miles, the area of its drainage basin about 331,000 square miles; but of this about one-half is comprised in the territory of Alaska.

Other rivers of the Pacific slope of Canada are mentioned in connection with British Columbia (p. 150), within which province their entire courses are included. The Fraser is the most important of these.

There are thus in Canada four great rivers of the first class—the St. Lawrence, Nelson, Mackenzie, and Yukon; but in addition to these there are many others which would in any less extensive and less well-watered region rank as important streams. By tracing on the map the courses of the remaining larger streams, and noting their relations to the four principal drainage basins just outlined, the manner in which all parts of the country are permeated by interlocking streams and water-ways will become apparent. There is in Canada no wide unwatered or streamless area, nor any great inland basin into which rivers flow and disappear by evaporation.

e. Climate.—Were climate dependent on latitude alone, that of all the southern and more important part of British North America should be much alike; but climate is in reality affected by all the circumstances of geographical position, including the latitude as of first importance, but embracing as well a number of modifying influences. Thus, as a matter of fact, climatic differences of great practical importance occur even in various parts of the southern half of Canada, while it is the distinctively Arctic character of the climate of the extreme northern parts of the continent which renders these unfit for permanent settlement. It is therefore not possible to speak of the climate of Canada as a whole with any degree of accuracy, and in order to understand the climatic conditions it is necessary to consider the influence of the adjacent oceans and to divide the intervening land area into districts similarly affected by these and other causes.

The only general statement which can be made respecting the climate is that it is for the most part of the "continental," as distinguished from the "oceanic" or "insular" type. This term is applied to the climates of the larger land-masses of the world in which the difference in temperature between the summer and winter months is very great. Thus over a large part of the interior of Canada the range in temperature is about 70°, while in England, which may be taken as an example of an oceanic climate in similar latitudes, the range is about 25° only. The climate of no part of Canada is however so typically continental as that of the region in the centre of the greater land-mass of Asia where the range exceeds 90°. There is also one comparatively limited region on the Pacific coast which enjoys an oceanic climate.

Without further considering the Arctic climate of the extreme north, with its prolonged and rigorous winter and

FIG. 1.—SUMMER VIEW ON THE LEWES, A TRIBUTARY OF THE YUKON RIVER (LAT. 62°). From a Photograph by the Author.

short though rather warm summer (which is, however, quite insufficient for the growth of cereals or other food plants), the greater part of Canada may, in respect to climate, be divided into three regions as follows : (1) The eastern region, characterised by great range of temperature and ample rainfall. This includes all the older provinces of Canada, with Newfoundland, and extends westward nearly to Winnipeg. It is naturally the great forest region. (2) The inland region, joining the last and stretching westward to within a short distance of the Pacific coast, embracing Manitoba, the North-West Territory and the greater part of British Columbia. This is characterised by very great range in temperature and moderate rainfall, with a tendency to aridity in certain tracts of its central and southern part. It includes the great prairies and open plains, but is also in large part more or less wooded. Where it overlaps the mountains of the Cordillera belt it loses its uniform character, the climate becoming varied and strongly contrasted within short distances under the influence of the bold features of the surface. (3) The Pacific coast region. This does not include the whole "Pacific slope," but a narrow belt only on the seaward side of the western mountain range of the Cordillera. The climate is here oceanic, with small range of temperature, and great rainfall and humidity.

It is interesting to note the effect of the high and wide mountain region of the west coast of Canada in confining the main part of the influence of the Pacific Ocean on the climate to quite narrow limits, and to contrast this with the conditions on the corresponding coast of Europe, where the absence of such a barrier permits the westerly winds from the Atlantic to modify the climate far inland.

Though it is convenient to divide the climatic regions of Canada in the way here done, it must be remembered that there is in most cases a gradual blending of each into the next. The sharpest line is that which bounds the Pacific coast climate, and this is definite only because it coincides with a mountain range.

To understand the causes which produce the climatic differences of the several regions, it is necessary to observe the relations which the northern part of the continent holds to the atmospheric circulation generally, and for this purpose some knowledge of the known laws of this circulation must be assumed. In applying this to the region in question, with due regard to its physical features, a ready explanation will be found for most of the local differences of climate which cannot here be spoken of in detail.

The circulation of the atmosphere, as a whole, depends on the varying amounts of heat received by different parts of the globe, from the equatorial regions to the poles, and Canada lies in the great belt of the anti-trade winds of the northern hemisphere, which tend to blow from south-west to north east. The continental lands of the northern hemisphere, because of the difference in amount of heat retained or lost by them as compared with the oceans, interfere with the regularity of the anti-trades, and this to so great a degree that the chief features of the winds and climate of Canada result from this secondary cause. The cold condition of the continent in winter, and the greater warmth of the northern parts of the Pacific and Atlantic at this season, produce a large constant area of great atmospheric pressure or high barometer in the western interior of the continent, while equally important areas of deficient pressure or low barometer are formed over the oceans to the east and west. In midsummer these conditions are exactly reversed, the heated land-surface causing an area of low pressure, while the cooler neighbouring oceans show an excess of pressure. The difference between the pressure in summer and in winter in the centre of the continent is equal to about four-tenths of an inch, as measured by the barometer, or nearly one-seventieth of the whole weight of the atmosphere.

It will be remembered that while the air tends to flow from areas of high to those of low pressure, it does not in so doing follow a direct line, but assumes a spiral course to such a degree that it may be considered as circulating around these areas with a downward and outward tendency in areas of high pressure, and an inward and upward tendency in those of low pressure. The direction of motion of the air in the northern hemisphere is with that of the hands of a watch in the first case, and against it in the second. Such great areas of high and low pressure affect the course of the winds, which again govern the rainfall, and have much to do with the direction of the ocean currents. These in turn react on the temperature itself, and all together go to produce the climatic conditions of any particular region.

The effect of these ruling areas of high and low pressure on the climate of Canada will be best understood by outlining those which have been described upon a couple of maps, and marking the directions which the winds should follow round them by a number of arrows. The cause of the prevalent north-west winds of the eastern provinces in winter will then be clearly apparent. Such winds have previously traversed a great extent of frigid Arctic lands at the season when the loss of heat from radiation is greatest. They are consequently very cold, and as they are advancing from colder to warmer latitudes they are likewise dry winds, incapable of precipitating much moisture. On the west coast of Canada at the same season the conditions are different, being the same with those of the similarly situated coast of Europe. The prevailing winds are here from the south-west. They are warm and moist, having crossed a great width of ocean surface, and as they advance into colder latitudes they deposit much of their moisture in the form of rain. The rainfall on the coast of British Columbia is moreover still further increased by the mountainous character of the land against which these winds flow. In the area of high pressure of the western interior of the country, the cloudless sky, characteristic of such areas, by favouring radiation, increases the cold; but in the western part of the region the general average of the temperature is raised by the frequent occurrence of strong winds, which blow across the Cordillera, and liberate heat as they become condensed on descending from the level of the mountains to that of the plains. These peculiar winds are known as "Chinook winds," and exercise an important influence on the climate of the inland plain.

In the summer months the reversal in the positions of

the areas of high and low barometer produces a quite different system of winds. Thus in the eastern provinces of Canada southerly winds prevail; and these, laden with moisture from the southern Atlantic, or Gulf of Mexico, as they advance into higher latitudes, produce the copious summer rains which are a notable feature of this region. As these winds meet with no high mountain range in their course, the rainfall which they cause decreases gradually and nearly uniformly inland from the south-eastern border of the continent; and as a smaller amount of moisture is sufficient for vegetation in the northern latitudes, it follows that the distribution thus resulting corresponds as nearly as possible with the requirements of the country.

On the west coast, at the same season, the North Pacific area of high pressure slightly overlaps the southern part of British Columbia, and gives rise to dry, cool, north-westerly winds in that part of the province. These winds are not dry merely because of their advance from cooler to warmer latitudes, but also because of the descending tendency found in the currents of an area of high barometer, in consequence of which they have not traversed the surface of any great breadth of sea before reaching the coast. The northern part of the coast of British Columbia, with that of Alaska, being at a greater distance from the Pacific area of high barometer, has, at the same time, prevailing westerly winds highly charged with moisture; and as a result of this, the rainfall of July is there twice as great as that of the southern part of the coast.

In the region of the great interior plains, the summer rainfall is in part afforded by southerly winds belonging to the same system with those which blow across the eastern provinces; but, as in order to reach the plains these traverse a great extent of land, the quantity of moisture which they are able to bring with them is small, and would doubtless alone be insufficient for the growth of crops. The position of the great mid-continental evaporative surface of Hudson Bay is, however, such that it supplies a notable addition, relieving the Canadian plains from the conditions of aridity which affect the corresponding region farther to the south, and causing them to be specially favoured in this

FIG. 2.—SUMMER VIEW IN HUDSON STRAIT (LAT. 62°) WITH ESKIMO. From a Photograph by Dr. R. Bell.

respect as contrasted with other inland regions. The driest part of the plains lies not far to the east of the Cordillera region.

The **temperature of different** parts of the country at **various seasons**, or the mean temperature of the year, is best shown by lines drawn through places having corresponding temperatures, and known as isothermal lines. The temperature depends not only on the position of each place in latitude, but also upon the direction and character of the prevailing winds, the height above sea-level, and other circumstances, among which, in the vicinity of the coast, the warmth of the sea-water is important. The Pacific coast of Canada is bathed by the Japan current, which in the Pacific is the representative of the Gulf Stream of the Atlantic (Fig. 1). The eastern coast, on the contrary, is chilled by a cold Arctic current coming from Davis Strait and the east coast of Greenland, which in the spring and summer brings much ice down with it (Fig. 2). The effect of these ocean waters does not make itself felt far inland unless conveyed thither by the winds, but in conjunction with the winds their influence is considerable. Thus the Arctic current just referred to has a noteworthy effect in reducing the normal temperature of Nova Scotia and Newfoundland in June and July.[1]

In the case of an extreme or continental climate the mean annual isothermals give a very imperfect idea of the temperature characteristics. What has already been said will prepare the student to find that over the greater part of Canada the isothermal lines hold widely different positions in summer and in winter. The facts may be seen on comparing two maps upon which these lines are drawn for July and for January. From a practical point of view the summer isotherms are the most important, as on the duration and intensity of summer heat the possibility of the growth of the various crops depends. The interior of Canada, to the west of its centre, is the region in which the summer and winter temperatures are most widely con-

---

[1] The two views, Figs. 1 and 2, taken in the same latitude, the former on the eastern, the latter on the western side of the continent, illustrate the difference of the summer climate in those regions.

trasted. The summer isothermal lines are here thrust up very far to the north-west, following the great inland plain and showing the occurrence of favourable temperatures in this vast area of fertile land.

It may help our conception of this important fact in climate to trace out one such isothermal line across the continent; and for this purpose we may take the line which represents a mean temperature of 60° in July. This may be assumed as a roughly approximate northern limit of practicable agriculture of any kind. Such a line passes through Newfoundland, and, touching the island of Anticosti, runs to the north end of Lake Mistassini. It then crosses the southern extremity of Hudson Bay, cutting the west shore of the bay, near the mouth of the Nelson. Thence it runs westward, striking the north end of Reindeer Lake, and then, bending to the north-west, crosses Great Slave Lake, and touches the southern point of Great Bear Lake. From this point it resumes a westward course, and crosses the Yukon river, a considerable distance to the north of the confluence of the Pelly and Lewes. Thence it makes a remarkable return to the south till it approaches the Pacific coast, and thereafter follows that coast southward to beyond the southern limit of Canada.

This last long southerly trend of the isotherm is particularly interesting in showing that similar temperatures are here found along a north and south line, instead of in their normal position along a line of latitude. Nothing could better illustrate the modifying influence of the cool summer winds from the Pacific. After reaching the Pacific coast, however, the particular line which we have been following ceases to be of any value as an indication of the conditions of agriculture, as it is no longer in a region of continental, but in one of oceanic, climate.

The comparatively local atmospheric disturbances known as storms are quite distinct from those larger features which have been explained above. It will be sufficient to note respecting such disturbances that in Canada, as elsewhere in similar latitudes in the northern hemisphere, the usual path of storm centres is from west to east, governed in great measure by the main direction of the anti-trade current.

There is, however, another important class of storms which originate near the West Indies, and travelling northward and then north-eastward either cross the eastern part of the United States, or sweep the seaboard, till they reach the eastern provinces of Canada. Such storms are often most destructive to shipping on the coasts of Nova Scotia and Newfoundland.

The effect of the continental climate of **Canada** on navigation is important. The cold of winter **results** in **the** closing by ice of all the rivers and lakes **as** well as the canals and some of the seaports. Thus the **St.** Lawrence is practically closed for about five months of **the** year, the average season of navigation extending from the latter part of April **to** the latter part of November. During the winter **the** Gulf of St. Lawrence and its approaches **are** also encumbered with **floating ice, and** for a certain period in each **year** all the **seaports as** far south as the eastern extremity **of Nova Scotia are** inaccessible. To this rule, however, **places on the eastern or** outer **coast of** Newfoundland, including **the harbour of St. John's, are** exceptions, and communication **is also** kept up between the mainland and **Prince Edward** Island by specially constructed steamers. The ports of the east coast **of** Canada which are open throughout the year are those **of** the outer coast of Nova Scotia and the southern coast of New Brunswick, **and of** these **the** most important are Halifax and St. John.

It is also to be noted that the Arctic current brings **down each** spring many icebergs and much floe-ice, which **in some** years drift far **south in** the western **part of the** Atlantic before they disappear. This ice **renders the** entrance by the Strait of Belle Isle uncertain in the spring. The length of the season of navigation by way of Hudson Strait and through Hudson Bay has not yet been accurately determined, **but** it is **believed** that it is sufficiently long to enable this route **to become** eventually important.

In the central inland regions of Canada the rivers and **lakes are** navigable for a period not exceeding six months, **and this is** still further reduced in the extreme north. On the **Pacific** coast, in consequence chiefly of the warm waters **of** the Japan current, none **of** the seaports are closed by ice at any season.

f. **Plants and Animals.**—The plants and animals to be found in any particular region in a state of nature, depend largely upon the climate of the region, and in comparing the flora and fauna of different parts of a wide uninterrupted land area like Canada, the diversity met with is attributable almost entirely to this cause. This is so much the case in respect to the plants that these may be employed as a rough index of the meteorology of any particular place in the absence of proper observations. Animals are not quite so trustworthy as an indication of climate, for some of them migrate with the seasons, and others make provision during the summer for the winter months, or hibernate. If, however, we compare the plants and animals of Canada or of North America, as a whole, with those of other large land areas of the world, a much greater degree of diversity is found, and this is the case even if we confine our comparison to places similarly situated in latitude and with similar climates. This fundamental diversity depends on the circumstance that the spread and migrations of plants and animals from one to another of the principal land areas of the world has been much impeded, or, in some cases, altogether prevented by dividing oceans or climatic barriers, which they have been unable to cross. From a comparison of the forms of life indigenous to different countries naturalists have been led to divide the whole land-surface of the world into regions which possess more or less clearly distinct characters. The North American continent is one of these regions, while Europe, together with the greater part of Asia and a small part of the north of Africa, forms another. The first is known as the Nearctic, the second (Eurasia) as the Palæarctic region—names referring to their respective positions in the so-called new and old hemispheres, and not implying that the forms of life met with in one are necessarily older than those of the other. These two regions resemble each other more closely than any others, while the Australian region is the most different from either of them.

The general resemblance of the plants and animals of North America and Eurasia, though it depends in part on similarity of climate, is such as to imply also that at some former period a land connection must have existed, and there is reason to believe that this connection was formed between the northern parts of Canada and those of Europe and Asia. The oceans on both sides are, as we have seen, comparatively narrow to the north, and are besides, not so deep there as elsewhere, so that a relatively small elevation of the sea-bed might produce such land bridges to the east and west. That such a connection was really formed is rendered still more probable by the fact that the plants and animals of the Arctic regions are nearly the same in both hemispheres, while distinct species become more abundant farther to the south. It is also to be noted, that if the forms of life of the temperate latitudes in the two hemispheres were interchanged by such a land connection, the climate to the north must at one time have been much less rigorous than it is now. The consideration of these circumstances, in fact, affords an interesting glimpse of a former period in which the geographical features differed much from those now existing.

When North America was first discovered by Europeans it was found that the native peoples, who were few in number and for the most part mere savages, had effected little change by cultivation or otherwise on the life of the country; and there is nothing to show that any plants or animals not indigenous to the continent were in their possession, or had been introduced by them. Within the limits of Canada the natives, generally called "Indians," cultivated in a few places, and on a small scale, maize or Indian corn, beans, pumpkins, and tobacco—plants which naturally belonged to more southern latitudes, but which are all indigenous to the New World. The only domesticated animal of the Indians of Canada was the dog. With the colonisation of the country began the introduction of plants and animals useful to civilised man; and some of these found the new conditions so well adapted to them that they ran wild, while others continue to require cultivation and care. Even now, however, the introduced plants and animals have spread only partially over a limited area of Canada, and though many of the native animals have become restricted in their range by being driven back into the wilder districts, or because systematically hunted for food or for their skins, none of them have been altogether extirpated, with the single exception of the great auk, a large, slow sea-bird which once inhabited islands near Newfoundland in great numbers. The bison or buffalo is, however, an example of a large and important animal which is now on the verge of extinction.

It is thus not at all difficult to state exactly which species of plants and animals are indigenous in Canada; and it is still easy to realise the appearance of all parts of the country when in a state of nature, even in the case of those districts of the eastern provinces which have been longest under cultivation.

As characteristic features of the flora of the northern part of the continent included in Canada, the great number of species of aster, solidago or golden-rod, and vaccinium or whortleberry, may be mentioned, with the comparative scarcity of those kinds of plants classed as umbelliferæ and cruciferæ.

Generally speaking, Canada is naturally a great forest region, and in the eastern provinces nearly all the land under cultivation has been cleared of trees by man. To this characteristically forest-clad character, however, two notable exceptions are found. Far to the north the forests are limited by the shortness of summer and the cold of winter, this limit following approximately the mean annual isothermal of 20°. Thus the northern part of the Labrador peninsula, with another great area to the west of Hudson Bay, bounded by a line drawn from the middle of the west shore of the bay to the mouth of the Mackenzie, is practically treeless. This northern region includes the desolate "Barren Grounds," distinguished by the abundance of mosses, lichens, saxifrages, gentians, willows, and other Arctic plants. The Arctic Islands to the north of the continent are entirely treeless.

The second exceptional unwooded region is that of the southern part of the inland plain, extending from the Red River, in the centre of the continent, westward to the

Rocky Mountains, and continuously northward, **though with decreasing** breadth, **to** the North Saskatchewan. Still **farther northward,** following the interior plain, smaller, more **or less** completely separated prairie tracts continue to occur, but the greater part **of** the surface be**comes** wooded. The treeless character of **this great region is primarily** due to its small rainfall, but its limits have been enlarged by almost annually-recurring **prairie fires—a** result which is doubtless the most important of those which can be traced to the native population. **These** open plains never possess desert characters **within the** limits of Canada, but are naturally clothed with nutritious grasses such as those named buffalo-grass and bunch-grass. They were the home and pasture-ground of the buffalo. Much of their area is adapted to agriculture, and already **fields of grain are replacing the** natural grasses, and **domestic cattle the buffalo.** The open plains separate the **Atlantic forests of the east** from the Pacific forests of the Cordillera ; but while **in the United States the separation between** these two **forest regions is complete, they join** and intermingle **to the north of the great prairie within the limits of Canada.**

Thus it happens that the trees and plants **characteristic of** these forest regions are not so distinct **as** they are farther to the south, such of them as are capable of enduring considerable winter cold being found in both regions. **There is nevertheless a very marked difference** in character **between** the southern parts of the Atlantic and **Pacific forests in** Canada, the most striking point being the **abundance** of round-headed, deciduous-leaved trees in the **east,** while spiry evergreens **of the pine and** spruce kind prevail almost exclusively in the **west.** There is besides a much greater variety **of** trees in the **Atlantic forest region** than in that of the Pacific. Thus **in the southern part of the** province of Ontario sixty-five species of trees are **known.** Of these **thirty-four occur in parts** of the province **of Quebec** and the Acadian provinces, while about fourteen **only** range westward to the vicinity of the Red River. In British Columbia there are about thirty-four species of trees, and of these but six are common **to the Atlantic** forest region, while the rest are peculiar to the Pacific forests. There are, however, in the two regions many representative trees which differ only in minor points from each other.

To the south of the Arctic treeless country the existence and characters of the forests depend chiefly on the amount of rainfall. The ample rains of the eastern provinces produce the Atlantic forest region, but this, though often dense, cannot compare in this respect, or in the size of its trees, with the rich and superb forests of that part of the Pacific coast region in which conditions of great humidity are combined with a long season of growth. This sub-region of gigantic and exceptionally dense forests is confined, however, to a narrow strip along the Pacific coast—the same which has already been described as enjoying an oceanic climate. It is interesting further to note that the southern part of this particular sub-region differs considerably from the northern in containing a number of peculiar plants, of which the western oak and arbutus may be specially mentioned. The latter is the only broad-leaved evergreen tree found in Canada. The limited range of these trees, with that of other plants and some animals which accompany them, depends upon the peculiar climatic conditions of the corresponding part of the coast, referred to on p. 19.

In the Pacific forest region, with few exceptions, the coniferous forest trees alone are of commercial value, but in the Atlantic region the wood of many kinds of trees is employed, though here also that of the coniferous species, and particularly that of the white pine, is most important.

Though the arboreal vegetation of the country best illustrates the general effect of climate and of other conditions on the distribution of its plants, the limits of the various herbaceous and shrubby plants are similarly affected, and the flora as a whole may be divided into Atlantic, Pacific, Prairie, and Arctic or boreal, regions on the lines above sketched.

In the whole Nearctic region, of which, as we have seen, Canada forms the larger part by area, about one-third of the genera of mammals and birds are peculiar, while most of those constituting the remaining two-thirds are found also in the Palæarctic region. The typically Arctic forms are found only in the northern part of Canada and in Alaska, but some of the animals of the southern part of the Nearctic region do not extend northward as far as the boundary of Canada. This is particularly the case with some of the mammals, which being unable to migrate very far with the change of seasons, are governed rather by the length and severity of the winter which they must endure, than by the favourable conditions which the summer may afford.

Of mammals found in Canada which are not known elsewhere in the world except to the southward in the same Nearctic region, and thus specially important as showing the difference between its fauna and that of Eurasia, the following may be mentioned: musk-ox, prong-horned antelope, Rocky Mountain goat, big-horn or Rocky Mountain sheep, tree-porcupine, musk-rat, pouched rats, racoon, skunk, and star-nosed mole. The resemblance to Eurasia is, on the other hand, shown by the identity or close similarity of the more abundant and larger animals, such as the caribou, scarcely differing from the reindeer, the moose, nearly identical with the elk of Northern Europe, the bison or buffalo, closely resembling the aurochs of Europe, the wapiti (sometimes misnamed the "American elk"), equivalent to the red deer of Europe, with the bears, wolves, lynxes, beavers, and hares.

The birds of the Nearctic region are on the whole less peculiar to it than the mammals, but the turkey, which reaches the southern part of Ontario, the humming birds, spreading far northward in summer, and the blue jays, are specially noteworthy.

The best known of the larger land animals of Canada as a whole, many of which are important from the value of their skins, or are hunted for food, are the following: The moose, found in the forest regions of the eastern provinces and westward, in forests, to the Rocky Mountains; the caribou, formerly common in some parts of the eastern provinces and still abundant in Newfoundland and across the whole northern part of the continent; the wapiti, red-deer or "American elk," once numerous over the whole southern part of Canada, but now confined to limited tracts in the west; Virginian deer, extending over the whole southern part of Canada; mule-deer, in the Rocky Mountain region; black-tailed deer on the Pacific Coast; mountain goat and mountain sheep or big-horn, in the Rocky Mountain region only; musk-ox, the most characteristic animal of the far northern regions, but not found elsewhere; cougar, or American lion, still occasionally seen in the southern parts of Quebec and Ontario, but more abundant in the Rocky Mountain region, and on the west coast; wild-cat or lynx, throughout the forest regions; the wolf, in several varieties, becoming white in the extreme north; the coyote, a small wolf, common in the southern part of British Columbia, and in the interior prairie country; several foxes; grizzly, cinnamon, and black bears, the two first restricted to the western half of Canada, the polar bear replacing the other species along the Arctic coasts; several kinds of hares.

In the western prairie region, the bison or buffalo formerly roamed in immense herds, but is now practically extinct. Together with the prong-horned antelope it was characteristic of the great plains, and the antelope, owing to its fleetness and timidity, is still moderately abundant.

Besides the above-named species the following are specially important as fur-bearing animals:—wolverine, fisher, pine-marten, ermine, mink, otter, beaver, and musk rat.

Of the mammals few are regularly migratory in their habits, the best-marked exceptions to the rule being the musk-ox and caribou, which each summer cross the barren-grounds and travel far into the Arctic regions, returning with the winter to the shelter of the northern border of the woodland country. The birds are very different in this respect, and as a direct consequence of the continental climate of Canada, few of them are permanent residents, while over 200 species are regular migrants. As might be anticipated, there are more resident birds on the Pacific side; while the migration is best marked where the winter and summer isotherms differ most in position.

Some of the birds of the eastern provinces go as far south in winter as Mexico and the West Indian Islands; those of the interior plain and the Cordillera, though following distinct lines of migration, also spend the cold months far to the south, returning to their homes in the north to nest and breed in the summer.

Except the turkey and possibly the Newfoundland dog, none of the animals native to Canada have been domesticated by civilised man, and most of them appear to be unsuited to domestication. The buffalo might in the course of time have become a useful draught animal, and the caribou of the northern regions may some day be utilised like the reindeer. All the well-known domestic animals of the older hemisphere, such as horses, oxen, sheep, and swine, have been introduced, but they continue to exist only in a state of domestication, and have not become feral as in some other new countries. On the western prairies, and in the southern part of British Columbia, horses and cattle are able to live throughout the year on the natural pasturage, but even in these places no wild horses or cattle are found.

The more important introduced plants are those which constitute the ordinary field crops, including those common to north temperate regions generally, and most of these have been so long under cultivation, and have become so much changed and improved under the care of man, that their origin is now doubtful. With few exceptions such plants have reached Canada from Europe—wheat, barley, oats, rye, buckwheat, peas, sorghum, broom-corn, turnips, beets, potatoes, and maize, are specially important. The two last are indigenous to the American Continent, but not to Canada, and the varieties actually grown have probably come by way of Europe. Flax, clover, many grasses, and other introduced plants, are also grown for fibre or fodder, as well as all the well-known garden plants of Europe, cultivated for food or for their flowers or foliage, with some forest trees. Besides useful plants many useless weeds have been accidentally introduced, including the dandelion, mullein, sorrel, buttercup, and several thistles. Many of the introduced plants, but more particularly the weeds, have now become perfectly naturalised, so that it is only by means of lists drawn out by the earlier collectors and by noting the spread of such species with that of settlement, that we know them to have been originally foreign.

The northern limits imposed by climate on the various staple crops are important, as these show what extent of the country may ultimately be occupied for agricultural purposes, and consequently that which is capable of maintaining a considerable population. Though certain industries, such as mining, fishing, lumbering, or the fur trade, may produce local settlements of some size, and these may in turn induce a limited cultivation of the soil, even under unfavourable circumstances, the wellbeing of the country as a whole must always depend chiefly on agriculture. As but a comparatively small part of Canada is yet cultivated, our knowledge of these limits is largely based on local experiments, and upon meteorological observations and the character of the native plants met with in different districts. The general northern limit of possible agriculture has already been defined in connection with the tracing out of the isothermal line of 60° in July (see p. 23). The limit of the profitable culture of wheat does not run so far to the north as those of barley, rye, potatoes, and some other crops, but it is more important than any of these. Its most northern point is found in the Mackenzie valley about the 60th degree of latitude.

The relative importance of the different agricultural products is noted in greater detail under the several provinces. It is sufficient here to state that maize, peaches, and the vine flourish in the southern part of Ontario; while the limits of growth of the more hardy crops extend farthest northward in the interior plain of the continent, and in valleys within the Cordilleran region in the neighbourhood of the Pacific.

g. **Native Races.**—When that part of the continent which now forms British North America became known to Europeans, it was found, in common with the rest of America, to be occupied by various native races, which, though in general sparsely distributed over vast tracts of country, left no portion of the continent entirely unpeopled.

These races were for the most part little better than savages. They were not acquainted with the art of writing, and possessed no means of recording events, nor any certain knowledge of their own origin; but as the result of investigations since made it seems probable that they reached North America at a very early date, and that by some means colonies were established both from Asia on the west and from Europe on the east. The native races are usually spoken of under the general name of "Indians," first applied to them by early European voyagers under the mistaken belief that America formed part of India.

To complete our idea of Canada as it was before the changes brought about by Europeans began, and to explain various circumstances connected with the spread of civilisation and the settlement of the country, it is necessary to know something of its aboriginal population, and this connects itself naturally with the subject of its indigenous plants and animals.

Though some of the Indians of Mexico and of South America had themselves reached a stage of imperfect civilisation, those of Canada had not advanced beyond the condition of rude hunters and fishermen. In the southern parts of Ontario and Quebec, however, some cultivation of the land is known to have been attempted, by which food was produced in limited quantity as an auxiliary to the results of the chase (see p. 26). It is further probable that some similar cultivation was carried on in the southern part of Manitoba, and that a native tobacco was grown in a few places in British Columbia. The cultivation, such as it was, tended to produce permanent village communities in these districts, and on the west coast, where abundance of sea fish was always at hand, fixed places of residence with wooden houses were likewise found. Elsewhere in Canada the Indians can scarcely be said to have had permanent abodes, though in most instances the scattered members of a tribe usually came together at some fixed point during the winter months. Most of the tribes were hostile one to another, even such as were closely related and spoke the same, or

nearly the same, language. Wars were continually in
progress, the fighting being carried on by means of ambuscades and massacres, and the Indians were in consequence
extremely wary and keen of apprehension, inured to
fatigue, stoical, and cruel. Because of their hostilities
among themselves they were unable in most cases to
present any united opposition to the whites, but they were
nevertheless a source of great and constant danger to the
scattered early European settlements.

In Canada the last serious Indian war was that of
1763, resulting from a combination of a number of tribes
against the English, and known as the Conspiracy of
Pontiac. From an early period in the history of this
country the policy pursued toward the Indians has been
that of acquiring their title to the lands by arrangement
and purchase rather than by force, and in some parts of
Canada many of the Indians have already adopted a
civilised mode of life. This is particularly the case in
the southern portions of Ontario, Quebec, and British
Columbia.

Throughout Canada many of the original Indian names
of places have been adopted and perpetuated by the
whites, but in most cases these have suffered abbreviation
or other changes in the process. In general the native
names are found to be of a descriptive character, and to
express some noted feature or product of each locality.
The following are instances of such names from different
parts of the country, and in several dialects: Nictau,
"forks of river"; Shediac, "running far back"; Matapedia, "roughly-flowing"; Quebec, "a strait" or "an obstruction"; Toronto, "a tree in the water"; Winnipeg,
"muddy water"; Saskatchewan, "rapid current." It is
further noteworthy that in many cases the principal
villages or places of resort of the Indians have since
become the sites of towns or cities. This depends partly
on the circumstance that the whites first sought such
places for purposes of trade, but chiefly on the fact that
the Indians selected localities where natural lines of travel,
such as rivers, converged or were interrupted by falls or
rapids necessitating portages; also such places as sheltered

havens or harbours on the sea-coast or the shores of the Great Lakes. The cities of Halifax, Quebec, Montreal, Toronto, and Victoria may be cited as instances.

The principal natural division found among the native races of Canada is that between the Indians proper and the Eskimo. The Eskimo inhabit the whole northern border of the continent with the adjacent islands, and because of their northern position have been little disturbed in their occupation or affected by contact with the whites. Though divided into many tribes all speak one language, and though scattered over so great an extent of country they are few in number. Like the Eskimo, the Indians to the south of them are broken up into numerous tribes with distinctive names, but among these a great variety of languages and dialects is spoken. It is found, however, that these are in many cases more or less closely related, being but local varieties of a few principal or stock languages, and this connection of the various languages affords the best means of classifying the tribes.

Tribes of the Tinneh or Athabascan group inhabit the whole northern interior of British Columbia with the greater part of the Mackenzie valley, and extend eastward to the west shore of Hudson Bay. They wander over vast tracts of country, and are for the most part hunters, though depending also on fish obtained from the numerous rivers and lakes. The country of the Algonkin tribes lies to the south of that of the Tinneh, stretching from the Rocky Mountains eastward to the Atlantic coast. Most of the Algonkin tribes resembled the Tinneh in their mode of life, but included on the eastern seaboard some whose chief occupation was fishing. The Algonkin people travelled principally by water, making use of the innumerable rivers and lakes by which their country is intersected, and constructing the well-known birch-bark canoes for this purpose. The Blackfoot tribes of the plains (Fig. 3) are closely related to the Algonkin stock, if not a part of it, and these, together with the Crees (another Algonkin tribe) and the Assiniboines (a branch of the Sioux or Dakota of a different family), together occupied the open plains of the interior of Canada. These "plain

FIG. 3.—BLACKFOOT INDIAN OF THE GREAT PLAINS.
From a Photograph by Ross.

Indians" depended almost entirely on the buffalo for food and clothing. As in the case of the other Indians, the dog was originally their only domesticated animal, but almost before they became known to the whites they had obtained horses from the southern tribes, who were in contact with the Spaniards in Mexico, and great changes had been produced in their habits in consequence.

The southern part of Ontario was the home of the Huron-Iroquois people, of whom colonies extended down the St. Lawrence valley farther than the position of Montreal. The Iroquois division of this family in Ontario formed a powerful and warlike confederacy, known as the "Five Nations," and at different times, as allies or foes, played an important part in the early history of the country. They were at deadly enmity with the Hurons, and eventually drove the remnant of these people from their homes. Like the other Indians the principal occupations of the Huron-Iroquois were hunting and fishing, but, as already noted, they had made some advance in agriculture, and possessed fixed towns.

The southern part of British Columbia constituted the territory of various tribes of the Salish family, also hunters, but dependent in great measure for their winter store on the salmon which annually ascend the rivers. On the coast of the same province many different tribes are found crowded together in a rather narrow belt, differing in language, but alike in habits, and all fishermen (Fig. 4). These coast peoples are more skilled in various forms of native handicraft than any elsewhere found in the continent to the north of Mexico; they are maritime in genius, and make long voyages in their shapely canoes hollowed from the trunks of the great western cedar.

In Newfoundland a race named Beothuks was found at the time of its discovery, but has since become extinct.

The first effect of the arrival of the whites in the eastern part of Canada was to direct the attention of the Indians more than ever to the chase of the fur-bearing animals; and at a later date many of them became the skilful *voyageurs* of the great fur companies, in the employment of which, especially from among the Iroquois and Algonkin races, men traversed the whole northern part of the continent, even to the Pacific coast. The natural mode of life of the Indians was such as to require for the support of a scanty population the control of a great area of country, and it has been estimated that on an average not less than 34

FIG. 4.—AHT INDIAN WOMAN OF THE COAST OF BRITISH COLUMBIA.
From a Photograph.

square miles of land was necessary for each Indian inhabitant. Thus the entire area of Canada, capable of supporting many millions of civilised people, could, at best, have maintained only a few hundred thousand Indians. The number of the natives inhabiting the country on its discovery is, of course, not accurately known. At the present time the remaining native population is estimated at about 125,000, being about one-fortieth of the entire population, and is distributed as follows: Newfoundland, none, or but a few Indian immigrants from Nova Scotia; Acadian provinces, 4000; St. Lawrence provinces (Ontario and Quebec), 30,000; Manitoba, North-West Territory and North-East Territory, 48,000; British Columbia, 38,000; Eskimo, along the Arctic coast, 4000.

h. **Discovery and Settlement.**—While the history of Canada requires separate treatment, it is useful, in order to understand the existing distribution of its population, to note some events in the progress of discovery and exploration, which depend directly on geographical features, and lead up to the stage of development and expansion now attained.

At a very early date the Norse Vikings had established colonies in Greenland, and it appears to be certain that more than one voyage was made by them, early in the eleventh century, to and along the American coast, including parts of Labrador, Newfoundland, and Nova Scotia. They were enabled to reach Canada at that time in their primitive vessels by making use of Iceland and Greenland as stepping-stones across the narrowest part of the Atlantic, but they formed no permanent settlements. In 1497, five years after the discovery of America by Columbus (and again crossing the narrow northern part of the ocean), Cabot, sailing from Bristol, coasted along part of Labrador and Newfoundland; but the exploration of Canada can scarcely be said to have begun before Jacques Cartier, from St. Malo in France, entered the Gulf of St. Lawrence in 1535, thirty-eight years later. In the year following, having heard of the existence of the great river named by him the St. Lawrence, he undertook a new voyage, and entering the wide estuary ascended to the places where the cities of Quebec and Montreal now stand, both at that time the sites of Indian villages. Thus it was that Eastern Canada became the object of enterprise from France, and long remained a French colony, while the attention of the English was chiefly directed to the more southern parts of the east coast of the continent.

In the St. Lawrence the French found an artery leading to the interior of the continent, but for many years the importance of this discovery was not realised, and the progress of exploration was slow. This was in part owing to the pressure of contemporary events in Europe, in part to the circumstance that the first comers became absorbed in the lucrative fur trade and rich fisheries of the new-found coast, and largely to the fact that the particular districts which first became known were unfavourable to colonisation. At a later date French settlements were formed along the St. Lawrence, which grew and prospered, and to the growth of these colonies, established before the cession of Canada to Great Britain, is due the preponderance of the French language to-day in the province of Quebec.

By the St. Lawrence valley the northern flank of the Appalachians was easily turned, and it continued for a long time to be the chief highway by which, during the seventeenth and early part of the eighteenth centuries, French explorers overran a great area of the interior, westward to the Rocky Mountains, northward to the sources of the Mackenzie, and southward along the Mississippi valley. At the same time as these advances of the French by the St. Lawrence route, Frobisher, Davis, Hudson, and other English navigators began that search for a North-West Passage, which was destined to continue for many years, and which resulted eventually in the complete exploration of the northern coast of the continent.

In 1670 Prince Rupert obtained from Charles II. a charter upon which the rights of the Hudson's Bay Company were based. This included a vast and scarcely-defined region of the centre of the continent, which became known as "Rupert's Land"; and, in pursuance of their fur-trading interests, the Company established their chief depôts at the mouths of the Churchill and Nelson rivers on Hudson Bay, and gradually pushed their explorations by means of the great connected system of waterways far into the interior.

At a somewhat later period, but scarcely before the

closing years of the eighteenth century, Spanish and English sailors successively reached the coast of that part of Canada now forming the Province of British Columbia, and thus established a fourth centre of exploration and trade with the natives. Here, however, because of the unfavourable character of the rivers and their relatively short courses, the progress of inland exploration was slow and restricted, and that part of the Cordilleran region removed from the actual coast became tributary to traders from the east, who followed the navigable rivers of the longer slope of the continent to their sources.

Returning to the St. Lawrence valley, which remained the principal means of access to the interior of the continent, it is instructive to note how closely the march of discovery depended upon it. In 1603 Champlain, who came to Canada from France in the interest of trade and colonisation, infused new vigour into projects of exploration. In 1609 he ascended a tributary stream from the south, the Richelieu, and reached the lake now known by his name, thus making known the remarkable valley which runs south by the Hudson to the Atlantic at New York. This valley, constituting the main gateway of Eastern Canada to the south, was subsequently to become the route of armed parties during the long-continued hostilities between the French colonists and those of New England; next, an important line of water-communication between the St. Lawrence and Hudson; and eventually the principal railway route from north to south.

The occupation by the hostile Iroquois of the country, along that part of the St. Lawrence near the Great Lakes, constituting a bar to direct westward advance of the French, Champlain in 1615 ascended the Ottawa for some distance, and leaving it, made his way to the west by rivers and lakes, with short intervening portages, to Lake Huron. His route by the Nipissing valley had long been employed by the Algonkin Indians, who, like Champlain, were unable to run the gauntlet of the Iroquois to the south. Their intimate acquaintance with the country had led them to utilise the wide depression which here runs between the Ottawa and Lake Huron, and

Champlain's journey under their guidance first made known to the French this covered way, which was afterwards used by them for many years, and which still later proved to be the most favourable line for the construction of this part of the Canadian trans-continental railway. The character of this depression is in fact such that it may probably before many years be made the route of a canal connecting Lake Huron with the Ottawa, by which the distance from the Great Lakes to Montreal, at the head of ocean navigation, would be much shortened.

Zeal for the conversion of the Indians to the Catholic religion, and the spread of missions among them, were with the French important motives of exploration at this early period. Following Champlain's footsteps, in 1665 the Jesuit Father Allouez advanced discovery to the westward on the Great Lakes, and was the first to bring back a report of the vast prairie country beyond them. A few years later, Marquette, from Lake Michigan, reached the Mississippi; and he again was followed by La Salle, who in 1682 descended the Mississippi to the Gulf of Mexico. Another intrepid explorer, Verendrye, again taking a line of water-communication known to the Indians, made his way from Lake Superior through the Lake of the Woods to Lake Winnipeg and the Red River Country, traversed parts of the Saskatchewan and Upper Missouri valleys, and was, it is believed, the first to see the Rocky Mountains in 1743.

Not long after the date of Verendrye's explorations in the far west, Canada (meaning at that time the St. Lawrence valley and its dependencies) was finally ceded by France to Great Britain in 1763. Quebec had been founded in 1608, Montreal in 1640, Frontenac (now Kingston) in 1673; and before the cession, French settlements along the St. Lawrence valley had assumed considerable proportions, the number of inhabitants being estimated at 65,000. Small French and English settlements had likewise been formed in Newfoundland, the first organised attempt at colonisation being that of Lord Baltimore in 1624. In Nova Scotia, known as part of Acadia till 1621, an important French settlement at Port Royal (now Annapolis), was established as early as 1604, and Acadia remained a battle-ground between the French and English till the date of its final cession to the latter power in 1713. The island of Cape Breton was, however, retained by France; and Louisburg, commanding the entrance to the Gulf of St. Lawrence, was strongly fortified, but was eventually also taken by England in 1758. Thus with the complete surrender of Canada to Britain the conflict between the French and English settlements in America, which had scarcely been interrupted for 150 years, and into which the native peoples were also drawn, came to an end.

Twenty years later, in 1783, the independence of the United States was acknowledged by Great Britain, and a line was drawn between the new states and the British possessions to the north. At this time the greater part of the population of British America was still centred in the lower portion of the St. Lawrence valley, and consisted chiefly of the French colonists. Most of the original French settlers of Acadia had been deported in 1755, and the Acadian provinces were held chiefly by a small number of English-speaking people.

Important changes followed the establishment of the United States. It became impossible for those who had taken any important part against the insurrectionary movement to retain their old homes, and thus a wholesale emigration, including many of the prominent and most intelligent people, occurred to the remaining British provinces. It is estimated that within two years of the recognition of the United States 20,000 refugees, known as "United Empire Loyalists," found new homes in Acadia, while about 10,000 emigrated to the southern peninsula of Ontario, then a forest wilderness. To these colonists is due the prosperity and rapid advancement of the provinces to which they came.

With the improved means of communication of later years, and the drawing together of distant parts of the world by the introduction of steamships and railways, the character and the nationalities of immigrants to British North America became more diverse, and has so continued to the present time, rendering it unnecessary to follow the progress of colonisation further in detail. The first attempt at the settlement of what is now the province of Manitoba by Lord Selkirk, in 1812, deserves, however, to be mentioned. His colonists reached the central region of the continent by way of Hudson Bay, crossing thence to the plains of the interior by the Nelson—the same route by which it is now proposed to connect Manitoba by rail with the northern seaboard. The opening up of British Columbia by the influx consequent on the discovery of gold in 1858 and 1859 is also noteworthy; and in still more recent years the establishment of special colonies in Manitoba and the North-West Territory, such as those of the Mennonites from Southern Russia, the Icelanders, and the Scottish crofters.

In 1784 the North-West Company, a fur-trading corporation, was established in Montreal; and by the employees of this and the older and rival Hudson's Bay Company the exploration of the western part of the interior of the continent was continued and completed as to its main features. Some years previously, Hearne, in the service of the Hudson's Bay Company, had travelled by land from Fort Churchill on Hudson Bay to the mouth of the Coppermine river on the Arctic coast. In 1789 Sir Alexander Mackenzie of the North-West Company followed the great river which bears his name to the sea, and four years afterward ascended the Peace river, crossed the upper part of the Fraser valley, and reached the shore of the Pacific, being thus the first to traverse the continent from sea to sea; and though Verendrye is supposed to have sighted the Rocky Mountains many years before, it was from Mackenzie's plain and unassuming narrative that the first description of the Cordilleran region was obtained. At a later date Simon Fraser descended the turbulent river still known by his name; Campbell and other explorers of commerce, crossing the Rocky Mountains farther north, travelled and traded along the Yukon and Porcupine rivers into what is now the centre of Alaska. Cook and Vancouver, in the service of Britain, had meanwhile made known the west coast of the northern part of the continent throughout its length. Thus in the early part of the present century the definition of the larger outlines of all Canada, as they now appear upon the map, may be said to have been completed.

In almost every case the pioneers of the fur companies travelled under Indian guidance, following as far as possible the great systems of interlocking waterways, and in many instances their routes still remain the most practicable ones through the north-west country. Few travellers deserve greater credit than those enterprising though modest men by whom the length and breadth of the great interior regions of the continent were explored, and the ultimate limits of Canada virtually established, almost alone and, generally speaking, in perfect friendship with the native races.

The names of places in a new country like Canada do not usually possess the same interest or significance as those of countries in which various races, speaking different languages, have succeeded each other in prolonged occupation of the soil, but they are still not without interest. In addition to the retention of many of the Indian names themselves (see p. 35), others are represented by their English or French equivalents. The great activity of the early French explorers, and the language spoken by the *voyageurs* of the fur companies, are shown by the general distribution of French names, not alone in the east, but even far to the west both in Canada and in the United States. Such are Detroit, Sault Ste. Marie, Isle Royal, Lac Dauphin, Lac la Biche, Rivière Souris, Côteau de Missouri, Qu'Appelle, and many others. This contrasts markedly with the prevalence of Spanish names in the southern part of the United States and in Mexico, where the early explorations were chiefly carried out by Spain, but is partly masked by the fact that many names, originally French, have subsequently been exchanged for their English equivalents; thus Lake of the Woods now replaces Lac des Bois, Cypress Hills, Montagnes de Cyprès, and Rocky Mountains, Montagnes Rocheuses.

In the province of Quebec the French language and French names of places have more than held their own throughout; and the distinctly religious bias of the early colonists is shown by the prevalence of the names of patron saints, and the relatively small number of local names derived from the soil of France. Where English-speaking colonists established themselves they very often planted in the new land the names of places from which they had come, such as Yarmouth, Newcastle, Cornwall, London, and many more. In other cases the names given were those of persons prominent in the history of the time, or of patrons or supporters of the colonists or explorers. Instances of this are found in Halifax, Carleton, King William's Land, Pitt Island, etc. The Arctic region is particularly notable for names of this character, from which the progress of geographical exploration may almost be traced by reference to history. In British Columbia there are, as in the east, many native names, and along the coast a number of Spanish names, such as Valdez, Malaspina, and San Juan, given by the early voyagers of that nation. Overlying these again is a preponderance of English names chiefly given by Vancouver in honour of persons prominent at the time, but without local significance.

i. **Population.**—The population of Canada, according to the census of 1891, is 4,829,000, the increase since 1881 being 504,600, or at the rate of 11·66 per cent in ten years. It is thus about equal to that of Ireland, and considerably greater than that of Scotland. Divided by the entire area of Canada it is found that there are less than two individuals to each square mile, while in the United Kingdom the density of the population is over 300 to the square mile. The population of Newfoundland is about 200,000.

In countries which have been long inhabited, the distribution of the population (apart from that of the great commercial centres, where other circumstances must be considered) depends closely upon the natural resources of the different districts. This is also the case to some extent in a new country like Canada; but much here depends as well on the relative facilities of access to various districts, and the history of the establishment of the growing settlements, while vast tracts, capable of maintaining eventually a dense population, still remain almost untenanted. Thus a very great inequality exists in the relative **density of population** in different **parts** of Canada, where **over three-fifths of the whole number of** inhabitants is included **in the provinces of the St.** Lawrence valley, Ontario, and **Quebec, and even in** these provinces the thickly-peopled **districts comprise** only their southern **and** more fertile **portions.** Grouping the figures for the **St. Lawrence and** Acadian provinces, it appears that about four-fifths of the whole population is contained in these provinces, leaving about one-fifth to be distributed over the **entire western** half of the Dominion, **which is at** least equally rich in agricultural and mineral resources, and may therefore be expected to increase in a rapid ratio now that means of communication are being provided throughout its length and breadth.

A century ago the civilised population of the whole of British North America slightly exceeded 100,000, and even fifty **years ago it was less than** 2,000,000, or about the same **as that of England at the date of the battle of** Crécy. The **present population of Canada** is probably about equal to that of **England and Wales at the time of** the accession of Queen Anne. Such comparisons, **of course,** give no accurate idea of the importance of the two countries relatively to that of others at the dates referred **to.**

k. **Political Divisions.**—Bearing in mind what has been **said of the modes of** colonisation of the country, it will be **easy to understand in what way the** political subdivisions **of the** Dominion of **Canada arose.** The map shows the boundaries of the eastern provinces to be in the main irregular in outline, these having been drawn with reference to the settlements and claims of the early colonists coming from various **directions. The straight lines,** separating the newer provinces **and** districts, on the contrary, plainly show that these were established for the most part in advance of settlement, and usually on arbitrary principles.

When Britain finally gained control of Canada, the **region which** had been known as Acadia became the colony **of Nova** Scotia, but in 1769 Prince Edward Island was made **a separate** colony, **and in** 1784, on political grounds, New Brunswick was also separated. The settlement of what is now the province of Ontario by the United Empire Loyalists and other English-speaking people, with the preponderance of the French element on the Lower St. Lawrence and the retention there of French laws, soon rendered necessary a separation between the eastern and western parts of what was then known as Canada. Lower and Upper Canada were thus constituted by an Act of the Imperial Parliament in 1791. The line between the existing settlements was drawn for the greater part of its length along the Ottawa river, but cut off part of the point between that river and the St. Lawrence which was added to Lower Canada, as it was already occupied by French-speaking people. Lower and Upper Canada became the provinces of Quebec and Ontario when confederation was accomplished.

British Columbia was at first the name applied to the mainland portion only of the present province, its boundaries to the north and east having been defined by an Act of Parliament. In 1866 Vancouver Island, which had for some years been a separate government, was made a part of British Columbia, and Victoria was selected as the seat of government for the entire colony. The province of Manitoba and the several districts of the North-West Territory were blocked out at later dates after the time of confederation.

The union of Lower and Upper Canada, Nova Scotia, and New Brunswick was brought about by a conference of delegates from the respective Governments, and finally established by an Act of the Imperial Parliament in 1867. This Act, defining the political status of the Dominion of Canada and of its constituent provinces, is known as the British North America Act. In 1870 Rupert's Land and the North-West Territory were added to the Dominion. In 1871 British Columbia was admitted as a province, and in the following year Prince Edward Island was similarly included, thus completing the union of all parts of British North America as the Dominion of Canada, with the exception of Newfoundland, which still prefers to remain a separate colony.

l. **Government.**—The history of events in British North

America from the inception of British rule to the time of confederation, has been that of the gradual development of responsible government, taking place together with the increasing population and importance of the country and as a consequence of these. The system of government finally established by the British North America Act is the outcome of this process of growth, and ensures the greatest measure of independent action compatible with the position of Canada as an integral part of the British Empire. It is nearly identical with that of the mother-country. The Governor-General, appointed by the Crown for a term of five years, is the representative of the sovereign, and governs through a Ministry, his constitutional advisers. As in the United Kingdom the Ministry consists of a certain number of members of a larger body, with the name of the Privy Council for Canada, and must possess the confidence of the majority in the House of Commons. All Acts are assented to by the Governor-General in the name of the sovereign before becoming law, the power being reserved by the Imperial Government of disallowing Acts which do not affect Canada alone, and which may be found injurious to the general interests of the Empire. The right of making treaties with foreign Governments rests with the Imperial Government, and the commander of the Canadian militia is appointed by that Government.

The Legislature consists of a Senate, analogous to the House of Lords in Great Britain, and of a House of Commons. The members of the Senate are appointed by the Crown on advice of the Ministry, and hold office for life. Members of the House of Commons are elected directly by the people upon a very wide suffrage, voting being by ballot. Measures must be passed by both these bodies before being assented to by the Governor-General and becoming law. The several provincial Governments are constituted on similar principles to that of the Dominion, but Ontario, Manitoba, and British Columbia have each but one legislative body. The North-West Territory is governed like a province, save that the Legislature comprises some members nominated by the Dominion as well as the elected members, and that certain matters are retained under the control of the Dominion Government which in other cases are dealt with by the local Governments.

The Government of the Dominion controls all matters of a general kind, while the provincial Governments manage all purely local affairs, the Acts of the provinces being subject to disallowance by the Dominion Government. As the Dominion Government controls indirect taxation, and the power of levying customs and other similar dues was surrendered by the provinces at the union, fixed subsidies are accorded to the provinces for the purpose of meeting the expenses of their Governments. Most of the provinces are further subdivided into numerous municipalities with elective councils which manage all subordinate local affairs, many of which would otherwise require special Acts of the provincial or Dominion Parliaments, and in this way self-government is ensured to the utmost possible extent.

While resembling in some points the form of government of the United States, that of Canada is more centralised and at the same time more democratic and more directly responsible to the people. The ruling principle of the constitution of the Dominion is that all matters not specially delegated to the provinces are centred in the general Government, which also controls the militia and defence of the country, and as already stated holds a power of veto over provincial Acts. In Canada, as in Great Britain, the Executive must command a majority in the elective House, and it therefore responds more quickly to the opinions of the electorate than is possible under the constitution of the United States.

Newfoundland is politically distinct from Canada, having a separate responsible Government. The Governor is appointed by the Crown, and there are two legislative bodies—the Legislative Council, the members of which are appointed for life, and an elective House of Assembly. The eastern coast of Labrador is under the political jurisdiction of Newfoundland.

The revenue of Canada is derived chiefly from customs

and excise duties, and most goods imported are **subject to duty.** Other **though minor** sources of revenue are the postal service, **railways, and** various public works. The revenue **per head of** population amounted in 1889 to $7·60 ; **but this** does not include the taxation for municipal **and** other local purposes **not** controlled by the general **Government.**

Previous to the date of confederation various monetary systems were in use in the different provinces ; **but the** decimal system is now universal, the dollar **being the unit.** Four dollars eighty-six and a half **cents are equal** to one pound sterling.

m. **Products, Industries, and Commerce.**—In Canada, as in other new countries, the principal industries are those directly connected with procuring and disposing of the natural products. Such raw materials, though in part consumed or **manufactured in** the country, are largely exported. Agriculture **in its** various branches holds the first place, **and, with the timber trade** and fishing, affords employment to a great **majority of the** population.

In the early history **of the** country **the fur** trade was for a long time the most lucrative pursuit ; **but at** a later **date,** in the eastern provinces, the timber **trade became and** long continued the staple industry. This led to the clearing of the forest lands, afforded a local market for the limited produce of the early farms, and naturally prepared **the** way **for the** extension of agriculture, which subsequently assumed the first **rank.** With the growth of population and wealth, mining, manufacturing, and other similar enterprises requiring a greater amount of capital and **skill,** tend to grow in importance. **In** the western prairie **country** lately opened to settlement, the march of events is not **the same. The** laborious process of clearing **the** land is passed **over, the settler takes** immediate possession, and the prairie becomes a farm.

So large a part of **the** entire area of Canada is naturally **adapted to** farming **or** fitted for pastoral occupation, that these **will** doubtless continue to be the chief sources of wealth. According to the census of 1881 45,000,000 acres of land were occupied, of which about one half was actually under cultivation. This is equal to more than twice the whole area of Scotland, and the area of cultivated land is probably greater than that similarly employed in the United Kingdom, but is still only a fraction of that which will eventually be utilised. Since the census of 1881 the cultivated lands have much increased, but precise figures are wanting. Under the headings of the several provinces the kinds of grains, roots, green-crops, and fruits produced are further noticed. Cattle, horses, sheep, and poultry, with the dependent production of cheese, butter, and eggs, constitute important industries in all the provinces.

Lumbering, or the production of timber of all kinds, is important chiefly in the provinces of Ontario, Quebec, and British Columbia, though prosecuted also to some extent in the Acadian provinces and in Newfoundland. The coniferous trees, of which the white pine, spruce, larch, Douglas fir, cedar, and hemlock may be specially mentioned, yield the greater part of the timber. Maple, walnut, butternut, hickory, basswood, elm and other trees, however, add their quota. A large proportion of all the timber cut is exported either in logs or sawn into boards and in other partially manufactured forms.

The fisheries constitute a great and practically inexhaustible source of wealth, the sea-fisheries being naturally the most important and maintaining a large and hardy seafaring population. The fisheries of the Great Lakes, with those of the rivers and many lakes of smaller dimensions, are, however, also productive. The fishing-grounds which have so far been most fully utilised are those of the eastern seaboard adjacent to the Acadian provinces and Newfoundland. In Ontario and Manitoba fishing is confined to the lakes and rivers. The coast of British Columbia abounds in excellent fish, but at present the only kind utilised on a large scale is the salmon.

The order of importance of the provinces of the Dominion and of Newfoundland in respect to the present value of products of the fisheries is as follows: Nova Scotia, Newfoundland, New Brunswick, British Columbia, Quebec, Ontario, Prince Edward Island, Manitoba, and the North-West Territory. The principal kinds of fish taken (including lobsters, which though zoologically distinct are conveniently classed here), arranged in order of the value of the catch of each, are as follows: Cod, salmon, herring, lobster, mackerel, whitefish, trout, haddock, hake, and pollock. The whitefish and trout are the most important of those obtained from the lakes. The aggregate value of the product of the fisheries of Canada for the year 1889 is estimated at over seventeen million dollars.

Mining and industries directly connected with minerals, though they have already attained considerable proportions and are increasing in this respect, must be considered as relatively little advanced. The principal coal-fields are situated in Nova Scotia, British Columbia, and the North-West Territory, in which provinces extensive metallurgical and manufacturing industries may be expected to develop. The existence of coal of good quality and abundant in quantity on both the eastern and the western coasts of the Dominion ensures an important future for the commerce and carrying trade of the country on both oceans. The portion of Canada most richly endowed with mineral wealth in various forms is undoubtedly that included in British Columbia, but its utilisation is as yet in its earliest stages.

At the present time coal exceeds any other mineral product in value, and the greater part of the whole output is employed within the country itself, though large shipments are also made to foreign ports, particularly from British Columbia. Other mineral products are chiefly exported, usually in a crude or but partially manufactured state. After coal, gold is the most important, and is principally obtained in British Columbia and in Nova Scotia. Considerable quantities of asbestos, copper, gypsum, apatite or phosphate of lime, pyrites, iron, and manganese are mined and sent abroad. Petroleum, salt, lime, building-stone, slate, clay for brick-making, and other materials are produced chiefly for home consumption. Speaking generally, few minerals known to commerce are altogether unknown in Canada, and many which have not yet attracted the attention of the miner, promise eventually to contribute to the wealth of the country.

The position of Great Britain as a manufacturing and commercial centre to which raw materials are brought from all parts of the world and from which manufactured goods are exported, is exceptional, and depends primarily on the abundance of coal, skilled labour, and capital, combined with the natural advantages due to its geographical position. In the United States, by means of a high protective tariff against the import of manufactures, the large home market is made to support extensive manufacturing industries, but on account of the high price of the goods thus produced the export of such goods is small. In geographical position and in proportion to its area Canada does not possess nearly the same advantages as Britain for foreign trade, but is equal in these respects if not superior to the United States, though the relatively sparse population, the high price of labour, and other circumstances have so far tended to limit manufacturing enterprises. Of late years, however, manufactures have been growing in importance, particularly such as deal with materials produced in the country itself or those which may advantageously be imported in the raw state and are required for consumption in Canada. Most of the Canadian manufactures are centred in the provinces of Ontario and Quebec, and these include especially the making of agricultural implements, railway rolling-stock, woollen-mills, saw-mills, tanneries, machinery, furniture, boots and shoes, paper and paper-pulp, etc. Cotton-mills, tobacco manufactories, and sugar refineries depend on the elaboration of imported raw products.

The total value of the imports of Canada in 1889 was $115,224,931, that of the exports $89,189,167. Thus the entire volume of trade, in addition to that conducted between different parts of the country itself, was over $200,000,000. Dividing this sum by the population, it is found that the amount of trade per head exceeds $40, being less than half the corresponding amount per head in the United Kingdom, but nearly double that in the United States. This commerce, though extending to all parts of the world, is principally conducted with Great Britain and the United States, that with these two countries being nearly equal in proportions and aggregating 88 per cent of the whole. Divided under general headings the following is the order in value of the chief exports: Animals and their products, produce of the forest, agricultural produce, produce of the fisheries, manufactured articles, produce of the mine. The exports of animals and their products, produce of the mine, manufactures, and fisheries are increasing in the order named. The imports are very varied, including woollen goods, iron and steel, coal, cotton goods, and various articles of food not produced in the country.

In respect to the tonnage of shipping owned, Canada ranks fifth among the countries of the world, being exceeded only by the United Kingdom, United States, Scandinavia, and Germany. Many of the vessels are engaged in fishing or in coastwise trade on the Atlantic, Pacific, and Great Lakes; others are employed in the general carrying trade of the world. The building of wooden ships was formerly an important industry in the Acadian provinces and in Quebec, but this is now much depressed in consequence of the general employment of iron ships, and the substitution of steamships for sailing-vessels.

The trade of Newfoundland, not included in that of Canada, aggregated in 1888 over $14,000,000.

n. Internal **Communications.**—In the early days of the settlement of British North America, intercommunication, when not by sea between places on the coast, was effected chiefly by means of the rivers and lakes. These were navigated by the early explorers in Indian canoes, and afterwards by boats, barges, and other larger craft. As settlement progressed, the narrow "trails" or footpaths, beaten out by the Indians through the eastern forest region, were replaced by wider roads adapted for carts or waggons. The St. Lawrence river, with its tributaries and the Great Lakes, continued however to be the principal artery of commerce; but its course is interrupted near Montreal by the Lachine Rapids, beyond which sea-going vessels could not ascend. Though but 86 miles above the influence of the tide, Montreal is over 900 miles inland measuring from the margin of the continental outline at Belle Isle strait. Stretching beyond Montreal westward to the end of Lake Superior the great waterway runs for a further distance of 1400 miles, and in order to facilitate its use as a means of communication efforts were early made to construct canals past some of the rapids, and thus to reduce the number of "portages" or places where goods and boats required to be carried by land.

The first canals attempted were intended for boats only, but these have since been improved and enlarged till the system of inland navigation opened by them has become the most important in the world. It is now possible for a sea-going vessel of moderate size to reach any of the Great Lakes; but as a matter of fact the inland navigation is carried on by specially-constructed vessels and steamboats, and a transhipment of freight going in either direction is made at Montreal, this method being found, for various reasons, to be the most profitable. The difference of level between Lake Superior and the Atlantic is 600 feet, of which all but 67 feet is accounted for by the various rapids and by the Niagara Falls. These impediments to navigation are surmounted by a total number of fifty-three locks on an aggregate length of 70 miles of canals. The Welland Canal, one of the most important, by which the fall at Niagara is overcome, now has a depth of 14 feet. In other parts of the system the depth is but 12 feet, but the whole will soon be increased to correspond with that of the Welland Canal. To accommodate the increasing dimensions of sea-going vessels, and because of the number and size of the steamships which have, to a large extent, superseded sailing-vessels, it has further been found necessary to deepen and improve the channel of that part of the St. Lawrence between Quebec and Montreal, and vessels drawing $27\frac{1}{2}$ feet of water can now ascend at all stages of water to Montreal.

Besides this main line of water communication there are several others of minor importance connected with the St. Lawrence, which have also been rendered available by the construction of canals. The Ottawa river has thus been made continuously navigable from Montreal to the city of Ottawa, while the Rideau Canal connects Ottawa with Kingston on the St. Lawrence, and the Richelieu and Lake Champlain Canal system completes a route from the St. Lawrence to the Hudson river, by which New York is reached.

Though the development of the railway system has in recent years much decreased the relative importance of the inland water communication, the canals are still largely employed for the conveyance of bulky and heavy articles, such as lumber, coal, and grain. The circumstance that the freezing over of the lakes and rivers interrupts all navigation for a considerable part of each year, causes the railway to be of even greater value in Canada than it is in countries with a less severe winter climate, so that the introduction and growth of the railway system really form a special epoch in its history. The railways have produced great changes in the respective importance of commercial centres, and in the value of farming lands, timber, and other natural sources of wealth; and places formerly remote and difficult of access have thus often become points on main routes of travel.

The more thickly-peopled parts of Ontario, Quebec, and the Acadian provinces are now covered by a network of railways, while the main line of the Canadian Pacific Railway affords an easy route across the hitherto almost impassable wilderness north of Lakes Huron and Superior to Manitoba and the western plains. In the region of the plains the character of the country is specially favourable to the construction of railways, and branch lines are there being pushed forward in various directions, even in advance of settlement. Between the plains and the Pacific Ocean the completion of the same line of railway has breached, for purposes of commerce, the great barrier of the Cordilleran ranges. Thus by means of the railway a free interchange of the products of all parts of Canada has been rendered possible, and a community of sentiments and interests otherwise impossible has begun to be realised, which must increase and spread as more such highways are opened and the population extends to wider areas.

In 1850 there were but 70 miles of railway in operation in what is now the Dominion of Canada; in 1889 the length of completed railways was over 13,000 miles. This is less by about 6000 miles than the total length of railways in the United Kingdom, a little less than that of the Indian lines, and greater by about 5000 miles than that of the lines in Australia. On the assumption that a railway efficiently serves the purposes of communication in a belt of country 20 miles in width on each side, the existing railways in Canada may be said to have opened up an area of about 500,000 square miles, or rather more than one-seventh of the whole. In reality, however, the country thus provided with means of communication is much less, for many parts of the various lines lie close together, and the belts of country estimated on their length therefore overlap.

To the north of the railway region there are vast tracts of country in which the means of communication are still scarcely less primitive than they were a century ago, where travel is accomplished by boats or canoes in summer, by dog-sledges or on snow-shoes in winter. Small steamboats have, however, lately been placed on some of the northern rivers and lakes, and it is now possible, with two comparatively short intervals of land travel by road, to pass from the railway system of the north-west to the Mackenzie, and to follow that great river by steamboat to the Arctic Ocean.

The total length of telegraph lines in Canada in 1889 was over 29,000 miles, a length exceeded by only seven other countries. The number of post-offices at the same date was nearly 8000.

II.—DOMINION OF CANADA AND NEWFOUNDLAND

NEWFOUNDLAND

Name and Size.—The Island of Newfoundland is the oldest British colony, and still remains politically distinct from the Dominion of Canada. Its name was probably given by Cabot during his first voyage, as it is met with shortly thereafter as *Terra Nova* and "New Islande," which soon passed into "Newfound Island," and then to its present form. It is supposed that the cape now named Bonavista was the first land seen by Cabot, and that its name is a corruption of *Prima Vista*.

This island contains 42,000 square miles, and is thus one-sixth larger than Ireland. It lies across the mouth of the wide indentation in the continent into which the St. Lawrence pours its waters, forming the eastern side of the Gulf of St. Lawrence. It is separated from Labrador, on the mainland to the north-west, by the Strait of Belle Isle, only 12 miles in width, while from Cape Breton, on the south-west, it is distant only 65 miles. The depth of the Strait of Belle Isle is not great, and a slightly increased elevation of the land relatively to the sea would make the island a part of Labrador, from which its actual separation may be regarded as accidental. The general form of the island is that of a triangle, of which one side, facing to the north-east, conforms to the trend of the adjacent eastern coast of Labrador. The other two sides face to the south and north-west respectively, but their outline is very irregular. The greatest length of the island from north to south is 325 miles, its greatest breadth from east to west 310 miles. It is the easternmost part of America, and was for a long time in its early history one of the best known, being resorted to on account of its valuable fisheries. Its geographical position, in later years, has caused it to become a landing-point for most of the transatlantic telegraphic cables, the actual distance from the eastern part of Newfoundland to the western extremity of Ireland being less than 1700 miles.

Surface.—Newfoundland has no mountain range properly so called, though a few isolated points slightly exceed 2000 feet in elevation. The greatest mass of high land is situated on its western side, where a large area rises to about 1000 feet, sloping down gradually to the level of the sea to the north-east and east. The island is composed for the most part of old crystalline (Laurentian) rocks, and of newer over-lying Silurian strata, arranged in a series of parallel folds, which run in north-east and south-west bearings. The higher parts of the land are plateau-like, and form wide flat-topped ridges, which depend for their existence and direction on the position of bands of the harder and older rocks. Where the newer rocks occur, tracts of low land and wide intervening valleys, which open broadly to the north-eastward, have been formed. The highland tract which is the most continuous and important on the western edge of Newfoundland is known as the Long Range. This and the adjacent parallel ridges may be regarded as forming the north-eastern termination of the Appalachian mountain system, which has already been referred to as so important a feature of the eastern border of the continent of North America. The interior of the country is not completely explored, but the higher parts are known to be scantily covered with forest of small growth or with stunted bushes, where sufficient soil exists for their support; while elsewhere mosses and lichens with small berry-bearing bushes occupy most of the surface. Such tracts are locally known as "barrens." In the immediate neighbourhood of the coast the forest is also stunted and gnarled, but in the wider lowlands and interior valleys trees of good growth abound and afford excellent timber, the most valuable kinds being the white pine, spruce, larch or tamarack, and birch. There are also some open pasture lands, and in the aggregate a large area of arable land, though that now actually under cultivation is not more than one-six-hundredth of the entire area of the island. Several large lakes and innumerable smaller lakes and ponds are scattered over the surface, and some of these occur even on the higher plateaux.

Coast.—The coast-line is exceedingly irregular, and for the most part rocky and rugged, but its irregularities are not without system, as an examination of the map will show that they conform in their outlines to the general direction of the structure of the island, the principal indentations being in fact the submerged extensions of the more important inland valleys. The Strait of Belle Isle is a similar and parallel though now submarine valley, and a depression of the land by an amount of 500 feet would produce another comparable, though narrower, strait between White Bay and St. George Bay. The larger sinuosities of the coast are themselves broken up into innumerable smaller inlets and coves, most of which form good harbours for small craft, and the total length of the coast-line is estimated at not less than 2000 miles. Most of the larger bays are situated on the north-east side of the island, comprising White, Nôtre Dame, Bonavista, Trinity, and Conception Bays. St. Mary's, Placentia, Fortune, and D'Espoir (often called Despair) are on the south side of the island, and St. George Bay and Bay of Islands on the west. The land separating the various larger bays frequently assumes the form of peninsulas, of which the most important is the Avalon Peninsula, constituting the south-eastern extremity of Newfoundland. It is connected with the main island by a neck of land not more than 3 miles in width at the narrowest place, and on it is situated the city of St. John's with other towns. The Burin Peninsula on the south side is also noteworthy from its size and the existence of considerable settlements upon it. In consequence of the penetration of the island in all directions by bays and inlets, communication between the different settlements and fishing-stations is chiefly by sea. The settlements are almost entirely upon the coast, and there is but one short line of railway, 120 miles in length, connecting St. John's with Harbour Grace and Placentia.

On the south and north-east sides of Newfoundland the coast is fringed by numerous rocky islands, of which St. Pierre and Miquelon require special mention as being the property of France. These islands are employed as stations by the French fishing fleet, and constitute the sole remnant of the once extensive possessions of France in North America. The French, however, also retain certain fishing privileges on the west coast of Newfoundland, which are secured to them by an old treaty, and give rise to the perpetual antagonism of the French and Newfoundland fishermen. The shortest route for steamships entering the St. Lawrence is by the Strait of Belle Isle, but in the spring and early summer the passage is usually made to the south of Newfoundland. For vessels sailing between Great Britain and Halifax, and even for those destined for ports in the United States, the shortest line is one skirting the south of the island. The bold outline of Belle Isle Island or the rocky front of Cape Race, the south-eastern extreme of Newfoundland, is generally the first land seen by the transatlantic traveller to Canada, and thus Newfoundland is still to-day, as it was to Cabot, the *Terra Primum Vista*. Both Belle Isle and Cape Race are now provided with excellent lighthouses.

Drainage System.—The rivers are numerous but small, and scarcely navigable except by canoes and boats, though useful as affording means of bringing timber from the interior, and important in connection with the cultivable land existing in their valleys. Most of the principal streams flow to the north-eastward, in conformity with the longer slope of the surface of the island in that direction. These include the River of Exploits, Gander, and Terra-Nova rivers. The Humber and St. George rivers reach the west coast.

Climate.—The climate is best suited for agriculture at some distance from the north-east and south shores, and is there such as to admit of the growth of wheat, and to favour that of barley, oats, potatoes, and garden vegetables. Though situated in the same latitude as the south of England and north of France the mean annual temperature is much lower. The cause of this difference has already been explained (see p. 22). The climate is, however, more equable, and at the same time more humid than that of the adjacent Canadian mainland on account of the modifying influence of the neighbouring ocean. In winter the thermometer seldom falls much below zero, while in summer it rarely attains 80° in the shade. The mingling of air, warmed and saturated with moisture by contact with the Gulf Stream water, with cold atmospheric currents from the mainland and from the often ice-encumbered surface of the Arctic current, produces frequent and dense fogs over the adjacent seas, but these do not usually extend far inland. The average annual rainfall is about 58 inches, and is thus not excessive. The climate of Newfoundland may therefore be stated to be naturally more favourable for grazing than for agriculture, though much of the interior will no doubt eventually be utilised for both purposes.

Products, Industries, and Commerce.—The coal-fields of Newfoundland, though they occupy but a small part of the surface, and are not at present worked, are believed to be of some importance. The largest and most promising is on the west coast, about St. George Bay. Copper is the only mineral product yet utilised at all extensively. Gypsum, pyrite, lead, nickel, iron, and other valuable minerals are known.

The resources of the island in timber are considerable, and already suffice to keep a number of sawmills in operation. Manufactures of a few kinds are carried on, but chiefly for local supply. Agriculture is not yet extensively pursued, though important tracts of fertile land have been found to exist in the valleys of the larger rivers, and in the vicinity of the principal inlets, including St. George Bay, where a large population will no doubt eventually be maintained.

The fisheries constitute the great industry of Newfoundland, upon which its prosperity and importance really depend, and by far the greater part of the adult male population follows a seafaring life. Nearly 1000 fishing vessels are owned in the island, besides numerous smaller craft. The cod fisheries are the most important in the world, and are carried on partly around the shores and in the bays of the island, and partly on the adjacent Grand Banks. The successful prosecution of the cod fishery requires a supply of suitable bait, which varies with the season, consisting in the early summer of capelin, and later in the season of squid or cuttle-fish and herring. The taking of "bait" in nets and otherwise constitutes almost an industry by itself, the prosecution of which is confined to the immediate vicinity of the coast, and is jealously guarded by the Newfoundlanders as against foreign fishermen. The cod, though the most important, is by no means the only species of sea fish caught and cured in large quantities, and the rivers abound in salmon. Within recent years the catching and canning of lobsters has assumed great proportions, and there are also many establishments for the production of cod-liver oil. Seals, whales, porpoises, and other marine animals abound in the adjacent seas.

The Grand Banks, being situated beyond the territorial jurisdiction of Newfoundland, are resorted to by numerous Canadian fishermen as well as by foreign fishing vessels from France and the United States. They lie for the most part to the east and south of the island, and are in all over 600 miles in length by about 200 in breadth, forming an extensive submarine plateau covered by a depth of water which averages about 40 fathoms, and ranges between 10 and 160 fathoms. Upon these banks marine life of all kinds abounds, and to them the cod and other species of fish resort in immense numbers. The fishing vessels frequenting the Grand Banks are known as "bankers," and are of larger size and better equipped than those in which the shore fisheries are prosecuted. The cod fishing lasts from June till about the middle of November.

The seal fishery is next in importance to the cod fishery, and is somewhat peculiar in its character. In the spring

F

FIG. 5.—SEALING STEAMERS IN THE ICE, HARBOUR GRACE, NEWFOUNDLAND. From the "Dominion Illustrated."

large floes of **Arctic** ice from Davis **Strait are brought
down** each year by the Arctic current, **and the sea about
the** coast of Newfoundland and Labrador **becomes encumbered** with field-ice, floes, "**pans,**" **and** detached cakes of
ice, to which the seals resort, and upon which their young
are born. The fishing vessels push their way into these icefields, and when **seals** are **met with,** the fishermen, dispersed
over the ice, **engage in their slaughter (Fig. 5).** The seal
fishery begins **in March and ends in May, and though in
some years 400,000 to 600,000** seals are killed, **the results
of the fishery are rather precarious** and **vary from year to
year.** Sealing is now chiefly prosecuted by **specially-constructed** small steamships, **and** from **10,000 to 12,000 men
are employed** in it. The **seals are valued for their blubber,
which is made into oil, and for their skins, but the** species
of seals taken here are different from the more valuable
fur-bearing seal of the North Pacific.

The commerce of Newfoundland consists **chiefly in the
export of the** products **of the fisheries to Great Britain,
Brazil,** Portugal, **the United States, Canada, and the West
Indies. Flour and meats, with clothing, and other manufactured articles are imported.**

Population.—**The total population, including the** scanty
fishing settlements **of the eastern coast of Labrador,** which
is politically **a** dependency **of Newfoundland, is** about
205,000.

Towns.—**St. John's (pop. 28,610)** is the chief town and
seat **of Government of Newfoundland.** The harbour is
stated to have been **named** by **John Cabot, and to have
been entered by him on his** patron's **day, 25th June 1497.
St. John's is** the commercial **centre of** the island, **and the
chief place of** export **of the product of the fisheries.** The
harbour upon which it is built **is situated on** the **east side
of** the **Avalon Peninsula, and opens to the Atlantic.**
Though **small, it is very secure, and well sheltered, and is**
entered **by a narrow though deep gap between high
cliffs. So narrow is the opening, that in** times **of war it
has been closed by means of a chain** stretched across it.

Harbour Grace, Carbonear and **Brigus** on **Conception Bay, Twillingate** on **Nôtre** Dame **Bay, and Bona-**

VISTA between Bonavista and Trinity Bays, are **settlements of some importance,** all dependent on the fisheries. HEART'S CONTENT on **Trinity Bay is** the landing-place of several **transatlantic cables.** Besides these are numerous smaller **settlements and** villages situated on **harbours** along the **coast and** having populations varying from **1500 to 500.**

DOMINION OF CANADA

(A.) ACADIAN PROVINCES

Under the name Acadian Provinces or Acadia, **Nova Scotia, New** Brunswick, **and Prince** Edward Island are included. These are perhaps more generally known as the Maritime Provinces; but as the province of Quebec is also in part **washed by the sea,** while that of British Columbia, at the opposite extreme of the Dominion of Canada, is equally entitled to be known as a maritime province, this name is not sufficiently distinctive. The name Acadia is derived from a native word *kadie*, meaning, when in combination with an object, a "place of abundance" of that object; it is still preserved in many local names, such as Shuhenacadie, or "place abounding in ground-nuts." It was adopted by the early French voyagers as La Cadie or l'Acadie, which has since become anglicised into Acadia.

Compared with the other provinces of Canada the three Acadian provinces are small in size, resembling in this respect the neighbouring north-eastern states of the American Union. They form a natural group, being similar in **their physical features,** such as the generally varied and **uneven forms of the surface,** which never attains a great altitude, **and alike in the variety of their soil and** mineral products, **their** large extent **of coast-line relatively to area, as well as in** their industries **and** people. **They bear to** the inland regions of Canada **somewhat the same relation** as that held by the **British Islands to the plains of** Central Europe.

NOVA SCOTIA

Name and Size.—This province first appears under the name which it has since retained in a charter granted by James I. to Sir William Alexander in 1621. It consists of a peninsula, Nova Scotia proper, and a large island, Cape Breton, which is politically united with it. The peninsula is connected with New Brunswick, on the mainland, by a low isthmus, 16 miles in width only at its narrowest part. The peninsula and Cape Breton Island together form a broad low elevation, with a north-east and south-west trend, parallel to that of the corresponding part of the length of the Appalachian highlands. It may thus be described as a hammer-shaped projection from the mainland which a slight subsidence of the land would convert into two large islands. The length of the entire province, including Cape Breton Island, which is separated from the peninsula by a narrow strait, is 360 miles, its average breadth being about 65 miles. The form of the land is such, that no part of the interior is distant more than about 30 miles from the coast. The area is 20,907 square miles, being thus less than that of Scotland by about 9000 square miles.

Though the coast of the Labrador peninsula lies to the east of Nova Scotia in longitude, the rigorous winter climate of that region, and the quantity of ice brought down along it by the Arctic current, cause the harbours on the southern coast of Nova Scotia to be the easternmost ones in the continental land of North America which are open to commerce throughout the year. Of these, Halifax harbour, 2910 miles from Liverpool, is the best known and most important. The 45th parallel of latitude, which passes through the centre of France, nearly bisects the peninsula of Nova Scotia, and the entire province is situated farther to the south than even the southernmost part of England.

Surface.—Though variegated in contour, the whole surface of the province is rather low and nowhere exceeds 1200 feet in elevation. Its dominant features consist of ridges running parallel to the length of the peninsula, and depending for their existence, exactly as in the case of Newfoundland, upon the lines of outcrop of the harder and older crystalline and metamorphic rocks. The most important of these elevations is known as the Cobequid Mountains. It is situated toward the northern coast of the peninsula, and runs, though with some breaks, from Cape Chignecto on the Bay of Fundy, to the east end of the peninsula, beyond which it is continued with a less elevation, in the northern part of Cape Breton Island. Another wide, though less elevated, tract of high land rises gradually from the southern coast, while in the south-western part of the peninsula a well-marked ridge of trap hills, known as the North Mountain, borders the southern shore of the Bay of Fundy, separating it from a long and direct parallel valley, the Annapolis valley, part of which is occupied by St. Mary's Bay and Annapolis basin, while the remainder includes much of the most fertile land of the province.

Generally speaking, the southern or outer side of Nova Scotia, though including some considerable tracts of good land, is rocky and barren; the best agricultural districts being situated toward the opposite or inner side, and thus facing toward the Gulf of St. Lawrence or the Bay of Fundy. About one-sixth of the whole area of the province is under cultivation or in use for pastoral purposes. The Annapolis valley is specially notable for its rich soil and garden-like and well-cultivated character. There are besides some large tracts of marsh lands along the shores of the Bay of Fundy with soil of almost inexhaustible fertility. These are classed as "salt marsh" and "dyked marsh," the first named being subject to occasional overflow by the sea and therefore useful only for the growth of fodder and for pasturage. The arable lands generally correspond closely with the extent of the newer and softer rock formations, particularly those of the Carboniferous and Triassic periods, the valuable lands of the Annapolis valley being based on red Triassic sandstones. The higher and more sterile and rocky lands of the province, both in the peninsula itself and in Cape Breton Island, often assume the character of peaty or shrubby moors, locally named "barrens" and still frequented by large game such as the moose and the caribou. In the Cobequid Mountains and other hilly tracts there are extensive **forests**, the most abundant timber being the spruce, though white-pine was also formerly to be found in some quantity.

Coast-Line.—The outer or Atlantic coast-line of Nova Scotia and Cape Breton, exposed to the full force of the ocean, is everywhere frayed into inlets and small bays resembling, though on a less scale, the **sea-lochs** of the west coast of Scotland, and affording many havens suited to fishing **vessels and** several large and **commodious harbours.** It is bordered by a great number of small and rocky islands. The north-west side, upon the Bay of Fundy, is more deeply indented by larger arms of the sea of irregular forms, while the semicircular sweep of coast fronting the Gulf of St. Lawrence is comparatively unbroken in its outline, but affords also some good harbours, though these are generally blocked by ice for a portion of the winter. The centre of Cape Breton Island is occupied by a land-locked and almost tideless expansion of the sea known as Bras d'Or (Arm of Gold) Lake, which opens to the north-eastward by two narrow passages. But for the isthmus of St. Peter's, less than a mile in width, Cape Breton would consist of two islands, and across this narrow isthmus a canal has been cut for purposes of navigation.

The Bay of Fundy (a name probably derived from the French *Fond de la bai*), separating the south-western part of Nova Scotia from the opposite shore of New Brunswick, with its arms Chignecto Bay and Minas basin, is celebrated for its tides, which are probably the highest in the world, the difference between high and low water being from 40 to over 50 feet in some places. At low tide muddy flats, often miles in extent, are laid bare, and the long estuaries of the rivers and streams are completely drained. The extraordinary height of the tides in this bay is due to its funnel-shaped form, and is greatest toward its narrow upper extremities, where in some places a dangerous broken wave or "bore" is produced by the rising water. The Strait of **Canso is** a narrow but deep channel which separates the peninsula of Nova Scotia from Cape Breton. It is about 15 miles in length and 1 mile wide, but opens on both sides into large bays—St. George Bay to the north, and Chedabucto Bay to the south. It is much used by **coasting** and fishing vessels, as by means of it the long **and often** rough voyage round the eastern extremity of the **province** is avoided.

Except Cape Breton Island, Isle Madame and Boulardie are the largest islands near the coast. Sable Island, distant 85 miles from the southern coast of Nova **Scotia in the** open Atlantic, is about 20 miles in length and 1 mile in breadth, and consists entirely of sand-dunes. It represents an unsubmerged part of one of the extensive fishing-banks which lie off the south-east coast of Nova Scotia, and has much decreased in size since it was first known. Its situation in the direct track of vessels renders it peculiarly dangerous to shipping. Many wrecks have occurred upon it, and it is therefore sometimes called the "Graveyard of the North Atlantic." It is provided with lighthouses and a life-saving station, but is otherwise uninhabited.

Drainage System.—In the nearly parallel-sided **belt of** land which forms the greater part of the Nova Scotian peninsula, the line of watershed lies well toward **the north at** both ends, but approaches the south coast about the **middle,** opposite Halifax, where the northern range of highlands is interrupted and its place is taken by the valleys **of the** Shubenacadie and some other smaller rivers which flow into Minas basin. **South** of this main watershed to the eastward, **the St. Mary** (length 50 miles) and Musquodobit (length 35 miles) are the largest streams, to the westward the La Have **(length** 45 miles) and Liverpool (length 60 miles) **rivers.** On the north the East river (length 35 miles) flowing into **Pictou Har**bour, and the Annapolis river **emptying** into the Bay of Fundy, **are** streams of some **importance.** But as most of the rivers **flow** northward and southward nearly at right angles to **the length** of the peninsula, which is nowhere wide, all are small and generally rapid and rocky; even the largest are navigable only for a few miles in their estuarine portions.

The Annapolis river is peculiar in running nearly parallel to the coast, being turned from its direct course by the trappean ridge of North Mountain. In the strip of land which connects the body of the peninsula with New Brunswick, the watershed lies near the Bay of Fundy on the south, the longer slope being toward the Gulf of St. Lawrence. The island of Cape Breton is so much cut into by the sea that it supports no large streams.

Lakes and ponds are numerous, but small, the largest being Lake Rossignol, Ship Harbour Lake, and Lake Ainslie in Cape Breton Island.

Climate.—This is not subject to such great extremes as in the case of the St. Lawrence provinces, but is very changeable. The rainfall is greater than it is farther inland, and fogs are rather prevalent along the coast, and particularly in the Bay of Fundy. In the western part of the province the average temperature is higher than in the eastern, where the spring is lingering in consequence of the influence of the cold waters of the Gulf of St. Lawrence. The climate as a whole is, however, remarkably healthy and conducive to longevity. The average annual precipitation for the province, including rainfall and melted snow, amounts to 44·44 inches. Mean highest temperature at Halifax, 87·6 ; mean lowest, 7·5 below zero.

Mineral Fields and Chief Industries.—The mineral wealth of Nova Scotia is known to be great, and is varied in character. Coal is the most important product, followed by gold. Gypsum, iron-ore, manganese, barytes, and grindstones are produced in smaller quantity.

The principal coal-fields are those of Pictou and of Cumberland counties, and that of the eastern part of the island of Cape Breton. The Pictou coal-field has been long worked, and is characterised by coal-seams of great thickness. Most of the coal is shipped by sea from the harbour at the mouth of the East river. Sydney Harbour is the chief port of shipment for the coal of Cape Breton. The seams here dip seaward, and are already worked at some distance beneath the sea-bed. From the Cumberland field, coal is shipped by way of the Bay of Fundy and by railway. Iron is manufactured to a limited extent, but most of the coal goes to neighbouring ports in the Dominion, a large proportion being consumed in Montreal.

The gold mines are in a belt of old slaty and quartzite rocks situated on the Atlantic slope of the peninsula, the gold being obtained from quartz which is mined and crushed, and not by the washing of alluvial gravels.

In the fisheries, which are very valuable and important, over 14,000 small vessels and boats with 27,000 men are employed; and the value of the catch obtained is more than one-third of the whole value of that taken in Canada. Cod, mackerel, lobsters, herrings, and haddock form a large part of the whole catch. The fisheries are conducted partly along the shores and partly on banks situated to the south of the Atlantic coast, and in the waters of the Gulf of St. Lawrence, while some of the fishermen also frequent the Grand Banks of Newfoundland, and the coasts of that island and of Labrador. A large tonnage of merchant vessels engaged in the carrying-trade in all parts of the world is also owned in Nova Scotia, and the building of wooden ships is still carried on to an important extent. Thus this province already fully realises the advantages of its commanding maritime position, the great extent of its coast-line and its numerous excellent harbours; and it is probable that as large a proportion of its inhabitants follow a seafaring life as that to be found in any other country on the globe.

Wheat, oats, and other similar field-crops are the staple products of that part of the province which drains to the Gulf of St. Lawrence, while the Annapolis and Cornwallis valleys—the old home of the French Acadians—are celebrated for their orchards, from which large quantities of fruit of the best quality are exported to Great Britain and the United States. Stock-farming and dairy-farming also constitute considerable industries. Lumbering is somewhat important, though timber of the first quality is now scarce, and the produce of the forest consists principally of spruce.

Manufactures of various kinds have also been established; but, relatively to the advantages which an abundant and cheap supply of coal should ensure, they are as yet but little developed.

Population.—As compared with the other provinces of Canada, Nova Scotia stands second in respect to density of population, the average number of persons to the square mile being about twenty-one. The total population of the province at the last census was 450,500, and as but few immigrants have established themselves in Nova Scotia for many years, by far the larger part of the people is native born. Arranged in order of importance with respect to nationality of origin, the greater part of the population is nearly equally divided between Scots and English, the Scots, however, somewhat preponderating. After these come Irish, Germans, and French, with small numbers from many other countries. The settlement of a large contingent of United Empire Loyalists in the province subsequent to the revolutionary war has already been referred to (p. 44). The French element of the population represents, for the most part, the descendants of the old Acadian colonists, most of whom were expelled by the British Government in 1755 because of their irreconcilable hostility. These people have been made the subject of Longfellow's poem "Evangeline." About the same time a large colony of Germans was established at Lunenburg, and in the county of this name, to the west of Halifax, most of the people of German origin are still centred.

For purposes of representation and government, Nova Scotia is divided into eighteen counties, forming two tiers, one facing to the Atlantic and the other to the northern coast. With the exception of this general difference, the lines between the several counties seldom coincide with natural features, but are arbitrarily drawn.

Towns.—HALIFAX (pop. 38,500) is the seat of the provincial Government, and the only city in Nova Scotia (Fig. 6). Known in early days by its Indian name Chebucto, this city was founded by the British Government, and received its present name in honour of Earl Halifax in 1749. It possesses a magnificent harbour, which is strongly fortified, and is the summer rendezvous and coaling-station of the North American squadron of the British fleet. It is the only place in Canada at which a permanent garrison is at

Fig. 6.—Halifax, Nova Scotia. From a Photograph by Notman.

present maintained by the Imperial **Government, and is
now a** maritime and commercial city. While **the trade of
other** parts of the province is largely carried on from local
ports, Halifax **absorbs** a considerable share of the whole,
and is also the chief winter port on the eastern seaboard
of Canada. The harbour is accessible at all seasons of the
year, and from its position on the main route of steamships
between Europe and America—about 600 miles nearer to
Liverpool than New York—is important as a place of call
or port of refuge. Some manufacturing industries are also
situated here. DARTMOUTH (pop. 6500) lies opposite
Halifax, and is separated from it only by the width of the
harbour. LIVERPOOL (pop. 2400), on the Atlantic **coast,
half-way** from Halifax to the south-western extremity of
the peninsula, is an important point in connection with
the timber trade. YARMOUTH (pop. 6000), situated at
the south-western extreme of Nova Scotia, though surrounded by a comparatively barren country, flourishes by
reason of its seafaring industries, and **is said to be the
most maritime place** of its size in the world. DIGBY, situ-
ated on Annapolis basin. ANNAPOLIS (pop. 950) was
founded by the French as Port Royal in 1605, **and thus
the oldest town in** America to the north of Florida, received
its present name on its **conquest by the English. It is**
situated on Annapolis basin **at the mouth of** the river of
the same name, and though **now a quiet** rural town has
often been the scene **of** conflict between the English and
French. It is the centre of the trade **in** fruit. WINDSOR
(pop. 2800), at **the** mouth of a small **river** named the
Avon, on Minas basin, is an agricultural **centre. Loyalists
coming here after the** American **revolutionary war replaced
the** French Acadians. TRURO (pop. 5100) **is beautifully
situated near the head** of Cobequid Bay, **at the extremity
of the south-east arm** of the Bay **of Fundy. It is surrounded by fertile lands,** and is the **seat of some manufactures and a railway centre.** AMHERST (pop. 3800), **situated
near the head of Cumberland basin, the** north-eastern
extremity of the Bay of Fundy, **near the** dividing line
between the **provinces of** Nova Scotia and New Brunswick,
is surrounded by a rich farming country, with widespread

marsh lands. PICTOU (pop. 3000) also possesses an excellent harbour, which opens to the Gulf of St. Lawrence, but unlike most of the harbours of the Atlantic coast it freezes over for a portion of each winter. The shipping points of the collieries of the Pictou coal-field are situated on the same harbour. NEW GLASGOW (pop. 3800) is one of these, and possesses besides some manufactories. The population of the adjacent part of the province is largely Scottish in origin, and farming is extensively prosecuted. ANTIGONISH, with a rather shallow harbour opening on St. George Bay, depends chiefly on the agricultural resources of the adjacent country, and is largely peopled by the descendants of Scots Highlanders. SYDNEY (pop. 2400) and NORTH SYDNEY (pop. 2500), both places on Sydney harbour, depend chiefly on coal mining for their prosperity, being the shipping points for the principal coal mines in Cape Breton. The harbour is excellent, and the place was selected as the capital of Cape Breton (at first politically separated from Nova Scotia) after the capture and destruction of the French fortress of Louisbourg.

NEW BRUNSWICK

Size.—This province has an area of 27,490 square miles, being thus considerably larger than Nova Scotia, and nearly as large as Scotland. Its form is that of an irregular quadrilateral, measuring about 200 miles from south to north by 160 miles from east to west. At its south-eastern angle it connects with Nova Scotia by the narrow Chignecto isthmus, the rest of its southern side being washed by the Bay of Fundy. Its eastern side borders on the Gulf of St. Lawrence, while to the north it joins the Province of Quebec, and is bordered on the west by the State of Maine.

Surface.—The general features of the surface of New Brunswick resemble those of Nova Scotia, but are drawn upon a somewhat larger scale and with greater uniformity. The highlands and lowlands depend very closely upon the character of the underlying rocks, but this influence has not so obviously affected the courses of the rivers and direction of the drainage. The surface consists chiefly of rolling plains and hills, and though it occasionally becomes mountainous no true mountain range exists. In order to form a clear idea of the two ruling systems of elevations, these may be compared to the two arms of a letter V, of which the apex lies at the south-western corner of the province. From that point a narrow belt of broken, hilly, and rather barren country, consisting often of several parallel ridges, with heights of 500 to 1000 feet, extends along the north shore of the Bay of Fundy nearly to its head, but not as far as the coast of the Gulf of St. Lawrence. The other and wider arm runs in a north-easterly direction from the apex to the southern shore of the Bay Chaleur. This includes the highest and most mountainous land in the province, with points such as Bald Mountain, Mount Teneriffe, and others having altitudes of from 2000 to 2700 feet. It also supplies the sources of several of the larger rivers, and it is characterised, like the southern hilly belt, by crystalline rocks and old hard Cambrian and Lower Silurian strata, much disturbed and folded. Between the two arms of the V lies a wide flat country, based on rocks of Carboniferous age, chiefly sandstones. This plain seldom attains a height of more than a few hundred feet above the sea, and slopes gradually to a low shore along the Gulf of St. Lawrence, where it spreads round the eastern end of the southern arm of the V connecting with similar low land in the northern part of Nova Scotia. To the north of the northern arm of the V, and parallel to it in direction, is a belt of undulating plateau country, with a height varying from 800 to 1200 feet. This is based upon Silurian rocks, and extends in width to the northern line of the province, beyond which it is bounded by much higher mountainous country running parallel to the St. Lawrence and forming the principal continuation of the Appalachian highlands, included in the Province of Quebec.

A large proportion, probably amounting to two-thirds of the entire area of New Brunswick, is adapted for agricultural occupation. The whole surface of the country was originally wooded, but up to the present time not much more than one-tenth of the cultivable land is cleared and occupied, the larger settlements being situated principally at no great distance from the coast or along the valleys of the more important rivers. The soil differs much in quality, varying from light and sandy to deep and rich. Some of the river valleys include a notable width of low alluvial land of excellent character, locally known as "intervale" land, while wide areas of marsh land, like those of the adjacent part of Nova Scotia, exist near the head of the Bay of Fundy.

Coast-Line.—While, owing to its nearly insular position and narrow irregular form, Nova Scotia possesses almost the greatest possible length of coast-line relatively to its area, New Brunswick presents a coast-line only about half as extensive. The southern coast, bordering on the Bay of Fundy, is generally rocky in character, but has several good harbours, including that of St. John. The western coast forms part of the semicircular south-eastern border of the Gulf of St. Lawrence, which is continued in the northern coast of Nova Scotia. It is characteristically low, shelving and sandy, but is penetrated by the rather large estuaries of several rivers, some of which form good harbours. The Bay Chaleur, celebrated for its fisheries, is a deep indentation 85 miles in length, which, in part, separates the province on the north from Quebec. This fine bay received its name (properly Baie des Chaleurs) from Jacques Cartier on his first voyage, on account of the great heat experienced by him there at the time of his visit. It is said to be without reef or shoal dangerous to navigation throughout. The southern entrance is partly enclosed by two large, low, wooded islands, named Shippegan and Miscou. These with Campo Bello, Grand Manan, and Deer Islands, near the mouth of the Bay of Fundy, are the most important in the province.

Drainage System.—The principal watershed of New Brunswick, which separates the rivers flowing to the Gulf of St. Lawrence from those reaching the Bay of Fundy, does not coincide with either of the tracts of highlands which have been described, but runs diagonally across the province from its north-west to its south-east angle. Its course is, however, very irregular in the middle of the province, where it makes a wide S-shaped flexure, sweeping first to the westward, round the sources of the Miramichi, then to the eastward, round those of the Salmon and Canaan rivers, branches of the St. John. On the north-easterly slope from this watershed the larger rivers are the Restigouche, Nepisiguit, Miramichi, and Richibucto. The opposite slope is principally drained by the St. John and its tributaries, with the St. Croix, Magaguadavic, Kennabecasis, and Petitcodiac rivers.

The St. John (length 360 miles) is much the largest of the rivers of New Brunswick, and forms in part of its upper course the boundary between that province and the State of Maine. It received its present name from Champlain at the beginning of the seventeenth century, and this afterwards became the name also of the city founded at its estuary nearly two hundred years later by Loyalist colonists. It is noteworthy, that though the general course of the St. John is nearly parallel to the line of the eastern coast of New Brunswick, it cuts across the principal lines of elevation and the usual north-east and south-west trend of the rocks of the province upon which the positions of these elevations depend. This river drains nearly half the entire area of the province, besides receiving much water from the adjacent State of Maine to the west, and several of its tributaries are themselves rivers of considerable size. It is continuously navigable by small steamers from the sea to the Grand Falls, a distance of nearly 200 miles, and is ascended to Fredericton, 85 miles from its mouth, by somewhat larger craft. Near the mouth of the river, at the harbour of St. John, it flows through a rocky gorge and is crossed by a reef, over which at high tide there is a fall inward, while at low tide there is a fall outward. This point can be passed only at certain stages of the tide.

Next in importance to the St. John is the Miramichi river (length 100 miles), flowing into Miramichi Bay, on the Gulf of St. Lawrence. At its mouth is the best harbour of the east coast of New Brunswick, and its estuary is navigable for vessels of considerable size for 18 miles. Here the towns of Chatham and Newcastle are situated.

The Restigouche (length 80 miles), flowing into the Bay Chaleur, is the third largest river. For part of its course it forms the boundary between New Brunswick and Quebec, but its upper waters are entirely within the province of New Brunswick. This river is specially noted for its salmon fishing, and is a resort of anglers. Dalhousie and Campbellton are situated on its estuary. The Nepisiguit (length 60 miles), which, like the last, flows into the Bay Chaleur, is also noted for its salmon fishing, and traverses valuable timber lands. It is a swift river, with a harbour at its mouth, where the town of Bathurst is built. The Richibucto, a small river, also has a good harbour for vessels of moderate draught at its mouth, where the town of the same name is situated. The Petitcodiac (length 55 miles), flowing into the extremity of the northern arm of the Bay of Fundy, traverses a well-settled agricultural country, Moncton, Dorchester and other towns standing on its banks. It is navigable by large vessels for about 25 miles from its mouth. The St. Croix (length 65 miles) for a great part of its length forms the boundary between New Brunswick and Maine. The towns of St. Stephen and St. Andrew are situated on its east side, and the harbour into which it empties, Passamaquoddy Bay, is justly celebrated as one of the finest on the continent.

Lakes are not so numerous in New Brunswick as they are in Nova Scotia. Grand Lake, over 20 miles in length, surrounded by a flat country based on sandstone, and flowing into the St. John river, is the largest.

Climate. — The climate of New Brunswick resembles that of Nova Scotia, but, in the interior, is somewhat more "continental" (see p. 15) in character. There the snow generally lies from December to April. The shores on the Bay of Fundy are subject to dense fogs. The winter is less extreme and the summer temperature more moderate than in the St. Lawrence provinces. Average annual precipitation for the province, 42·64 inches. Mean highest temperature at Fredericton, 90·6 ; mean lowest, 27·4 below zero.

Mineral Fields and Chief Industries.—Though rocks of the Carboniferous period—in which the coal deposits of the eastern part of North America, like those of Britain, are generally found—occupy a large part of the surface of New Brunswick, including its whole eastern and much of its central part, the coal-seams known to exist are thin and are worked only on a small scale for local purposes. Gypsum is, however, obtained in considerable amount from rocks of this age, and small quantities of manganese and antimony are mined. The manufacture of grindstones, and the quarrying of freestone for building purposes in the same Carboniferous rocks, are of some importance, and at St. George, in the south-western part of the province, red granite is quarried and worked into various forms for architectural uses.

Agriculture, fishing, and lumbering constitute the occupation of the greater part of the population. Wheat, barley, oats, and buckwheat, with potatoes and other ordinary root crops, green crops, and hay, are the staple agricultural products; but from what has already been stated with respect to the area of cultivated land, it will be apparent that farming is yet capable of great expansion.

The fisheries are second only in importance to those of Nova Scotia, giving employment to more than 10,000 men. They are chiefly prosecuted on the shores of the province itself, either in the Bay of Fundy or Gulf of St. Lawrence. In the first-named the fishermen are not interrupted by ice in the winter, but in the Gulf the shores are partly blocked with ice during several months of the year. The kinds of fish caught are similar to those taken in Nova Scotia, but the salmon, smelt, and shad here form a more important part of the catch, and oysters are obtained at certain places on the Gulf shores. A considerable proportion of the fish taken in winter is not cured, but sent by rail to various markets in a frozen state.

Timber in various forms constitutes the greater part of the exports of New Brunswick, most of it going to Great Britain. Spruce is obtained in the largest quantity and generally shipped in the form of "deals." White pine, larch, birch, maple, cedar, and other kinds of wood are also abundant; and in obtaining and dealing with these products of the forest a large number of men are engaged, and many saw-mills are employed. "Spruce logging," as it is called, is chiefly carried on in the winter, the logs being drawn on the snow to adjacent streams, down which they are afterwards "driven" to the various mills.

Manufacturing industries have grown up to some extent, but are not important as compared with the natural industries just referred to. Many sea-going vessels are owned in the province, and these are engaged not only in carrying to various markets the produce of the country itself, but also in the general carrying-trade in all parts of the world. Wooden vessels are built; but the general adoption of iron in shipbuilding has reduced this business to small proportions. Flour, salted meats, and manufactured articles are imported from the western provinces of Canada and from the United States, and manufactured goods from Britain.

Population.—The number of people within the limits of this province at the last census was 321,300. As in the case of Nova Scotia, but a small part of the entire population is not of native birth. The proportions existing between the nationalities of origin of the different elements in the population again resemble those in Nova Scotia, though there is in New Brunswick a somewhat greater number of French-speaking inhabitants. In respect to density of population relatively to area, New Brunswick stands third among the provinces, being exceeded in this respect only by Prince Edward Island and Nova Scotia.

The province is subdivided for political purposes into fifteen counties, of which eight include portions of the coast-line, the remaining seven lying entirely inland. The boundaries of these are in almost all cases straight lines, drawn with little reference to the physical features of the country.

Towns.—FREDERICTON (pop. 6500) is the political capital of the province of New Brunswick, and is prettily situated on the bank of the St. John river. Its commerce is chiefly connected with timber. ST. JOHN (pop. 39,000), the largest city and the commercial centre of the province, is built at the mouth of the river of the same name, and was originally called Parrstown (**Fig. 7**). In 1877 fully half of

FIG. 7.—ST. JOHN, NEW BRUNSWICK. From a Photograph by Notman.

the city was destroyed by fire, but it has since been rebuilt, fine brick buildings in many cases replacing the older ones of wood. Besides the export and import trade, and some manufactures, the people of St. John own shipping to an amount of more than 100,000 tons. ST. ANDREW (pop. 1700) and ST. STEPHEN (pop. 2700) are small towns to the west of St. John on the St. Croix river, chiefly dependent on industries connected with timber and fishing. To the west of St. John, and near the head of the Bay of Fundy, are SACKVILLE and DORCHESTER, small towns in a rich farming district with extensive marsh lands. MONCTON (pop. 8800) is a railway centre and contains several manufactories. The tide flowing up the estuary of the Petitcodiac comes in here as a "bore" six feet in height. WOODSTOCK (pop. 3300) stands on the bank of the St. John river, sixty-five miles above Fredericton, in a fertile farming country.

The following seven towns are the principal ones on the eastern shore, often locally called the "north shore," of the province. They are named in order from south to north, and all are situated on harbours or the estuaries of rivers. SHEDIAC (pop. 1500), RICHIBUCTO (pop. 1200), CHATHAM (pop. 5000), NEWCASTLE (pop. 2500), BATHURST (pop. 800), DALHOUSIE (pop. 800), CAMPBELLTON (pop. 2200). These places are all largely supported by lumbering and fishing. Chatham is rather noted for shipbuilding, and is the fourth largest town in the province.[1]

PRINCE EDWARD ISLAND

Name and Size.—This island was originally a part of the French territory of l'Acadie, and was known as Isle St. Jean, which name it retained for a number of years after the cession by France, the present name being adopted at the beginning of this century in compliment to Prince Edward, Duke of Kent, father of Queen Victoria, at that time commander of the forces at Halifax. It is much the smallest province of Canada, its whole area being 2133

---

[1] The number of inhabitants given for these seven towns is approximate only, as they are not separately enumerated in the census.

square miles, or 1,365,400 acres. The island lies in the southern part of the Gulf of St. Lawrence, opposite the coasts of **N**ova Scotia and New Brunswick, from which it is separated by **N**orthumberland Strait, comparatively shallow and varying in width from nine to twenty-five miles. The island is irregularly crescent-shaped, with broad ends, but its outline is cut up by numerous bays and inlets, due to the action of the sea upon the soft sandstone rocks of which it is composed. At two points it is less than five miles from shore to shore. Its greatest length is 150 miles, greatest breadth 35 miles.

Surface.—Being formed of red sandstone rocks which differ little in their resistance to weathering and waste, the surface is generally uniform in character, and nowhere exceeds 500 feet in height. It is usually either nearly level or undulating, becoming hilly in a few places. The soil is almost everywhere fertile, and, like the underlying rocks, red in colour. Only a small part of the entire province remains in a state of nature, while about one half of the whole is actually under cultivation. It may appropriately be called the "Garden of Canada," and more nearly resembles the appearance of some parts of England than that of most other places on the American continent.

Coast-Line.—The coast is much broken and very irregular in the details of its outline, several large and many small bays and inlets constituting excellent harbours, particularly for small fishing vessels. Some parts of the coast are bordered by low red sandstone cliffs, while others are shelving and sandy. The sea adjacent to the island is nowhere deep, and it thus affords favourable feeding-grounds for fish. The subsidiary islands are small and unimportant, several of these bordering the north shore consisting of sand-dunes or low sand-bars.

Drainage System.—The small size of the island and its broken outline leave no room for any considerable drainage-basins, and the numerous small streams which exist scarcely merit the name of rivers.

Climate.—This resembles that of the neighbouring parts of Nova Scotia and New Brunswick, the progress of spring being often somewhat retarded by the cold and occasionally ice-laden waters of the Gulf. Fogs are not common.

Industries.—No mineral deposits are worked. The rocks of the island are those of the Trias, Permian, and upper part of the Carboniferous formations. Coal may exist in the lower part of the last-named formation, but if so it must be at a great depth. Agriculture in its various branches is the chief occupation of the people, and the soil yields an abundant return for the labour expended on it,— the principal crops being wheat, oats, barley, potatoes, and turnips. Oats and potatoes are exported in large quantity, and the horses bred in the island are noted for their excellence. A deposit found in some of the estuaries known as "mussel mud" is much used as a fertiliser. It consists largely of broken shells with vegetable and animal matter derived from the marine life. Though the island is the best fishing-station in the Gulf, the attention of the people is comparatively little directed to the fisheries. Large fleets of fishing vessels visit this part of the Gulf, but the people of the island generally limit their fisheries to the vicinity of the shores. Oysters are obtained in abundance on Northumberland Strait. In aggregate value of their product the fisheries rank next in importance to agriculture. Manufactures are unimportant and local in character. A number of sea-going vessels are owned on the island, and shipbuilding is prosecuted to some extent. The island is traversed from end to end by a line of railway. From the middle of December to the middle of April the ordinary navigation of the adjacent waters, including Northumberland Strait, is generally more or less interrupted. At such times mails and passengers are carried across the Strait in specially-constructed steamboats of great strength and power.

Population.—Prince Edward Island is more than twice as thickly peopled as any other province, there being about 51 inhabitants to each square mile. The total population is 109,000. The people are for the most part native born, about half being of Scottish descent, with large proportions of English and Irish origin, and of descendants of Acadian French, the original settlers. The island is

divided into three counties, each of which extends **across** its whole width.

Towns.—CHARLOTTETOWN (pop. 11,400), **the largest town** and seat of the local Government, is situated **on the** south side and near the middle of the island, at the mouth of a long inlet known as Hillsborough river. It possesses a large and excellent harbour and is the principal port of shipment, with a thriving trade. SUMMERSIDE (pop. about 2900), also situated on the south side of the island but nearer to the western end, is the principal oyster mart. ALBERTON, GEORGETOWN, and SOURIS are smaller towns. The characteristic feature of the island **is,** however, the almost continuous lines of comfortable farmhouses which border the roads and highways, **seldom** clustering together even **into villages.**

(B.) ST. LAWRENCE PROVINCES

Under **this** geographically descriptive **name, the two** most populous and important provinces of Canada—Quebec and Ontario—may be included. Before the Confederation of the various provinces **of** British North America, Quebec and Ontario were known as Lower and Upper Canada, or Canada East and Canada West, the name Canada being confined to them. Now that this name has been extended to the whole area of the Dominion, the term St. Lawrence Provinces is a convenient and appropriate one by which to designate them. The drainage-basin of the great river and its estuary, from the lower end of the island **of** Anticosti westward, comprises an area of about 530,000 square miles in all. Of this the Great Lakes, forming **the** upper reservoirs of the river, together with the estuarine portion of the river, cover an area of about 130,000 square miles, deducting which from the total area leaves a land superficies of about 400,000 square miles. Of this eight-tenths belong to Canada, the remainder to the United States. The whole of the Canadian portion is included in the provinces of Quebec and Ontario. Generally speaking, **the St. Lawrence flows near the** southern side of its drainage-basin; and the whole northern and wider slope, together with, in Quebec, a large part of the southern slope as well, is included in these two provinces. The only part of the United States which lies north of the St. Lawrence river, in its widest sense, is a small district to the west of the head of Lake Superior. Though thus fundamentally united as parts of the hydrographic basin of the St. Lawrence, Quebec and Ontario, in other respects, are not by any means so uniform in physical character, nor do they resemble each other so closely as do the provinces of the Acadian group. Quebec has a long line of sea-coast, while Ontario lies altogether inland, but possesses a great length of lake shore. The elements of the population also differ, French-speaking inhabitants largely preponderating in Quebec, while in a small minority in Ontario. Both provinces contain large connected areas of the most fertile land, as well as extensive barren and rocky tracts, scarcely, under any circumstances, susceptible of cultivation.

QUEBEC

Name and Size.—The name applied to this province is derived from the Indian name of the place where the city of Quebec now stands (see p. 35). It contains an area of 228,900 square miles, being thus larger than France or Germany, and somewhat less in size than Austria-Hungary. In form it is rudely triangular, the shorter base of the triangle lying to the south-west on the side of Ontario, the much-produced apex extending north-eastwards as far as the Strait of Belle Isle. From this apex to the base, near Lake Temiscamang on the Ottawa river, the greatest length of the province slightly exceeds 1000 miles, while its greatest width exceeds 400 miles. The funnel-shaped estuary of the St. Lawrence, with the large island of Anticosti in its mouth, cuts into the south-eastern side of the triangle, not very far from its apex; and then turning to a south-west bearing, which is continued by the river, divides the province into two very unequal parts, the portion cut off on the south-eastern side having an area of only about 50,000 square miles.

Surface.—The river and estuary of the St. Lawrence, in the province of Quebec, follow the trend of a belt of low country of variable width, but often wide, which is named the St. Lawrence plain, in order to distinguish it from the much more extensive hydrographical valley. This plain lies between the northern extension of the Appalachian highlands on one side, and the base of a part of the great Laurentian plateau on the opposite or north-western side. Practically the whole width of the north-eastern part of this low country is covered by the estuary of the river up to a point about 100 miles below the city of Quebec, above which the estuary narrows and the plain gradually increases in width, owing to the divergence of the bordering highlands, till wide lowlands are found to spread on both sides of the river.

The Appalachian highlands, in this their northern part, consist of a series of more or less nearly parallel ridges, of which the most elevated lie toward the north-west side, or that nearest to the St. Lawrence. Their general direction, from the place at which they enter the province on the south, is north-eastward till they approach the shore of the St. Lawrence estuary, when they turn to an easterly bearing and run through the Gaspé peninsula. At the extremity of this peninsula they decline in height and pass beneath the waters of the Gulf, to reappear in a much reduced form in the island of Newfoundland. South of the Quebec boundary, and east of Lake Champlain, the Appalachian highlands are known as the Green Mountains, but their extension through the province of Quebec is generally designated as the Nôtre Dame Range. As in other cases, the existence of these highlands is here found to depend upon the occurrence of upturned ancient crystalline and metamorphic rocks, and in general it is observed that the more elevated ridges are composed of the older rocks.

The south-western part of the Nôtre Dame Range consists rather of hills than of mountains properly so called. These heights, with the exception of a few prominent points, seldom exceed 1000 to 1500 feet in height, and present a rolling but not a rugged surface, comprising much land suited to tillage or pasturage. But on entering the Gaspé peninsula, and throughout its centre, the elevation of the range is much increased, so that it becomes entitled to be described as a mountain region. This tract, known as the Shickshock Mountains, has a length of about 65 miles in the Gaspé peninsula, being separated from the neighbouring shore of the estuary of St. Lawrence by a belt of lower hills and ridges about 12 miles in width. The higher points of the Shickshock Mountains, such as Mounts Bayfield, Albert, and Logan, reach elevations of from 3500 feet to 3800 feet, which, in these latitudes, rise above the upward limit of forest growth. Hence the summits are treeless and rocky.

The Gaspé peninsula, as a whole, is a block of table-land with a height of about 1500 feet, from which the Shickshock Mountains stand out; but it is remarkable that in this table-land these mountains do not form the watershed. The streams flowing to the St. Lawrence estuary rise to the south of the Shickshock Range, and flow completely across it in deep gorges cut down to within 500 or 600 feet of the sea-level. In the south-western part of the Nôtre Dame Range the rivers tributary to the St. Lawrence behave in a similar manner, their sources being found beyond the main ridges of the range. While the meaning of this peculiar structure cannot be fully explained, it evidently points to the great antiquity of these river-courses, and seems to show that they may have originated at an earlier period than that in which the higher parts of the range attained their present elevation.

The St. Lawrence plain, which is most important in the south-western part of the province, is 30 miles in width to the south of the river, opposite the city of Quebec. To the south-east of Montreal, where it runs across the international boundary on the 45th degree of latitude to become the Champlain valley, it has a width of 50 miles. The front of the Laurentian plateau, forming the opposite side of the plain, leaves the St. Lawrence about 20 miles below the city of Quebec, and at Montreal is about 30 miles distant from the river. To the west of Montreal it runs up the Ottawa, nearly coinciding with that river, for about

100 miles, when it turns southward, **to reach the St. Lawrence** river again at Kingston, not far below the outlet of Lake Ontario. The western extremity of the **plain thus** circumscribed, however, is included in the adjoining province **of Ontario.**

Much of the surface of the **St. Lawrence** plain, which has an area of about 10,000 square miles in the province of Quebec, is almost absolutely level, while no part of it reaches a height of more than a few **hundred feet above the sea,** and most of it is less than three hundred **feet in elevation.** It is based almost throughout upon nearly horizontal or but little disturbed Silurian rocks, most of which are **limestones, but** its surface is often composed to a variable and **often great** depth of clays and sand, left by the sea **at the time of** the latest considerable submergence of this part of **the continent,** and in places still including marine shells in abundance. The only prominent points found in the plain are certain isolated hills or low mountains, of which that behind the city of Montreal is one. These owe their existence to the superior hardness of the rocks of which **they** are composed, and mark **the positions** of very **ancient** centres of eruption, **probably of old** volcanic **vents.** There **are** six or **seven such hills in all,** varying from 500 to **1800** feet in height, and all **of them are** visible **from** the summit of "Montreal Mountain," from which also the eye ranges over a great part of the St. Lawrence plain and its bordering highlands. The soil of the plain is in general very fertile, but in consequence of its early occupation in the history of the country, and the careless methods of cultivation adopted, the natural **fertility** of **much of its** area has become reduced. The original French settlers found the surface one almost unbroken **forest, but long** before the cession of New France to Britain, **a** great part **had been** cleared and brought **under** cultivation. Part of the plain **to the** south-east **of Montreal,** together with the rolling and hilly country beyond it, is generally known as the "Eastern Townships."

With regard to the entire province **of** Quebec, the arable lands may be divided into three classes, of which those of the **St. Lawrence plain form** the **first.** The lands of the second class are those near or within the area of the Nôtre Dame Range, which have already been alluded to; the third, those of parts of the Laurentian plateau, which is next described.

To the north of the St. Lawrence, Quebec includes a vast tract of country of a peculiar type, belonging to the Laurentian plateau, which likewise extends throughout the whole northern portion of the province of Ontario (see p. 110). A limited part of this great region in Quebec assumes rugged and mountainous characters. This is situated not far to the north of the estuary of the great river, between the city of Quebec and the Saguenay, forming a range of highlands nearly parallel in direction to the river, in which some points probably exceed 3000 feet in height. The Laurentian region as a whole, though by no means level or flat-topped, may be most fittingly described as a plateau. Its slopes often emerge gradually or with no very conspicuous acclivity from the level of the plain to the south, but in other places (particularly along some parts of its border which front directly on the Gulf of St. Lawrence) its surface rises rapidly to a height of about 1000 feet. The average height of the highest parts of the plateau, near the watershed between the rivers flowing to the St. Lawrence and those draining to Hudson Bay, is seldom more than 2000 feet, and in many places is several hundred feet lower, 1500 feet being about the average elevation of the entire Laurentian region. Though the actual differences in elevation are thus considerable, the width of the plateau is such that its general slopes are very light. At some distance from its margin the surface is usually hummocky, composed of low rocky hills of monotonous outline, which have been reduced to rounded forms by the prolonged action of denudation, and the passage over them of ice during the glacial period. These hills are often arranged in ridges, which run in bearings corresponding with those of the rocks of which they are composed, and their height above the intervening valleys is usually small in the central parts of the plateau, but towards its borders the valleys become much deeper, and bold cliffs, with elevations notable because of the reduced height of the adjacent country, are frequently met with. Lakes are exceedingly numerous, being counted by thousands in that part of the plateau included in Quebec. Most of them are small, but many attain considerable dimensions and are very complicated in form. Some parts of the region which have been carefully surveyed in Quebec and Ontario consist almost in equal proportions of water and land (see p. 117). The lakes are almost invariably connected in irregular chains by streams and rivers, which in flowing from lake to lake usually form rapids or low falls and pursue most serpentine courses. The waters draining to the north and south often interlock in such a way as to produce a very irregular line of watershed. The streams of the inner parts of the plateau eventually collect to form the larger rivers, which fall more rapidly toward the edges of the plateau, and these often afford good water-power for mills and other industrial purposes.

The innumerable lakes which bespangle the whole area are one of its most remarkable features, and though these often appear to be scattered at random on the map, where the country has been closely examined it is found that the lake-basins are intimately associated with the less indurated belts of rock. The plateau as a whole consists of gneissic and granitic rocks, geologically known as "Laurentian," and of softer and darker-coloured though generally still crystalline strata, classed under the name "Huronian"; and where these last-named rocks spread most widely the larger lakes as well as the more extensive tracts of level land usually occur. The lakes, together with their network of connecting streams, afford a means of traversing almost any part of the country with light birch-bark canoes, which may be transported without difficulty across the narrow intervening "portages" or past the various rapids and falls.

The surface of the Laurentian plateau as a whole is rocky, but in the state of nature it is almost uniformly overspread with forest; pines and spruces cover the hills, while broad-leaved trees are often abundant in the valleys. The greater part of the timber obtained in the province is derived from these forests, but large tracts have been burnt, and in some cases the **hills** have thus been so completely denuded that little **remains** but the bare rock itself. **Though thus on the whole** of a barren character, the **Laurentian** region contains in all a large amount of land **susceptible of** cultivation **in** valleys or limited plains lying **between** the rocky hills. In these, gravelly, sandy, and clayey deposits have accumulated, often **in the form of** a series of terrace-like flats, and such areas are found especially along the courses of the larger rivers and toward the centre of their hydrographical basins. **The most important** of these alluvial areas included in the Laurentian **district** within the province of Quebec is that surrounding **Lake** St. John, at the head of the Saguenay; but along each of the larger river valleys, following in the steps of the "lumberer," **lines of settlements are** gradually being formed.

It is not possible **to give any precise statement of** the area **of** arable **lands within** the province of Quebec, **but** the unoccupied land susceptible of agriculture is believed to amount to about 20,000,000 acres. The area actually under tillage in 1881 was over 6,000,000 acres, or about one-twentieth of the whole area of the province.

Coast-Line.—The length of the coast-line of the province, embracing that of the estuary of the St. Lawrence as far up as the city of Quebec and that of the island of **Anticosti, but** not including all its smaller sinuosities, is **about** 1500 miles; but the gulf narrows so gradually into the estuary, and the latter into the river, that it is difficult to apportion definitely their respective **coast-lines. The head** of the gulf, however, is generally assumed to **be at** Point de Monts; and about 40 miles below the city of Quebec the water becomes altogether fresh, though **the** influence of **the** tide extends for 100 miles farther.

The **coast of** the **southern** part **of** Gaspé peninsula **on Chaleur** Bay is moderately elevated, but that **of the** eastern **end** of the peninsula is much bolder and more broken, the principal indentation being named Gaspé Bay. Cape Gaspé, **at** the northern entrance to this bay, presents to the sea **a** fine range of limestone cliffs 600 feet in height; and at Percé an isolated limestone crag, which has been worn by the waves into a natural arch, stands off the coast. The northern coast of the peninsula is also **high, with** bold cliffy headlands, and coves with small scattered fishing-settlements. Farther eastward, with a lower coast, the estuary **of the** St. Lawrence becomes fringed almost continuously **by** settlements. **Vessels** entering the river generally follow this side, and its uninterrupted line of white **cottages is** a striking feature. **The works** carried out **in** the part of the river above the **city of** Quebec, by which the largest **vessels** are enabled **to reach** Montreal, **are noticed on** p. **57.** The northern coast of **the gulf** and **estuary of the** St. Lawrence, as seen from **the sea, is** generally **bold and rocky,** and **in some places assumes an almost mountainous aspect.** It is nevertheless dotted **with** little fishing-villages, and **above the** mouth of the Saguenay is pretty thickly settled.

The large spindle-shaped island of Anticosti—140 **miles** in length, but **without good** harbours—consists **of low wooded land rising gradually to** its north side, **where it breaks off in cliffs.** The name is derived from the Indian, meaning "place where bears are hunted." The Magdalen Islands, situated in the **centre of the gulf, are also** politically attached to Quebec. **This little group is** about 20 **miles in length,** and is formed **of low** projecting masses of **rock** connected by lines **of** dunes and sand-bars. Many small and generally **rocky** islands also occur along the north shore **of the gulf,** of which the Mingan Islands, opposite the **island of Anticosti, are** the best known. The **largest of the many islands of the upper part of the** estuary **and of the river** are—**Isle aux Coudres, 60 miles below** Quebec city; the island of Orleans, just below **that city and 20 miles in length;** Montreal Island, **30 miles in length; and the smaller** adjacent **Isle Jesus. All these are rather low, and afford good** cultivable land.

Drainage System.—Quebec abounds in large and long rivers, **of which the St. Lawrence is** the main stem. **These** naturally **group** themselves into two series—those reaching the St. Lawrence from the south-east or shorter slope, and those coming in the opposite direction from **the**

H

Laurentian plateau. The principal rivers of both series generally flow on bearings nearly at right angles to that of the great river. Of the rivers on the south-east side the most important are those which drain the wide triangular area of the province between the cities of Quebec and Montreal. These include the Chaudière (length 110 miles), Becancour (length 75 miles), and St. Francis (length 140 miles). The first joins the St. Lawrence nearly opposite the city of Quebec, while the second flows into the expansion known as Lake St. Peter. Both rise to the south-east of the hilly country representing the Nôtre Dame Range, where their tributaries nearly meet. The Becancour, with other smaller streams, drains the region between these two rivers and to the north-west of the hilly country. The Yamaska (length 87 miles) and Richelieu (length 72 miles), also reaching the St. Lawrence at Lake St. Peter, run nearly parallel from south to north through a low country. The Richelieu is the outlet of Lake Champlain, and with the aid of canals forms part of a system of communication between the St. Lawrence and Hudson rivers. The Yamaska and St. Francis are also navigable for parts of their length.

The rivers which reach the south-east shore of the estuary of the St. Lawrence below Quebec, though some of them, like the Métis, are locally important in connection with the timber trade or as salmon-fishing streams, and though frequently of considerable size, are among the smaller ones of this province, and need not be separately enumerated. The same remark applies to the rivers of the Gaspé peninsula.

On the north side of the gulf and estuary, to the east of the Saguenay, the larger of the very numerous rivers which come from the Laurentian plateau are as follows, in order from east to west: Esquimaux, Mecatina, Natashquan, St. John, Moisie, Manicouagan, Outardes, Betsiamites, and Sault-au-Cauchon. Of these the Manicouagan and Outardes have courses exceeding 200 miles in length, while those of the others reach or surpass 100 miles. The general character of all these rivers, upon none of which any settlements exist away from the coast, will be understood from what has already been said respecting the Laurentian country. They are notable for the excellent salmon-fishing which they afford, and the Betsiamites is employed to a considerable extent for driving logs.

The Saguenay, St. Maurice, and Ottawa are the largest tributaries of the St. Lawrence.[1] Their farthest sources are situated about 200 miles to the northward of Montreal, in such proximity that a *voyageur* ascending any one of the rivers may, by portaging, without much difficulty reach the waters of either of the others. From their common point of origin on the higher part of the Laurentian plateau the Saguenay first runs eastward, and then turns to the south-east, flowing into Lake St. John under the name Ashouapmouchewan. Into the same lake-reservoir several other large rivers flow, including the Mistassini (length 160 miles), Peribonka (length 140 miles), Metabechuan (length 90 miles), and their united waters, on leaving it first, take the name Saguenay (Fig. 8). The lower part of the Saguenay, for about 60 miles from its mouth, is a true fiord, up which the tides flow from the gulf, and which is bordered by bold hills and precipices of solemn and impressive grandeur. The river proper discharges into one side of this fiord at a little distance from its termination at Ha-Ha Bay. Including the fiord-like lower portion, which is exceedingly deep, the length of the Saguenay is about 280 miles.

The Ottawa from its source flows first for about 180 miles by a very devious course toward the west, after which it turns southward, then south-eastward, and eventually eastward, thus making altogether a great U-shaped turn, open to the east, and joining the St. Lawrence near the upper end of the island of Montreal. Where it first turns from its westward course, it enters Lake Temiscamang (Indian, "Deep-water lake"), the largest of many lakes through which it flows. The whole upper part of this river has the character common to most of the streams

---

[1] The Saguenay derives its name from the Indian, meaning "water which runs out"; the Ottawa from the name of an Indian tribe, which appears to mean "wide-eared." Fig. 8 illustrates the character of a stream in the Laurentian region.

FIG. 8.—MARGUERITE RIVER, A TRIBUTARY OF THE SAGUENAY, WITH BIRCH-BARK CANOE. From a Photograph by Topley.

of the Laurentian plateau, but where it finally assumes an easterly direction it falls into an important and somewhat peculiar valley, the same which has already (p. 42) been mentioned as connecting the valley of the Ottawa with Lake Huron. This is known to be a feature of great antiquity because of the occurrence in it of old Silurian rocks, which are not found on the higher parts of the Laurentian plateau. The Ottawa thus possesses rather peculiar characters, and differs considerably from all other tributaries of the St. Lawrence in the nature of its lower valley, besides being the largest of its feeders. The length of this great river is 615 miles, and the area of its drainage-basin, within the province of Quebec, exceeds 40,000 square miles. Its principal affluents join it from the north, and some of these are themselves large rivers, of which the Noire (length 115 miles), Coulonge (150 miles), Gatineau (250 miles), Du Lièvre (170 miles), and Rouge (120 miles) may be named. The navigability of the Ottawa as far as the city of the same name has already been noted (see p. 57).

The St. Maurice, reaching the St. Lawrence below Lake St. Peter, drains the greater part of the country between the basins of the Saguenay and Ottawa. It is 280 miles in length, with a drainage-basin of about 17,000 square miles, and is fed by numerous tributaries, of which the Trenche (length 102 miles), Matawin (length 120 miles), and Vermilion (length 100 miles) are the largest. Part of its course is also navigable.

These three great branches of the St. Lawrence, the Ottawa, St. Maurice, and Saguenay with their affluents, afford the means of bringing timber down from the most remote parts of the province, and constitute the chief outlets for the products of the northern forests, their importance being in the order in which they are here named.

Lake St. John is the most important if not the largest lake in the province. It is relatively at a low elevation, being but 350 feet above sea-level, and has an area of about 360 square miles, with an approximately circular form. Lake Temiscamang, on the Ottawa, is 40 miles in length. Both of these are within the Laurentian region;

and to the eastward of the Saguenay there are several other large lakes, similarly situated, but of which little is known, in addition to the multitude of smaller lakes and ponds distributed over all parts of its surface. In or near the Nôtre Dame Range are the following lakes: Memphramagog (length 22 miles), Massawippi (length 8 miles), St. Francis (length 15 miles) drained by the St. Francis river; Megantic (length 9 miles), drained by the Chaudière; Temisquota (length 26 miles), flowing by the Madawaska to the St. John river of New Brunswick; and Matapedia (length 12 miles), discharging southward by the river of the same name to the Restigouche.

Climate.—In an area so great as that of the province of Quebec, part of which borders the Gulf of St. Lawrence, while the other extremity lies far within the Continent, the meteorological conditions are naturally varied. The climate of the St. Lawrence plain from the city of Quebec south-westward is the most favourable for agriculture, and the advance of spring is here very rapid, and summer heat great, bringing not only wheat but maize and the hardier kinds of grapes to perfection. Along the shores of the gulf the cold adjacent waters cause the spring to be protracted and cool, to such a degree that below the Saguenay wheat cannot be grown with profit. To the north of the great river, on the Laurentian highlands, the limit of the profitable growth of wheat is also soon reached, but the conditions in the low country about Lake St. John are exceptionally favourable, and in few parts of the province in which fertile soil is to be found is agriculture of one kind or another impracticable. The winter is characterised by cold clear weather, with an abundance of snow; and for nearly five months in the year the rivers, including even the St. Lawrence above the city of Quebec, are bound by frost, but form at that season excellent roads by which produce is brought to market, and local trade is carried on by means of sleighs. Average annual precipitation of the southern and inhabited part of the province, 36·6 inches. Mean highest temperature at Montreal, 89; mean lowest, 22·5 below zero.

Mineral Fields and **Chief Industries.**—This province

is at a disadvantage in containing no coal-fields, the coal required for manufacturing purposes being brought chiefly from Nova Scotia. The principal minerals obtained and exported **are** asbestos, apatite or phosphate of **lime**, used as a fertiliser, and copper—their relative importance being in the order given. The asbestos is procured by quarrying or mining operations in a limited district of the south-eastern part of the " Eastern Townships," the apatite **from** the Laurentian rocks to the north of the Ottawa river, and the copper in the " Eastern Townships." Gold is obtained from alluvial deposits, in limited quantities, in the valley of **the** Chaudière. Iron ores occur in many places, but are as yet scarcely worked. Mica and **plumbago** have been worked to some extent, **and antimony, silver, and many** other metalliferous metals are known. **Slate is** quarried to the south-east of Montreal, and building-stone of good quality, with clay well adapted for brick-making, is abundant. Marbles of various kinds, together with serpentine and other ornamental stones, are found in numerous localities, but have so far not become **the** basis of important industries.

Much the greater portion **of** the population is engaged **in agriculture,** or in pursuits resulting directly from it. **Oats** and hay are the two most valuable crops, followed in order by potatoes, peas, and beans, wheat, barley, and buckwheat. Stock-raising and the production of butter and cheese are of great and increasing importance.

The timber trade stands next in importance to agriculture, and furnishes a large part of the exports of **the** province, besides keeping many saw-mills and **various** subsidiary industries in operation. **White and red pine,** chiefly obtained on the tributaries **of the Ottawa, are** the most important woods, followed by spruce, larch, cedar, birch, maple, and others. The timber is **cut** during the **winter** by gangs of **men** sent into the **woods** for the purpose, and the logs are hauled on the snow to the bank **of** the nearest stream. When the **ice** breaks up in spring **the** logs are "driven" down the stream to some convenient point, where they are formed into "cribs," and these again, when the size of **the river becomes** sufficient, are collected into large rafts. The logs then go either to some saw-mill, or are shipped in the **form** of "square timber" without further treatment.

Fishing is of importance chiefly along the shores of the **Gulf of** St. Lawrence and **in** the lower and wider parts **of the estuary.** The kinds of fish taken are the same as **those in the** neighbouring Acadian provinces, but the aggregate value of the catch is much less than that of Nova Scotia, New Brunswick, or British **Columbia, being about** equal to that of Ontario.

Manufacturing industries increase in importance annually, the abundance of water-power to be found in **the** province to some extent compensating for the absence of coal-fields. In the order of their importance, and excepting saw-mills and flour-mills, the principal branches of manufacture are as follows: Leather, including tanning and **boot and shoe** making, iron manufactures, sugar-refining, furs and hats, cotton factories, woollen-mills, india-rubber factories. Most of **the** articles produced are for use within Canada. The **trade of this** province, in consequence **of** its position on the St. Lawrence, is very large, including most of that in transit to or from the western **provinces,** as well as considerable quantities of grain from the western part of the United States.

Population.—The total number of inhabitants exceeds **1,488,000, and of** these nearly eight-tenths are descendants **of the** original French colonists, the remaining two-tenths being principally people of English, Scottish, or Irish extraction, including a considerable proportion of immigrants from these countries. The natural rate **of** increase of the French-speaking portion of the population **since the time of** the cession of **Canada, when the colonists did not** number more than 70,000, is remarkable. The English-speaking portion of **the** population is found principally in the larger towns and **in** twelve counties lying to the south-**east of the river between** Montreal and the city of Quebec, **known as** the "Eastern Townships." Though **a** considerable part **of the** St. Lawrence plain is rather **densely** inhabited, the great area of the **northern** part **of the** province is very sparsely settled.

For purposes of local government, Quebec is divided into sixty counties of extremely variable size, which, however, bears to some extent an inverse ratio to the density of population. The inspection of a map upon which these divisions are represented will show that most of the smaller counties, clustered thickly and irregularly together, lie to the south of the St. Lawrence and to the west of the city of Quebec, in which region the oldest and some of the most important settlements are situated. To the north of the river, on the contrary, where the land at first taken up lay along its border only, the county lines were generally produced north-westward at right angles to the frontage on the river, in a manner totally independent of physical features or other considerations.

Towns.—QUEBEC (pop. 63,000), the seat of Government for the province, is situated on the north bank of the St. Lawrence, on a point of land between that river and a small affluent named the St. Charles (Fig. 9). It was founded in 1608 by Champlain, nearly on the site of an Indian village named Stadacona, and is remarkable for the beauty of its situation, the historic associations connected with it, its strong fortifications, and magnificent harbour. The city consists of an "Upper Town" and "Lower Town," covering respectively the summit of a bold promontory named Cape Diamond, and spread along the low land at its base. The two parts of the city are connected by steep streets. The natural strength of the position, commanding the St. Lawrence at a narrow point, rendered Quebec from the first a military stronghold, and its walls have been assaulted six times in the course of its history. The position of Quebec causes its commercial interests to be large, and it ranks third in this respect among the cities of Canada. It is the great port of shipment for timber. The most important manufacturing industry is boot and shoe making, very extensively prosecuted. Other manufactures are of comparatively small dimensions. Shipbuilding is carried on, and a considerable number of vessels are owned. The town of LÉVIS (pop. 7300) is situated opposite Quebec on the south side of the river.

MONTREAL (pop. with suburbs 238,600), 150 miles above

FIG. 9.—CITY OF QUEBEC. From a Photograph by Topley.

Quebec, and the head of ocean navigation, is the **largest city and commercial metropolis of Canada** (Fig. 10). It is built on **the** large island **of** the same name, facing the St. Lawrence and spreading from **the** river **to** the **base** of the **acclivity** known as Mount Royal **or** "Montreal Mountain," **which was** named by **Cartier** and from which **the** name **of the** city has been derived, though the **first settlement was** originally founded by Maisonneuve **in 1643 under the name** of Ville Marie. The city extends for several miles along the river, with fine **wharves and a** massive river-embankment. The buildings are largely constructed of **gray limestone,** though brick **is also extensively** employed. Besides being the **point of transhipment and of** export **for produce of all kinds from the west, and a** distributing **centre for imports, Montreal is also more largely** engaged **in** manufactures **than any other city in Canada.** Boot and shoe factories, cotton-mills, **tobacco** factories, breweries, tool and sewing-machine factories, clothing factories, nail-works, india-rubber **factories,** and rolling-mills are among **the most important, but** scarcely **any** manufacturing industry **is altogether** unrepresented. Montreal is also a great railway centre, and numerous machine-shops connected with the several railways are there established. The Mountain Park, with its magnificent outlook over the surrounding plain, is a feature of special interest to visitors. Fig. 10 gives a view of Montreal in winter with the St. Lawrence river frozen over, the St. Lawrence plain extending beyond it; and Belœil Mountain, one of the isolated elevations which rise above the plain, in the distance.

HULL (pop. 11,200), on the north side of the Ottawa river, 115 miles from Montreal and separated from the city of Ottawa only by the river, which is here the boundary between the provinces of Quebec and Ontario, is largely dependent on the saw-mills in which timber from the Upper Ottawa is worked up, but contains a match-factory, paper-pulp factory, and other industries. THREE RIVERS (pop. 8300), on the **north** side of **the** St. Lawrence, 80 miles below Montreal at the confluence of the St. Maurice, was, before the foundation of Montreal, the most important place **above** the city of Quebec. Its chief commercial

FIG. 10.—MONTREAL, WINTER VIEW. From a Photograph by Notman.

interests are connected with the timber trade. RIVIÈRE DU LOUP (pop. 5000), on the south side of the St. Lawrence estuary, nearly opposite the mouth of the Saguenay, is a railway centre and the farthest eastern considerable town in the province.

The following seven towns are situated to the south of the St. Lawrence and west of the city of Quebec: SOREL (pop. 6700), between Montreal and Three Rivers, at the head of Lake St. Peter, is a point with considerable trade. Steamboats such as those which ply upon the river are built here, and barges and similar craft suited for inland navigation are owned. ST. HYACINTH (pop. 7000), on the banks of the Yamaska river, 30 miles east of Montreal, stands upon the St. Lawrence plain and is chiefly built of red brick. It is notable on account of its manufactures of various kinds. ST. JOHNS (pop. 4500), on the Richelieu river, 20 miles south-east of Montreal, played an important part in the early history of the country as a fortified post commanding the line of approach by the Champlain valley, and is now a centre of local trade with some manufactures. SHERBROOKE (pop. 10,100) is the chief place of the "Eastern Townships," and is largely peopled by English-speaking inhabitants. It is built on the St. Francis river, at the mouth of its tributary the Magog, and being well supplied with water-power has become the seat of several manufacturing industries. RICHMOND (pop. 2000), an agricultural centre on the St. Francis river, with some manufactures. COATICOOK (pop. 3100), situated near the International boundary and containing several factories. VALLEYFIELD (pop. 5500), on the south side of the St. Lawrence, at the foot of the Côteau Rapids, which supply unlimited water-power utilised by a cotton-mill, paper-mill, and other factories.

In addition to these here named, there are many small towns and villages scattered over the province, forming local agricultural or trading centres or depending on lumbering or fisheries.

ONTARIO

Name and Size.—Ontario is the Huron-Iroquois name of one of the Great Lakes, meaning "Great Lake" or "Fine Lake," and was given to the old province of Upper Canada at the time of confederation. The total area of the province as now recognised, exclusive of that of the adjacent portions of the Great Lakes, is 222,000 square miles, being thus a little less than that of Quebec. It extends from the western boundary of Quebec to the eastern line of Manitoba, with a length of over 1000 miles, while its greatest width from south to north is about 700 miles. To the south it is bordered by the Great Lakes and the river St. Lawrence, while its northern extremity includes a part of the southern shore of Hudson Bay. Its form is very irregular, but if it be compared to that of an obtuse triangle of which the wide base stretches along the Great Lakes, and the apex is truncated by the southern extremity of Hudson Bay, we must then add to the eastern end of the base a large arrowhead-like projection which extends south-westward between three of these lakes and is usually known as the "Ontario peninsula."

Surface.—The physical features of Ontario are as varied as those of Quebec, and there is a general resemblance between those of the two provinces, based particularly on the great importance of the St. Lawrence valley and of the Laurentian plateau in both. In respect to surface Ontario is naturally divided into four main regions —(1) The region bordering on Hudson Bay, comprising low wooded country, underlaid for the most part by flat limestones of Upper Silurian and Devonian age, which form a wide margin round the south-western part of the bay. (2) The Laurentian region, which occupies the greater portion of the northern part of the province and is continuous with that of the northern part of Quebec, with similar characteristics (see p. 94), is, for the most part, a forest country with much valuable timber, but is very sparsely inhabited. The watershed on the Laurentian plateau in Ontario is generally somewhat less elevated than in Quebec. "Muskegs" or peaty and grassy swamps are more abundant on some parts of its surface; and along the north shore of **Lake Superior** its border is notably rugged and high. Though generally rocky **and unfit for agricultural occupation**, considerable tracts of good land **occur in** some places. A projecting point of this Laurentian country runs south, and crosses the St. Lawrence just **below** the outlet of Lake Ontario, producing there the picturesque archipelago known as the Thousand Islands. (3) To the east of this point the region included between **the** St. Lawrence and Ottawa rivers is the western end of **the** fertile St. Lawrence plain, already described (see p. 92). (4) A line drawn almost **due** west from the Thousand Islands **to** the **north-east angle of the** Georgian Bay of **Lake** Huron, nearly **follows the** southern edge **of** the corresponding part of the Laurentian plateau; **and to the** south of this line, extending to the lake shores, **is a** wide region of moderately elevated, nearly level, and fertile country, of which the Ontario peninsula is a part.

This last region is the richest and most thickly-peopled **part of the province**, and as such requires **some** further notice. It is naturally subdivided into two **portions— a** *lower plain* to the eastward, **and an** *upper plain* **to the** westward, **these** being separated **by the line of the** Niagara escarpment, which is the ruling physical feature. This escarpment is formed by **the** outcropping edge of a thick and massive limestone formation, which slopes gradually away beneath the **surface** to the south-westward, but is broken off abruptly with a steep face toward the lower plain to the north-eastward. It derives **its name from the** fact that the limestone outcrop to **which it is due is the same which** produces the **famous** Niagara **Falls, where the river,** flowing from Lake Erie, plunges over it to **the lower level of Lake Ontario.** Crossing the river at this point, **the Niagara escarpment runs** westward along the south **side of the upper** part of Lake Ontario to the **extremity of the lake,** and thence north-westward to the long promontory **which** separates Georgian Bay from the main extent of Lake Huron. **This** promontory is named the Bruce peninsula, and beyond it the ridge produced by the same limestone outcrop is continued by the line of the

Manitoulin Islands to the head of Lake Huron, where it crosses into the State of Michigan, and curves to the south along the west side of Lake Michigan. The Georgian Bay, with the channel to the north of the Manitoulin Islands, occupies the same position between the Niagara escarpment and southern edge of the Laurentian country as that held by the lower plain farther east. Where the escarpment fronts on the lower plain to the eastward it is often a rocky, broken cliff resembling a sea-cliff, and it is even probable, from the relative levels, that when the sea last covered the St. Lawrence plain (p. 93) it actually found for a time its western shore at the Niagara escarpment.

The lower plain has an area of 16,000 square miles, with a flat or undulating surface which never reaches a height of 1000 feet above the sea, its lowest part being on the shore of Lake Ontario, 247 feet above sea-level. It is deeply covered with gravels, sands, loams, and other alluvial deposits, and constitutes a fine agricultural region, draining chiefly to Lake Ontario, but in part also to Lake Huron. The upper plain, to the south-west of the line of the escarpment, has an area of about 10,000 square miles, and its highest parts average about 1200 feet above the sea. From these it slopes away in two directions toward Lakes Huron and Erie. Like the lower plain it is pretty thickly covered with gravels, sands, and clays, and its rolling surface often resembles that of parts of the plains west of Manitoba, except in its numerous belts of woodland. Its soil is of remarkable fertility. Practically the whole of Ontario was a forest country before the arrival of the first colonists.

Coast-Line and Great Lakes.—With the exception of about 120 miles of the shallow coast of the southern extremity of Hudson Bay, which includes a harbour suitable for small vessels at the mouth of the Moose river, the coast-line of Ontario is entirely that of the Great Lakes. This, without measuring its minor sinuosities, but including that of the short lengths of river which connect the Great Lakes, exceeds 1700 miles. By means of the Welland Canal and a short canal at the outlet of

Lake Superior, by which the interruptions caused by the Niagara Falls and the rapid known as the Sault Ste. Marie are overcome, the whole of this coast is accessible to shipping, and though for some months in the winter the freezing of the narrower waters and the accumulation of drift-ice in the large lakes prevents navigation, an extensive commerce is carried on by water.

The total area of the Great Lakes is 94,750 square miles, being thus considerably greater than that of Britain, and with the exception of Lake Michigan, which is wholly within the United States, the northern half of this area belongs to Canada, Ontario being the only province which borders on the lakes. This great system of inland waters stands at four distinct levels, the lowest being represented by Lake Ontario, 247 feet above the sea (area 7250 square miles, length 197 miles, greatest depth 738 feet); above this is Lake Erie, 573 feet above sea-level (area 9900 square miles, length 246 miles, greatest depth 210 feet). That part of the St. Lawrence by which this lake discharges to Lake Ontario is known as the Niagara river, and a great part of the difference in level between these two lakes is accounted for by the Niagara Falls, 167 feet in height. Below the fall the river flows for some distance between perpendicular cliffs 200 feet in height, between which the fall has gradually receded by cutting away the limestone rock over which it plunges. The length of river connecting Lakes Erie and Huron is without interruptions to navigation, and the height of Lake Huron is 581 feet above the sea (area 23,800 square miles, length 247 miles, greatest depth 702 feet). Georgian Bay, though nearly separated from the main lake, and Lake Michigan are at the same level. The height of Lake Superior, the highest of the Great Lakes, is 602 feet above the sea (area 31,500 square miles, length 377 miles, greatest depth 1008 feet).

Many excellent harbours are found along the coasts of these lakes. The northern shores of Lakes Ontario and Erie are low, and with the exception of a few peninsulas and points formed of low land, their outlines are little broken. The western shore of Lake Huron is similar in character, but to the north, along the Bruce peninsula and Manitoulin Islands, it is often rather bold, with limestone cliffs and numerous indentations. The northern coast of Georgian Bay is chiefly composed of Laurentian and the associated Huronian rocks, and, though not notably high, is often broken into a maze of rocky inlets. The north side of Lake Superior is bold, rocky, and irregular, resembling in physical character parts of the Riviera of the Mediterranean, though so different in respect to climate, and for the most part a wilderness. The most important islands belonging to Ontario are Wolf Island, at the outlet of Lake Ontario; Long Point Island and Pelee Island, in Lake Erie; the Manitoulin Islands, St. Joseph and Sugar Islands, in Lake Huron; with Michipicoten and St. Ignace Islands in Lake Superior.

Drainage System.—Ontario includes portions of three great hydrographic basins, that of the St. Lawrence with its tributary the Ottawa, that of the rivers flowing directly to Hudson Bay, and that of Lake Winnipeg which discharges by the Nelson, also to Hudson Bay. The two first cover the greater part of the province, the last-named including a relatively small area of its western extremity. The principal watershed is that of the Laurentian plateau, which, leaving the province of Quebec 40 miles north of Lake Temiscamang, runs westward to within about 40 miles of the north-east shore of Lake Superior, and then sweeps round the north shore of that lake at an average distance from it of about 60 miles. This part of the watershed is very sinuous in detail, and in one place it approaches the lake to within about 20 miles. It follows from the position of this watershed that the rivers flowing to Lake Superior are comparatively short and rapid, while the longer and gentler slopes are those toward Hudson Bay and the basin of Lake Winnipeg.

The principal rivers flowing to Hudson Bay are the Albany (length 440 miles), constituting part of the north-western border of the province, Moose, and Abittibi [1] (each about 260 miles). The country drained by these is as yet

[1] So named from the lake at its head, the Indian name meaning "middle" or "intermediate" lake, from its position on the watershed.

almost uninhabited. The larger streams which unite to form the Winnipeg river and reach Winnipeg Lake are the English river and Rainy river.

The Pigeon river, coinciding with part of the boundary between Ontario and the United States, the Kaministiquia, Nipigon,[1] draining the large Nipigon Lake, the Pic, with several smaller streams, enter Lake Superior. The Missisaga, Spanish, Wahnapite, and French rivers are the most important of those which flow into Lake Huron on the north, the last-named draining Nipissing Lake (Indian, "little lake").

The principal tributaries which reach the Ottawa river on its southern or Ontario side, all below Lake Temiscamang, are as follows in order down-stream: Montreal, Petawawa, Bonnechère, and Madawaska. These drain country of the Laurentian type, and all have courses somewhat exceeding 100 miles in length. The direction of flow of these rivers is south-east or east, which, taken in connection with the southward courses of the tributaries of the Ottawa on the north side in Quebec (see p. 101), shows a remarkable difference between the two slopes of the drainage-basin of that river, and indicates the structurally important character of the valley which it occupies. Below, the Madawaska, the Rideau, and Petit Nation rivers drain most of that part of the St. Lawrence plain which is included in Ontario. Both these have their sources not far from the north bank of the St. Lawrence itself. The mouth of the Rideau is at the city of Ottawa, where it forms a fall.

In that portion of Ontario described as the lower plain (p. 112) the largest river is the Trent, navigable in parts of its length, which pursues a very tortuous course of about 170 miles, flowing through a number of lakes and falling into the Bay of Quinte on Lake Ontario. The Nottawasaga and Severn rivers drain parts of the same plain, flowing northward to Georgian Bay. The Severn is the outlet of Lake Simcoe. The principal rivers of the upper plain are the Saugeen (length 70 miles), Grand (length 110 miles), and Thames (length 120 miles). The

[1] Meaning probably "clear water."

first two rise near together in the highest part of the plain, not far from the southern extremity of Georgian Bay, the Saugeen flowing to Lake Huron, the Grand river, which is navigable for some distance, to Lake Erie. The Thames is the largest river of the south-western part of the Ontario peninsula, being navigable for 18 miles from its mouth. It empties into Lake St. Clair, between Lakes Huron and Erie.

Besides the Great Lakes, Ontario contains a great number of smaller bodies of water. The upper plain of the Ontario peninsula is almost destitute of them, but several considerable lakes occur in the lower plain, and of these Lake Simcoe (30 by 18 miles) is much the largest. Along the northern border of this plain, where it meets the edge of the Laurentian region, is the remarkably irregular chain of lakes through which the Trent river flows. The entire surface of the Laurentian region is strewn with countless lakes, with characters similar to those found in the like region in the province of Quebec (Fig. 11). Muskoka Lake (length 15 miles), to the east of the southern part of Georgian Bay, is noted as a summer resort. Nipissing Lake (length 50 miles), between the northern part of the same bay and the Ottawa river, occupies part of the notable depression referred to on p. 101. Abittibi Lake (length 45 miles), draining by the river of the same name to Hudson Bay, lies in the centre of the Laurentian plateau, and is surrounded by rough rocky and wooded country. Nipigon Lake (length 70 miles), situated to the north of Lake Superior, is about 40 miles in width, and contains a number of high rocky islands. Rainy Lake (length 53 miles) lies along the southern boundary of Ontario, near its western extremity. Its waters flow by Rainy river to Lake of the Woods (length 70 miles), which owes its name to the great number of wooded islands studding its surface. Lac Seul or "Lonely Lake" (length 100 miles) discharges by the English river, and Lake St. Joseph (length 65 miles) gives origin to the Albany river. Both these lakes form part of the north-western boundary of the province.

Climate.—In consequence of the southern position of the Ontario peninsula, and the modifying influence of the

DOMINION OF CANADA—ONTARIO

extensive water-surface of the surrounding Great Lakes, which tends to reduce the extreme of summer heat, and that of winter cold, the climate of this part of the province

FIG. 11.—MAP OF A SMALL PIECE OF THE LAURENTIAN PLATEAU-COUNTRY TO THE NORTH OF RAINY RIVER, ONTARIO. Showing the characteristic features of its Lakes, with intercommunicating Streams and numerous Rapids and Portages. The Figures on the Lakes indicate the depth in feet.

is in some respects more favoured than that of any other part of Canada except the coast of British Columbia. Maize and peaches are grown in this district as staple crops, and the time during which snow lies upon the ground in winter is short and irregular. Along the Ottawa

valley and to the northward, the climate closely **resembles
that of the western portion of Quebec in the same latitudes
(see p. 102), while in the** western extremity of this long
province it **approaches in** character **to** that of the adjacent
province of Manitoba (see p. 128). Average annual precipitation of the southern and inhabited part of the
province, 33·5 inches. Mean highest temperature at
Toronto, 90·1; mean lowest, 12·7 below zero.

Mineral Fields and Chief Industries.—Like Quebec,
Ontario contains no coal-fields, but this is to some extent
compensated for by the existence of petroleum, **large quantities** of which are obtained in certain districts **of the
Ontario peninsula,** from wells bored into the underlying
Devonian rocks. Natural gas has also lately been discovered in the same part of the province in deep borings.
Salt, obtained in the form of brine **from** deep wells in the
western portion of the peninsula, near Lake Huron, is an
important product; and considerable quantities of **gypsum
are mined in the** vicinity of Grand river. The metalliferous **minerals occur for** the **most part within the Laurentian** region (generally in the rocks **classed as Huronian),
or in** the rocks of the older formations adjacent **to it.
Silver is** mined in the vicinity of Thunder Bay **on Lake
Superior.** Copper and nickel ores have been discovered,
and are being **rapidly developed** in the Sudbury district
north of Lake Huron. Iron ores are worked to a limited
extent for export, in several places, and numerous deposits
are **known.** Apatite or phosphate **of lime** is procured in
that part of the Laurentian area which **lies** between the
Ottawa **river and Lake Ontario.** Building-stone **in**
many varieties is abundant, as **well** as clays employed in
brick-making. The **value of the petroleum** procured has
in past years **been greater than that of any** other mineral,
but in 1890 **was exceeded by that of nickel.**

Though the mineral wealth of the province is thus
considerable, **agriculture** is the most important industry.
Wheat, barley, oats, and maize or Indian corn, potatoes,
mangel-wurzels, turnips, and hay are the most important
crops. Stock-raising and dairy-farming, and particularly
the production of cheese and butter, are largely carried on.

Fruits of many kinds are extensively grown, particularly in the south-western part of the Ontario peninsula.

Lumbering, in all its branches, stands next to agriculture in importance, and is prosecuted in the manner already described under Quebec (see p. 103). Manufacturing ranks third, embracing many diverse industries, such as the making of agricultural machinery, cotton and woollen mills, saw-mills, furniture manufactories, boot and shoe factories, meat and food preserving establishments. The fisheries also employ a considerable number of men, and are about equal in value to those of Quebec, though entirely confined to the inland waters, of which those of Lake Huron are the most productive. The largest class of exports is that derived from agricultural industries, including animals and their products, followed by products of the forest, the mines, manufactured articles, and fish. The chief imports are coal, obtained generally from the United States, sugar, tea, iron, and iron manufactures, with numerous other manufactured articles. With the exception of coal, the larger part of the bulky exports and imports find their way through Montreal, but a considerable proportion of the trade is carried on by railway with the United States, or across the Eastern States to the ports of Boston and New York.

Population.—The population of Ontario is 2,113,000. Of this number about three-quarters were born in the province, while the remaining fourth are immigrants from various countries or from the other provinces. The original settlers in the province were principally the United Empire Loyalists (see p. 44), and to their energy in bringing the wilderness lands into cultivation its rapid early progress is chiefly due. A considerable number of French-speaking people inhabit the eastern counties, situated in the western part of the St. Lawrence plain, and some are found in the extremity of the Ontario peninsula, while many colonists from Quebec are settling on the Upper Ottawa and in the Nipissing valley. There are as well some inhabitants of German origin in the Ontario peninsula.

Ontario is divided into forty-five counties, and five

FIG. 12.—KING STREET, TORONTO. From a Photograph by Notman.

large districts without county organisation. The counties are generally of moderate size, but rather unequal in this respect, and are all included between the Ottawa river and Nipissing valley on the north, and the St. Lawrence and Great Lakes on the south. In their irregularity of form, and the varied direction of the lines by which they are separated, they resemble those of that part of Quebec to the south of the St. Lawrence. By far the greater part of the entire population is concentrated in the southern portion of the province. The districts include a great area to the north of the Great Lakes, and are separated by straight north and south lines.

Towns.—TORONTO (pop. 189,000), named York by the early colonists, is the seat of the provincial Government, and the second largest town in Canada (Fig. 12).[1] It is situated on the north shore of Lake Ontario, at a good harbour, sheltered by a low island. The land upon which it is built is nearly flat, and does not rise more than 100 feet above the lake. The streets are wide, and laid out at right angles. Its progress has been very rapid within late years, and it possesses many handsome buildings, and a fine park. Though largely engaged in manufacturing industries, its chief importance is as a commercial city and distributing-point for manufactured and other goods, either imported or produced elsewhere in the province. The fertile and well-peopled country of the whole southern part of the province is tributary to it, and it is an important railway centre. OTTAWA (pop. 44,200), the third largest city in Ontario, and the capital of the Dominion of Canada, is built on the south bank of the Ottawa river, at the mouth of its tributary, the Rideau (Fig. 13). The Ottawa here descends about 60 feet over the Chaudière (Kettle) Falls, affording a magnificent water-power, while the Rideau also forms a fall at its mouth, from the curtain-like appearance of which it derives its name. The most important industry is the timber trade, of which Ottawa is the centre—the water-power being utilised by numerous large saw-mills, in which the logs brought down by the river are cut into

[1] The Iroquois original of the present name is Karonto, meaning "The place where there is a tree in the water."—H. HALE.

FIG. 18.—PARLIAMENTARY BUILDINGS, OTTAWA, WITH RAFTS OF TIMBER ON THE RIVER. From a Photograph by Topley.

merchantable form. The Government buildings are large and architecturally fine, and occupy a high point of land facing the river, in full view of the Chaudière Falls.

The following cities and towns of Ontario are arranged as nearly as possible in order of importance, according to population: HAMILTON (pop. 49,000), a substantially built city on the extreme western end of Lake Ontario, overlooked by the bold escarpment of the Niagara limestone, is a commercial centre with rather varied manufacturing industries. LONDON (pop. 32,000), appropriately situated on the Thames, in the centre of the rich land of the Ontario peninsula about midway between Lakes Erie and Huron, is a commercial town, and contains petroleum refineries and manufactories of agricultural machinery, furniture, etc. Many of the streets are lined with trees, whence the name "Forest City" sometimes given to this place. KINGSTON (pop. 19,200), originally established by the French as a defence against the Iroquois, with the name of Fort Frontenac, has been of great importance in the history of Canada, particularly during the war of 1812, when it was the rendezvous of the naval force on Lake Ontario. Much of the produce brought down from the upper lakes is here transhipped to barges for carriage to Montreal. There are some manufactories, including locomotive works. The buildings are largely constructed of gray limestone quarried in the neighbourhood, and the name "Limestone City" is thus often given to Kingston. BRANTFORD (pop. 12,700), on the Grand river, is a point of shipment for produce, with manufactures of agricultural implements. GUELPH (pop. 10,500), on the Speed, a branch of the Grand river, manufactures organs, pianos, sewing machines, carriage and waggon gear. ST. THOMAS (pop. 10,300) is chiefly important as a railway centre. WINDSOR (pop. 10,300), at the extremity of the Ontario peninsula, and opposite the city of Detroit in Michigan, is one of the points at which trains are transferred by ferry from Ontario to the United States. The surrounding country is a fruit-growing district, producing pears, peaches, and grapes. BELLEVILLE (pop. 9900), on the Bay of Quinte, an inlet of complicated form from Lake Ontario, is a shipping place for produce and lumber. PETERBOROUGH (pop. 9700) is a centre for the distribution of supplies for lumbering and agricultural districts. STRATFORD (pop. 9500), in the middle of the peninsula, is important as a produce market and railway centre. ST. CATHERINES (pop. 9200) is situated in the angle between the Niagara river and Lake Ontario, in the midst of a fine fruit-growing country. CHATHAM (pop. 9000), on the lower part of the river Thames, near the extremity of the Ontario peninsula, is an agricultural centre. BROCKVILLE (pop. 8800), on the St. Lawrence due south of the city of Ottawa, has chemical works and some manufactories. It is important in connection with the cheese trade. WOODSTOCK (pop. 8600) manufactures agricultural implements and furniture, and lies in a very fertile region. GALT (pop. 7500), on the Grand river, is noted for its manufacture of edge-tools and woollen goods. OWEN SOUND (7500), an important harbour on Georgian Bay, possesses shipbuilding, tanneries, button and shirt factories, and fruit, particularly plums and apples. BERLIN (pop. 7400) lies between Stratford and Guelph, the surrounding country being largely settled by people of German origin. CORNWALL (pop. 6800), on the St. Lawrence, near the eastern extremity of the province, has a paper-mill and other manufactures. SARNIA (pop. 6700) lies near the outlet of Lake Huron. A long railway tunnel beneath the river-bed here connects Ontario with the State of Michigan. LINDSAY (pop. 6100) stands on a tributary of the Severn in a farming district. BARRIE (pop. 5550), built on an arm of Lake Simcoe, is a produce market. PORT HOPE (pop. 5000), a harbour on the south shore of Lake Ontario, manufactures agricultural machinery. COLLINGWOOD (pop. 4900), a port on Georgian Bay. COBOURG (pop. 4800), on Lake Ontario near Port Hope, has large car works.

There is considerable general uniformity in the interests of the numerous smaller towns throughout the thickly-peopled southern portion of Ontario, and manufacturing industries of various kinds are to be found in nearly all of them, the facilities for distribution of the various products being excellent by reason of the numerous lines of railway.

The two following towns, though smaller than any of those previously noted, are the most important in the further western portion of the province. PORT ARTHUR (pop. 2700) is situated on Thunder Bay of Lake Superior. Valuable silver mines are worked in its vicinity, and large quantities of grain from Manitoba and the North-West are shipped for further carriage on the Great Lakes. RAT PORTAGE, at the northern extremity and outlet of the Lake of the Woods, possesses a magnificent water-power, and is becoming important in connection with timber and flour-milling.

MANITOBA

This new province, often called the "prairie province," obtains its name from that of Manitoba Lake, which again is derived from two Cree Indian words meaning "spirit narrows," applied to a strait in that lake. It is almost exactly square in form, the southern side of the square being the 49th degree of latitude, and the length of the sides nearly 270 miles each. The area is 73,956 square miles, or about 8000 square miles less than the combined areas of England and Scotland.

Manitoba is nearly in the centre of the land-mass of the North American continent, and almost exactly midway between the western and eastern extremes of the Dominion of Canada, a line drawn north and south through the centre of the province being within less than ten miles of equidistant in longitude between the extreme of Labrador on one side and the boundary between Canada and Alaska on the other. The width of country on each side of this central line, to the east and west, is measured by about 43° of longitude.

Surface.—The north-eastern part of Manitoba, to the shore of Lake Winnipeg, with a strip along the southern part of its eastern boundary bordering on Ontario, covers a portion of the rocky, hummocky, and generally-wooded Laurentian plateau, with characters similar to those already noted. The entire central and western part of the province lies within the area of the great inland plain of the continent, in which the hard ancient rocks are uniformly covered by much newer and softer strata. In correspondence with this change, the country here assumes a nearly level character, such irregularities as may still exist in the surface of the underlying rocks being further concealed by deep alluvial deposits, gravels, and clays.

The lowest part of the surface of Manitoba is that of the Red River plain, which runs from south to north with the Red River in its southern part, and Winnipeg, Winnipegosis, and Manitoba Lakes, with the flat land surrounding them to the north. The least elevated portion of this plain—that including the lakes—has a height of about 700 feet above the sea; while the height of its upper part, where it crosses the southern boundary of Manitoba, is about 100 feet greater. The width of the plain on this boundary is 52 miles, but increases farther north, and becomes greatest where the plain is partly submerged beneath the lakes. Though to all appearance a perfectly level prairie, that part of the plain through which the Red River runs slopes down at the rate of about a foot in a mile to the north, while on both sides of the river it rises toward its borders with a considerably greater inclination. The average height of the whole of that part of the plain to the south of the lakes is about 800 feet, and the area of this part is about 7000 square miles. It is wooded only along the banks of the streams, and is covered with a great depth of rich alluvial soil, supporting a luxuriant growth of grass. The soil represents the fine sediments of an ancient lake which at one time covered the entire plain, and of which the old high beaches, consisting of sand and gravel, in parallel lines, can still in many places be traced.

On the east a narrow border of higher and partly wooded plain, attaching to the edge of the Laurentian region, borders this lower prairie. On the west it is more definitely bounded by an escarpment, which enters the province on the south under the name of the Pembina "mountain," and is continued northward by the Riding, Duck, and Porcupine "mountains." This escarpment is about 500 feet in height in its southern part, but even higher to the north, and is breached by several valleys, of which that of the Assiniboine is the most important. It constitutes **the front** of a second plain of greater height and **somewhat** more irregular surface, which **occupies** the **whole** south-western part of the province, and **extends far beyond its limits.** .

While the Red River cuts **but a** shallow **trench in its** plain, the rivers and streams **of the second and higher** plain generally flow in deep **valleys which often contain** belts of woodland, though the **plain itself is usually tree-** less, except to the north in **the** vicinity **of the great lakes,** where it is wooded like the lower country **which borders** these lakes and separates **them one from another.**

The soil of the second prairie level is usually excellent, though more varied in character and not so deep and clayey as that of the Red River plain.

Drainage System.—Manitoba possesses no **coast-line** except that of the large lakes already mentioned. Its **area is entirely** comprised within one river basin, that of the Nelson. The lakes of the Winnipeg group have an aggregate area **of about 12,700** square miles, **but a** part of this lies **to the north of the limit of the province. Within** the province the largest river entering these lakes is the Winnipeg, fed by the Lake **of the Woods, and navigable only by canoes, with** many **portages. The Red River rises far to** the south, and **flows for about 100 miles** through Manitoba to the south **end of** Winnipeg **Lake.** It is navigable by steamboats and barges, with the exception of a short length between **the** city of Winnipeg and the lake, where it is interrupted by a shallow rapid. The Assiniboine, its principal tributary (named **from a tribe** of Sioux Indians, Assiniboines **or "** stony **Sioux "), after a** long **southerly course parallel to the general direction of** Winnipegosis **and Manitoba Lakes, turns to the eastward near the west line of the province, and joins the Red River at the city of** Winnipeg. **Though very tortuous,** this **river can also be navigated by small steamboats for** a long distance. The Souris (Mouse) river, **a shallow stream,** is the largest tributary of the Assiniboine. Owing to the wearing away of their alluvial banks, **all** these rivers traversing the plains **are** usually clouded with fine sediment.

Lake Winnipeg (height 710 feet) is 250 miles in length, Lake Winnipegosis (height 830 feet) 130 miles, and Lake Manitoba (height 810 feet) 120 miles, but all are rather shallow. In addition to these larger lakes, Lake Dauphin, Swan Lake, St. Martin Lake, and Shoal Lake are of some importance. That part of the Laurentian plateau included in the province is characterised as usual by many rock-bound lakes and ponds, while numerous shallow lakes occur also both on the surface and in the deep river-valleys of the second prairie level.

Climate.—In consequence of its geographical position in the centre of the continent, far removed from the influence of both oceans, Manitoba exhibits the "continental" climate in almost its extreme form. The winters are characterised by clear and very cold weather, with a rather scanty snowfall. The summer is hot, though with cool nights toward spring and autumn; and is of about the same length as in the more southern parts of Ontario and Quebec. Vegetation advances with great rapidity on the incoming of spring. The rainfall is less than in the eastern provinces, but is generally ample for the growth of crops. Average annual precipitation for the province, 19·5 inches. Mean highest temperature at Winnipeg, 94·7; mean lowest, 43·3 below zero.

Chief Industries.—Brine springs, gypsum, and iron ore are known in that part of the province adjacent to the Winnipeg group of lakes, but none of these materials are yet utilised. Stone for building purposes is scarce throughout the entire prairie region, though found in some places not far from Winnipeg and employed in that city. Clay for brick-making is abundant.

The wealth of the province lies in its fertile and easily tilled soil, and the most important industry is agriculture—wheat, oats, barley, and potatoes being the principal field crops, in the order named (Fig. 14). The conditions are, however, favourable for the growth of almost all the ordinary crops of the other provinces, and particularly so for flax and hemp and also for stock-raising and dairy-farming. With the rapid advance of settlement its products are becoming more numerous and varied, and "mixed farming," as

Fig. 14.—Wheat Field on the Manitoba Prairie. From a Photograph.

opposed to the almost exclusive cultivation of wheat, is growing in favour. In 1886 an area of about 753,000 acres was actually under cultivation, but this has since been much increased.

The lakes abound in fish, and the annual product of the fisheries is already notable. Manufacturing industries are inconsiderable. Lumbering is carried on to some extent for the supply of local needs in the northern and eastern parts of the province. The chief export of Manitoba is wheat, while most manufactured articles used in the province are imported.

Population.—In 1870 the population of Manitoba was about 12,000, of which 10,400 was made up of "half-breeds" or Indians. This has increased to about 155,000. The original settlers of the Red River valley were in the employment of the North-West and Hudson's Bay Fur Companies, generally Scotch or French Canadian, who took up lands on the borders of the river. These were added to by the romantic, though only partially successful, colonisation enterprise of Lord Selkirk in 1812 (see p. 45); but for many years thereafter the colony increased very slowly, being exceedingly remote from the thickly-peopled parts of the continent. Since means of access to the region have been afforded by railways, its settlement has advanced with increasing rapidity, the immigrants coming from various countries, but in considerable proportion from the province of Ontario. Colonies of Mennonites from the south of Russia, and of Icelanders, have settled in the province in late years, and the original "half-breed" population now forms but a small part of the whole.

Manitoba is divided, for political purposes, into four large counties, each consisting of a number of municipalities. The greater part of the fertile land has already been surveyed, the main divisions being along north and south and east and west lines, separating square blocks with sides of six miles in length. Each of these is known as a "township," and contains 36 square miles or "sections" which are further subdivided into "quarter-sections" of 160 acres. The same system of survey extends over the North-West Territory.

Towns.—WINNIPEG[1] (pop. 25,600) is the provincial capital of Manitoba. It is built on the level plain of the Red River, on the west bank of that river at the confluence of the Assiniboine, and is the chief commercial and railway centre, with already many substantial and handsome buildings. In 1870 the population of Winnipeg, then known as Fort Garry, was about 250. ST. BONIFACE (pop. 1550) stands on the east bank of the Red River, opposite Winnipeg, with which it is connected by a bridge, and of which it is virtually a suburb.

PORTAGE LA PRAIRIE (pop. 3400), on the main line of the Canadian Pacific Railway and near the Assiniboine river, 60 miles west of Winnipeg, is one of the older settlements of the province. An important agricultural centre with flour-mills. BRANDON (pop. 3800) is 132 miles west of Winnipeg, and also on the main line of the Canadian Pacific Railway where it crosses the Assiniboine. It is prettily situated on the south side of the river-valley, and stands in the centre of one of the best farming districts in the province.

The large number of smaller towns and villages of Manitoba are very similar in general character, being local agricultural centres and distributing-points. In most such towns along the various lines of railway one or more "grain elevators" are prominent features. These are high buildings for receiving, storing, and delivering grain to the railways, and are generally visible for a long distance across the flat surface of the prairie.

NORTH-WEST TERRITORY

Size and Subdivisions.—Under this name is known the entire region extending from the boundaries of Manitoba and Ontario west and north-west to the province of British Columbia, and to the boundary-line between Canada and Alaska. The area of this territory is 1,792,027 square miles; and a portion of it only has been blocked out into large districts for administrative purposes, while the

[1] From the lake and river similarly named, meaning "muddy water."

remaining and larger part has not yet been subdivided. The names of the districts which have so far been established are as follows: KEEWATIN (area, to the Arctic coast, 282,000 square miles) is a large provisional district extending indefinitely northward from Manitoba. ASSINIBOIA (area 89,535 square miles) and ALBERTA (area 106,100 square miles) are bounded to the south by the 49th parallel, and lie between Manitoba and British Columbia. SASKATCHEWAN (area 107,092 square miles) and ATHABASCA (area 104,500 square miles) lie to the north of the last two.[1]

Surface.—This great territory includes several distinct types of country, of which the most important are: (1) The northern extension of the Laurentian plateau, bordered on the west by a line drawn from the head of Lake Winnipeg to the west end of Athabasca Lake, and thence through Great Slave Lake and Great Bear Lake; (2) the great inland plain, to the west of this line, and between it and the Cordillera; and (3) to the north of the province of British Columbia, part of the Cordillera belt itself.

Though as yet imperfectly known, that part of the Laurentian plateau comprised in the North-West Territory is believed to be alike in general character to the geologically similar regions already described (see p. 94), save that to the north of the 60th degree of latitude it becomes more or less completely destitute of forest, and constitutes what is known as the "barren grounds," a resort of the caribou and musk-ox. The northern part of the Cordillera included in the North-West Territory maintains the characters of the same belt of country as found in British Columbia (see p. 142), but with less elevated and more irregular ranges, including larger intervening tracts of low land, which are for the most part covered by forest till the shores of the Arctic Ocean are approached. The broad, physical features of the interior continental plain have already been noted (see p. 9); but its southern, wider, and

[1] The names of these districts are derived as follows:—Keewatin, Chippewa (Algonkin), for north-west wind. Alberta, from one of the Christian names of the Princess Louise. Assiniboia, Saskatchewan, and Athabasca from native names of rivers, already explained.

economically more important part, included in the districts of Assiniboia, Saskatchewan, Alberta, and Athabasca, requires to be further characterised.

This southern part of the inland plain is highest along the base of the Rocky Mountains, from which it slopes gradually, but not quite uniformly, down to the belt of low land found along the margin of the Laurentian plateau. Thus in the south-west angle of Alberta the plain has an elevation of about 4000 feet, from which it descends to the north end of Lake Winnipeg, a distance of 700 miles, at an average rate of nearly $5\frac{1}{2}$ feet to the mile. Farther north, in Athabasca, the height of the western margin of the plain is less, being about 3000 feet only.

Two low transverse watersheds traverse this part of the interior continental plain. The first, crossing and recrossing the 49th parallel of latitude several times, and making no very wide departure from this line to the west of the Red River, separates the tributaries of the Missouri on the south from the streams which eventually reach the Nelson river. The second, from a point not far to the north of Winnipeg Lake, pursues, like the first, a somewhat sinuous westerly course, crossing and recrossing the 54th parallel. This divides the basin of the Nelson river on the south from the Mackenzie basin, and in part from that of the Churchill river, on the north. Both these watersheds are low and diffuse in character, forming features which, though hydrographically important, are rendered apparent only by the changed direction of the drainage.

The great interior plain of this part of the continent nearly coincides with the area occupied by imperfectly consolidated and almost horizontal strata of Cretaceous age. Its characters, and particularly its unbroken surface, depend chiefly upon the wide and uniform spread of these subjacent deposits; but the definition of the two transverse watersheds is believed to have been brought about chiefly by the action of denudation, by which the drainage-basin of each of the great rivers has gradually been lowered, leaving in the vicinity of the sources of their tributaries some higher remnants of the old surface. In dependence, chiefly, on the climatic conditions, and most directly upon the differences in amount of rainfall, the whole northern and north-eastern part of that portion of the interior continental plain here described is generally wooded, while its south-western part is almost treeless, and extends for hundreds of miles in wide sea-like prairies. The line between the wooded and open regions is by no means definite; for while many considerable areas of prairie occur within the forest country, wooded belts follow most of the large river-valleys far into the otherwise treeless plains. Almost the whole of the district of Athabasca is a woodland country, yet, in the vicinity of the Peace river, attractive natural prairies of from ten to twenty miles in length are common. A general line of separation may, however, be drawn between the forest and prairie regions. Such a line, beginning in Manitoba near the southern end of the Winnipeg group of lakes, would run north-westward to the vicinity of the confluence of the North and South Saskatchewan rivers, thence westward to Edmonton on the North Saskatchewan, and then south-westward to the base of the Rocky Mountains near the Bow river. The total area of the prairie country thus defined (including the prairie land of Manitoba), to the north of the international boundary on the 49th parallel, is about 193,000 square miles, or considerably more than twice the size of Great Britain. Here the surface of the plain becomes green with a new growth of grass at the first approach of spring, and in June is gay with brilliant flowers. In August the sod is already burnt to a tawny yellow by the long, hot days of summer, except along the borders of the lakes or of such stream-courses as still contain a little water. This great tract of prairie, with its contiguous woodland border, constitutes the most valuable portion of the North-West Territory, being for the most part fertile, and everywhere producing an abundance of nutritious natural grasses suitable for grazing purposes. It lies to the north of the arid plains of the upper Missouri, and to the south of the forest country, where to prepare land for cultivation much preliminary work is necessary in clearing the ground.

We have seen that the southern and northern transverse watersheds approximately correspond with the 49th and

54th parallels of latitude. Between these lines of latitude a belt of country 350 miles in width is comprised, which contains the whole of the great prairie region, with some part of the forest country (see Fig. 15). This, from the eastern base of the Laurentian plateau to the base of the Rocky Mountains (again including the plains of Manitoba), contains an area of about 295,000 square miles, of which about 20,000 square miles only on the south belong to the Missouri drainage, and about 10,000 square miles on the north to the Mackenzie basin, the whole remaining area being within the hydrographic basin of the Nelson river, and much the larger part in that of the Saskatchewan and its tributaries. Within this area the surface of the plain rises rather abruptly to the west along two lines, thus defining three tracts of prairie country. The first and lowest is that of the Red River plain already described (p. 127). The second forms the south-western portion of the province of Manitoba, and extends far beyond it, forming a great part of the extent of Assiniboia and Saskatchewan. It is bounded by the edge of the third plain, which runs from southeast to north-west under the name of the Missouri Côteau. This second plain has an area of about 105,000 square miles, of which some 71,000 square miles is prairie country. Its mean altitude is about 1600 feet above the sea, and it generally affords an excellent soil. The third plain or prairie level has an average altitude of about 3000 feet, and an area of about 134,000 square miles, much the larger part being entirely devoid of forest. Its surface is more irregular and diversified than that of the last because of its greater height, and the consequent greater effect of rivers, rain, and other denuding agents upon it. Those portions of its surface which still remain but little modified, form isolated tablelands such as the Cypress Hills, and Wood Mountain, deeply seamed by ravines and valleys. The soil is often excellent, but the climatic conditions are more favourable to stock-raising than to agriculture.

Along the base of the Rocky Mountains the hitherto horizontal strata underlying the plains are found crushed together into wave-like parallel folds, which, in consequence of the varying hardness of their different rocks, have resulted in the production of series of more or less regular ridges, with long intervening valleys. This broken belt of land is known as the foot-hills. It is partly wooded, and with the clear cold rivers from the mountains running through it, and vista of distant snow-spotted peaks to the west, is singularly attractive in appearance. The North-West Territory, to the south of the 54th degree of latitude, also includes politically that part of the Rocky Mountain range which lies to the east of the watershed, but physically this mountain border is a part of the Cordillera.

Drainage System.—The courses of the larger rivers of the North-West Territory have already been sufficiently indicated on p. 13, and in connection with the foregoing notes on its surface and its slopes. Because of its numerous rapids, the Nelson river between Lake Winnipeg and Hudson Bay is navigable only for boats, and then with numerous portages. The Saskatchewan river, above the Grand Rapids near its mouth, is navigable by small steamboats to Edmonton, 650 miles, and its south branch is similarly navigable for about 400 miles above its confluence. Part of the Athabasca is also navigable by small steamboats, but its lower course is interrupted by rapids. A series of rapids 20 miles in length again interrupts navigation on that part of the Mackenzie known as Slave river, between Athabasca and Great Slave Lakes; but below these the Mackenzie is continuously navigable to the Arctic Ocean, a distance of about 1300 miles. With the exception of two short breaks caused by rapids, the Peace river is navigable for similar steamboats for about 580 miles. The Liard river is navigable from its confluence with the Mackenzie for about 200 miles, and many other streams might be navigated for considerable distances by small steamboats of a similar kind. Those usually employed on such rivers are flat-bottomed, and are propelled by a large paddle-wheel at the stern.

The chain of large lakes which follows the border of the Laurentian plateau north-westward beyond the Winnipeg group of lakes has already been alluded to (see p. 10).

FIG. 15.—VIEW ON THE GREAT PLAINS, WITH INDIAN ENCAMPMENT, WESTERN ASSINIBOIA. From a Photograph by the Author.

Of these, Athabasca Lake (length 185 miles), Great Slave Lake (length 340 miles), and Great Bear Lake (length 200 miles) are the most important. The heads of all of these are in the rocky Laurentian region, while their lower ends extend into the inland plain. The portion of the Laurentian plateau included in the North-West Territory holds, as elsewhere, innumerable lakes, and some of them are here very large; while the surface of the inland plain itself, both in its wooded and prairie portions, is dotted with lakes and ponds, which are usually rather shallow. In this respect the part of the great plain included in Canada differs much from its southern extension in the United States, where lakes are rarely found. This abundance of lakes in the Canadian region depends upon the irregular distribution of the surface deposits of clay, sand, and gravel which has been brought about during the glacial period, the effects of which do not here extend far to the south of the 49th parallel of latitude. Many of these lakes in the prairie country are without outlet, and are then generally saline. Such lakes and ponds are particularly abundant in the south-western and more arid parts of Alberta and Assiniboia, where they are often completely emptied by evaporation before the close of the summer.

Mineral Fields and Chief Industries.—The most important mineral deposits of the North-West Territory are those of coal and lignite or brown coal. These are contained in the Cretaceous rocks, and are therefore much newer than the coals of Nova Scotia and Great Britain. The total area of the coal fields south of the 56th parallel (beyond which they are very imperfectly known) is not less than 60,000 square miles. Bituminous coals are found near the base of the mountains in Alberta and Athabasca. To the east of these, and extending nearly to Manitoba, are lignite fields. Anthracite coal occurs in limited tracts in the mountain country. These fuels are already worked to a certain extent in a few places, but the demand for them is as yet rather small. Iron ores are known but not worked, and the mineral resources of the northern part of the Laurentian region are still unknown. Vast deposits of mineral tar exist in the district of Athabasca, and it is believed that petroleum can be obtained by sinking wells, though the experiment has not yet been made. Throughout the whole of the great plain stone for building purposes is scarce, but there is generally an abundance of clay for bricks.

Agriculture and stock-raising are the leading industries in the North-West Territory at the present time, and both are capable of almost unlimited expansion. Twenty years ago the whole western part of the prairie was roamed over by countless herds of buffalo, hunted by Indians who often still employed the primitive bow and arrow. The buffalo is gone, and the Indians now live peaceably on their various reservations; but the utilisation of the natural resources of the country has only begun. The principal stock-raising or "ranching" country lies along the eastern base of the Rocky Mountains, while the larger agricultural settlements, which have so far been formed, are in those parts of Assiniboia and Saskatchewan nearest to Manitoba; but smaller scattered settlements exist as far north as the head waters of the Athabasca, and west to the Rocky Mountains. The fur trade is almost the sole industry of the great northern region, and is carried on by barter with the Indians at trading-posts belonging for the most part to the Hudson's Bay Company.

Climate.—The eastern parts of Assiniboia and Saskatchewan are alike in climate to Manitoba (see p. 128); farther to the west, in the same latitude, and notwithstanding the increased elevation of the plains, the winter is found to be shorter and less severe. This change depends on the general meteorological conditions explained on p. 19. The lower elevation of the surface in Athabasca, together with its westerly situation, to a great degree counteracts the effect of its higher latitude. The result of these conditions on the character of the weather is such that along a line drawn north-westward from the city of Winnipeg, through the centre of Athabasca, the advance of spring and the progress of vegetation, including the dates of sowing and of reaping, are almost simultaneous and identical. The dry climate of the southern part of the inland plain, with the increase of rainfall to the north, upon which the change from prairie to woodland depends, may best be shown by comparing the amount of the total annual precipitation in the three following places, which are nearly equidistant from the base of the Cordillera :—

Medicine Hat	Lat. 50°	Rainfall 10·3 inches	(Prairie)
Edmonton	Lat. 53° 30'	Rainfall 11·6 inches	(Woodland and prairie)
Dunvegan	Lat. 56°	Rainfall 20·0 inches	(Woodland, with patches of prairie)

At Medicine Hat, in the western part of Assiniboia, the mean highest temperature is 98·9 ; mean lowest, 43·8 below zero.

Population.—The entire population of the North-West Territory is estimated at 143,000, including about 47,000 Indians and a considerable number of "half-breeds." The "half-breeds" are most numerous along the Saskatchewan river. The remaining and greater part of the population consists of immigrants from many different countries, most of whom are settled in the eastern parts of Assiniboia and Saskatchewan districts, and in the south-western part of the district of Alberta. A force of about 1000 mounted police maintains order in the Territory.

Towns.—No large towns have yet grown up in the North-West Territory, but there are numerous small centres of population which are fast increasing in size. In Assiniboia are—REGINA (pop. 1500), on the main line of the Canadian Pacific Railway. This is the seat of government for the North-West Territory, and headquarters of the mounted police. It is built on a perfectly level plain. MEDICINE HAT (pop. 750), near the western boundary of Assiniboia, where the Canadian Pacific Railway main line crosses the South Saskatchewan. QU'APPELLE (pop. 700), also on the main line of the Canadian Pacific Railway, surrounded by fine land. In Alberta are—CALGARY (pop. 3900), on the main line of the Canadian Pacific Railway, is beautifully situated in the valley of Bow river near the outer edge of the foot-hills, and is the principal "ranching" centre. LETHBRIDGE (pop. 1200), on the Old-Man river, a branch of the Belly river, is the site of the largest coal mine in the Territory, with railway connection with the Canadian Pacific Railway, and southward with lines in the State of Montana. EDMONTON (pop. 600), on the North Saskatchewan, is now connected by a branch line with the Canadian Pacific Railway. In Saskatchewan are—PRINCE ALBERT (pop. 2000), on the North Saskatchewan, near the confluence of the South Saskatchewan, surrounded by an excellent farming country. BATTLEFORD (pop. 650), on a point of land at the confluence of the Battle river with the North Saskatchewan, wasformerly the seat of Government for the Territory.

NORTH-EAST TERRITORY

By this name is known the whole of the Labrador peninsula north of the province of Quebec, and east of the Atlantic coast-strip, which is politically attached to Newfoundland under the name of Labrador (see p. 67). With the exception of a few trading-posts, some wandering bands of Indians and Eskimo along the northern coast, this country is uninhabited. Its character is very imperfectly known, but in it are many large lakes drained by long rivers to Hudson Bay on the west, or Ungava Bay on the north. It is believed to be a rocky and hilly Laurentian region throughout, partly forested, but becoming almost perfectly barren and treeless toward the north. It is highest in its southern and eastern parts, and along the Atlantic coast becomes even mountainous. The fisheries of the Atlantic coast are rather important, and those of Hudson Bay may become equally so; but apart from fish, fur-bearing animals, and the probable existence of mineral deposits, the whole region possesses little real value.

BRITISH COLUMBIA

Size and Outlines.—This province has an extreme length of about 1250 miles, measured from its south-eastern to its north-western corner. Its greatest width, measured from the outer coast of the Queen Charlotte Islands to its north-eastern corner, is 650 miles, and its area is

383,300 square miles, being thus the largest of the provinces of Canada. It is bounded to the north by the 60th parallel of latitude, to the south by the 49th parallel, save on the coast, where the southern end of Vancouver Island extends beyond that line. The southern half of its eastern boundary follows the line of watershed in the Rocky Mountains, but the northern half coincides with the 120th degree of longitude. It thus includes the whole of the Cordillera or mountain belt of the western part of Canada, except its extreme northern part and the rather narrow eastern slope of the Rocky Mountains, which lie within the North-West Territory. Its north-eastern corner, moreover, embraces a large triangular region of the interior continental plain, adjoining the district of Athabasca.

Surface.—If we exclude the tract of plain last referred to, the whole of British Columbia belongs to the Cordillera region of the continent, and is characteristically a country of mountains. The breadth of the Cordillera belt, from the coast to its north-eastern margin, is, throughout the southern and greater part of British Columbia, about 400 miles. South of the International boundary it becomes much wider, and it is also considerably wider in the northern part of this province. In this narrower part of the Cordillera the constituent mountain ranges are more regular and more nearly parallel than elsewhere, their general direction being, like that of the coast, north-west and south-east. But even here this broken country presents so great an intricacy of detail, and exhibits so many local conditions, that its ruling features only can be explained. Broadly viewed, the dominant and most important mountain systems are the Rocky Mountains on the north-east side of the belt, and the Coast range which borders the Pacific. The intervening country comprises the Interior Plateau, together with various ranges which have been grouped together as the Gold ranges, as well as other detached mountains and irregular mountainous tracts.

The average width of the Rocky Mountain range proper in the southern part of British Columbia is about 60 miles, but this decreases to the north-westward till, in latitude 56°, it is about 20 miles only. Still farther to the north-west this range is more irregular. The southern part of the range includes many peaks exceeding 10,000 feet in altitude, and farther north-westward, about the sources of the North Saskatchewan, it appears to culminate in Mount Brown (about 16,000 feet), Mount Murchison (about 13,500 feet), and other lofty summits. Still farther in the same direction, with the decreased width and less regular trend above referred to, it becomes less elevated. Granites and other crystalline rocks are scarcely found in this range, but massive limestones abound, and these, breaking off at right angles to their planes of bedding, produce crags and lines of cliff which give a special character to the scenery. Glaciers of some size exist in this range about the sources of the Bow and North Saskatchewan.

The Coast range is often, though incorrectly, regarded as a continuation of the Cascade range of Oregon and Washington. This range in reality originates almost exactly on the southern boundary of British Columbia, and runs without any important interruption or change in character for over 900 miles in a north-westward direction. It has an average width of about 100 miles, from which it varies little, and a large number of its summits reach heights of 7000 to 8000 feet, while some exceed 9000 feet. Its submerged valleys on the coastward side constitute the remarkable fiords there met with. The rocks composing it are chiefly granites, with the addition of much hardened and altered stratified rocks of various kinds. Glaciers and snow-fields are abundant throughout the higher parts of this mountain system, being maintained by an abundant snowfall, which the chain receives in consequence of its position athwart the stream of moisture-bearing winds from the ocean.

To the south-west of the Coast range, and thus beyond the margin of the main mountain belt of the Cordillera, a partially submerged and broken parallel range forms Vancouver Island and the Queen Charlotte Islands. This is similar to the Coast range in its general characters, and is composed of like rocks. Its highest known mountain, in Vancouver

Island (Victoria Peak), is 7484 feet above the sea. Several other summits in this island surpass 6000 feet, and some in the Queen Charlotte Islands probably attain 5000 feet. The mountains of the Gold system, including the Selkirk (Fig. 16), Purcell, Columbia, Cariboo, and other ranges, lie along the south-western side of the Rocky Mountains proper, from which they are separated by a remarkably long and straight though not wide valley, which is occupied in various portions of its length by several of the larger rivers. These ranges are as yet very imperfectly known, but many of their peaks are scarcely inferior in height to those of the Rocky Mountains. Mounts Sir Donald (10,645), Macdonald (9440), and Tupper (9030), all overlooking the pass through which the Canadian Pacific Railway runs, are among those of which the heights have been ascertained. The various ranges of which this somewhat irregular mountain system is composed consist partly of granitic rocks, but largely of old and much-altered rocks of many kinds, most of which are of sedimentary origin. Many small glaciers and some of considerable dimensions are found in these ranges.

Between this mountain system and that known as the Coast range is a region which has been called the Interior Plateau of British Columbia, having a width of about 100 miles. Though the surface of this region is by no means flat, and is often indeed so much broken that in a less elevated country it might be regarded as mountainous, it is here characterised as a plateau by comparison with the lofty and rugged ranges which border it. It is not so continuous in its general north-west and south-east bearing as are the Rocky Mountains and Coast range, being practically closed by mountains which are thrust between these main ranges, in the vicinity of the 49th parallel, and again in a similar manner in about latitude 55° 30'. It is thus about 500 miles in length. Its general elevation decreases gradually from its south-eastern to its north-western end, and it is traversed by numerous trough-like valleys which are deepest where its elevation is greatest. These have been excavated by rivers and streams, which have been largely instrumental, in the long course of time, in destroy-

Fig. 16.—View in the Selkirk Range, British Columbia, where crossed by the Canadian Pacific Railway.
From a Photograph by Notman.

ing the original uniformity of its surface. Water, standing at an elevation of 3000 feet above the present sea-level, would flood most of these valleys in the southern part of the plateau, while in its northern portion a large extent of its area would then be completely submerged. If the irregularities of the Interior Plateau were reduced by planing off the prominences, and employing the material of these to fill in the hollows, its mean level would be about 3500 feet.

Beyond the mountainous country which, as we have seen, closes this plateau to the north-west, the interval between the Rocky Mountains and Coast range contains more irregular ranges not definitely referable to the Gold system; and though there are also wide tracts of lower land, these are more or less completely isolated.

The soil of the arable tracts contained in the province is exceedingly diverse in character, but is often very rich; and the nature of the surface with respect to vegetation is as varied as its relief. To the changes in humidity and climate generally, which would naturally result from increasing distance from the ocean coast, and from difference in latitude, is superadded in this case that produced by the bold physical features of the country.

The coast, on account of the influence of the sea on its climate, is in general thickly covered to the water's edge with forests of magnificent growth, affording fine timber, but rendering the clearing of the ground for agriculture difficult. The largest tracts of low land suited to cultivation are situated on the southern and eastern shores of Vancouver Island, the north-eastern part of the Queen Charlotte Islands, and at the mouth of the Fraser river. The first is based on Cretaceous rocks, softer than those which project to form the mountainous interior of the island. The second coincides with a region of nearly horizontal rocks of Tertiary age, and is deeply covered with deposits left by the sea at a still more recent geological time. The third forms a triangle narrowing to the point at which the Fraser breaks through the Coast range (Fig. 17), and is largely a delta region floored with sediments brought down by that river. The Coast range is everywhere covered with forest except where too rocky to

Fig. 17.—Cañon of the Fraser River where it breaks through the Coast Range of British Columbia. From a Photograph by Notman.

support the growth of trees, or over such parts of its summits as are too elevated.

Much of the southern part of the Interior Plateau, including nearly all of the principal valleys and their slopes, is either open and grassy or but dotted with trees, while the intervening higher tracts of plateau are generally wooded. The arable land is almost entirely confined to the valleys, which are however sometimes notably wide. The northern and lower part of the plateau is preponderantly a forest country, but with many small areas of prairie, especially along the banks of the rivers and lakes. It comprises much good land, but has scarcely yet been entered by settlers. Still farther to the north-west, the region between the Coast range and the Rocky Mountains is almost everywhere covered with forest.

In the Gold ranges thick forests are characteristic, and the trees are often of fine growth and afford excellent timber, though most of the higher parts of the mountains are bare and Alpine in appearance. The southern part of the long valley which separates these ranges from the Rocky Mountains is open or thinly wooded, but to the north it is filled with forest. The higher parts of the Rocky Mountain range justify the name of that range in possessing scarcely a vestige of soil, but the western slopes are usually thickly wooded, while the eastern slopes are more thinly covered with forests, and small natural prairies occur in the valleys on this side.

Coast-Line.—The part of the Pacific coast belonging to British Columbia, though its general trend is uniform, is singularly intricate in detail, being not only dissected by long fiords, but also fringed by an archipelago of numerous islands of all sizes, from that of Vancouver Island to mere rocks. It resembles the western coast of Scandinavia, but is drawn to a larger scale, the fiords being deeper and the mountains which border them higher. The character of the coast of the mainland is best explained by referring to the origin of its features. Like most mountain ranges the wide Coast range is traversed by two principal sets of valleys, one parallel to its length, and the other more or less nearly transverse. These are continued on the seaward side into the fiords and straits. They have been excavated chiefly by the prolonged action of streams, during a former period at which the land stood higher relatively to the sea than it now does. Subsequently, when the land sank to its present level, the sea filled all the lower parts of the old river-valleys, producing a maze of islands where these valleys were lowest and widest and the general height of the mountains was least, and long separate fiords in the central and higher parts of the mountain system. The two systems of valleys first referred to, varying in direction somewhat with the slightly irregular trends of different parts of the mountains, may be distinctly traced in the coast-lines of the submerged border on a good map. Features of the same character, though on a smaller scale, are found on the outer coast of Vancouver Island and in the southern part of the Queen Charlotte Islands.

The fiords of the coast are generally called "Inlets," "Channels," "Canals," or "Sounds." From south to north, the more important are Howe Sound, Jarvis, Bute, and Knight Inlets, Dean Inlet, with Bentinck north and south arms, and connecting channels, forming a complicated system; Gardiner Channel with Douglas Channel and connecting waters, Observatory Inlet and Portland Canal. The general characters of all these and of the many smaller fiords are much alike. Their width is usually from one to three miles, their shores rocky and abrupt, and rising toward the heads of the longer fiords into mountains from 6000 to 8000 feet in height. The water is deep, usually much too deep for anchorage, but at the head of each arm a delta-flat, formed by an entering river, is commonly found.

Many good harbours exist along the coast, but the two best and most important of those on the mainland are Burrard Inlet, near the mouth of the Fraser, upon which the city of Vancouver is built, and Port Simpson, near the northern end of the coast of the province, and adjacent to the southern extremity of the "coast-strip" of Alaska.

Vancouver is the largest island, having a length of 285 miles, with a greatest width of 80 miles, and an area of about 20,000 square miles, or nearly the same as that of the province of Nova **Scotia.** Harbours abound **along** its coast—that of Esquimalt, **near** its southern extremity, **being** one of the best. It is separated from the mainland by Fuca Strait, the **Strait of** Georgia, and Queen Charlotte Sound. **The tides,** flowing round the **two ends** of the **island, meet in** the northern part of the Strait of Georgia; **and in the** narrowest part of the Channel **(Seymour Narrows),** to the north of this strait, the tidal **current flows with such** great velocity that it is **dangerous for vessels to pass** through except at high **or** low **water, when for** a brief **space** the flow ceases.

The Queen Charlotte Islands form a horn-shaped archipelago, running to a narrow point at the south. They are separated from the islands adjacent to the mainland by Hecate Strait, **20 miles** wide at its narrowest part. There **are three large islands, Graham,** Moresby, and Prevost, with **many of smaller size. The islands of** the archipelago **fringing the mainland are too** numerous to admit of separ**ate mention, though several** of them are large. Those **adjacent to** Vancouver Island **in** the Strait of Georgia, though relatively small, are important because occupied for purposes of agriculture or sheep-farming. From the southern extremity of Vancouver Island to the northern **border** of the coast, a distance of about 550 miles, an **almost** completely sheltered route, navigable for the largest **vessels,** exists between the islands and the mainland.

Drainage System.—A small part of the extreme north **of British** Columbia is drained **by the sources of the Yukon; and a** large area to the **north-east lies in the hydrographic basin of** the Mackenzie, being **drained by** the Liard and Peace rivers and their tributaries. It is noteworthy that both these important rivers rise **far within the region of the** Cordillera, from which they gather **a large part of their waters, and flow thence across the line of the Rocky Mountain range to reach the great inland plain.** The remaining and largest part **of** the province **is drained by rivers which** flow directly **to** the Pacific. **Of these the Fraser is the** most important, followed by the Skeena, Nass, and Stikine. The upper part of the Columbia river drains a considerable area in the south-eastern angle of the province. All these streams gather their waters from the inner part of the Cordillera belt, between the Rocky Mountains and Coast range, and eventually flow across the last-named mountain system to reach the sea. Not only is this the case with these larger rivers, but several much smaller streams, such as the Homathco, Bella-Coola, Salmon, and Taku, which rise a short distance only within the Coast range, flow boldly toward it, and follow profound valleys through the mountains to the heads of some of the larger fiords. This circumstance indicates former conditions of the physical geography of the region very different from the present, but the geological history of these river-valleys is not fully known.

Because of the bold mountainous character of the country, the courses of all the rivers are very sinuous and indirect; and on account of its considerable elevation, most of them are either rapid throughout, or are interrupted by numerous rapids and falls, rendering them of comparatively little utility for purposes of navigation. The Fraser (length over 600 miles) is the most important river in the province. Rising in the eastern slopes of the Rocky Mountains, and flowing at first north-westward, it turns sharply upon itself and runs nearly due south for about 300 miles, after which it rounds gradually to a westerly direction, and, cutting through the southern part of the Coast range, empties into the Strait of Georgia. Its estuary is navigable for sea-going vessels to New Westminster, and small steamboats ascend as far as Yale, about 80 miles farther. At this point the cañon by which the river traverses the Coast range begins, and for many miles its course is a succession of wild rapids. Its whole upper waters are swift, but there are some reaches upon which steamboats can run. The largest tributary of the Fraser is the Thompson, and above Kamloops Lake, through which it flows, both branches of this river are navigable by steamers for considerable distances. The Nechacco, Quesnel, and Chilcotin are other large rivers tributary to the Fraser.

Portions of the Columbia river within the limits of the province are also navigable, including the long Arrow Lakes. The Skeena and Stikine rivers can be ascended with difficulty by small steamers for over 100 miles in each case, but the other smaller rivers of the coast are scarcely navigable even for canoes on account of their rapid fall. None of the rivers of Vancouver Island are navigable except by canoes or boats, and even then with difficulty.

Lakes are numerous, and in the Coast range often occupy the upper parts of valleys of which the lower parts are sea-fiords. Generally speaking, the lakes of the province have long narrow forms, and are to be regarded as filling portions of the river-valleys of which the natural drainage has become interrupted in some way. A remarkable series of such long parallel-sided lakes occurs within or near the Gold ranges, including Kootanie Lake (length 64 miles), the Arrow Lakes (united length 87 miles), Shuswap Lake (greatest length 45 miles), Adams Lake (length 38 miles), and Quesnel Lake (length 47 miles). Okanagan Lake (length 65 miles), Kamloops Lake (length 18 miles), with other considerable lakes, lie in the southern part of the Interior Plateau. François (length 58 miles), Babine (length 87 miles), Stuart (length 40 miles), and Tacla (length 46 miles) lakes form the larger members of a remarkable group in the northern part of the same plateau. Chilco Lake (length about 40 miles) and Harrison Lake (length 35 miles) lie partly within the Coast range. Dease Lake (length 24 miles) is the source of one branch of the Liard river, while Frances Lake (length 30 miles) feeds another. Several more large lakes, on or some way beyond the northern border of the province, drain to the Yukon. Some large and many small lakes also occur in Vancouver Island.

Climate.—The climate of British Columbia is very varied, being much affected by its physical features (see p. 17). The total annual precipitation ranges from 15 inches in the valleys of the southern interior, to $29\frac{1}{2}$ inches at Victoria, 65 inches on the border of the adjacent mainland, and 100 inches or more on outer parts of the coast to the north. Even on the coast snow occasionally falls to some depth in mid-winter, particularly to the north, but it does not lie long on the ground. The southern part of the Interior Plateau is a markedly dry country, with occasional severe cold in winter and great heat in summer;

DOMINION OF CANADA—BRITISH COLUMBIA

while farther to the north-west in the same region, lying between the Rocky Mountains and Coast range, the rainfall is greater, and the weather generally much resembles that of the central part of the province of Quebec (see p. 102). In the higher mountain regions the conditions become Alpine, but it is noteworthy that the westward slopes of each of the main ranges are moist, while the opposite slopes are relatively dry. This depends on the eastward flow of the atmospheric currents, which precipitate their moisture where forced to ascend on the windward side of each of the principal mountain systems and descend on the lee side as dry winds.

All the ordinary crops of temperate climates may be grown on the coast, though the summer is not hot enough to ripen melons, grapes, and maize; but these, as well as the ordinary field crops, can be grown in the valleys of the southern part of the Interior Plateau. The small rainfall of this latter region, however, renders artificial irrigation necessary; and long ditches are constructed for this purpose, by which the waters of the mountain streams may be distributed over the fertile lands. In the northern parts of the Interior Plateau irrigation is not necessary, but these have hitherto been but little cultivated. Though scattered and more or less completely isolated from each other, the cultivable lands in the province are in the aggregate extensive. Many places offer special advantages for fruit-growing, and the open grass-lands of the southern interior are already largely utilised for stock-raising purposes. At Victoria the mean highest temperature is 82·6; mean lowest, 13·5. The thermometer seldom touches zero.

Mineral Fields and Chief Industries.—The discovery of gold first brought population to British Columbia, and gold mining has since remained one of the most important pursuits. Since the beginning of such mining about $55,000,000 worth of gold have been produced, nearly all from gravels and alluvial deposits, from which it is obtained by various processes of "placer mining." The treatment of the quartz-veins from which the "placer" gold has originally been derived is now only beginning.

The coal-fields of the province are important and

extensive. Those at present worked are situated on the inner coast of Vancouver Island, the centres of the industry being Nanaimo and Comox, and a large proportion of the coal raised is sent to California. Anthracite coal is known in the Queen Charlotte Islands, and coals and lignites of different kinds in many other places. Mines of silver, in association with lead ores, are being opened up in the southern part of the Gold ranges; but their development has been so recent that no large quantities of ore have yet been exported. Iron ores abound, the best-known deposit being on Texada Island in the Strait of Georgia. Platinum is obtained in some of the gold washings, and altogether this province promises to become the most important mining region of Canada in the near future.

Fishing and lumbering rank with mining as the staple industries of the province. Salmon are exceedingly abundant in most of the rivers, and many salmon-canneries have been established, from which the product is exported to various parts of the world but principally to Great Britain. The coast fisheries, including those of halibut and herring, have so far received little attention, though capable of affording an almost inexhaustible food supply. Many small vessels are engaged in the fur-seal fishery, which is carried on in the open ocean. These vessels are owned principally in Victoria, whence they sail in the early spring, following the seals in their annual migration northward to Behring Sea. The fur-seals are quite distinct in habits and otherwise from the seals taken on the Atlantic coast, and much more valuable than these.

Lumbering is carried on for local purposes in the interior, but more extensively on the coast, where there are large saw-mills cutting for export. The most important timber tree is the Douglas fir, which on the coast frequently attains a height of 200 to 300 feet, with a diameter of eight to ten feet (Fig. 18). The size of the logs and the short time during which snow lies on the ground cause the timber business to be conducted in a different manner from that usual in the eastern provinces. The logs are generally brought from the places where they are cut ("logging camps") to the shore on "skid-ways," after

Fig. 18.—Forest of Douglas Firs, Vancouver Island. From a Photograph.

which they are formed into rafts, and these are towed to the various mills. The lumber produced is exported to various places on the coast of the Pacific Ocean. The western cedar is another valuable timber tree, and many other kinds of wood are obtained in lesser quantity.

The agricultural products of the province are as yet inconsiderable, and in consequence of the isolated positions of the best farming regions, must continue to depend largely on the establishment of local markets and the growth of other industries. Manufacturing is carried on to a limited extent.

Population.—The population of the province is about 100,000, and is chiefly concentrated in the southern parts of Vancouver Island, on the mainland coast and in the Interior Plateau, though local centres dependent on gold mining exist far to the north. It embraces immigrants from almost all parts of the world, being more varied in character than that of any other province of Canada, and including a considerable number of Chinese.

Towns.—VICTORIA (pop. by civic census, 23,000), originally a post of the Hudson's Bay Company, sprang into importance on the discovery of gold in 1858 (Fig. 19). It is situated on a small but secure harbour at the south-eastern extremity of Vancouver Island, and is the capital and largest city of the province. It has a considerable amount of shipping and various local industries, but is chiefly important as a distributing point. Three miles from Victoria is the spacious harbour of ESQUIMALT, the station for the British fleet in the North Pacific, with a large graving dock. VANCOUVER (pop. 14,000), on the south side of Burrard Inlet and the terminus of the Canadian Pacific Railway on the Pacific, was established in 1885, but was almost completely destroyed by fire in the following year. It has since advanced rapidly. It is a centre of the lumber trade and possesses other growing industries, besides being an important shipping point and the landing-place of the trans-Pacific steamship service. NEW WESTMINSTER (pop. 6600), situated on the north bank of the Fraser, about 12 miles from the sea and 10 from Vancouver, from which it is separated by a tract of low forest-covered hills,

FIG. 19.—PART OF THE CITY OF VICTORIA, VANCOUVER ISLAND. From a Photograph by Notman.

is another thriving place. Its importance depends largely on the salmon-canneries and on saw-mills. NANAIMO (pop. 4600), on a harbour of the same name on the inner coast of Vancouver Island, nearly opposite the mouth of Burrard Inlet, and 60 miles north-west of Victoria, is the centre of the coal trade. Several large colleries are situated in its vicinity. KAMLOOPS (pop. 1000) is the most important trade centre and distributing point in the interior of the province. It is built on the south side of the Thompson, at the confluence of its two branches, and a few miles from the head of Kamloops Lake—the main line of the Canadian Pacific Railway passing through it. The adjacent country lies in the dry belt, and is largely utilised for stock-raising. Other small towns in the interior constitute local distributing points depending on agriculture, stock-raising, or mining. The low lands about the mouth of the Fraser river have agricultural centres, and a number of villages and settlements along the coast depend on the fisheries and on trade with the Indians.

III.—THE WEST INDIAN COLONIES

Geographical Position.—The West Indies constitute a vast archipelago, the islands of which form a chain, running from the low peninsula of Florida in North America to the northern coast of South America, near the mouth of the Orinoco, in a north-westerly and south-easterly bearing, parallel in trend to that of the highlands of the isthmus of Central America. These islands, numbering in all about 1000, are included between the 10th and 27th degrees of latitude north of the Equator, and extend from 59° 30' to 85° west longitude. They are thus situated in the same latitude as the southern half of India, and at about the same distance in longitude from Greenwich as that country, the west longitude of the centre of the archipelago being nearly the same as the east longitude of the eastern part of India. Their name perpetuates the mistaken idea of Columbus, who, when he first reached the islands, supposed them to be the western shore of India. The distance from England to the nearest part of the West Indies is about 600 miles greater than that to New York, and about 1000 miles greater than that to Quebec.

The West Indian Islands separate the Gulf of Mexico and the Carribean Sea from the Atlantic, being, in fact, the projecting points on a wide submarine ridge which has much deeper waters on both sides. Their close geographical relation to the American mainland is made evident by the soundings, which show that an elevation to the amount of 1000 fathoms, though little affecting the size of the Atlantic as a whole, would unite all the islands in two land areas, the wider of which would attach to North

America, the narrower to South America. These would then be separated by but one narrow channel to the east of the island of Porto Rico, while a branch of the northern and wider land would connect by way of Jamaica with Central America, wholly isolating the deep Gulf of Mexico.

Form and Size.—The south-eastern part of the archipelago forms a nearly simple chain, running first in a northerly direction for about 600 miles, and then to the westward for a similar distance; the western promontory of Hayti and the island of Jamaica continue on this last bearing, but two divergent north-westward branches are thrown off, one of which is represented by Cuba, the other by the Bahama Islands, and between these the point of the peninsula of Florida comes in from the north.

From the island of Trinidad to the most northern reef of the Bahamas, the total length of the West Indian archipelago is nearly 2000 miles; and though presenting rather an unimportant appearance on the map of the world, the aggregate area of the West Indies is about 95,000 square miles, of which that of the British Islands makes 13,754 square miles. The islands are geographically divided into three principal groups—(1) THE BAHAMAS, including a great number of islands, some of which are very small. (2) THE GREATER ANTILLES, including the four largest islands—Cuba, Hayti, Jamaica, and Porto Rico. (3) THE LESSER ANTILLES, comprising a number of medium-sized and small islands. These last are further subdivided into the Leeward Islands, forming the northern part of the group, and the Windward Islands forming its southern part, the line of separation running between Dominica and Martinique, on the 15th degree of latitude.

The islands of the archipelago not under British authority are divided between Spain (Cuba, Porto Rico, etc.), France (Martinique, Guadaloupe, etc.), Holland, Denmark (St. Thomas, with its important harbour, and other islands), and Venezuela (several small islands adjacent to the coast of that country), while Hayti is independent and comprises two negro republics, named Hayti and St. Domingo respectively. The French, Danish, and Dutch possessions are confined to the Lesser Antilles, with the exception of some small islands on the Venezuela coast and remote from the main chain, which also belong to Holland.

Climate.—The climate of the West Indies is tropical, but the intensity of the heat is to some extent modified by the ocean, while in the higher parts of such of the islands as are mountainous the temperature is still further reduced. The southern part of the group has a mean annual temperature of about 80°, while that of the northern part is about 75°, and the range in temperature shown by the means of the various months is small. Snow is unknown. In most of the islands there is a short wet season of a few weeks in April, followed by a short dry season. The longer wet season begins in July, and at this time storms are apt to occur. These are known as hurricanes, and are equal in violence to the typhoons of the Indian and Pacific Oceans. The islands lie in the trade-wind belt, and the prevailing direction of the atmospheric currents is from the north-east. The rainfall is generally ample.

Plants and Animals.—In the state of nature almost all the West Indian Islands were characterised by a luxuriant forest growth, but many of them have since been largely cleared by man. Ferns and orchids are abundant, and bananas, plantains, mangoes, guava, cactus, avocado-pear, and tamarind are among the characteristic plants. The native vegetation is on the whole intermediate between that of Mexico and the northern part of South America. Except in Trinidad and neighbouring small islands, which lie so near to South America as to belong to that continent zoologically, the native animals of the West Indies are rather peculiar. The most characteristic South American forms—monkeys, carnivora, and sloths—are wanting; and besides bats, which are numerous, only a few kinds of rodents and insectivora are found, and these are confined to the north-western portion of the islands beyond the deep-sea channel east of Porto Rico, which has already been mentioned. From these facts, and from the zoological relationship of the animals, it is concluded that the West Indies, by a former elevation of the land, were at one time connected with Central America, but that this elevation

M

was not sufficient to bridge the deep channel just alluded to. Over 200 kinds of birds are found to be permanent residents of the islands, and about a third of these are not known elsewhere. Some eighty-eight species of birds from the North American continent spend the winter in the

FIG. 20.—JAMAICAN CACTUS AND PINGUIN HEDGES.

West Indies. Maize, tobacco, cotton, sugar-cane, coffee, cocoa, indigo, ginger, various spices, and many other tropical products, including fruits, are cultivated, and the ordinary domesticated animals have been introduced.

Population.—When discovered by Columbus, the northern part of the West Indies was peopled by a native race called the Arawaks, the southern part by a fierce and warlike race named the Caribs, but both are now nearly extinct. For some time after the discovery of the islands, the Spanish alone took any interest in them, but early in the seventeenth century the English, French, and Dutch began to form settlements, and the history of the islands became chequered by many conflicts between their European owners. Negro slaves were imported in large numbers from Africa to work on the plantations, but in 1834 the Act of Emancipation came into force in the British Islands, and slavery was abolished, the Imperial Government making a grant of £20,000,000 to reimburse the owners for their loss. The present population, numbering in all about 1,179,000, is thus largely composed of blacks, or mulattoes. Since the abolition of slavery, East Indians, known as "coolies," and Chinese in considerable numbers, have been imported for plantation work.

Government.—The form of government differs in the several British Islands or groups of islands, but none possess a full constitution and responsible Government. They are either Crown colonies in which the Crown initiates legislation, or representative Governments, of which the members are in part elective and in part appointed by the Crown, the Crown retaining a power of veto on legislative measures. Trinidad is an exception, as here all the members of the legislature are appointed by the Crown. Jamaica has a Privy Council and Legislative Council of nine appointed members, and a House of Assembly of twenty-four elected members. The Bahamas have a Legislative Council of nine members, and an elected representative assembly of twenty-nine members. In the Leeward Islands the General Legislative Assembly consists of ten nominated and ten elective members, while the Windward Islands, though under one Governor, have no General Assembly, each island in the group having its own legislature, laws, and financial arrangements.

Products, Industries, and Commerce.—The growth of the sugar-cane at one time nearly monopolised the cultivable lands of the British West Indian Islands, and is still most important. It is increasing after a period of decline, as the result of improved methods of cultivation and manufacture. Rum is an important product derived from the cane. Large quantities of fruit and other tropical products, including spices, dye-stuffs, fibre plants, medicinal plants, coffee and cocoa, are now grown and exported. The larger islands also furnish timber adapted for cabinet-making and other arts. Trinidad exports asphalt, and salt is obtained by the evaporation of sea-water in the Bahamas. The imports are chiefly manufactured goods, bread-stuffs, salt fish, and other foods not produced in the islands. Trade is carried on chiefly with Britain and the United States, and to some extent with Canada, Newfoundland, and various other countries.

THE BAHAMAS

Name and Size.—The meaning of the word Bahama is uncertain, though it is perhaps of native origin.

This group of islands is about 600 miles in greatest length, running in a north-west and south-east direction, between Florida and the north shore of Hayti. Most of the larger islands are united in subordinate groups by wide shallow banks, and are surrounded by numerous rocks and "cays," a name derived from the Spanish *cayo*, meaning a reef, shoal, or islet. There are in all twenty-nine larger islands, 661 cays, and over 2000 rocks. The total land area is about 5800 square miles. (Estimates differ.) The principal islands are New Providence, Abaco, Harbour Island, Eleuthera, Inagua, Mayaguana, Ragged Island, Rum Cay, Exuma, Long Island, Long Cay and the Biminis. All these are ports of entry, but Nassau or New Providence is the only important harbour. In addition, though not ports of entry, are Grand Bahama, Crooked Island, Aklin Island, Cat Island, Watling Island (or San Salvador), the Berry Islands, and Andros Island.

Surface.—All the Bahamas are low and flat, being composed of coral rock, or of coral sand which is sometimes blown into dunes or hills 100 or 200 feet in height, and in places becomes hardened by the percolation of rain-water through its calcareous substance. In their material and character of surface these islands resemble the adjacent part of Florida. Because of the small size of the islands and porous nature of the rock, fresh water is in general obtained from wells, in which it rises and falls with the tide. Running water occurs only on Andros Island, the largest of the group.

Chief Industries.—These are fruit-growing and obtaining and preparing sponges for market. Bananas, oranges, and pine-apples are largely exported to the United States. Cocoa-nuts are also grown, and the cultivation of a fibre plant known as Sisal hemp is now attracting much attention. The sponge is procured on the neighbouring banks, either by diving, or from boats by means of long hooked poles. Salt is produced by the natural evaporation of sea-water.

Population.—The number of inhabitants is 49,800, of which about 14,000 are whites, the remainder being the descendants of liberated Africans. A considerable number of Loyalists removed to the Bahamas at the close of the American revolutionary war. The small island of San Salvador was the first American land discovered by Columbus in 1492. The islands were first colonised by the English in 1629, but afterwards fell into the hands of Spain for a time. Turks and Caicos Islands, at the south-eastern extremity of the group, are politically dependencies of Jamaica.

Town.—NASSAU (pop. 5000) is the capital and only important town. It was a busy place during the Civil War in the United States, when it became the centre from which blockade-running was carried on. It is noted as a sanitarium and winter resort.

JAMAICA

Name and Size.—Jamaica is one of the four islands which constitute the Greater Antilles, and is the largest of the British West Indian Islands. Its name is but little altered from its native form, Xaymaca, meaning "land of wood and water," or, in other words, fertile land. Unlike the Bahamas, which lie along the outer or Atlantic edge of the submarine plateau of the West Indies, Jamaica is a projecting part of the broad ridge which runs from this

plateau to the continent, and separates the two deep
basins of the Carribean Sea. It lies 90 miles to the south
of Cuba, and about 100 miles from the nearest part of
Hayti, and is 144 miles in length by 49 miles in greatest
breadth, with an area of 4193 square miles.

Surface.—Jamaica is bold and mountainous, so much
so that it is said Columbus explained its character to
Queen Isabella of Spain by crumpling a piece of paper in
his hand, and exhibiting it in place of a description of the

FIG. 21.—PORT ROYAL, JAMAICA.

island. It is the unsubmerged part of a mountain ridge of
which some of the higher points are composed of granites
and other hard crystalline rocks, including old altered
limestones, but the greater area of the island is formed of
a much newer white limestone. The principal range runs
through the centre of the island from east to west, and
from this many ridges run down to the coast-line, separating the valleys of the numerous streams. In the western
and middle parts of the island the mountains are rather irregular in direction and height, and much lower than those

of the eastern end. Here the central **range is known as** the Blue Mountains. Several of its **summits rise to 6000** feet, and its culminating point, Blue Mountain **Peak,** attains a height of 7360 feet. The main range of the **Blue** Mountains throws off subsidiary ridges to the north and south, which again divide into numerous still smaller ridges in such a manner as **to occupy** nearly all this end **of** the island from shore to **shore.**

On the south side of the island the highlands and ridges often reach quite **to the** coast, but the inclination of the northern side is more gentle, **and** the surface is diversified by low hills, clothed with pimento groves and **intersected** by beautiful valleys. The whole **area of low land,** contained in the valleys and several small plains, is inconsiderable, and occupies little more than a tenth of **the surface.** The plains are of alluvial formation, the largest being that of Liguanea, near Kingston, 30 miles in length. Others are found in the valleys of the Morant **and** Plantain Garden rivers, with smaller flats about **the mouths** of several of the principal streams. About **another tenth** of the surface is entirely valueless, **consisting of morass, rocks, or** "cock-pit" country—the last being **a name** given **to a** rugged limestone region characterised by funnel-**shaped** depressions produced by the solvent action of rain-water on the limestones. Caverns, **formed** in the same manner, **are** rather numerous. The whole area of the island is equal to 2,683,520 acres, of which over 600,000 acres in all are actually under cultivation or care. Vegetation is luxuriant even to the mountain-tops.

Coast-Line.—The coast-line is more indented **as well as** bolder on the south side of **the** island than **on the north.** Kingston is the most important harbour, being **large** and almost completely land-locked. It is protected on the seaward side by a long, low, sandy point known as the Palisadoes. Numerous smaller harbours and bays form points of call along both shores of the island, **but many of** them are not well **sheltered from the sea.**

Drainage System.—The **rivers** generally flow **to the** north or south from the central highlands, and, though numerous, drain comparatively small areas. To the **general**

directions of flow there are a few exceptions, of which the Plantain Garden river and the Montego river are the most important. The first-named flows eastward for the greater part of its length, between the Blue Mountain range and a range of coast hills, and discharges eventually in Holland Bay near the east extremity of the island. The Montego flows westward to the bay of the same name on the north coast. Most of the rivers are rapid, and subject to heavy floods. The Black river only is navigable, for a length of 30 miles, by small craft. Some of the rivers in the extensive limestone districts of the western half of the island run to "sinks," where they disappear in crevices or caverns of the rocks beneath. The principal rivers of the south coast are—Morant river (length 15 miles), Rio Cobre (length 38 miles), flowing into Kingston harbour; Rio Minho (length 45 miles), and Black river (length 30 miles). On the north, the Great river (length 20 miles), Montego river (length 12 miles), White river (length 13 miles), Wagwater (length 19 miles), the name being a corruption of Agua Alta; Rio Grande (length 18 miles), and Plantain Garden river (length 20 miles). The upper streams of the Rio Grande and of other smaller rivers draining the northern slopes of the Blue Mountains are noted for their romantic scenery and numerous waterfalls.

Climate.—The tropical heats of the lowlands are modified by the sea breeze during the day and the land breeze at night; and in ascending the mountain ranges a temperature of 80° or 85° is exchanged for one of 45° or 50°. Because of the diversity in climate resulting from the high altitudes of the central parts of the island, a great variety of plants may be profitably cultivated.

Chief Industries.—The growth of the sugar-cane and the production of sugar, molasses, and rum are the most important industries. Coffee, fruits (including oranges, citrons, bananas, and pine-apples), spices, tobacco, nutmegs, and fibre-yielding plants are grown in the lower country. Pimento (or allspice), ginger, and cinchona are the principal crops of the higher regions, while various woods are also cut for export. Maize flourishes and Guinea grass is largely used as a fodder plant. The exports and imports are on the whole very similar in character and destination to those of the Bahamas.

Population.—This, according to the census of 1881, was 580,800, including 14,400 whites, 444,200 blacks, 110,000 mulattoes, and a number of East Indians and Chinese. The total population was estimated in 1889 at about 634,000. Jamaica is divided into three counties, for political purposes—Surrey, Middlesex, and Cornwall—and each of these is again subdivided into several parishes. Sixty-four miles of railway are in operation, and telegraphs and good roads intersect the island.

Towns.—KINGSTON (pop. about 40,000), situated on the harbour of the same name, and built upon a flat plain which rises gradually from the sea, is the seat of Government and largest town. PORT ROYAL, on the point of the Palisadoes spit at the entrance to the harbour, now a naval station, but formerly an important place, and notorious as a resort of privateers, was almost completely destroyed by a terrible earthquake in 1692. SPANISH TOWN (pop. about 5700), 13 miles distant from Kingston, was at one time the capital, and has some points of historic interest. SAVANNA-LA-MAR (pop. 2500), on the south coast near the west end of the island, and PORT MARIA (pop. 6700), MONTEGO BAY (pop. 4650), and FALMOUTH (pop. 3000), on the north coast, are the remaining larger towns, besides which there are many villages.

LEEWARD ISLANDS

Under this name are included those islands of the Lesser Antilles which lie to the north of latitude 15°. The islands under British authority are grouped into five presidencies, each with a local legislature, but all subordinate to one governor. These are Antigua, Montserrat, St. Christopher and Nevis, Dominica, and the Virgin Islands. The whole population of the Leeward Islands is about 126,000.

Antigua (and **Barbuda**).—Antigua was so named by Columbus, its discoverer, from a church in Seville, Ste.

Maria de la Antigua. Its area is nearly 108 square miles, equal to 68,980 acres, of which 20,000 acres are under cultivation. The island is composed of volcanic rocks, partly covered by coral limestones. Its north-east part is low and sometimes marshy, but it rises to the south-west and becomes more broken, attaining a greatest height of 1210 feet. The shores are much indented, and afford several good harbours, but the surface is less wooded than that of the neighbouring islands. Sugar, rum, molasses, pine-apples, and arrowroot are the chief products, but droughts sometimes interfere with these industries. The population of Antigua is about 35,000. ST. JOHN'S (pop. about 10,000), the chief town, is also the seat of the central Government of the Leeward Islands federation. BARBUDA and REDONDA ISLANDS are dependencies of Antigua, with an aggregate area of 62 square miles. Barbuda is flat, with a fertile soil. There is a good roadstead, but no sheltered harbour. Cattle, horses, pigs, and poultry are raised for sale in the neighbouring islands. Population about 1000. Redonda, little more than a rock, exports phosphate of alumina.

Montserrat.—Named by Columbus from a mountain in Spain. The area of this island is only 47 square miles, about two-thirds of which are mountainous, but the remainder is fertile and well cultivated. The highest point reaches 2500 feet, and the island is picturesque in appearance and healthy. The principal industry is the cultivation of lime trees and the production of lime-juice, though sugar is also made. There are a *soufrière* and several hot springs on the island. The population is about 11,000. PLYMOUTH (pop. 1400) is the principal town, and is situated on a roadstead, there being no good harbour.

St. Christopher and Nevis (with Anguilla).—The estimated population of this group of islands is now about 45,000. St. Christopher is commonly known as St. Kitts; it was discovered by Columbus and possibly obtained its name from that of the great navigator himself. Its area is 68 square miles. The highest point of the island, Mount Misery, has an elevation of 3711 feet, and this and the other highlands are formed of volcanic rocks, upon the flanks of which coral limestones rest. From the central mountains the land sweeps down to the coast, which is bordered by a continuous line of estates under high cultivation. Sugar is the chief product, but sweet potatoes, bananas, bread-fruit, etc., are grown for the support of the population. BASSETERRE (pop. 7500), on the south coast, is the chief town and seat of Government. The population of the whole island in 1881 was a little more than 29,000. NEVIS, which is separated from St. Christopher by a strait about three miles wide only, was so called by Columbus after the snow-capped mountain (Nieves) near Barcelona. It has an area of 50 square miles, about half of which is cultivable. It consists of a single conical mountain, the point of which rises to a height of 3200 feet, and around the base of which the cultivated lands spread. Sugar, rum, and molasses are the chief products. The population in 1881 was nearly 11,900. ANGUILLA, the name meaning "little snake," given for its lengthened form, is situated about 60 miles north of St. Christopher, the French and Dutch islands of St. Bartholomew and St. Martin intervening. It is about 16 miles in length, with an area of 35 square miles. Cattle, phosphate of lime, and salt are the principal exports, and these go for the most part to the neighbouring island of St. Thomas. The salt is obtained from a "salt-pond," about two miles in circumference, in the centre of the island. Tobacco, maize, and various roots are also grown. The population is 2500, and of this only 100 are Europeans.

Dominica.—This island is 29 miles in length, with an area of 291 square miles, of which nearly one half is suited for cultivation, 55,000 acres being under culture. It is a volcanic island, with high and rugged mountains, of which Morne Diobloten, the most elevated, attains 5314 feet. The volcanic forces though latent are not extinct, a slight eruption having occurred in 1883. There is a "boiling lake" at an elevation of 2425 feet, and many hot springs, while much sulphur, produced by numerous *soufrières*, is found. Many rivulets descend from the higher mountains, and the soil is good, producing crops similar to those of the neighbouring islands. The population is about 29,500, including about 300 Caribs. The white element of the population is chiefly French, and the blacks speak a French *patois*. The capital, ROSEAU (pop. 4500), stands in a remarkably picturesque situation on the south-west coast.

The Virgin Islands were so named by Columbus after the "11,000 virgins" of tradition. They comprise about 50 islets and rocks, some high, which in part belong to Britain and in part to Denmark. The total area of the British islands is about 64 square miles, the largest of them being Tortola, Virgin Garda, and Anegada. Population about 5000. Tortola is rugged and without forest, with a scanty water-supply, but forms one side of a magnificent harbour, Drake's Bay, partly enclosed by the neighbouring islands. There is good pasturage on the Virgin Islands, and sugar and cotton are produced in small quantity. On Virgin Garda there is a copper mine. The capital, ROADTOWN (pop. 400), is on the island of Tortola.

THE WINDWARD ISLANDS

Under this name are included the southern islands of the chain of the Lesser Antilles, all of which are British, except the French island of Martinique. The population of the British islands is about 148,000, of which only five per cent is white. The islands, with their dependencies, are grouped under three local Governments, those of Grenada, St. Vincent, and St. Lucia, with a Governor-in-Chief.

Grenada.—This island has an area of 133 square miles, or 85,120 acres, of which about one-fourth is under cultivation. It is of volcanic origin, mountainous, and very picturesque. The line of principal elevation runs from north to south, and several summits exceed 3000 feet. A circular fresh-water lake named the Grand Étang, on the summit of a mountain ridge, and a second lake named Lake Antoine, which is believed to have subterraneous communications with various streams, are interesting features. Hot springs and mineral springs are abundant. Sugar was formerly the chief product of the island, but cocoa is now the most important. Nutmegs and other spices are produced, and various woods, and turtles are among the exports. The population, including that of the Grenadines, is 55,500. ST. GEORGE, the capital of Grenada, is beautifully situated on a land-locked harbour, and was at one time strongly fortified. The GRENADINES are small islands and rocks, with a total area of 8462 acres, forming a chain which runs northward from Grenada toward St. Vincent. These are in part dependencies of each of the two larger islands mentioned.

St. Vincent, so named by Columbus from the calendar saint of the day on which he discovered the island, comprises an area of 140 square miles. It is a wholly volcanic island, characterised by sharp peaks, the highest of which rise to about 4000 feet in the centre, but opening out into valleys toward the coast. The greatest extent of flat land is on the north-east side. Two craters, known as *soufrières*, occur in the mountains of the northern part of the island, from one of which a great eruption, with lava streams and showers of ashes, occurred in 1812. The products of St. Vincent are similar to those of the neighbouring islands; but the arrowroot grown here is specially good. Population, 47,600. KINGSTON (pop. about 6000), the capital, is on the south-west coast of the island.

St. Lucia.—This is the northernmost of the Windward Islands and the largest and most picturesque of the group. Its area is 237 square miles. The name it bears was bestowed by Columbus in the same way as that of St. Vincent. This island is also of volcanic origin, with *soufrières* and hot springs. High mountains, with broken and fantastic forms, run north and south through the island, and two remarkable and conical peaks, known as the Pitons, rise from the sea to heights of about 3000 feet, guarding the entrance to the port of Castries. The valleys are very fertile, and some parts of the island are wooded and afford good timber. Among the principal products are sugar, cocoa, and logwood. It is historically interesting because of the numerous conflicts waged upon it or about its shores between France and England. Of these the fight between the **fleets of** Rodney and De Grasse **in** 1782, upon which **the dominating** influence of one **or** other of these **powers** depended, is the most noteworthy. The population, **including** over 2000 coolies, is 45,000. CASTRIES, (pop. 8000), the seat of Government and **chief town,** built **on a fine harbour** of the same name, is a naval station **and coaling depôt, and** is now being strongly fortified.

BARBADOS

Barbados is supposed **to derive** its name from a Spanish word designating a peculiar "bearded vine." It lies about **100** miles to **the** east **of** the volcanic chain **of** the Windward Islands, **and differs** completely from those islands in character, **being largely** composed of **coral rock, resting on** sandstones **and other soft Tertiary rocks.** It is surrounded by coral reefs, and the highest point on the island, Mount Hillaby, is only 1100 feet above the sea. **Barbados is about the size of the Isle of Wight,** having an area **of 166 square miles or 106,470 acres,** of which all **but** about **7000 acres is under cultivation.** Numerous gullies and valleys **radiate from the** high **eastern** part of the island, having been cut out by the **action** of water flowing either on the surface or through **the porous coral** rock beneath. "Sink-holes" are characteristic in some places, and caverns in the coral rock **are** not **infrequent;** while **so much** of the drainage takes a subterranean course **that streams** are almost completely wanting, and water is chiefly obtained **from wells. The** most important interests are agricultural, **the chief products** being sugar, molasses, **and rum; and on** account of its position the island **is as well** a centre of trade for the other islands. Petroleum **is known** to occur, but is little utilised. Barbados **has always been a** British possession, and disputes **with Newfoundland** the title to being the oldest **colony. The population is about 180,000,** and is remarkably **dense, averaging about 1080 to the** square mile. About **one-twelfth of the whole is white.** The blacks on this island **are unusually industrious and** thrifty. A railway, twenty-three miles in length, has been built. BRIDGE-TOWN (pop. 25,000), the capital and largest town, is built along the shore of Carlisle Bay, an open roadstead, the land rising in soft-outlined cultivated slopes and hills behind it.

TRINIDAD

This large island lies close to the South American coast, by which it is almost embayed. Its general form is that of a rectangle 48 miles in length from north to south, by about 30 miles in width; but the north-western and south-western points of this figure run out into spurs, and include between them the shallow Gulf of Paria, the water of which is rendered turbid by the discharge of the Orinoco river. The area of the island is about 1754 square miles, or 1,287,600 acres. Its dominant physical features are three rather narrow but nearly parallel ranges of mountains or hills. One of these runs from east to west along the north shore, its western extremity producing one of the long points, the islands off which are merely detached portions of the same range which resumes its continuity on the adjacent mainland coast. The main ridge of this range varies from 1600 to 2200 feet in height, while its highest point, Tucutche, rises to 3000 feet. The southern coast range is less continuous and less elevated than the northern, but holds a somewhat similar relation to the other long spur of the island. It is highest in its eastern part, where the peaks, now termed the Three Sisters, suggested to Columbus the name given by him to the whole island. The third range, in the middle of the island, includes numerous ridges and hills, the highest point of which, Tamana, is 1025 feet. The hardest and oldest rocks of the island are those which stand out in the northern mountain range, and both these and the softer sandstones and calcareous rocks, which form the greater part of the island, are continued on the neighbouring continent, of which Trinidad is merely a detached portion. The soil of Trinidad is fertile, but about a tenth of the surface only is under cultivation, the remainder being covered by luxuriant tropical growth, and in some places, particularly in the northern range, by noble forests. The principal rivers, which are not large, flow to the east and west, and in the vicinity of both coasts there are extensive swamp lands.

The most remarkable natural product of the island is asphalt, which occurs in various forms from a hard solid substance to an asphaltic oil. The celebrated Pitch Lake, with an area of about 100 acres, is situated near the shore of the Gulf of Paria on the long south-western point of the island. The asphalt or mineral pitch is largely exported

FIG. 22.—PITCH LAKE, LA BREA, TRINIDAD.

for use in pavements. Sugar, molasses, rum, cocoa, with cocoa-nuts, and other fruits are the most important agricultural products, but timber is also exported. The population numbers 196,200, largely made up of blacks and coolies, and with considerable French and Spanish elements. Fifty-four miles of railway are open.

PORT OF SPAIN (pop. 31,900), the largest town and capital on the north-east angle of the Gulf of Paria, is built on low land near the border of the sea. It is one of the finest towns in the West Indies, but vessels have to lie at anchor from one and a half to two miles out, goods and passengers being landed in boats. SAN FERNANDO (pop.

6335) is an important town, also situated on the west coast, and connected with the capital by railway.

Tobago is an island lying 18 miles north-east of Trinidad, with an area of 114 square miles, about one-seventh of which is under cultivation, most of the land being covered with forest. The higher parts of the central range of hills reach 2000 feet. It is a dependency of Trinidad with a population of 20,600 ; and its agricultural products are similar to those of the main island. There is reason to believe that this island was that which Defoe had in mind in writing his well-known narrative of *Robinson Crusoe*.

IV.—CENTRAL AMERICAN COLONY

BRITISH HONDURAS

THE name Honduras, which is also that of a Central American republic, is supposed to be derived from the Spanish *hondura*, "depth," given to Honduras Bay. This colony is the only British possession in Central America. It includes a strip of coast to the south of the peninsula of Yucatan, extending between 15° 54' and 18° 29' north latitude, with a length of 174 miles, and runs back from the coast-line for a distance of about 60 miles with an area of 7562 square miles. The position of British Honduras in latitude is nearly the same as that of Jamaica, of which island it was at one time a dependency. Inland and to the south it is bounded by Guatemala, to the north by Mexico.

Surface.—The coast-line is considerably indented, but the shore is low, shoal, and fringed with islands, coral reefs, and cays. The largest island, Turneffe, lies opposite the mouth of the Belize river. While the line of cays and reefs forms a natural breakwater, the navigation among them is very dangerous, and their intricacies afforded refuge to the buccaneers who at one time frequented these shores. From the coast, low land, which is occasionally swampy, extends for 10 to 20 miles; but farther inland the country becomes irregular and hilly, and in certain districts is even mountainous with elevations reaching 4000 feet in the Cockscomb Mountains. The higher regions are based upon metamorphic rocks and limestone. Most of the surface is still covered with dense forest, but this is intersected by regions of open woodland known as "pine ridges," which afford fair pasturage.

Drainage.—The drainage of the whole country is toward the Gulf of Honduras, the Belize or Old river (length 200 miles), New river, and Hondo river being the principal streams. The last-named forms the line of boundary between the colony and Mexico.

Climate.—The climate is moist, and the average temperature is about 80°, but falls as low as 60° during a part of the year. It is besides tempered by the sea-breezes from the eastward, which prevail during nine months of the twelve. The wet season lasts from June till October.

Industries.—The chief and only important industry is wood-cutting—mahogany and logwood being the most valuable trees. Some sugar and india-rubber with various fruits are also exported, and nearly all the staples of the West Indian Islands can be grown. The queen conch shell is collected and exported for the manufacture of cameos.

Population.—This is about 30,000, the great majority being negroes. There are some descendants of Caribs from St. Vincent, and a few natives in the inland regions. The Government is that of a Crown colony in which the members of both the Executive and Legislative Councils are appointed by the governor, not elected.

BELIZE (pop. 5800), the capital and largest town, built on both sides of one mouth of the river of the same name, stands upon low land with groves of cocoa-nut and tamarind trees.

V.—SOUTH AMERICAN COLONY

BRITISH GUIANA

This colony is situated on the north-east coast of South America, to the east of the mouth of the Orinoco. From the coast it runs southward, with Dutch Guiana on the east and Venezuela and Brazil on the west and south. Its southern or inland limit approaches to within less than one degree of the Equator, its northern extremity being in 8° 40′ north latitude. Its length is thus about 550 miles. The boundary on the side of Venezuela is not yet accurately determined, but the area exceeds 109,000 square miles, and the seaboard is about 300 miles in length.

Surface.—The coast is shallow and difficult of approach by large vessels; and flat country, deeply covered with alluvium, extends for about 50 miles from the sea, beyond which the surface gradually rises to an elevation of about 200 feet at the northern edge of a low tableland. Farther inland the elevation continues gradually to increase, and ranges of hills appear, forming the culminating points between the valleys of the large rivers, and running southward to join the Sierras or mountain ranges which separate the sources of these rivers from those of others flowing to the Amazon. Mount Roraima, in the western part of British Guiana, is the highest, attaining an elevation of about 8600 feet. It is an isolated block of high plateau surrounded by nearly perpendicular cliffs, but has lately been successfully scaled. Beyond the alluvial belt of the coast the rocks underlying the country and forming the ranges of hills and mountains are granites, gneisses, and schists, covered in some places by softer sandstones. More than half of the entire surface is occupied by dense and luxuriant tropical forests, but some wide savannahs or open grassy plains are found in the southern part of the country. The cultivated land is less than one six-hundredth of the whole. Agriculture is chiefly confined to the vicinity of the coast or to the banks of the rivers, and much of the cultivated land, being subject to overflow by the sea, is protected by dykes and intersected by canals much like those of Holland.

Drainage.—The principal rivers flow from south to north, the Essiquebo (length 300 miles) and Berbice (length 170 miles) being the largest. The Corentyn (length 240 miles), also a large river, forms the line of division between British and Dutch Guiana or Surinam. All these rivers receive numerous considerable tributaries, and on the Potaro, one of the branches of the Essiquebo, a fall 822 feet in height occurs. The Essiquebo and Berbice are navigable for vessels of considerable size for 50 miles from the sea, and communication with the interior is chiefly carried on by means of boats on the rivers.

Climate.—This though hot, the mean annual temperature being about 80°, is not unhealthy, and is tempered by easterly breezes which blow throughout the year. The long dry season lasts from August to November, followed by the short wet season, December and January; the short dry season February and March, which is succeeded by the long wet season beginning before the end of April. Hurricanes are unknown.

Plants and Animals.—These are of the South American type. The bully tree, greenheart, purpleheart, crabwood, and the lofty mira tree, with cabbage-palms, mahogany, and the Brazil-nut tree, abound, and the forests are characteristically bearded with moss, ferns, orchids, and such like plants. The wild flowers are notably gaudy, and the *Victoria regia* is a native of this region. The tapir is the largest quadruped, and cougars, jaguars, anteaters, armadillos, and agoutis, deer, monkeys, and alligators are common. The manatee or sea-cow, a peculiar marine animal, frequents the estuaries of the rivers.

Chief Industries.—The products resemble those of many of the West Indian Islands, sugar constituting over

90 per cent of the exports. Coffee, **cotton, rum, molasses, cocoa,** nuts, timber, and dye-stuffs are also exported. Some **attention** has **been** given to placer gold-mining of late **years, but the** mineral wealth of the country is as yet very imperfectly known.

Population and Government.—The population numbers 282,000, a large proportion being East Indian immigrants. **Negroes, the** descendants of freed slaves, Chinese, and the remnants of half a dozen native tribes, with some Europeans, make up the remainder. **The** country **was first** settled by **the** Dutch **at a very early date,** and afterwards changed owners several times. **As in** the West Indies, slavery was abolished **in** 1834. British Guiana is a Crown colony with a partially representative government of a somewhat complicated character; a certain number of representatives being elected under a high franchise. Dutch laws and institutions **are maintained in accordance** with treaty provisions.

Towns.—GEORGETOWN (pop. 50,000), handsome **and well built, is the capital** and most important place. It is situated at the mouth of the Demerara river, which, though comparatively small, is navigable for 100 miles. A railway, 20 miles in length, connects Georgetown with Mahaica. NEW AMSTERDAM (pop. 10,000) is the only other important **town.**

VI.—ATLANTIC ISLANDS

BERMUDA

THE Bermudas form a group of islands situated in mid-Atlantic, in 32° 15' north latitude, 64° 51' west longitude, 580 miles from Cape Hatteras in North America, and 2970 miles from London. The name is that of the Spanish voyager Bermudez, who first sighted and was wrecked upon the islands. The group is 18 miles in length and 6 in greatest breadth, and consists of about 300 small islands, of which 15 only are inhabited, the rest being mere rocks. The islands are formed of white coral rock, and are surrounded by extensive and dangerous coral reefs. Main Island (length 14 miles), St. George, Ireland, Somerset, and St. David's are the largest. The total land area is about 20 square miles. The surface is low, the highest land being less than 200 feet above sea-level. As there are no streams, water is obtained partly from wells but chiefly from rain collected in tanks. The soil is moderately fertile, and a species of cedar is the most abundant tree. Six or eight North American species of birds are residents, and a number of others from the same continent visit the islands occasionally. The climate is mild and equable but rather damp. During the winter months it is most salubrious, and at this season the islands are frequented as a health resort. Onions, potatoes, and early vegetables are the chief products, most of which go to supply the markets in New York. Arrowroot is grown in limited quantity, and the fisheries are rather valuable. The resident population is estimated at 15,700, besides which there is a considerable garrison, while several vessels of the British North

American Squadron may often be found stationed there. There is a strongly fortified dockyard, and the defensive works, together with the intricate character of the approaches to the harbour, render the islands an almost impregnable fortress. Bermuda is governed as a Crown colony by a Governor who is also Commander-in-Chief, assisted by an appointed Executive Council and a representative House of Assembly. HAMILTON (pop. 2100) is the chief town and seat of Government.

FALKLAND ISLANDS

These islands, constituting the only important group in the South Atlantic, lie about 350 miles east of the southern extremity of South America in a southern latitude corresponding to that of the south of England in the northern hemisphere. The group consists of two large islands, nearly equal in size and separated by a narrow strait, surrounded by more than 100 smaller islands and rocks. The two larger islands are known as East and West Falkland respectively, and have an aggregate area of 5300 square miles, the total estimated area of the group being 6500 square miles. The coast-line is generally rugged and much indented, and the land is often hilly, the highest point reaching an elevation of about 2300 feet. Trees do not grow on the islands, of which the surface is characterised by moorland and bog interspersed with patches of barren rock, but affording on the whole a great extent of fine pasturage.

Between the Falkland Islands and Patagonia the depth of the sea is everywhere less than 100 fathoms, and the similarity of the plants and animals to those of the adjacent mainland leads to the belief that the islands at one time formed part of the continent. A wolf-like fox and a species of mouse are the only indigenous land mammals.

The surrounding ocean renders the climate equable and humid, though the actual rainfall is not excessive. The mean temperature for January (midsummer) is about 49°, that for July 39°.

In former years the Falkland Islands were chiefly important in connection with the whale and seal fisheries, and as a port of call for vessels. At the present time the principal industry is sheep farming, but horses and cattle are also numerous. The huts of shepherds are sparsely scattered over the tussocky uplands. Wool, hides, and tallow, together with live sheep or frozen mutton, are the principal exports. Less than 100 years ago the southern fur-seal resorted in great numbers to the Falkland and other islands for which these served as a central point, but the reckless slaughter of these animals on their breeding-places ashore has since resulted in their almost complete extermination.

The population of the Falkland Islands numbers about 2000. The Government is that of a Crown colony and includes under its jurisdiction the barren island of South Georgia (area 1000 square miles), which is situated about 800 miles to the south-eastward.

STANLEY (pop. 700), situated on East Falkland, is the seat of Government and only town.

ST. HELENA, ASCENSION, TRISTAN D'ACUNHA

Out in the Atlantic Ocean, 1200 miles from Africa, lies St. Helena, a little islet of no importance so far as its size is concerned, yet well known and often referred to. It is a rocky place 10 miles long by 8 miles wide, with dark-coloured cliffs rising abruptly 2000 feet above the sea. There is only one landing-place, and even there the little strip of beach is backed by precipices rising so steep and so high that there used to be no way of getting up to the top of the island but by climbing long ladders fixed for the purpose. But now the inhabitants have cut a road slanting up the face of the rock. On the beach lies Jamestown, the capital of the small colony. It has little room for future growth, and seems little likely to need any. Its trade used to be derived from passing vessels that called in on their long voyage across the Atlantic Ocean; but the opening of the Suez Canal has greatly diminished the number of ships that pass this way. A garrison of 200 soldiers is kept to defend the place as a store for the British navy, and there are about 150 English people on the island. The bulk of the population consists of negroes, who number about 4000. They have many neat cottages among the valleys up above, where fountains, supplied by the clouds which rest at dawn upon the mountains, make everything green, though rain is rarely known to fall. The island is really part of an extinct volcano, which once rose from the crest of the submarine ridge which here traverses the bottom of the ocean.

Another peak of this long-submerged ridge is now the Island of Ascension, 750 miles to the north-west. It is about 8 miles long and about 5 miles broad, yet it contains no less than forty extinct craters, one of them rising 2700 feet above the sea. The bare and steep shores are almost as difficult of access as those of St. Helena. Only 360 people live on the island, and these are mostly in the pay of the British Government; for the chief use of the place is to keep stores of all kinds for war-ships. Rain rarely falls in this island, but the heavy clouds of the early morning supply it with moisture, and make it well suited for vegetation. Thus these upland valleys produce most of the food wanted by the people on the island. At one season of the year gigantic turtles visit the place to lay their eggs; they are then caught, and used by the people for food.

Far in the midst of the South Atlantic, half way between Africa and South America, lie three small islets belonging to the British Empire, of which the largest, 6 miles in diameter, is called Tristan d'Acunha after the Portuguese sailor who first discovered them. About 100 inhabitants live in this remote solitude, cut off from the world except when a passing vessel calls in for provisions, or for the seal-skins that may have been gathered by the inhabitants.

VII.—MEDITERRANEAN POSSESSIONS

In the great **inland sea of the** Old World, the shores **of** which were the cradle **of** the human race, the prowess of the British **people** has **secured** several possessions which **possess a vast** importance **in regard to** the **general** inter-**communication** and defence of the empire. **Of these the most westerly** is **Gibraltar, a rocky** fortress commanding the entrance to the Mediterranean. Nearly two centuries have passed **away** since it **was** won **from** the Spaniards. Such is the natural strength of the place that, although the **Spaniards, assisted by** the French, have made **vigorous attempts to regain it, they have** failed. **On one** occasion **they kept 30,000 men battering it for two years,** but the **garrison held it** safely **for our** empire. How far it could **now** withstand the enormous projectiles **with** which modern ironclads are armed is open **to** question. Gibraltar is a mountain mass about 3 miles long, rising out of a low and sandy **coast. On three sides the rocks tower in great** precipices, which, **in some places, are 1000 feet high,** so that not only is it **impossible to effect the ascent on these** sides, but it is **difficult to fire cannon-balls into the top of the fortress. On the western side, on which alone there is any** possibility of **an ascent, the slopes are steep, but not so rocky.** Here **grow clumps of palms, amid which** wild **monkeys find their home. At its top this slope** is fortified with ·**immense care. Embrasures in the** solid **rock, with multitudes of** guns, appear one above the **other** away to the top, where the watch-tower and the signal-mast rise 1400 feet above **the sea.** Gibraltar is **a** Crown colony, ruled **by** a Governor-General appointed by **the home Government.** It has a population of more than

25,000, of whom nearly 6000 are soldiers forming the garrison. It is a coaling station, and a port of call for vessels bound to or from the various ports of the Mediterranean.

Farther east, in the middle of the Mediterranean Sea, two islands lie side by side, of which the larger, **Malta**, is of great importance to British navigation. This island is 17 miles long and 9 miles broad. On the south its cliffs rise boldly from the sea, and are almost inaccessible; but on the north the shores are broken into several

FIG. 23.—GIBRALTAR.

harbours, of which the best resembles a large artificial dock. On this inlet lies the chief town and seaport, called Valetta. Landing at this place the visitor finds himself in front of flights of stairs, which he must climb, for the whole island is high. In the town itself the streets at first are really stairs, but the upper and busy part is a city of stately but much-decayed splendour. The narrow streets are bordered with lofty mansions, the projecting balconies of which are wrought with so much taste and beauty as to suggest, what is really true, that this city was once the abode of merchant-princes. Fine churches, spacious convents, and marble-fronted palaces everywhere delight the eye. Almost every language of Europe may be heard spoken by the people of mingled nations who frequent the streets. The great majority of the regular inhabitants of the place speak a kind of corrupt Italian; but there are many English in the town, and the garrison itself numbers 4000. The whole population of the island is upwards of 165,000 people, who are mainly employed in connection with ships, of which no less than 4000 visit the place each year. As many of these require to tranship part of their cargoes, they provide plenty of work. But Malta is partly engaged in productive industries. It exports oranges, figs, and grapes, and is noted for the excellence of the honey which it produces, its fine gardens being well adapted for bees. Malta has a partly representative Government. It is ruled by a Governor appointed by the Queen, and he is assisted by an executive council and council of Government consisting of six official and fourteen elected members.

Gozo, the neighbouring island, is much smaller, and has only 1600 people. It gets none of the shipping trade which makes Malta so busy, for it has no good harbour.

In the extreme east of the Mediterranean Sea lies the Island of Cyprus, which, in virtue of a treaty made with the Sultan of Turkey in 1878, is administered by Great Britain. It is 140 miles in length, and supports a population of about 200,000 people. Seen from the sea it presents many scenes of great beauty, with a noble background formed by the lofty Mount Olympus, whose peak, 7000 feet above sea-level, is often, even in these warm latitudes, lightly feathered with snow. But a nearer inspection reveals many evidences of decay. The villages among their trees are picturesque, but usually dirty, and their inhabitants squalid and idle. Ruins of ancient temples remain as memorials of the prosperous days of the island in old Hellenic times, when its copper-mines gave it an importance all over the East. But Persian conquerors swept over it, and Egyptian masters ruled it. Long afterwards came the Arabs, who made it flourish in their own way; but from them it was taken by the

Venetians in their days of greatness. It was still, however, fairly prosperous when the Turks seized and ruined it with their greed and mismanagement. Look at those fields, once rich with harvests, now overgrown with thistles. Yonder has been of old a vineyard, but it is now a wilderness. Over all the island we are impressed by seeing what the place must once have been, and how forlorn and hopeless it now is. The island is administered by a British Commissioner, and under his rule it is to be hoped that justice, liberty, and light taxes may soon change the appearance of the place and the condition of the population. Of the people, about 46,000 are Mohammedans, the rest almost all belong to the Greek Church.

VIII.—THE SOUTH AFRICAN COLONIES

The vast and populous continent of Africa holds within it a multitudinous life which has little connection with the outside world. There are numerous tribes who live and die, make war and peace among themselves, unknown to us, and knowing nothing of us. Bold explorers are even now working hard and suffering much in order to place these people in touch with civilisation, and to give them a part in the general life of the world. In the meantime, however, it is chiefly on the margins round the coast that the inhabitants of Africa are in communication with the rest of the human family. All the interior is held by dark-skinned races, generally thick in the lips and flat-nosed, with hair so frizzly as to be popularly called "wool." In short, they are mostly of the type known as "negro." These people are far from being savages, but their civilisation is of a primitive kind. The higher civilisation has been brought by strangers who dwell round the shores.

In the north the Arabs have the chief control except in Algeria, where they have been overcome by the French, who now occupy that country. The extreme south of Africa is held as a colony by the British; but on the east and west coasts various nations contend for the control. Germany, France, Portugal, Spain, and Great Britain all have portions which they claim, and which are, in a certain sense, colonies of theirs, though, as a rule, they have as yet only very partially occupied them. The shores are in general too hot to form the permanent homes of Europeans, but the high plateaux of the interior have healthy climates, and may yet become important settlements for European races.

History and Settlement.—At present the most important of the British possessions in Africa is the southern apex of the continent terminating in the Cape of Good Hope. This portion originally belonged to the Dutch, who formed a small station not far from the Cape about two centuries ago. It was at first intended only as a place of call on the long and tedious voyage from Holland to the Dutch possessions in India. But by degrees Dutchmen began to settle in the country, and form farms in it, employing the natives as slaves to tend their flocks. Thus in a hundred years a colony of Dutchmen grew up all round the Cape. But at the beginning of this century, when England was at war with France, the Dutch took sides with the latter, and as each country tried to do as much damage as possible to its enemies, the British took this colony from the Dutch. When peace was made they gave it back again; but war broke out anew, and the British once more took possession of the Cape. This time when peace was made they kept it. It thus happens that in the present day, though the colony belongs to the British, its population is, to a large extent, Dutch.

For twenty years the Dutch lived contentedly enough under the new rule, but when the British, in accordance with their principles, wished to abolish slavery and free the Kaffirs whom the Dutchmen kept in bondage, the latter refused to part with them and rather than give them up they left their homes, and, carrying wives and families, slaves and sheep and cattle across the river Orange, they took up unoccupied land, and formed what they called the Orange Free State. At a later date a second migration took place, when large numbers went across that tributary of the Orange river which is called the Vaal, and formed another free state called the Transvaal.

There is therefore nowadays a very mixed state of affairs at the Cape. The south is a British colony called Cape Colony, but in it half of the white people are Dutch. Farther north, upon the east coast, there is another colony called Natal, also belonging to the **British Empire**, but also with many Dutch settled in it. Then **there are two free** states peopled by Dutchmen, though having **no connection** with Holland. And **yet to** these latter states **numbers of** Englishmen **are** being **attracted** by gold, diamonds, or good opportunities for trade. So that the population begin to seem quite as much **English as** Dutch.

Coast-Line.—Before entering on a description of these colonies let us look **at their coast-lines.** Commencing on the west, at **the mouth of the** Orange **river, we might naturally think that the** entrance to so large **a stream would give a good harbour for** ships, but it **is blocked up with sand, forming a great** bar. The sand **is brought down by the river, and would** be carried **out to sea and deposited there but for** the action **of currents in the** ocean hereabouts, which cause the sand to be washed back into the long bar on which the Atlantic rollers **are ever** breaking in a line of tumbling foam. Inside **of the** bar the river spreads **in** a sheet of glassy water **on which** float numberless wild geese, ducks, and **sea-gulls;** while on its margin the flamingoes stand **in long scarlet rows,** churning up **the mud** in **search of food.** This coast for a long way is singularly **wanting in good harbours, and** looks **miserably** barren and **uninhabited.** The fine land lies inland.

Southwards the shores gradually **improve. At** TABLE BAY **there is plenty of verdure.** The mountains, which rise **behind the bay to a height of 3000** feet above the sea, **are covered with forests of pine-trees** almost to their **summits; and** from **amid the foliage numbers of pretty houses** peep out, showing **their gable-ends and ornamented roofs. At the** head of the **bay stands Cape Town, where the Dutch first** settled. It is a **large place now, and its wharves are busy** with many ships. **And yet** Table Bay **is not really a very safe harbour. It is** somewhat open **to the waves of the Atlantic, and** therefore a long **breakwater has been built to** shelter vessels when unloading. The entrance is somewhat impeded **by a** little rocky island, round which lie sunken reefs. **At** night the **navigation is** guided by **a lighthouse.**

O

A long ridge of land, which extends out into the sea towards the south, forms what is known as the Cape Peninsula, ending in the CAPE OF GOOD HOPE, a high cliffy promontory, breasting the rollers and the icy blasts from the south, which sometimes blow fiercely against its weather-worn face. Sailors four hundred years ago called it the Cape of Storms; but others who came after, when their hopes of reaching India round its stormy point seemed likely to be realised, gave it its present name. It rises into two bold peaks, of which the higher bears a lighthouse 800 feet above the waves.

On the south-eastern side of the headland lies a wide inlet called FALSE BAY. Its name has been suggested by its character for navigation. The inlet is well enclosed, and looks as if it ought to form a fine harbour, but its mouth faces towards those gales from the south which are the most to be feared on this coast; and it is blocked with sandy shoals and rocks, so that on the whole the fair promise of the bay is belied. On the eastern shore of this indentation a range of hills runs southward into a promontory called Cape Hanglip, with a long line of rocks at its base, beyond which the coast is again bare and desolate, as far as CAPE AGULHAS—the most southerly point of Africa. This headland projects in a long, low reef of sandstone, on which the sea breaks, in heavy weather burying it in foam; but behind this the rock rises into two square hills, on one of which another lighthouse has been placed. Here, although in sailing past we should not ourselves be likely to notice it, our vessel would be impeded in her easterly course by a strong current, called the Agulhas current, the waters of which are a little warmer than those of the surrounding seas, for they sweep round from the hottest part of the Indian Ocean. It flows past both sides of the island of Madagascar and creeps along the coast, till, meeting the drifts of cold water which come from the Antarctic Ocean, it is deflected to the north. This meeting takes place off Cape Agulhas, and causes fogs to rise where the warm and the cold waters mingle. Hence in bad weather during the continuance of these fogs vessels turn into Mossel Bay, where a projecting tongue of land makes a safe anchorage in front of a small seaport. Beyond the projection of Cape Recife the coast retires into Algoa Bay, which **though** open, and in some winds affording indifferent anchorage, must yet be reckoned **the best** on the south coast. There has accordingly grown up a large and important seaport on its shores, called Port Elizabeth.

From this point onwards, **for** about 400 miles, the coast has no good harbours. At first wild and rocky, or occasionally sandy, with high and barren hills behind, it begins to grow more verdant farther **north**. Evergreen **shrubs cover the hills with rich** dark foliage, among which **many** little waterfalls may be descried even from the sea. **The** streams from these cascades enter the sea by estuaries **which** are unfortunately blocked **with** sand so as to be unavailable for harbours, while the river-mouths are still further impeded by the groves of mangrove trees that grow out of the water.

An inlet small and unimportant in itself, but a place of note on a coast so destitute of seaports, called PORT NATAL, has become a frequented harbour, with a **town built along** its shores. Northward the general character of the **coast** becomes increasingly tropical. **The hills** descend to near the shore and are covered with foliage, **the trees** being often large and handsome; aloes and huge cactus plants are occasionally mingled with the forest. Population, too, is more numerous; the people being dark in skin and not **much clad.** A day's sailing along these cheerful coasts takes **the** traveller past the British territories, **and into Delagoa Bay,** where the shores are claimed by the **Portuguese.**

Configuration.—As he sails along the coast of South Africa the traveller notices what seems to be a line **of** hills running **with almost** unfailing regularity behind the shore. But when he lands and examines these heights he finds them not to be hills **in** the proper sense, but rather **the** outer seaward slopes **of** the high tablelands which occupy the interior of the country. Ascending these slopes from Mossel Bay on the south coast, he finds himself on grassy plains where numerous flocks of sheep are pastured. Crossing these plains for about thirty or forty miles he reaches the base of a second line of slopes, mounting which he reaches the top of another plain called the "GREAT KARROO." This is a wide stretch of what is popularly called "desert," though, as a matter of fact, its red sandy surface is covered far as the eye can see with bushes. These are mostly of one kind, called "karroo bushes," but mingled with them are others, greener and not so dry, called "milk-bushes." For months at a time no rain falls over this region; but after a week of steady downpour such as comes occasionally, a short sweet grass springs everywhere with multitudes of wild-flowers. Even in the dry season, the valleys or "kloofs," where some little streamlet or "fontein," as the Dutch call it, flows, are kept green along a narrow strip, on which are built the solid-looking houses of the Boers or farmers. Their brick walls are whitewashed, and their roofs are of thatch, old and brown; round them stand the "kraals" or enclosures for the sheep or cattle, and close to the stream lies the garden with its vines, figs, oranges, and pomegranates. But on the Karroo these houses are far apart; twenty, thirty, or forty miles may divide the nearest neighbours. At night beyond reach of the sounds from the farms deep silence reigns over these monotonous leagues of stunted bushes, broken sometimes by the whine of the jackal or the howl of the hyæna, or perhaps by the startled cry of the spring-boks or some other kind of antelope that come down to the water's edge to drink in the moonlight.

Beyond this plain, which is about 70 miles broad, rises a main ridge of mountains, here called the NIEUWVELD or New Mountains. Its peaks are wild and bare, and in winter are snow-clad; but the ridge is easily crossed, and on the other side lies a tract which looks like a plain, but which slopes gradually down to the Orange river. It is a grassy land of gentle undulations, in the hottest part of the year dry and burnt up; but otherwise green enough, with bushes and small trees dotted lightly over it so as to make a sort of park. Here many animals once roamed which are no longer to be seen, such as the zebra, elephant, and buffalo. The neighbourhood of white men has led to their extermination, and the survivors can only be found in the country farther north, where they are less molested. The only large animals now to be seen are a few herds of the antelope and gazelle species.

The ordinary route across these broad plains is by the railway which goes from Cape Town to the Orange river, but if the traveller desires to strike to right or left he may take what used to be the only mode of travelling, by bullock-waggon. At the wayside stations on the railway these waggons may be seen standing waiting for the loads they are to take away to the farms. To the great lumbering vehicles are fastened some sixteen bullocks with wooden yokes round their necks. In front of the team stands the Kaffir leader with nothing much in the way of clothing on him. Alongside the animals the driver walks with a long bamboo-whip in his hand, by means of which he urges on his slowly-moving line of animals. Twenty years ago this mode of locomotion was the only one available, and it required nearly a month to drag a waggon across these sandy plains, which are more than 250 miles in width from mountains to river.

The central mountains, though they receive different names in different parts of their course, are in truth but one continuous chain; so that it would be no great exaggeration to say that a person might walk along the top of them from one end of the colony to the other without getting down. On such a journey, extending 600 miles in all, he would look down on the level stretch of the Karroo to the south, while to the north he would have wide prospects over the grassy plains which slope imperceptibly to the Orange river. At the west end lie the ROGGEVELD MOUNTAINS, with a somewhat flat summit, about a hundred miles long and 5000 feet above the sea, flanked on its southern side by a precipice that descends like a wall towards the Karroo. The ridge becomes higher towards its eastern end, and there turns northward in a curve, after which it is called the Nieuwveld, already referred to. Its peaks are high and bold, some of them attaining the height of 7000 feet. Farther east come the SNEEUWBERGEN or Snowy Mountains, at the farther end of which rise the steep slopes of the peak called

Compassberg, whose **naked** rocks tower 8300 feet above sea-level.

Farther **east** mountains of greater average elevation, called the STORMBERGEN or Storm Mountains, take their **place in** the range, and lead by a long curve to the **highest ridge** of all, called the DRAKENBERGEN or Dragon Mountains. This range, nearly 400 miles in length, is **throughout** its course almost unbroken. Only two passes cross it, and these are 5000 feet high, so that in winter they are buried under snow. Hence although the Orange Free State lies nearest to the coast of Natal, it suits the people of that country better to send their goods south to Port Elizabeth than to take them only half the distance over these wild mountains. Still a certain amount **of** traffic is carried on in the summer months across this great **range by** bullock-waggons. The journey by either of the **passes lies through** much rugged scenery, and the waggons **take at least two days to cross the mountains.**

The Drakenbergen Mountains send off numerous spurs to right and left so as **to** roughen Natal on the one **side and** Basutoland on the other with great tracts of hilly ranges. The highest peak, MONT AUX SOURCES, rises 10,500 feet above the level of the sea. Its long spurs **are** covered with forests, and between them lie deep valleys in which grow **tree-ferns,** and tender ferns of all kinds. In the spring wild-flowers abound; here grows the box-tree, whose wood **is so much** used by the engraver. Down in the woody **dells the** laughter-birds flit past like a flash of light. Among the rocks the traveller may sometimes see a troop of baboons with the patriarch of the tribe bringing up the rear as they sullenly retreat to their inaccessible fastnesses.

Where the terraces rise along the south coasts they are in some places bordered by a sort of rim, consisting of a range of mountains which, perhaps, look like mere hills **from** the north, but seem much more imposing when seen **from** the south. None of these are of any great height **except the** Winterbock Mountains, which reach 6000 feet in their loftiest peak. Similar rims occur at the edge of the second terraces, but these are much higher. The Olifants or Elephants Mountains, the Wittebergen or White Mountains, the Zwartebergen or Black Mountains are all high and rugged, while the easternmost part of this rim, called the Winterbergen or Winter Mountains, rises to nearly 8000 feet.

Drainage System.—There are few lakes in South Africa, and none of any importance. The rivers, therefore, gather their waters on the mountain sides, either from melting snows upon the winter peaks, or from springs in the upland valleys. The long ridge which traverses the country from east to west forms a watershed, which sends the streams on the north side into the Orange river, while those to the south seek the ocean by shorter courses. The ORANGE RIVER is thus by far the largest stream of South Africa, for no other has an opportunity of gathering many tributaries. It rises in a wild corner, until recently untrodden by civilised foot, and even now but little known. From Mont aux Sources, in the midst of the Drakenbergen Mountains, several ranges run out as radii from a centre; the angles between them form long, deep valleys, into which streams descend from the forest-covered slopes. Flowing through solitary forests and ferny hollows, and then through grassy valleys, past the quaint villages of the Basutos, they reach the dry and dusty plain. Thus the Orange river is formed by the junction of all these little rivulets. The Caledon, its first large tributary, rises among the same hills, but flows in a valley farther to the north. Then, the main river, increased to a current of smooth deep water, though of no great breadth, forms the boundary between Cape Colony on the south, and the Orange Free State on the north.

For a time the Orange river is fringed with low alluvial banks, but ere it is joined by the slow and sluggish waters of the VAAL it begins to have the high banks, dotted with mimosa bushes, and the deep channel, which continue characteristic of it till it reaches the sea. To the south of its route lie the plains already described; to the north stretch for many hundreds of miles the vast and almost perfectly level plains called the Kalahari Desert. But the latter region is not in truth a desert; it has been so called because in summer wells and streams are scarce. In the wet season, however, grass grows to an astonishing height, and at certain times of the year the whole plain is carpeted with water-melons. Here the superabundance of food is accompanied by a corresponding profusion of animal life. The zebra and quagga, with the gnu, the buffalo, and scores of different species of antelopes and goats, rove in countless thousands over the plain; the giraffe waddles along in ungainly fashion, while the elephant in the season lives on melons, and descends at evening where a break in the banks allows him a path to frolic and bathe in the waters of the Orange river. Countless herds of smaller animals, both gnawers and flesh-eaters, make their home among the tufts of grass. The lion is more common here than anywhere else in the world, and the leopard prowls in pursuit of feebler animals. The hyæna and the jackal howl at nightfall, and, most formidable of all, the great two-horned rhinoceros wanders down at twilight to drink and amuse himself in the river. Yet it is not a full-volumed current, and in the summer shrinks and almost ceases to flow in its lower course. Some tributaries, which look most important on the map, such as the Brak and the Hartebeest, though raging torrents in the rainy season, are absolutely dried up throughout a large part of the year. For the last three or four hundred miles of its course the Orange river is broad, but generally with a dirty, sluggish current, until the rains have set in, when it rushes along, deep, impetuous, and destructive, carrying vast quantities of mud and sand to form in the sea a bar at its mouth. Though more than a thousand miles in length, the Orange river is thus of little or no importance for navigation.

All the other rivers of South Africa are comparatively short, as they rise in mountains not far from the sea. Only one or two of them exceed 200 miles in length. To the west the Olifants river takes its origin in the Olifants Mountains. It flows for the first half of its course in a long mountain valley, and then carves out for itself a deep bed through level terraces ere it descends to the Atlantic. In the dry season it is a slender current, here trickling over a little fall, there creeping with slight motion in a glassy pool; but in the rainy season it fills its bed and overflows its banks. The waters spread in sheets of thin mud, from which a fine sediment of rich soil is deposited, whereon the Dutch "Boers" raise fine crops of corn.

The Breede river flows south from the Olifants Mountains towards the Southern Ocean. Unlike the Olifants river it is navigable by small vessels for some 30 or 40 miles from its mouth. The Gauritz, gathering its waters from the Nieuwveld Mountains, after a shallow and fitful course, discharges them into the Southern Ocean. Of much the same character is the Camtoos, which, however, is deep for the last few miles of its course, and might be made useful for that distance but for the bar at its mouth. The Great Fish river and the Great Kei river rise in the Stormberg, and cut their way through the upper terraces in great "kloofs" or gorges. Neither of them is deep enough to be fit for navigation, but like most South African streams they have a use little less important, for they provide the settlers with water, and so make these dry but grassy plains and valleys capable of being employed as pasturages for millions of animals. All these rivers were once the home of the hippopotamus, but the Dutchmen held that the food which one of these monsters required would support a score of sheep; they therefore waged an unrelenting war against them, and not a single hippopotamus now exists in Cape Colony.

In Natal the largest river is the Tugela, which descends from the Drakenbergen Mountains. It is a much more constant stream and of fuller volume than any of those that have just been mentioned. From the rugged hills of its sources it descends through plateaux where goats, sheep, and cattle are pastured, then through flats in which patches of maize and other green crops show where the farms are worked by Kaffir labourers, and thus to the low-lying coast, where plantations of sugar, arrowroot, and tobacco succeed each other till it reaches the Indian Ocean, where mangrove forests line the muddy shores.

Climate.—No part of the world has a finer climate than Cape Colony, though, like every other place, it has at times some disagreeable weather. It is never very cold there, although often enough the mornings may seem as raw and the evenings as chilly as they ever are in England. But there is nearly continuous sunshine; the sky remains almost constantly blue. Indeed the chief complaint against the climate of South Africa is that for long intervals the sky is too clear and the sunshine too persistent. Yet it is never distressingly hot; the temperature of the months of December and January, which are decidedly the warmest in the year, reaches a maximum average of about 94° Fahrenheit. The only trying times in the Cape climate are those days when hot winds blow from the north-west, dry, dusty, and oppressive. Under their breath plants wither up, beasts lie panting with outstretched tongues, and birds lose all their sprightliness. A cool south wind, wafting the breath of ocean over the parched land, at once restores the animation of the landscape. Over the larger part of South Africa the climate is mild and equable, with from 20 to 30 wet days spread irregularly through the year.

There are districts, however, to which the foregoing description of the climate will not apply. In the Great Karroo for instance, lying as it does between two mountain ranges, rain-clouds so rarely come that not so much as a drop of rain may fall for two long years. When at last the clouds do chance to pass over one range they never succeed in crossing the other also, but break and pour down upon the thirsty red soil. For several days the rain descends as if the heavens were opened; the dry watercourses become foaming torrents of great width and impetuous speed.

Plants and Animals.—South Africa has many interesting peculiarities in the way of vegetation; but these are chiefly to be observed among the smaller plants. The forest trees do not strike a visitor as greatly different from those which he would see in England. The beautiful silver-trees that grow round Cape Town present probably the most notable exception. Forests are not common in the west, but grow more frequent towards the east, till in Natal there is an abundance of tall and handsome timber, filling the great mountain hollows which occupy so much

of that colony. South Africa is **the land of heaths.**
Nearly four hundred distinct species are found there;
and **over** all the country, even where the soil is poorest,
their spikes of brilliant colour—pink, crimson, or white—
glow from amidst the duller vegetation of the plains.
Mesembryanthemums are far more plentiful in this part of
the world than in any other. Their fleshy leaves when
crushed are found to be full of water, yet the plants grow
in exceedingly dry places **and possess** but small roots for
the support of such large masses of foliage. They gather
their supplies **of moisture** chiefly from **the heavy dews**
which settle on them during the night. **The hotter the
weather and clearer the sky at** night, **the** fresher and
brighter appear their marigold-shaped flowers of yellow,
pink, and purple. The carrion flower **with its** large
and showy blossoms invites the traveller to approach
and smell them, till he learns by trial that their foul odour
justifies the **name that has** been given to the plant. The
most charming flowers **of** South Africa are the bulbs of
many kinds, some of them peculiar to this corner of the
world. The **ixias, the** sparaxis, **the gladioli, and many**
lovely **kinds of iris** make **the** hillsides **in the springtime**
great masses of resplendent colour.

South Africa possessed **an** abundance and great variety
of wild animals; but, as we have seen, **the** settlers have
extirpated most of them in order to have more room for
their flocks. The hippopotamus is completely extinct in
Cape Colony, and extremely rare **in** Natal. The rhinoceros
is now very seldom seen south of the Orange river. Only
a few elephants are now found **in** Cape Colony, and only
a very few still haunt the woody parts of Natal. They
are not easily seen, though occasionally there has been **a**
difficulty **in the** telegraphic department when a herd of
them **has amused** itself with pulling up telegraph-poles.
An occasional lion may still skulk about on the plains
south **of the Orange** river, but they are very much more
numerous to the north **of** that river. **The** leopard is still
not uncommon, and monkeys of different kinds **are
numerous;** baboons haunt the rocky mountains, while
little long-tailed monkeys live among the trees of Natal.

The hyæna and the jackal still prowl over the thinly-settled country. The boar makes its lair deep in the tangled thickets; the zebra and the quagga, the giraffe and the buffalo, used to be found all over South Africa, but they are now practically banished from it; they are still, however, numerous to the north of the Orange river. Various species of antelopes and gazelles, such as the spring-bok, the eland, the riet-bok, the gnu, and so forth are still plentiful; while of smaller animals, such as the Cape ant-eater, hares, shrews, and rat-like animals, there is great abundance.

In regard to bird life, South Africa is extremely rich. On the plains there used to rove many ostriches. They are now almost unknown in their wild state; but the colonists breed and rear them in ostrich-farms for the sake of their feathers, a single ostrich yielding to the value of twenty or thirty pounds a year. Away on the plains north of the Orange river these birds still wander in native freedom. On the rivers long lines of flamingoes, scarlet or delicate pink mingled with others of pure snow-white, may be seen. With their curiously twisted bills and long thin legs like stilts, they wade in shallow ponds, or in brackish waters near the sea-shore, where they stir up the mud with their feet and devour the small animals that live at the bottom of such waters. The ungainly, though interesting, pelican is also a common bird in South Africa; while vultures are only too abundant,—the worn-out horse or sickening ox left anywhere on the plains will soon attract an ominous crowd to flutter over the expected feast. Eagles, owls, and other birds of prey are well supplied with food in lands that teem so richly with life. Serpents, including several sorts of venomous snakes, are found in South Africa, the boa constrictor being especially common in Natal.

Native Races.—The earliest inhabitants of the south of Africa were two allied races called by the Dutch *Hottentots* and *Bushmen*. They were both of a dirty brown colour, and of low stature, the Bushmen averaging only a little more than four feet, the Hottentots hardly exceeding five feet. Only a few Bushmen now exist, chiefly in the Kalahari desert, where they make a sort of nest for themselves in the midst of the bushes. In a few other parts of the colonies they skulk among the rocks, dwelling in caves or in clefts upon the mountain-side, and living chiefly upon what they can steal from more settled people. The Hottentots were distinctly superior, as they built huts for themselves in little villages. Both races were noted for their dirty habits, dressing their woolly hair with grease and soot, and never washing their bodies; but rubbing them over sometimes with grease, sometimes with clay. The Bushmen were actually naked, the Hottentots almost so, and both races killed their old parents as well as such of their children as they considered to be a burden to them. There are about twenty thousand Hottentots now in the south of Africa, but they are wholly altered from what they were. They wear old clothes given them by white men, and act as servants or shepherds or bullock-drivers on the farms. A few wild hordes still wander on the plains south of the Orange river, but the race is steadily dying out.

These aboriginal tribes would in all probability have disappeared, even if white men had not settled in their land, for the dark races which we call Kaffirs and Zulus were pressing them hard upon the north, and slowly exterminating them. These are men of a deep brown or deep gray colour, tall and well made. The average height of the men must be close upon six feet; while the breadth of their shoulders, their fine limbs, and their well-set heads make them enemies whom any man would respect. They live in villages of huts which look like large bee-hives, being made of branches stuck into the ground in a circle, and with their tops bent over to touch each other, so that they may be tied into a roof. Then the sides are woven with reeds and plastered with clay. These races also go nearly naked, men and women having no clothing but a slight band round the waist. They are clever in the management of cattle, which form their chief riches, and also in the tilling of small plots of ground.

Political Subdivisions.—The two chief colonies of South Africa are Cape Colony and Natal, which are regularly occupied and governed by the British; but there are various territories occupied by natives, among whom the British at present merely keep order; Kaffraria and Basutoland lie between Cape Colony and Natal; Zululand lies to the north of Natal; Griqualand West lies to the north of the Orange river; British Bechuana still farther north. All these will one day become colonies, as there is a tendency for Englishmen to settle in them. North of these lies the Bechuanaland protectorate, and farther north what is called Matabeleland, and reaching up to the Zambesi there is Mashonaland. All these are under British influence, the negro tribes which inhabit them being supposed to live under British protection; though, as a matter of fact, the great majority of them neither know nor care anything about it.

CAPE COLONY

Area and Population.—The extreme southern part of Africa is occupied by what is known as Cape Colony; because it was first formed by white men at the Cape of Good Hope. It now extends over an area of 200,000 square miles, or more than twice the surface of Great Britain. It has a million and a half of people in it, but of these only 370,000 are white people, and of the whites more than half are of Dutch descent, and speak a language which is corrupted from the Dutch. Of the other whites, large numbers are German, or of German descent, and a large number more are the descendants of French Protestants who emigrated to the colony at a time when ecclesiastical persecution would not suffer them to remain in their own country. Thus only a small fraction of the population is British, though most of these people of other races seem contented and even proud to belong to our empire. Seven hundred thousand of the people are dark-skinned; but these also are much mixed in their descent. First comes the degraded remnant of the primitive races, just described—small, dark-yellow in their complexions, and far from prepossessing in their looks or in their habits. Then there are the Kaffirs, who conquered the land from these aboriginal people in bygone years, but who have themselves been conquered by the white men. For a long time these people were slaves to the Dutch; but they now act as servants on the farms—waggoners, shepherds, cooks, and so forth. Again of the dark-skinned races, a number are Arabs from the Red Sea, and Malays from the East Indies, who have settled in the country to grow vegetables, to work as carpenters or joiners, or to act as servants to the white people.

The British population is chiefly settled along the south coast, the west coast being dry and barren, the east coast swampy and unhealthy. They form the mercantile classes, and occupy the seaports, of which the chief are Cape Town, Port Elizabeth, and East London. In these towns English is the language chiefly spoken. But away from the coast, among the inland highlands, the farmers are almost all Dutch, with Kaffir servants and labourers. There they live in simple fashion, in their old brick houses, with long low roofs of brown thatch and quaint-looking gables, and with their fields and "kraals" around them. Many of these farms, however, show the progress of invention in the mother country; corrugated iron is replacing the thatch, and wire fences the old stone walls.

The British authorities find some little trouble in governing a people so greatly mixed. If justice is done to the blacks, it is difficult not to offend their masters the whites; and we have seen that the Dutch in past years left the country for that very reason. Difficulties also arise between the English and the Dutch. For instance, in the Parliament which meets at Cape Town, what language is to be used? Half of the members are Dutch farmers who can speak only a little English; half are English who understand Dutch imperfectly. At present the only way to meet this difficulty is to let each party speak its own language, but few can follow with complete intelligence so mixed a debate. All Acts of Parliament and public notices are printed in both languages. In schools and churches they use English or Dutch according as the British or Dutch elements prevail in the district.

Government.—The colonists manage their own affairs

without interference from the British Government. They elect an Upper and a Lower House; but only those who are fairly well off are allowed to vote. The Queen is represented by a Governor who is sent out from London.

Towns.—The capital and most important city of Cape Colony is CAPE TOWN, which occupies a charming situation on the shores of Table Bay. It lies in the very lap of a high mountain range. Behind it to the left rise the long

FIG. 24.—TABLE MOUNTAIN AND DEVIL'S PEAK, CAPE OF GOOD HOPE.

slopes of the Table Mountain, clad in pine-trees all the way up to where a line of precipices forms the edge of the flat table from which the mountain derives its name; a white cloud which often hangs from the edge of the summit is called the "table-cloth." To the right there is a lower mountain called the Lion's Head; its sides also are covered with dark trees up to its sharp-pointed summit. Amid the forests as seen from a distance occasional white specks sprinkled here and there are the gables of the villas which the merchants of the town have built upon those breezy heights. In the town itself, among many shops and dwellings of the familiar kind, others, solid-looking and flat-topped, recall the Dutch origin of the town. English, French, German, and Dutch; Kaffir, Arab, and Malay, all bustle along the streets. The wharves, shops, and tramways which are so busy during the earlier part of the day begin about four o'clock in the afternoon to grow silent; especially if the day has been very **warm**. **For as** evening approaches every **one who can afford it** goes off to his country home by tram-car or suburban railway to Wynberg, Constantia, **the** Paarl, or **some** other suburb ten or fifteen miles away. There in their lovely gardens, **fragrant with** overhanging bushes of honey-suckle, **passion-flower, and clematis; or** on their broad verandahs, in cool attire, **they** enjoy the evening breeze from the neighbouring sea.

The harbour of Cape Town, enclosed and defended by **a** breakwater, used to be constantly filled with vessels, calling on their way round the Cape either for water or for provisions. But the opening of the Suez Canal has made a great difference in this respect. The vessels which **now** call are fewer in number; but the prosperity of the city has not declined, for this passing trade was not particularly profitable. At the present time the traffic is more genuine, inasmuch as the vessels which arrive are loaded with goods **solely** for the people of the country, and carry away the native products. Thus **as the** colony is becoming better peopled, and its **resources** are developed, Cape Town is increasing in size. **Its** population now numbers 80,000 persons.

The second town of **the** colony, **PORT ELIZABETH, at the head of** Algoa Bay, is more like an English town in appearance; for the Dutch element is almost wholly absent in its population. In the year 1820, 4000 English emigrants landed **here and** founded the town, which from that time has **thriven** and grown **to be a** place of 20,000 persons. Like Cape Town, it lies **in** a hollow of the hills, which are here of **no** great height. Formerly all goods had to be landed here by means **of** surf-boats, **as** the harbour was much exposed to the south-east wind; but now a good breakwater has been built, so that vessels can lie at rest

P

against the piers or **jetties**. The country round about is by no means fertile, but among the hills, and in the interior, millions of sheep are pastured, whose wool is brought down to this port for shipment.

Nearly a hundred miles **by railway to** the north-east, GRAHAMSTOWN, the chief interior town, stands on top of **a range** of grassy hills, **at a** height of almost 2000 feet **above sea-level.** However hot the other parts of the colony may be, here it is generally **cool. The wide streets of the** town are well planted with **trees, and outside the business** streets, the houses **are all** embowered **in gardens among** orange-trees and oleanders. This is the inland **centre of a** wide wool-growing district; moreover, the place **has of late years become** surrounded **by** ostrich farms, where **ostrich eggs are hatched in** incubators, **and where** the **young birds are tended with care, and allowed, when a little older, to run about in fields enclosed for their use. They are fed daily on maize, and when they are old enough the feathers are twice a year cut from their tails and sent to Europe.**

GRAAF-REINET, **another of these inland towns, lies in the** midst **of beautiful country, and** serves **as centre to a** wide pastoral district. It is a thoroughly Dutch **town;** the old-fashioned houses with their gables rising from among the **trees** of well-grown gardens; their whitewashed walls, **gay with** climbing plants, **and the** thatched roofs, brown **with age,** all lying basking in the pleasant sunshine, with **the lofty Compassberg** raising **his bold blue cone** in the **distance.**

KING WILLIAMSTOWN, **which lies more to** the east, **is a larger town, forty miles from the coast, and** has for its seaport EAST LONDON. **Its streets are** solid, and have a look of quiet prosperity. The population of the town is about 6000, of whom **a** considerable proportion are of German **descent.**

On the banks **of the** Orange river there are two large **towns,** COLESBERG **and** ALIWAL NORTH, both centres of pastoral districts, **and** engaged in receiving the wool and **the** ostrich feathers **which** come from **the** farms; and in sending **out to** them the provisions **and** other necessaries which are required by the people in the country districts.

VIII SOUTH AFRICAN COLONIES—CAPE COLONY

Chief Exports.—The chief exports of Cape Colony are wool to the value of more than two million pounds sterling each year; ostrich feathers to the extent of upwards of half a million; hides to nearly the same value; but chief of all, diamonds to the extent of more than four millions a year. These diamonds come from a district only recently added to the colony. This is called **Griqualand West**, and is now the richest diamond field in the world. Diamonds were first found there in 1867, but it was not till four years later that the wonderful wealth of the place was recognised. Then there poured in adventurers from every part of the world, but the great majority of them British. Since then they have extracted forty million pounds' worth of diamonds.

At first the precious crystals were dug out of a hill of blue clay; and near that hill a town called KIMBERLEY began to be formed by the miners. At first it was merely a collection of tents; but when they found that the production of diamonds continued, they put up huts and shanties. Then came store-keepers, inn-keepers, bankers, and diamond merchants, who erected more solid buildings, and thus the place has grown, till now it is quite a city, with more than thirty thousand inhabitants. Its broad streets are well planted with trees, traversed by horse-trams, and lit by electricity. It has, however, a new and somewhat unsubstantial look in all but the central streets. In the outskirts, the houses are mostly of wood, and their iron roofs have an unpleasant glare in the strong South African sun.

A great deal of the laborious work of the mines is done by natives, whom it is difficult to detect if they secrete for themselves the diamonds which they have found. To meet this difficulty, there is a law forbidding any one from buying diamonds from the natives, and indeed only certain persons licensed for the purpose are allowed to buy diamonds at all. The name of this district is derived from the word "Griqua," which is the name of those half-caste children whose fathers are Dutch and whose mothers are Kaffirs. It is nearly a century since they settled in this part of Africa, and gave their name to those dry plains. The east of the district is now mostly occupied by the **diamond-seekers**; but the west is still left very much to the **Griquas** and their primitive ways. It is a **land of quiet** pastoral pursuits, where sheep and fine-haired goats rove under blue skies, on green hills, or down on the **sandy plains** where the milk bushes afford them nourishment in the drought of summer, when the **coarse grass** is all burnt up.

NATIVE PROVINCES ATTACHED TO CAPE COLONY

North of Griqualand **West** lie two great districts which have within the last **few** years been added to the British Empire, though **as yet** almost wholly inhabited by darkskinned tribes. **These are the Crown colony of Bechuanaland and the Protectorate of Bechuana.** They both derive their names from the Bechuanas, a partially **civilised negro** race, who inhabit the land in considerable numbers. **They** are tall, stout, woolly-headed people, and as a rule goodnatured. Like most of the South African tribes they dwell in villages composed of round huts with high conical roofs, each surrounded by a fence made of **stakes with mats** fastened to them. They grow corn, and store it in **granaries** which they build near their houses, and they are **now** becoming accustomed to the rearing and tending of sheep. **They** wear by way **of** ordinary clothing only a **tiny** apron round their waists, and for full dress a short cloak **of** skins hung from their shoulders. When paying visits they smear their bodies with grease and red clay, and if a young girl desires to be particularly attractive she adorns her face with patterns in red, yellow, and white clay. The men are good hunters, and kill the zebra, buffalo, and antelope with great address by driving them into enclosures in which they slay them with spears. They **snare the** elephant **and** rhinoceros by making pits, into **which these** animals **fall.** They have acquired some of the mechanical arts, and have among them tolerably good blacksmiths. They **lead** an easy good-tempered sort of life, with plenty of music, dancing, and feasting, but it is

VIII SOUTH AFRICAN COLONIES—CAPE COLONY   213

still whispered that they have not given up their ancient fondness for human flesh, and that babies are still, in spite of the British authorities, eaten in secret at some of their festivals. The climate is delightful, for though the land lies in warm latitudes, it is nearly 5000 feet above sea-level, and therefore has a pleasant bracing temperature.

The Governor of Cape Colony is commissioner of this district. He keeps a force of native police at Vryburg, a small town in the east of Bechuanaland. But the chief native town is Mafeking.

North of the Crown colony of Bechuanaland lies what is known as the Protectorate of Bechuana, a district comprising in the west the so-called desert of Kalahari, but in the east elevated plains and hilly ridges, peopled with negro tribes who live in villages and exhibit a certain rudimentary civilisation. Few white men live here, but the British Government has a telegraph line running through the heart of the country to Shoshong, a native town which until the year 1889 was the capital, situated in a valley among the rocky hills, in which a tributary of the Limpopo takes its rise. It has a certain amount of trade, since it is the place where the natives sell the ivory and other products from the interior of Africa, in exchange for the products of civilised lands. The present capital has been fixed at Palapye. From Shoshong the goods are carried in ox-waggons across the plains 400 miles to the nearest railway station, which used to be Kimberley, is now Vryburg, and will soon be Mafeking. The round huts which composed Shoshong were inhabited by 30,000 negroes.

Between the Orange Free State and Natal lies a tract of country nearly 10,000 square miles in area, called Basutoland. It is inhabited by a fine tribe called the Basutos, who number about 180,000. They are now under British rule, their country having been constituted a protectorate with a resident British Commissioner, who lives at Maseru, the chief village. Less than 500 Europeans live in the country, mostly missionaries and Government officials, with a few traders, but the settlement of Europeans is not encouraged. Lofty mountains, including the Drakenbergs, and their spurs form the most notable feature of the region. The river-valleys include fertile patches well grassed, and filled with endless profusion of springs and streamlets, shaded by groves in which the ring-dove loves to build. Here and there a hut may be seen down in a valley and surrounded by fields of maize and sorghum. Quite as often the village stands perched on the top of an eminence or rocky spur for the purpose of security against attack. It is usually surrounded by a fence or else a prickly hedge. Inside, the brown huts are ranged in narrow lanes, leaving a wide space in the centre to which the cattle are driven in order to be safe against the leopard and the hyæna, which are common enough in these parts. In the very middle stands the chief's hut, where he lives with his thirty or forty wives. The British authorities are steadily improving the country, and in spite of the hilly nature of the ground many good roads have now been made upon which the Basutos send their grain, cattle, and a little wool, to be exchanged in Cape Colony for clothes, blankets, and ironmongery.

Kaffraria is a district on the east coast lying between Cape Colony and Natal. It is now a province of Cape Colony, though almost entirely inhabited by native tribes, who number, it is thought, about half a million. They are not as a rule the original inhabitants of the district, but rather a mingled crowd of Kaffirs who have been crowded out of the southern parts when the white man took possession of them. The land is generally fertile, and the Kaffirs have settled down to a semi-civilised life. On the ground that ascends from the shores, and the terraces that rise, slope after slope, to the high tableland of the interior, native villages are sprinkled thickly enough. The men are good-looking, with dark skins and woolly hair, and tend the cattle on the grassy hillside, while the women, much smaller and lighter, work down in the hollows on the little farms, where melons, millet, maize, hemp, and tobacco, and even a little cotton are easily grown. There are about ten thousand white men scattered through the district, and among the Kaffirs dwell more than twenty gentlemen sent by the Governor of Cape Colony to live among the people and act as magistrates, so as to prevent the dreadful wars which used to cause such devastation among these tribes.

NATAL

In the colony of Natal those Kaffirs called Zulus form the chief part of the population, although the colony is independent and ranks second among the British possessions in Africa. It has its own Governor, and its own Parliament, a Legislative Council, consisting of thirty members, of whom twenty-three are elected by all citizens who possess a little property or who pay at least ten pounds a year as rent. But the other seven are nominated by the Colonial authorities in London; and to that extent the colony is not left so unfettered as other colonies of its size. But the people of Natal hope ere long to obtain the full system of parliamentary government, with two Houses, and the power to select their own Ministers. The difficulty which prevents this being done at once is that the white people are so few and the blacks are so many, that the community cannot be treated exactly as if it were mostly composed of well-educated people who understand the management of civilised states. There are 46,000 whites, but the Kaffirs number 450,000, and there are besides 41,000 Malays and Hindoos who have been brought from the south of Asia to act as servants and workmen.

Behind the mangrove flats and the occasional cliffs of sandstone which form the coast the soil is rich and fertile. Here the settlers have made plantations of sugar, coffee, and cotton. Inland the land rises, the soil becomes light and sandy, yet rich enough to support fine grasses, which wave in high fields over many miles of hills and hollows. At intervals the houses of the settlers appear dotted over the land, with groups of fine cattle and herds of sheep. Altogether Natal has 200,000 cattle and half a million of sheep. The landscapes are generally fine, as the country is varied with large clumps of evergreen shrubs, patches of Cape gooseberries, huge cactus plants, and aloes, together with groups of forest trees, on which climb creeping-plants with sweet-scented blossoms. Still farther into the interior the land becomes more rugged; the conical and rugged hills project their masses of red and gray granite from the steep slopes of short grass, on which a quarter of a million angora goats find their pasture. The hair of these animals forms a valuable article of export.

About a sixth part of the colony has been set apart for the exclusive use of the Kaffirs, who have little farms of their own on which they work industriously, and are fairly successful.

Natal has as its nominal capital the town of PIETER-MARITZBURG. It derived its name from two Dutchmen who first settled in this part fifty years ago; but it is now always called Maritzburg by the people of South Africa. It stands in the hilly district upwards of fifty miles from the coast, and is surrounded by pastoral lands. It contains a population of 16,000 persons, of whom only 6000 are white. Of the latter a considerable proportion are officials and soldiers whom the British Government keeps here for the defence of the colony against the wild tribes of Zulus in the north. A good deal of the trade of the town is carried on by the Hindoo pedlars, who make it their headquarters, obtaining there the iron pots, blankets, crockery, cloth, and other articles which the Kaffirs on the farms are likely to buy from them. The streets of Maritzburg are solid and well built, with a number of churches gathered in the heart of the town. A distant view of the place shows red-tiled roofs and white walls, contrasting with the vivid green of the poplars and willows which abound in the streets and gardens.

Although the government of the country is carried on at Maritzburg, the largest town and the chief commercial centre of the colony is D'URBAN, or, as it is now more often spelt, Durban. It stands on the only good harbour of that part of the coast, and contains about 20,000 people, of whom about one half are English, the others being mostly blacks. Its streets slope up gradually from the harbour, with many well-built banks and public offices. The general aspect of the buildings is thoroughly

English; but the visitor, who might be tempted for a moment to fancy himself back in the old country, would soon be recalled from that illusion by the sight of crowds of Zulus thronging the pathways. A drive out of the town would remind him that he is in a tropical, or at least a semi-tropical, climate—for the merchants' villas are mostly set down among groves of bananas and bamboos. Durban exports the wool, hides, sugar, and angora hair which Natal produces; likewise a small part of the ostrich feathers and wool produced in the Orange Free State, and part of the gold obtained in the Transvaal, for these states have no seaport of their own.

North of Natal lies a fertile district on the coast called **Zululand**. It is a protectorate ruled over by the Governor of Natal, but not yet formally attached to that colony. Its population, amounting to about 400,000, consists almost wholly of Zulus, who have been strong enough to preserve, to some extent, their independence. These dark-skinned people dwell in villages of thirty or forty huts, which are made after this fashion. Long and flexible poles are stuck in the ground, and their tops are bent over till they meet; the poles are then tied in a point at the top, and cross-pieces of stick are fastened from rib to rib so as to make a sort of skeleton, which is covered with mats woven out of grass. A door is left about as high as one of our tables, through which the inhabitants creep on all-fours. On the floor of hardened clay a fire is kindled to cook the family meal, but no exit save the door is provided for the smoke. A Zulu is under no great concern about clothing. He puts on a tiny apron and a string of beads, and is then completely dressed. But he is always careful to have his head shaven except a knot on the top—a solitary tuft, of which he takes religious care. The Zulus are good warriors, as we have found to our cost in our many wars with them; but they have at last settled down in quiet fashion under the care of British magistrates, who reside in various parts of the country to see that justice is done.

The surface of Zululand is much like that of Natal. On the coast grow mangrove swamps, which in the hot climate are too malarious for Europeans to dwell near them. Above these flats grassy hills slope upward, on which the Zulus pasture numbers of small cattle, goats, and sheep with large fat tails. The valleys between the hill ranges display tracts well wooded and watered by streams from the Drakenbergs. On the most fertile river-flats the Zulus clear away the mimosa scrub, and grow fields of maize and sweet potatoes. The agricultural work is done by the women. The men, who would stoop to nothing so menial, leave behind their wives—two, three, or four according to their means of buying them—and set out to hunt the antelope, buffalo, or gnu, or to enjoy the chase of the wolf, hyæna, lion, or possibly the rhinoceros. A few elephants are still left in the valleys, and a few hippopotami in the river; but these animals will soon be quite extinct.

Internal Communication in South Africa.—The longest railway in South Africa is that which joins Kimberley to Cape Town. The express which leaves the diamond-fields every week has a journey of 700 miles to perform over the long plains, through the gorges of the mountains, across the Great Karroo, and down by long grades to the coast. Another line starts from Port Elizabeth, and runs north to Colesberg, near which it joins the line already mentioned. A third line runs from East London to Aliwal North on the Orange river. One or two other short lines bring up the total length of railway to about 1900 miles in Cape Colony. In Natal a railway has been carried from Durban to Maritzburg, and thence to the foot of the Drakenberg Mountains, which it skirts for a long distance, the slopes themselves being too formidable to be crossed at present. The great lumbering waggons, therefore, still go slowly up the passes, carrying produce to and fro between the railway terminus and the Transvaal.

5000 miles of telegraph wires now stretch through South Africa over deserts and through forests. Natal and Cape Colony are thus well in touch with the world in general; but Bechuanaland and Basutoland are still much isolated, though in the former there is a telegraph line to Palapye.

IX.—BRITISH WEST AFRICA

From Cape Verde to the **River** Niger the west coast of Africa is largely under British control, but four special portions of it form recognised British colonies. These are Gambia, Sierra Leone, Gold Coast, and Lagos; while the country round the mouth of the Niger, though not yet formally annexed to the British Empire, is occupied by a British company, and is reserved for annexation at some future time. All these lie along the coast, their boundaries being rarely more than 50 miles inland. They are all too unhealthy for Europeans ever to make their homes there in any great numbers. The few white men who dwell there stay for only a few years, and require to take much care of themselves if they wish ever to return to their native lands.

In December a wind called the Harmattan blows as a parching breath from the Sahara Desert of the interior. Through January its pestilent breath sucks the life and strength out of the white man, though the negro seems not to be inconvenienced by it. When it declines in February there comes the season of tornadoes; then, from great banks of cloud that advance from the south-east and cover the land with silence and gloom, lightning and thunder are discharged, and the wind howls over the land, ripping up all that is not securely fastened. One of these hurricanes lasts from three to four hours, and is followed by some days of pleasant freshness. After the tornado season comes the period of rain, when for days together the dull sky will pour down lukewarm showers through the still, hot, and oppressive air. Vegetation springs up luxuriantly but soon falls, and by its rapid decay breeds a deadly kind of fever. No wonder that this coast is known as the "white man's grave," though strange to say the natives swarm upon it, and seem to thrive. The Englishmen to be seen here are clerks sent out by British firms to transact their business for a few years, after which they return. The British also keep a considerable number of soldiers in forts along the shore.

As these colonies are so narrow their main characteristics may be described with the account of their coast-line. From Cape Verde southwards the shores continue low but verdant. The first inlet is the mouth of the Gambia river. A short way up this stream, and situated on a sandy point, stands Bathurst, the capital of Gambia, where a few English houses with broad verandahs, amid heavy foliage, are surrounded with clusters of brown cones like large bee-hives, which are the houses of the natives. Less than a hundred white people live here, most of them being attached to the commissioner who rules the colony. The natives, who number about 14,000, are engaged partly in bringing in the products of the country for sale, and partly in loading and unloading the vessels which arrive. The colony carries on a considerable trade, vessels constantly calling to take away ivory, bees-wax, india-rubber, and various sorts of precious woods which the natives bring from the interior in exchange for iron goods, cloth, and rum, which they carry on their heads back to their homes.

Beyond the River Gambia a cluster of islands with large warehouses is occupied by the French, to whom the opposite coast also belongs. But after a brief interval the coast again becomes British territory. This is the colony of Sierra Leone, which was first colonised a hundred years ago as a place to which the British Government could send those negroes whom it rescued from slavery. A town thus grew up of more or less civilised black men and women, whose descendants are now good British subjects. They are ruled by a Governor sent from London. They export half a million pounds' worth of nuts, palm-oil, ginger, and hides each year.

At the mouth of a small river, Freetown, the capital,

rises on a sloping hill crowned with an old fortress, and a large building forming the barracks for 400 British soldiers. A military force is required here for the defence of the inhabitants from the fierce tribes of the interior. Besides the soldiers there are not 300 white people in the place, but it swarms with negroes, mostly fairly well clad and looking comfortable. The women and girls carry immense baskets of oranges and pine-apples on their heads, or sit behind their fruit calling out its merits and prices. The main street, which is long and straight, is shaded by groves of lime-trees, mangoes, and guavas.

The coast is now low and the water so shallow that vessels cannot come nearer than 14 miles from the shore, which is lined with mangrove-trees, and stretches inland in a long monotonous level of green. But behind rise the bold slopes of the Kong Mountains, richly covered with tropical forests. Here lies a small independent republic called Liberia. It was founded in 1821, as a place where slaves, liberated in America, could come and live in their own climate. After passing over 400 miles of Liberian coast we see once more British territory in what is called the **Gold Coast**. The shore, still low and swampy, is backed by dark hills covered with forests. On a bold granite hill, which juts out into the sea from the low shores, stands Cape Coast Castle; and sheltered behind it a little town called by the same name. Behind the rock and under the white buttresses of the fort there is a landing-place. On the slopes above this stand the Governor's residence, the hospital, the barracks, and some storehouses; a little farther off lies the town, consisting of about twenty good stone houses, surrounded by two thousand frail abodes, the huts of the natives, over which wave clusters of palm-trees and of tamarind. The main street is a cool and shady avenue of india-rubber trees which meet overhead. Farther down the coast another similar town, called **Accra**, is inhabited by a few Englishmen, who live in old time-worn houses surrounded by a multitude of negroes.

The Gold Coast extends for 350 miles, and is succeeded to the east by the territory called, with sad suggestiveness, the **Slave Coast**. But the slave-traffic with all its hideous accompaniments is now abolished, for the British have stopped the transport of captives from the interior. The headquarters of the colony of Lagos are at a town of the same name, on a small island at the mouth of a broad and sluggish river, forming a sort of lagoon over which the natives in their canoes bring produce of different kinds for sale to the white men.

The Gold Coast and Lagos are colonies of much the same kind as Gambia and Sierra Leone. Each is ruled by a Governor and Legislative Council appointed by the mother country. The exports of each amount to about half a million pounds' worth of palm-oil, gold, and ivory each year.

Here the shores are low and flat, scarcely ever rising 10 feet above sea-level. The maritime part of the land consists of sand and mud covered with brushwood, and dense crops of tropical weeds with low clumps of mangrove here and there, or an occasional cocoa-nut palm-tree. But beyond this flat country the giant forest rises stately and tall like a green cliff above the sea of shrubs.

A little farther eastward the shores are lined with a green scum of sickening odour. All sorts of vegetable matter seem to be floating in the sea, and to be cast up on the shore, causing pestilential vapours to hang over the place. This vegetable matter is brought down to the sea by the great River Niger. This vast body of water finds its way by many channels to the sea. These various mouths are known as the "Palm-Oil Rivers," on account of the article which the natives chiefly bring down for export. The villages lie tolerably thick on the banks of all the branches of the river, with an occasional "factory," as the English warehouses are called. Only a few bold people, who have seasoned themselves to it, dare to settle in this district of dense forests, tangled jungle, gloomy waters, overhung by palms and steaming beneath the mangroves which rise from out the black and evil-smelling mud. But territory commanding the navigation of so large a river as the Niger, may eventually become of importance as the key to wide and productive lands in the interior. It is under the domination of Great Britain. Eastward, beyond the main mouth of the river, what is called the Calabar coast is under British influence. Behind rise the long slopes and bold shoulders which lead up to that great mountain called the Cameroons, whose topmost point is 13,000 feet above sea-level. The Calabar coast terminates opposite Fernando Po, beyond which to the south, Africa has been partitioned among the French, Germans, Spaniards, Portuguese, and the Congo State.

The whole of this Niger district is known as the **Niger Protectorate**, or officially, the NIGER TERRITORIES and the OIL RIVERS DISTRICT. It contains between ten and twenty millions of negroes, who trade with Englishmen, bartering palm-oil, ivory, ebony, and other articles produced in tropical Africa in exchange for guns and gunpowder, cloth, tobacco, and fancy goods. The district called the Niger Territories is governed by the Royal Niger Company, and includes the large and populous native empire of Sokoto. The Oil Rivers District is an important maritime region extending all the way along the coast from Lagos to the Cameroons.

X.—BRITISH EAST AFRICA

On the east coast of Africa, a vast territory, lying between the Zanzibar coast and Lake Victoria Nyanza, has recently been ceded to an association of merchants called the "Imperial British East Africa Company," of which the headquarters are in London. The district is populous, with negro tribes, peaceful in their habits and quite worthy of being called semi-civilised. They sell cotton, ivory, india-rubber, spices, and various sort of gums to the British traders who take their vessels to Mombasa, where a harbour, protected by an island that lies right across it, gives shelter to their ships.

The British coast stretches for nearly 400 miles from German East Africa northwards to the Equator. The islands of Zanzibar also, though lying opposite to the German territory, have been placed under British influence (Fig. 25). The form of the ground from the sea-coast inland resembles that of South Africa. Terrace after terrace, with long intervening slopes, lead like gigantic steps to a height of 4000 feet. Plains of long grass, wherein buffaloes, antelopes, giraffes, and zebras abound, give place to forests of teak and ebony wood, where trees of graceful foliage also are found, from which are derived those gums which painters use in making their varnish. These woods harbour the civet-cat, lynx, lion, and leopard; likewise apes and monkeys. The villages of the natives are formed of huts of the usual beehive shape, generally surrounded with a prickly hedge. The people themselves are strongly made and almost naked, their only clothing being short kilts of hairy skin, or of home-made cloth; while their woolly hair is shaved from the front of their heads and elsewhere screwed up into little tufts stiffened with fat. Round their settlements are spread good fields of potatoes, yams, or beans, or, where the soil is suitable, of rice or sorghum.

Above the plateau rise the two giant peaks of Africa, Mount Kilimanjaro and Mount Kenia, of which the former lies partly, and the latter wholly, within British

FIG. 25.—ZANZIBAR.

territory. Though on the Equator, they are high enough to be for ever tipped with a cap of gleaming snow. Now the natives of that part of the world, being unacquainted with snow, and having never tried to climb these lofty eminences, believed that the glittering peaks were made of solid silver. European travellers, however, have ascended both of the mountains, and have made known the gradual change in the character of the vegetation as the ground rises into the colder upper air. From the surrounding table-land rich clover slopes begin to mount upward, with native villages in every hollow. Then follows a belt of jungle, succeeded by a forest of tall trees, frequented by many wild beasts. Still higher lies another grassy region, rich with **the scent of** clover-flower, and **yielding** magnificent prospects over the **smiling plains away to the sea.** Slopes of heather now **rise upward,** growing barer and barer **as the realms of cold are** neared. Far above the ordinary level **of the clouds** the mountains show nothing but bare **rocks; and** lastly **on the** chilly summit there are **fields of snow and** cliffs of ice. Kilimanjaro has two peaks **or horns, one of** which is 21,000, the other **18,000** feet above **the sea, the** intervening hollow being **15,000 feet** high. Mount Kenia is about 18,000 feet above sea-level.

From **the summits of these** mountains the traveller **can** perceive, **more than a hundred miles to** the west, **the waters of one of the greatest lakes upon the** face of **the earth, the Victoria Nyanza.** Formerly this sheet of water served as the western boundary of the British territory; but now a tract extending along the northern and **western shores as well is** included within the British "**Sphere** of influence," while **Germany holds all to** the south. Though so immense a sheet of water, this lake is 3300 feet above sea-level, being situated on the top of the great table-land which occupies all this central part of Africa. **The** shores of the lake are finely diversified; plains **of tall** grass alternating with forests of teak, tamarind, and cotton-wood, wherein elephants, **buffaloes,** leopards, **lions, zebras,** antelopes, **and large numbers of gray monkeys are to be seen. The country is thickly** inhabited **by negro races, who dwell in houses like small** haystacks. **The numerous islets of the lake are covered** with forest trees; while **in the water the** hippopotamus may be seen disporting, **the mothers perhaps** swimming about with their young **ones on their** backs, and the crocodile waiting for its prey. Across **the** bays canoes **make** their way, **manned** by almost naked negroes, **bringing** their ivory **and** other merchandise for sale to **the** English, German, **and** Arab traders, who cause it to be carried on the heads of porters to Mombasa for shipment **there.**

Besides **the territory under** the jurisdiction of the East

Africa Company large regions or states, which are ruled by native chiefs, come within what is called the sphere of British influence. The chief of these states are RUANDA, UGANDA, and UNYORO. No doubt in the future they will be largely colonised by emigrants from Europe. They have a good climate and are believed to be rich in minerals and other natural products.

FIG. 26.—MOMBASA—ENGLISH POINT.

British Zambesia and Nyassaland.—To the south of Lake Victoria Nyanza lies another great lake, Nyassa, a sheet of water 350 miles long, and about 40 miles in average breadth. It makes a noble waterway, more especially as the Shiré river which flows out of it to join the Zambesi is navigable through its whole course of nearly 300 miles, except at one place where a number of falls occur. Hence the Lake Nyassa is one of the most promising lakes of Africa, and a British Company has a steamer or two upon it. The whole of the surrounding region is dotted over with British Mission Stations (Blantyre, Livingstonia), so that it is now in the sphere of British influence, or practically a protectorate; and is destined doubtless in course of time to become a colony. All the land to the south as far as the Zambesi is thus sure to become part of the British Empire, and to join with Matabeleland and Mashonaland, having only the Zambesi to divide them. The British South African Company obtained in 1889 a charter enabling it to organise the northern part of this region, and it has made considerable progress in its task, pushing the railway and telegraph system steadily northward. Some parts of the region are said to be rich in minerals. Doubtless at some future time this inland territory will become a valuable colony. It will then be reached not only from the Cape, but much more expeditiously from the east coast by way of the Zambesi. It is a great difficulty in this part of Africa that while the British hold all the interior, the Portuguese possess all the coast, and serious international collisions have been with some difficulty avoided. The river Zambesi has now been declared an international waterway.

There is yet another tract of East Africa, a large portion of which is vaguely under British control, though not yet formally annexed. This is the large peninsula which juts out to the east and terminates in Cape Gardafui. It may be called Somali Land, for it is occupied by a people called the Somali, a mixture of Arab and of negro blood. Their features recall those of both races of their ancestors, but in religion they are Mohammedans like their Arab forefathers. They are more civilised than any tribe of purely negro descent, being good weavers, ironsmiths, and workers in leather. They have schools and churches of their own sort. At BERBERA, which is their chief seaport, the British keep a commissioner, who takes an active part in managing the affairs of the country, though not in fact its ruler. Berbera consists of some 5000 or 6000 frail houses made of a frame of bamboo or other light poles, and roofed with skins or with palm leaves. In the monsoon period, when the winds are favourable, the town swarms with Arab and Hindoo traders, who bring articles of their own or of

European manufacture to barter for the gums, aloes, myrrh, and other valuable products which the country yields. The interior is as yet but scantily explored, and offers a field for the bold and adventurous to add to our knowledge of the earth. So far as we know, it consists of a grassy plateau on which wander the pastoral tribes of the Somali tending their camels, ponies, fat-tailed sheep, and small cattle.

XI. — POSSESSIONS IN THE RED AND ARABIAN SEAS AND INDIAN OCEAN

In the Red Sea, off the coast of Arabia, lies the bare, rocky, and sandy island of Kamaran, about 15 miles long and 5 miles broad. Its chief advantage is that it affords good and sheltered anchorage. It forms one of a chain of possessions which the British Empire has acquired on the highway from Europe to India.

Near the entrance to the Red Sea there is an important fortified British coaling-station called **Aden**, situated on the south coast of Arabia. Rain is scarcely ever known to fall here; nothing is seen on all hands but naked black rocks, rising in a semicircle behind the town, and forming the crater of an extinct volcano, of which the seaward side has been breached. Part of the inside of the crater forms a good harbour, and part affords a little level ground for the town to stand on. But it is the harbour which has made the town. Steam-vessels which pass through the Suez Canal on their way to India, China, or Australia, take in coal at this port. There is, therefore, a fleet of slower ships employed in carrying coal to this harbour, where it is stored in large stacks. The town which has sprung up in connection with this traffic has now 35,000 inhabitants. These are mostly Arabs, who form their houses by sticking a few bamboos into the ground and weaving round them a few palm leaves. The government of Aden is in the hands of a political resident, who also has command of the troops that form the garrison, but he is under the jurisdiction of the Bombay Presidency.

Included in the government of Aden is the bare rocky

island of **Perim**, lying in the middle of the strait of Babel-mandeb. Its position gives it command of the channel. A lighthouse has been erected on it. The lighthouse-keepers and a few soldiers are its only inhabitants, and even these are changed every two months.

The island of **Socotra**, which lies off Cape Gardafui, is also a part of the British Empire. Geographically it is attached to the continent of Africa, but the British Government have placed it, as well as Aden and Perim, under the control of the Governor of Bombay. It was annexed in 1886. It consists of a rocky table-land, about 1000 feet in height, surrounded by a low plain, probably consisting of sand thrown up by the sea in the monsoon periods. This border plain is barren and useless, but on the higher land there grow the best aloes that the world produces; and the tree called the dragon's blood, which yields a valuable gum, is also found there. Although 70 miles long, and of considerable area, the island has only 4000 persons in its population. These are Arabs, and are Mohammedan in their religion. They lead a quiet and somewhat lazy life, tending flocks of sheep and goats, and exporting small quantities of wool and aloes.

Farther north, off the coast of Arabia, lie the **Kooria Mooria Islands**, which were acquired by the British Government from the Sultan of Muscat. They have yielded an inferior kind of guano, but are barren and almost uninhabited.

The **Bahrein Islands** form a group in the Persian Gulf, of which the largest is 27 miles in length and 10 in breadth. They have been placed under British protection, with an English political agent. They carry on a considerable trade, especially with British India. The great industry is the pearl-fishery, which employs about 400 boats, with from 8 to 20 men in each.

But of much greater importance than those just enumerated are the islands which lie in the Indian Ocean to the east of Africa. **Mauritius**, to the east of Madagascar, is 38 miles long and 25 broad. Such is its fertility that 360,000 people live on it, making it one of the most densely populous districts on the earth's surface. But of these people 258,000 are Hindoos, who have been brought over by white men to work in the sugar-plantations, which form the chief industry of the place. At the beginning of this century the island belonged to the French, and still the majority of the white people are of French extraction. But when England and France were at war in 1810 the English took all the French colonies, and this was not one of those which were given back.

It has a town, called PORT LOUIS, of singular size for so small an island, and presenting a curious assemblage of people gathered from widely-separated countries. Here may be seen Hindoos in white robes and many-coiled turbans, swarthy Arabs in little red caps, Chinese with their black hair in long tails, Frenchmen talking their native tongue, and Englishmen in light summer clothing —all jostling each other on the busy streets. It is a place of much trade, and contains 62,000 people. It possesses a large Roman Catholic cathedral, some Protestant churches, a bazaar, a hospital, a theatre, an observatory, and Botanic Gardens. It boasts also a college with a large staff of professors; and this small island has no fewer than 140 schools within it. The visitor who comes to Mauritius may at first wonder why the island is reputed to be so fertile. Rough and ill-made roads lead through country which seems mostly covered with boulders; but as he rises towards the interior he sees that the volcanic rocks, of which the land has been formed, have been worn down by the weather to make a productive kind of soil, which has been washed down into the valleys, where it forms fertile fields. There used to be boulders in these valleys also, but the planters have gathered them up and made them into rough walls, which mark the plains off into squares, wherein the sugar-cane is grown. Many thousands of dark-skinned men work in these plantations; and between £150,000 and £200,000 are received for the raw sugar which is annually sent away from this little island. Some parts of the island, however, present only scenes of wild and desolate grandeur, especially among the ancient craters, of which there are two of considerable height. **The chief** is about 3000 feet high. Visitors often climb to the summit of its peak, though there is some danger in the last part of the ascent.

Besides Port **Louis** the island has several other small **towns**. It is ruled by a Governor sent from England, but he is assisted by a council partly elected by the inhabitants, and partly nominated by the colonial authorities in **London**. The British keep a battalion of soldiers in Mauritius.

About 300 miles east of Mauritius lies the island of **Rodriguez**, a rugged volcanic mass, about 12 miles long and 6 broad. In its fertile valleys sugar and a little cotton are grown. Although it is part of the British Empire its inhabitants are mostly French, as the island belonged to France before the English took it. These French planters have Hindoo and negro servants to work in their fields, and the population, all told, amounts to only 1800 persons.

Ruled by the same Governor are the **Seychelles Islands**, which lie about 1000 miles north of Mauritius. They are a group of peaks which rise to the surface, and have been surrounded by extensive reefs of coral, so that they look as if resting on an immense area of coral, whereas it is the coral which is resting on them. They are about forty in number, the largest, called MAHÉ, being about 8 miles long. As they lie close to the Equator they are hot in climate, but they form one of the most lovely spots on the face of the earth. Little sandy bays, protected by coral reefs, lie in perfect calmness, their pale green waters rich with marine life of exquisite beauty; on the beach stand picturesque old French houses, surrounded with abundant palms and gorgeous tropical flowers. Behind these the islands are masses of verdure, rising up into bold peaks in their interiors. Everywhere the cocoa-nut waves on high its clusters of feathery leaves. A large part of the population consists of Hindoos who have been brought over to gather the nuts of these trees, which form the most important export of the islands. But another characteristic product is to be seen in the plantations where the vanilla plant is grown, a kind of parasite, which is made to take root on old logs or stumps of trees. From its handsome flowers there spring the long pods that are **so much** used in flavouring.

Numerous islets, scattered over the Indian Ocean, are claimed as portions of the British Empire. Of the **Chagos Islands**, the largest, called Diego Garcia, $12\frac{1}{2}$ miles long and $6\frac{1}{4}$ miles wide, with 700 inhabitants, has now become a valuable coaling-station for steamboats. It also exports a good deal of cocoa-nut oil. These islands, together with numerous small islets—the St. Brandon or Cargados Islands, the Oil Islands, the Eagle Islands, the Cosmoledo Islands, and a number of uninhabited rocks—are considered to be dependencies of the colony of Mauritius. Among the smaller of the British possessions in the Indian Ocean are two rocky islets, **St. Paul** and **New Amsterdam**, that lie half-way between Africa and Australia. **They** have **no permanent inhabitants, but** men sometimes **dwell on** them **for a time, attracted by** the fisheries of the **surrounding seas, and by the prodigious** numbers of sea-birds which gather on **these lonely rocks in the** breeding season.

The **Laccadive Islands**, lying about 200 miles **west** from the Malabar coast of the Madras Presidency, of which they are a dependency, number **fourteen,** of which nine are inhabited.

The **Maldive Islands** lie 500 miles west of Ceylon, of which they are a dependency. They are, in truth, an **enormous** bank of coral, stretching, north and south, **to** the extent of nearly 500 **miles,** with a breadth of about **70 miles.** This coral bank rises here and there out of the water, so as to form eighteen groups of little islands, each island being an atoll. Their surface is rarely more than 6 feet above sea-level, and from a little distance **the cocoa** trees, with which they are well covered, seem to be growing out of the **ocean.** The inhabitants, nearly 150,000 in number, are short people **of** a dark copper colour—quiet, inoffensive Mohammedans, who find occupation in sending **fruit,** turtles, and fish to the markets of Ceylon and India.

The **Nicobar** and **Andaman Islands**, in the Bay of Bengal, form part **of the** Indian Dominions of Britain. They are described in *The Elementary Geography of India*, etc., by Mr. H. F. Blanford.

XII.—POSSESSIONS IN THE SOUTH-EAST OF ASIA

Straits Settlements.—Along the eastern shores of the Strait of Malacca lie several British colonies, which are small in area, but of an importance out of all proportion to their size. The chief is the island of Singapore, situated at the extremity of the Malay Peninsula. It is 26 miles long, and just half as broad as it is long. It stands in a large bay, and is divided from the mainland by a channel only a mile or two in width. Its surface consists of decomposed gneiss, which makes a soil of the most brilliant red; so that the voyage round it and through its straits and labyrinth of small attendant islands is singularly picturesque, the red cliffs and dark-red shelving banks being overhung with green plantations of coffee, tea, cotton, and pepper, while cocoa and other palms spring here and there from their midst. A piece of the original tropical jungle may occasionally be seen in all its luxuriance.

Singapore owes its importance to the fact that it lies so conveniently in the course of communication between the nations of the East and those of the West. In 1819 the English first put up a warehouse on the island as a place where vessels might call on the voyage from China to India; then in 1824 they bought the island from a Malay prince, and began to form a regular town. Then came Chinese by thousands to settle round it and trade; after that, when the Malays found that work was always to be had there in loading and unloading vessels, they too began to gather; and thus three different quarters of the town have arisen. Along the seashore is a carriage-drive,

Fig. 27.—Singapore from the East.

behind which stand the handsome houses of the English
residents. Some of the English, however, prefer to live
on a little hill a mile or so inland; for Singapore, being
almost on the Equator, is excessively hot. The Europeans
on the island generally look pale and sickly, as the climate
is so decidedly unhealthy. Round the English quarter
there lies a broad Chinese part, with narrow streets of
wooden houses, of which many are cook-shops and warehouses for fancy goods. Outside of this, again, there
stretch acres of poor-looking huts, which the Malays make
out of bamboos for their own use. These frail dwellings
are only a slight protection against the tigers which
swim across from the mainland, and it is said that for
many years on an average one man a day was eaten
on Singapore Island by these animals. The population of the island is about 182,000; but of these less than
3000 are white people. They are almost all kept busy by
the arrival and departure of steamers, which call while
passing, or which unload their cargoes in order to have
them distributed by small native vessels throughout the
adjacent populous islands.

Farther north, on the Strait of Malacca, lies the ancient
town of Malacca, which was first founded by the Portuguese nearly four hundred years ago. Two hundred years
later the Dutch took it from the Portuguese, and it was
to their East India trade much as Singapore now is to
ours. In 1825 the English purchased it from the Dutch.
It has some considerable trade with the interior of the
Malay Peninsula, but there are not 50 English resident
in it; almost the whole of its 100,000 people are
Chinese or Malays, or half-castes between Portuguese and
Malays. The ruins of a fine old cathedral and many heaps
of stones that once were churches, public buildings,
colleges, and so forth, tell how much importance Malacca
possessed in olden times. In Singapore the Chinese out-
number the Malays, but in Malacca the Malays are nearly
four times as numerous as the Chinese.

Penang, also on the Strait of Malacca, lies 240 miles
north of Malacca. It is sometimes called Prince of Wales
Island. It is only 15 miles long, and has a rugged surface,

FIG. 23.—THE FISH MARKET, SINGAPORE.

with mountains over 2000 feet high. It has a pretty town called George Town on its north extremity. The whole island has a thriving look, the Chinese having fine plantations of cloves, nutmeg, allspice, and ginger, and on the low alluvial flats that face towards the mainland there are fine crops of rice and maize. A strip of land on the opposite shore of the Malay Peninsula forms the province of Wellesley, which is about 45 miles long, and has an average width of about 8 miles. Penang and Wellesley go together to form one colony; between them they have about 230,000 people, but not 1000 of these are Europeans, the remainder being Chinese, Malays, or Hindoos.

Singapore, Malacca, Penang, and Wellesley are all ruled by an English Governor, who lives at Penang. He is assisted by an Executive Council and a small Legislative Council.

The chief articles of native produce that are exported from these settlements are tapioca, rice, sugar, and spices; of their immense trade, all the rest is merely transit trade.

Nearly the whole Malay Peninsula forms a kind of British protectorate. It is divided into populous states, each state with its own native ruler; but at the capital of each there lives a British commissioner, whose advice is asked and generally followed in all important matters. Perak is the most important of these places. It promises to be a populous district on account of the productive tin-mines that are now being worked in all directions throughout it.

North Borneo, Labuan, and Sarawak.—The large and fertile island of Borneo is mostly claimed by the Dutch. The northern shores, however, have until recently retained their independence. But in 1840 they were visited by a remarkable Englishman, Sir James Brooke, popularly known as Rajah Brooke. He helped one of the native sultans against some rebels, and in return he was made Governor of the province of Sarawak, at the western end of the north coast of Borneo. By degrees he came to be a sort of Prime Minister over all this northern part of the island, and by his vigour in putting down piracy, in establishing law and order, and in encouraging cultivation and trade, he quite altered the prospects of the place. With his wife's fortune he purchased Sarawak, and settled down as an independent sovereign; in 1846, when the British Government bought the little island of Labuan, off the north coast, he was made Governor of it. All the rest of his life he lived in Borneo, promoting the good of the people, and encouraging English settlement. His nephew carried on the same work after him, and now British influence is dominant over all this district. The territory of North Borneo is placed under the control of the British North Borneo Company. It has a population of 175,000 Malays, with a few Chinese. Many parts of this district are richly cultivated, the rice-fields being well planted and neatly fenced. Beyond them lies the giant tropical jungle, above which the great granite peaks of mountains rise to 12,000 feet in height.

Up in the hill-country live the Dyaks, a people of mild look, but with an evil reputation for murder, and a habit of collecting human heads. It is in the forests of these uplands that the sago-palm is found. The pith is taken out of it and sent down to the coast, where the British North Borneo Company turn it into sago. Brunei is the name given to the north-eastern part of Borneo. It is under the rule of a sultan, who keeps an imposing state with palaces and courtiers in theatrical splendour, but who really follows the instructions given him by a resident British commissioner. The capital of this little state is built over the water; it is a fairly large city, but every house is founded on bamboo posts rising out of the river—streets, courtyards, market-places, and so on, are all water, and are traversed only by boats.

Labuan has no white people except the Governor of the island, with his family and two officers; most of the rest are Malays—hard-working, industrious people. Sarawak has a capital of the same name—a town of 25,000 inhabitants, who are Malays and Chinese. The population of the district is said to be nearly 300,000.

The chief occupations in Borneo, Labuan, and Sarawak are the growing of tobacco, sago, and pepper, and the gathering of gutta-percha, wax, gums, india-rubber, and bamboos from the dense tropical forests which cover so much of the land. But they are all rich in gold, and also in coal—a mineral which will yet make Borneo a most important part of the world.

Hong-Kong.—The British Empire possesses a little island called Hong-Kong at the mouth of the Choo-kiang or Canton River, on the coast of China. It is only 11 miles long, and not 5 miles broad at its widest part; yet it is of immense importance in the vast stream of commerce that flows to and fro between England and China. As the visitor approaches it, a high hill looms out among the

FIG. 29.—HONG-KONG LOCOMOTION.

clouds, and soon after, at its foot, are discerned thousands of masts and funnels, lying like a forest in the harbour of the town of Victoria. Chinese junks and small vessels rigged with bamboo laths and palm-canvas sails are plying out and in, giving an air of strange restlessness to the scene. Behind the masts rise rows of stately warehouses, one above the other, so steeply that the foundations of the one row are on a level with the roofs of another. Halfway up the hill-side the warehouses and Chinese houses cease, and then a well-made road winds to the very top of the mountain, 1800 feet above sea-level, where the wealthy merchants of Hong-Kong have built their villas, surrounded with semi-tropical shrubs. Trees are not common on the island, as the soil is poor and stony. The traveller who lands at one of the wharves encounters a crowd of Chinese, running, pushing, singing, and shouting in the most perfect good-humour; while the boat-women work their barges in and out of the port, coming from or going to the immense city of Canton, which lies 100 miles up the river. In the narrow streets many English soldiers and sailors may be seen, for the British Government always has a strong force here to protect imperial interests; but the bulk of the crowd consists of Chinese, who number about 220,000, while the Europeans are not 9000.

XIII.—AUSTRALIA

Discovery and Settlement. — A hundred and thirty years ago, after the end of the keen rivalry between the French and English for colonial predominance in India and in Canada, there lay a wide region far away to the south still unoccupied by civilised men. Both nations turned their eyes in that direction, and vaguely thought of adding Australia to their possessions. But the distance was great, and the land was not known to be prolific in jewels, precious metals, spices, and the other costly tropical products that had offered such great attractions in India, the East and West Indies, Peru, and Mexico. The successive voyagers who had touched its shores brought home accounts of the remote island-continent. It was known to be peopled by roving tribes of blacks, who lived a primitive life in a rude, though not actually degraded, condition. These people, in companies of from thirty to a hundred, wandered by day from one hunting-ground to another, the men stalking naked ahead with clubs and bundles of spears in their hands, while their wives, partly clothed, carried the little children and the household utensils, staggering on behind, heavily laden, but with plentiful laughter and chatter. At evening the tribe would camp for the night under shelter-places of leafy branches. Sometimes they would stay for a week or two at one camp if the opossums were numerous. But these tribes were sparsely scattered over the country. Every man, woman, and child would have had 8 or 10 square miles as a single share if the whole land had been divided equally among all its people.

At last this primeval simplicity was broken up by the

first invasion and **settlement** of **white men.** In the year 1787 **the English sent out** to Australia seven hundred **convicts, men who had been** sentenced to long terms of **imprisonment, and for whom no** sufficient gaol accommodation could be easily provided in England. These, **with the soldiers and** others in charge of them, made **a little community of** about a thousand persons **who at the beginning of the year** 1788 settled down at Sydney **on the east coast of Australia.** For twenty years they **continued to be** almost entirely a convict settlement, **supported by the British** Government, **which every** year **sent out fresh batches of prisoners.** But free settlers then began to seek the shores of Australia; while hundreds of the convicts, when set free, began the **life of** farmers or of sheep-growers, and **being removed from** the temptations of their old haunts, became industrious and prosperous colonists.

The English were likewise the first to occupy **New Zealand, and so by far the larger** part of that collection of **islands known as** Australasia, being the island-continent of Australia itself, and the groups of islands surrounding it, passed permanently into their hands. A century has seen an immense change in this region. The original 1000 people, mostly poor and miserable exiles, have grown to nearly 4,000,000, with great cities and abundant **fields**; with 120,000,000 sheep and 10,000,000 of cattle; **with 14,000 miles** of railway and all the busy adjuncts of **a prosperous** civilisation. During this period the native **races have been** slowly disappearing. Elaborate pains have been taken to preserve them and to make them comfortable. But like wayward children they have generally chosen the vices rather than the **virtues of** their visitors. **Their** own quarrels among themselves, their love of drink, the spread of infectious diseases, and in the more northern colonies, conflicts **with the white** men who refused to let **them spear** and eat **the** sheep on the stations, have caused **them to become in many** places extinct. Yet wherever **Australia is** not settled, or only thinly settled by white **men, in the** centre, **the** north, and the **west,** the black **tribes are still numerous.**

After the first colony was founded at Sydney, a branch

was started at Hobart. These settlements succeeded well, mainly on account of the introduction of sheep, and the discovery that the Australian climate was peculiarly adapted to the growth of wool.

Free settlers in 1836 founded colonies at Melbourne and Adelaide, which also prospered side by side at an equal rate till the year 1851, when the discovery of gold in the country 100 miles north of Melbourne attracted many hundreds of thousands of men, whose energies made that part of Australia for many years the most prosperous and most important. A colony at Perth was founded in 1829 by free settlers, and another at Brisbane in 1824 by a detachment of convicts sent from Sydney. All of these have grown into free, energetic, and wealthy communities, which, enjoying their separate parliamentary government, are called colonies. A short account of each of these colonies will be given in later pages of this volume. We shall first consider the physical geography of Australia as a whole.

Coast-Line.—Australia, viewed as a continental area, takes rank as the least of the continents of the globe. It is the only one which lies wholly south of the Equator; although it does not stretch so near to the South Pole as South America. If we consider it as an island, it is the leader, as it were, of that immense assemblage of islands of all sizes which lie south and south-east of Asia, dotting the Indian and Pacific Oceans.

Its greatest length is 2300 miles from east to west. If a traveller, starting from Brisbane, were to attempt to cross the country along this line he would pass first through beautiful well-settled country; then, from homestead to homestead, across the great plains which are occupied by millions of sheep. But after journeying 1000 or 1200 miles he would enter on uninhabited lands that have been only three times crossed, and then only by experienced explorers with camels. The western half of Australia is excessively dry, though not as a rule what is properly called a desert, for shrubs and grass grow nearly everywhere. The vegetation is of a kind that requires little water, and the night-dews and occasional rains keep it alive; but there are no streams, and ponds occur only at intervals of 100 or 200 miles, so that the journey across this region is one of extreme hardship and difficulty.

The greatest breadth of Australia is about 2000 miles from the promontory of Cape York to the southern coast at Melbourne. One might traverse this eastern division of the continent from south to north and pass through settled country all the way, as far as the peninsula which runs out into Cape York, where the country is a dense mass of thick and difficult tropical jungle, and its natives are savage and hostile.

Australia is a remarkably compact continent, its coasts being little broken into by arms of the sea. To form some idea of the look of the country from the outside let us in imagination sail round the whole coast, and suppose that after crossing the Indian Ocean we first sight the land at CAPE LEEUWIN, on the south-west of Western Australia. The big bare hill of that promontory, with its yellow burnt-up grass, dotted here and there with stunted and wind-tossed shrubs, looks pleasant enough as a change from the monotony of a long sea-voyage. For a day we skirt a shore of undulating hills, grassy, but generally looking yellow and dry. These terminate in rocky cliffs, vexed for ever by the long rollers that travel ceaselessly up from Antarctic Seas, and break in white foam upon the rocky ledges. Our steamer may require to get more coal, and for that purpose may turn into the pretty little bay, King George's Sound, running up among grassy hills, whereon we notice for the first time those trees which we shall see all over Australia, the gum-trees, scraggy-looking trees with gnarled arms and leaves of a dull and not refreshing green. But dotted lightly over the grassy sward, as they are here, they give a park-like look to the country. From the neat little town of Albany, where vessels coal, we sail eastwards with a hilly shore just barely in view. We see many little headlands and pebbly bays, and the shore is fringed with numberless islets. But after a time the coast bends northward into that great curve known as the Great Australian Bight. We now have to coast along 600 miles of one of the most monotonous shores in all the world. It is like a dead wall of rock, rising 200 but more often 500 or 600 feet from the sea. Its face of dirty white or reddish-brown is flecked at the base by the white spray of the breakers. We cannot see over it, and only an occasional stunted bush here and there gives a suggestion of the dreary uninhabited wilderness behind. Near the centre of this great bay runs the boundary between the colonies of Western and Southern Australia. At the eastern end of the bight the land runs out into a horn, which was called CAPE CATASTROPHE by Captain Flinders, because the boat which he sent ashore to look for fresh water, with a master, a midshipman, and six seamen, was found a day or two afterwards floating bottom upwards; and not one of the crew was ever found.

Rounding this headland into the long Spencer Gulf, we ascend what looks like an estuary, narrowing gradually up to a point as if about to lead us into a river; but if any river did ever flow into it, it has long dried up, and its bed is filled with sand, which makes a dreary plain all round the head of the Gulf. But in the wider part of the inlet the shores are pleasant, the undulating hills being openly timbered like a gentleman's park. CAPE SPENCER, a hill about 250 feet high, ends in three cliffy points, with black wave-beaten rocks at their base. Of the Gulf of St. Vincent, so called after one of England's naval heroes, the western shores are low, but grassy and pleasant enough to look on, while the eastern shores also continue flat for six or eight miles inland, beyond which the blue ridges of the Mount Lofty Range rise as a charming background. On the plain between the shore and the hills we note increasing signs of a civilised and thriving population. First, scattered in all directions, come villas, then steeples, chimneys, and spires, and floating over them all that faint haze of smoke which marks a busy city. This is Adelaide.

The narrow passage between Kangaroo Island and CAPE JERVIS was facetiously named by Flinders, Backstairs Passage, while he called the broader strait lying between Kangaroo Island and Cape Spencer after his vessel Investigator Strait. Cape Jervis is a high bold headland formed by the termination of the green and grassy Mount Lofty Range.

The coast now bends northward into an inlet known as Encounter Bay, for it was here that Flinders, exploring eastward, encountered the French navigator Baudin, working his way westward. For a hundred miles nothing can be seen on shore but lines of sand-hills thrown up by the waves; they are of some height and of dazzling whiteness, with a few bushes growing here and there from their summits. Behind them lies a great stretch of sandy desert, with a narrow lagoon called the Coorong running close to the foot of the sand-hills. The shores now become higher and more rocky, and two green hills form prominent landmarks inland. These are well known as extinct volcanoes, and one of them has its crater filled with a lake of exquisite loveliness. CAPE NORTHUMBERLAND forms a line of bold but not remarkable cliffs, and CAPE NELSON, the most westerly headland of the colony of Victoria, rises as the middle rock of three that jut out picturesquely into the sea, sheltering Portland Bay, a wide curve with green shores of no great height, and the little town of Portland at its head.

Coasting still eastward along a low shore we pass the busy town of Warrnambool, beyond which the land begins to rise into rugged cliffs with the Otway Ranges mounting up behind them—slope after slope of mountain ridge, deeply clothed in some of the most gigantic timber that the world has to show. This bold and delightful scenery continues round CAPE OTWAY. On the flat-topped summit of this bare rocky headland a fine lighthouse has been built, from which at night a powerful white light flashes from minute to minute to warn the mariner from this dangerous shore.

Steaming for a hundred miles along a coast which gradually grows lower and lower, we steer through a narrow entrance into PORT PHILLIP—an inlet completely land-locked, about forty miles long, and of nearly the same breadth. At its head stands the great city of Melbourne, the capital of Victoria. Without a break for some fifteen miles wharves and piers and bathing en-

closures line the shores, with rows of villas and mansions
behind, and beyond these again the crowded streets of
the capital of the colony of Victoria. From Port Phillip
eastwards sand-hills for some distance skirt the land until
the coast rises abruptly at CAPE SCHANCK into a picturesque cliff, with a mitre-shaped rock protruding from
it. A fine piece of rocky coast, with charming bits
of marine scenery, brings us to the western entrance of
Western Port, so called by Bass, who discovered it, because
it was the most westerly point reached in that wonderful
voyage of his when, with a whale-boat and a crew of six
men, he sailed 600 miles on the open ocean, and explored
300 miles of utterly unknown coast.

Beyond Western Port the shores continue high, as far
as the mountainous headland known as Wilson's Promontory, the most southerly point of Australia. It is covered
with magnificent timber, and five peaks raise their rounded
tree-clad tops into the blue of the Australian sky, while
in its recesses are charming valleys, filled with tree-ferns
and a luxuriant vegetation of musk-trees and blackwood.
Rounding this bold projection we reach the shallow Corner
Inlet, from which at low tide the sea retires, leaving a
wide stretch of sand with streaks of water in the hollows.
The shore presents a continuous line of low sand-hills along
what is called the Ninety Mile Beach; but behind these
lie some pretty lagoons, and occasionally, when the sand-
hills decline a little, a vista of the blue tops of the lofty
Gippsland Mountains far away inland may be seen. Skirting some more low and bare-looking coast we reach CAPE
HOWE, where the colonies of Victoria and New South
Wales meet. This is an important station for Australian
traffic. Night and day there is scarcely an hour but some
steamer may be seen passing, while sailing ships and small
craft make the stream of vessels almost uninterrupted.
Hence on the little Gabo Island, close to the cape, a
village of cottages has sprung up, beside the lighthouse,
wherein live signal-men, lighthouse men, telegraph opera-
tors, and others connected with the station.

Our course lies now nearly north-north-east along a
bold and attractive coast-line. Lines of cliffs from 50

to 100 feet high, their dark faces of red, gray, and yellow
stone carved into many a fantastic form, alternate with
little bays on whose beaches of sand or snowy pebbles
the rollers break with a never-ending murmur. For 150
miles this scenery continues until at BOTANY BAY a small
inlet, some 10 or 12 miles long, indents the coast, along
the shores of which lie the suburbs of the city of **Sydney**,
the capital of New South Wales. But to see the city
itself we sail some 10 miles farther, and, passing between

FIG. 30.—SOUTH HEAD, AND ENTRANCE TO PORT JACKSON.

two bold and rocky heads, enter the waters of the far-
famed PORT JACKSON, which opens up into many arms
and scores of bays, and is dotted with little islets. The
city has been built round the harbour, and the hundreds
of steamboats which here play the part of the omnibuses
and tramways of other towns, give a singularly lively
character to the scene.

Northward from Port Jackson the coast-line continues
generally rocky, with many inlets and capes fringing
a pleasant country inland, and allowing the outlines of blue
hills to be seen behind as a charming background, until
at CAPE BYRON it mounts into a bold precipice, tree-clad

on its rounded brow. This is the most easterly cape of Australia.

Past Point Danger (so named by Captain Cook from its surf-beaten rocks) the coast-line is that of the colony of Queensland. A passage leads into the almost landlocked Moreton Bay, one end of which is so broad and the other so narrow that when its name was first given it was thought to be a bay, though it is more properly a strait. Its shores are low; on one side lie two sandy islands partly covered with low and scrubby woods, on the landward side patches of mangrove swamps fringe the coast. These trees, which grow out upon a muddy shore into the sea-water, indicate that we are nearing the tropical latitudes. But along the greater part of the shores stretch beaches of clear sand, behind which from time to time may be seen villas and an occasional hotel, marking the distant outskirts of the city of Brisbane, which lies itself too much inland to be visible from the sea.

North of Moreton Bay long sandy flats and shallow ponds are varied only by slightly raised sand-hills, which support a poor sort of vegetation. But inland the outlines of noble mountain ranges may be descried to the west. Passing again through a narrow entrance, set between a long flat waste called Sandy Island and a much more pleasant shore on the mainland, we enter Hervey Bay, a shallow sheet of water with nothing of interest except the boats with their harpooners in front, watching for the dugongs, which are killed for their oil.

The scenery now again becomes more interesting. The shores are often high, and pleasantly wooded to the water's edge; where they are low, green mangrove flats stretch out into the sea; and, busy among the muddy roots of these trees, flocks of duck and curlew may be noticed, and the great pelican filling his bag with fish. So we enter Keppel Bay and then Broad Sound, and observe the increasing dignity of the mountains as they approach more and more nearly to the coast.

But in the navigation of this part of the Australian coast a remarkable change is soon apparent in the surface of the sea. The water, no longer undulating with the broad rollers, becomes quite calm, and presents a striking green colour. Far **away to** the **east** lies the Great Barrier Reef — a massive rampart of coral, 1000 miles **in** length, raised by the coral polyp from the bottom of **the** sea. We may hear at times the hoarse thunder of the **ocean** rollers on the outer side of this barrier, and may see the surf and spray thrown up against the spotless blue **of the sky,** but the lagoon channel inside is protected like a vast natural harbour. Could we **look down** through the transparent water upon the growing coral we should see **fish** of many stripes, with strange prickles **and wonder**ful frills, lazily wandering in and out among bunches **of** pink, blue, **white, and purple** coral. For a thousand miles the steamer **sails on this calm** sea, but anchors at night, for the **navigation is dangerous.** Coral reefs, often only a few feet above the water, oftener still not above water at all, make it necessary to travel only half speed by day and to lie still during the darkness.

At length we reach HALIFAX BAY and round CAPE MELVILLE, which projects as the rugged end of a line of lofty hills. The cape, like the hills themselves, is densely covered with tropical foliage, and from its face have fallen great ruddy-coloured boulders of granite which now stretch in a line a mile and a quarter long out into the sea.

North of this point the country, unlike what we have already seen, is quite uninhabited by white men. From the sea the land looks inviting, but it is covered with great jungles of tropical forest in which rove fierce tribes of naked blacks. It terminates in CAPE YORK, a bold promontory, with an island at the end of it which leaves a passage only 500 feet wide. But the water being deep, the channel is navigable and affords a view of the bold rocky scenery topped with luxuriant vegetation and occasional palms. Here too may be seen gigantic ant-hills, made of red and yellow clay, standing twenty feet high or more, and looking like miniature cathedrals with spires, pinnacles, and buttresses. In rounding Cape York we pass through TORRES STRAITS, so called after the Portuguese mariner who first sailed through it. The scenery is exquisitely lovely, and we shall never forget it

if we see the sun set among those innumerable coral islets
dotted with palms, their foliage reflected seemingly far
underneath those waters of wonderfully delicate yet
gorgeous tints. Yonder comes a fleet of pearling boats
with their noisy South Sea Islanders, whom they have
taken out as divers to bring up pearl oysters from the
bottom of the strait. They are all on their way to the
various islands where the headquarters of the pearling
fleets are stationed.

The GULF OF CARPENTARIA, into which we now pass,
so called after General Carpenter, a Dutchman who 250
years ago was the first to explore it, is large but not
very interesting, its shores being uniformly flat—often
only the edge of sandy plains; at times showing low cliffs
of clay with a tuft of cabbage palm here and there, but
also presenting, where the rivers enter the sea, wide expanses
of low and somewhat dreary mangrove. The gulf is of
no great use at present, as few people live round its
shores. Its eastern half belongs to the colony of Queensland, the western half to the northern territory of South
Australia.

Coming out of this gulf we round CAPE ARNHEIM, a
smooth grassy projection with rolling hills behind it, and
sail along sandy shores fringing well-wooded lands, until
we reach the Coburg Peninsula. As we round the extremity
through Dundas Strait we have on our right-hand side
Melville Island, which lies in front of an almost land-locked
bay called Van Diemen's Gulf. Its shores are red bluffs of
no great height, but from their edges forests of tropical
trees run inland far as the eye can see. As we sail
through Clarence Strait we may chance to see some shipping making for PALMERSTON—a small town on the southern
shore which is of some importance as it is the only town
upon the whole of the north coast of Australia. From
Cambridge Gulf all the way round to the middle of the
Great Australian Bight the coast-line is that of the colony
of Western Australia. The northern shores west of
Cambridge Gulf are of most miserable aspect; giving
little promise of the fine pastoral lands that generally lie a
hundred miles or so inland. The coast is bare and sandy,

save where in the little bays its flat shores are filled with monotonous stretches of mangroves.

CAPE LONDONDERRY is a forlorn and dreary promontory except at the season when the Malays come over with their boats in crowds to get trepang, a kind of sea-slug found on tropical shores and sold among the Chinese. The shores of KING SOUND consist of dreary mud-flats, nor is EXMOUTH GULF more inviting. The navigators who have at various times explored it cannot well map out its western shores for they are formed by mud islands so low and flat that it depends upon the state of the tide where the dry land may be supposed to begin, and there is in fact no actual line of shore, the mud-flats running away inland with no very evident margin.

From the NORTH-WEST CAPE, a long low stretch of sand over which the waves of the Indian Ocean roll for a mile or more, the coast-line bends southward into Shark Bay, an inlet well sheltered by a row of islands; it received its name from Captain Dampier, who caught a monstrous shark in it. Here we again reach civilised habitations. For a thousand miles and more the coast has been inhabited only by the blear-eyed and unlovely native population. The little town here planted serves as the seaport of the pastoral districts lying inland, and other places of the same sort may be seen farther south. Steep Point, one of the horns of Shark Bay, is the most westerly point of Australia. The land is fairly well occupied by white men in the more southerly parts of this coast till we reach Geographe Bay, fringed by sand-hills on which grows a little stunted vegetation. It terminates in a horn called Cape Naturaliste, densely covered with low bushes.

Configuration, Surface.—If we divide Australia into two parts by a line from the head of the Australian Bight to Van Diemen's Gulf, then it may in general be said that all the eastern part is fully known, and mostly occupied by white men; while the western part is only partially explored, and is mostly occupied by thin and wandering tribes of blacks. Bold explorers, Warburton, Forrest, and Giles, have traversed this second part in three parallel lines, from east to west; they found no want of fine country,

with **many** grassy districts pleasant **to view, but the
scarcity of** water made their travelling **excessively difficult
and dangerous.** White men will before long carry **their
sheep** into these regions and contrive to store the rainfall
as they now do in the west of New South Wales and
Queensland, but at present there is no inducement for the
settlers to go far inland from the coast of West Australia.
Thus an immense area is **still unoccupied,** and indeed
unknown, except that we **can judge of the whole** by the
samples seen by the travellers, who report **that** regions of
prickly grass or of stunted shrubs predominate, but yet
with many an oasis of fine sheep country.

There is none of this **western half very level, and yet**
the ranges, though spread everywhere over the country, are
so inconsiderable in length and in height as to form no
important features. This half of Australia may be regarded
as a vast undulating plain, gently swelling here and **there**
into table-lands up to 1000 feet in height, and **dotted**
in all directions with hills, which sometimes rise into
mountain peaks of 2000 or even 3000 feet **in height.**

The eastern **half is more** diversified and **can be more**
definitely described. It contains a belt of table-land running parallel with the east coast from Cape Melville in the
north through Queensland to Cape Howe on the southern
border of New South Wales, and then bending westward
through the colony of Victoria, **which it** almost completely
traverses. **In all** this **great** length of over 2000 miles
of upland there is no break. There are places indeed where
the level of the **ground sinks to** no more than 1000
feet though its general elevation is about **2000 feet;
but** it is impossible anywhere to pass inland **from**
the east coast without traversing this plateau. **The**
engineers who have constructed the railways of the colonies
have naturally sought to cross the table-land at **its** lowest
parts; yet some have been compelled **to take** their lines
2000 or 2500 feet high in order to cross, **while** the lowest
lines ascend to 1200 or 1400 feet.

This table-land is cooler than the **rest** of the country,
hence in New South Wales it forms the wheat-growing
district of the colony; while in Queensland its undulating

surface, known as **downs,** makes one of the most magnificent districts in the world for the rearing of fat cattle. The settlers who live on the top of the table-land grow fruits belonging to colder climates than those cultivated by their neighbours on the lower level. Otherwise there is nothing very characteristic in this long table-land. It **varies** in breadth from 50 to 200 miles, but rarely exceeds 100 miles. Its surface is traversed lengthwise by mountain ranges, which make the scenery everywhere varied. Most of the peaks are of considerable height, ranging from 3000 to 7000 feet above sea-level, but they lose some of their apparent elevation from standing upon such high ground.

Among the confused ranges that traverse the table-land it is possible to make out one continuous line of ridges generally **higher than the others.** This backbone, of **which** the **rest may be** considered branches, is called the GREAT DIVIDING RANGE. It forms the crest of the table-land from beginning **to** end, and is therefore not less than 2000 miles in **length.** A little **south of** Cape Melville it starts boldly **in the fine** ridge called the Bellenden Ker Range, **whose** peaks rise **from** the rocky coast in a steep slope to the height of 5000 feet and more. They catch the moisture-laden clouds that float in from the steaming tropic sea, and on their sides an immense **rainfall descends,** making the country one vast forest of **jungle vegetation.** The gold miners who have so often **landed** on these shores, hoping to reach the gold-fields inland, have told of the steep spurs, the sudden gullies, the dense foliage of palm and stinging nettle trees, the giant trunks interlaced with creeping vines, the climbing of precipices, and the lowering by ropes into deep chasms; but they have always come back discomfited. The road from the coast crosses the ridges far to the south of these forbidding hills.

As the Dividing Range is followed south the distance **between it** and the coast increases, though **it is** generally visible **from the sea.** The Leichardt Ranges, the Denham Range, **the** Expedition Range are all high and densely covered with luxuriant forests. On reaching the border of New South Wales the main ridge sends out a branch called the Macpherson Range, which terminates on the coast in the bold headland of Point Danger.

Entering New South Wales the Dividing Range is at first known by the local name of the NEW ENGLAND RANGE, a ridge varying from 3000 to 5000 feet above sea-level. Its cliffs of granite rise from amidst solemn forests which spread like a leafy ocean on every side. Here gather the waters of foaming torrents which tumble down the steep slopes or over the cliffs in magnificent waterfalls. Two or three branches of the range run out to the coast, and in these there are situated still higher peaks, of which many have not yet been ascended by man. The highest, Mount Seaview, is estimated to exceed 6000 feet in height.

At the end of the New England Range the main ridge turns west and forms the LIVERPOOL RANGE, whose highest peak is 4500 feet high. The table-land now becomes higher, and the ridges upon its summit less distinct. They are known as the BLUE MOUNTAINS, and are famous for their remarkable scenery. The traveller who approaches them in one of those trains that leave Sydney several times a day to cross them, would first observe them as a great wall of rocks and trees, stretching north and south as far as the eye can see, and offering a seemingly impassable barrier, half a mile high, which no one could climb. But the railway has been skilfully engineered, so that by a series of gigantic zigzags, the trains are brought to the top, whence a view is obtained over all the plain, which stretches for 50 miles away to the sea. The summit along which the railway runs is a flat, uninteresting country, sparsely covered with small trees. Yet from any of the stations access may be obtained to numerous gullies where, in the cool and moist air, the most lovely and delicate ferns and mosses grow in incredible profusion. The abrupt edges of the table-land form the most remarkable feature in the scenery of the Blue Mountains. Some of them descend in sheer precipices down to the forests, 1400 feet below, and sweep in long curves from which here and there we see the waterfalls in slender

S

cascades. Immense **gulfs**, now filled with trees in place of water, were once **arms of the** sea, at a remote time, when Australia **was submerged** except this table-land, which formed a long row of narrow islands. The railway, after traversing 50 miles of elevated ground, descends by **still longer** and more remarkable zigzags to the plains of the **interior.** During the whole of this elevated journey the traveller sees on every side the houses of people who come out to live in this cool and bracing climate, away **from** the heat and dust of Sydney.

To the south the Blue Mountains become lower, though still charming in their scenery, till they break up in **a** somewhat confused **mass of** parallel ridges, from which emerges at length the highest range of Australia, known popularly as **the** AUSTRALIAN **ALPS.** Its highest peak is Mount Kosciusko, **so called by the Polish** traveller who **first ascended it, and saw** from its **bald** forehead the vast **valleys in which** the River Murray gathers **its** waters. From that point, **7000 feet above** sea-level, **the country** extends on every hand **like a sea of** sombre-tinted **trees,** rising and falling in vast waves where the forest covers long ranges or dips into valleys. The whole range is wild, not with precipice and jagged peak, but with interminable forests, tangled and difficult to pierce.

These ranges now cross into Victoria, with many peaks **of from** 5000 to 6000 feet in height, the highest being **MOUNT BOGONG,** snow-clad for half the year. The ranges diminish in height as they reach the centre of Victoria, but their scenery improves; in these ranges and their branches occur the deep and shady gullies wherein grow the stately white-gum trees, the tallest in the world, lifting up their smooth white stems from 300 to 400 feet; and here also are stately tree-ferns in endless profusion, rising from 20 to 60 feet from the ground.

Opposite **Port Phillip the** ranges are lost for a little; **the** railway lines going north from Melbourne cross the table-land and climb some 1400 feet, but have no ridge to traverse, **although low** timber-clad hills **are** seen on all sides. So the plateau continues, these hills becoming higher, till they end in rugged ranges called the VICtorian Pyrenees and the Victorian Grampians, with peaks nearly 4000 feet high. But here the table-land comes to an end, and these ranges in part rise boldly out of the broad grassy plains whereon the squatters of Western Victoria pasture millions of sheep.

There are no other mountains of much importance in Australia. Near Adelaide, in South Australia, the Mount Lofty Range and the Flinders Range are green and pretty, with many rounded summits rising to 3000 feet in height; in their fertile valleys the orange and the grape are grown by industrious farmers. Near the borders, between New South Wales and South Australia, there lie the Barrier Ranges, not high, but famous of late years for their silver mines, which have caused a little city called Silverton to grow up in the midst of a broad desert.

The Dividing Range marks off the coast plains of the east of Australia from the interior plains. These are very different from one another in aspect, for the rain-clouds, which mostly float in from the Pacific Ocean, are stopped by the mountains, and shed their waters on the eastern side, making all that strip of country green and woody. But none of the rain reaches the interior, which depends for its moisture mainly on what comes from time to time fitfully and irregularly from the Indian Ocean.

At Sydney the rainfall is five times as great as it is only 100 miles away on the other side of the mountains, and ten times as great as in most parts of the interior. Hence as one travels from Sydney towards the interior one sees from the railway carriage at first plenty of farms, fields, and meadows, with hedges and clumps of trees. On the top of the table-land everything still seems green; but on the other side he descends into a level dusty desert, along which he travels for 400 miles to Bourke, with little sign of population. Yet all this country affords pasture for enormous flocks of sheep; and if the traveller leaves the railway and drives along the dry, monotonous, sandy roads on either hand, he comes upon pleasant homesteads every 10 or 12 miles, where care and industry make fruit trees grow and even gardens smile. When rain does visit these plains it falls very heavily, and soon thereafter, beneath the warm sun, the grass grows with amazing quickness. Then is the merry season of plenty for the sheep, when the grass is high and the dams are full of water. But months may succeed during which no more rain descends, and then the grass disappears almost entirely, and the sheep begin to seek the places where salt-bushes grow in scrubs or thickets, on the leaves of which they subsist until the next showers come. But if rain should be withheld for six or eight months in a hot summer season, the distress from want of food and water becomes terrible. In a recent season 11,000,000 sheep died of thirst upon these pastoral plains.

Drainage-System.—From this inequality of rainfall we may readily infer the main characteristics of the river-systems of Australia. Along the east coast and in the south-east corner where the rainfall is abundant and fairly uniform, the rivers are deep and perennial streams of water. But throughout the rest of Australia one might live for years close to where long rivers are marked upon the map and never see a drop of water in them; till at length a season of excessive rain would arrive, when one might have to flee for his life from the rising river, which would now spread as a broad rushing torrent from one to ten miles in breadth.

Noticing then this great difference in the nature of the rivers, let us consider the two systems separately. Those of the first or permanent system are rarely of any great length. They rise in the Dividing Range, and have but a short course to reach the sea; some of them, however, begin their courses by flowing north or south between the ranges before they turn to the sea, and so make their lengths much greater. Especially is this the case in Queensland, where the Burdekin, Fitzroy, Burnett, and Brisbane rivers are all thus lengthened. The BURDEKIN is in most of its course not more than knee deep, but here and there it spreads out into broad reaches that reflect the rugged ranges on either side, unbroken, save when an alligator lifts his jaws out of the water as he crawls up the sandy shores, or when a flock of pelicans cease their sleepy watch and flutter with awkward wings across the surface. The FITZROY is formed of two streams which, when they have joined their waters, give rise to a placid current navigable for small craft. The BURNETT is a similar stream which, in its lower part, flows through a country rich with maize-fields and sugar-plantations, and past the wharves and mills of the little town of Bundaberg. The BRISBANE is entered by scores of steamers at its low and sandy mouth bound for the busy city of Brisbane, whose streets and suburbs line both sides for many a mile, and whose wooden wharves are noisy with the bustle of loading or unloading cargo.

In New South Wales the CLARENCE RIVER is broad at its mouth, and continues as a deep and smooth stream to the town of Grafton, where it is still half a mile wide. It is diversified with many wooded islets; on its banks the sugar-cane grows close to the water's edge, while its rich flats are well covered with tall fields of maize. The MACLEAY is a similar stream, and so in some respects is the HUNTER also. This latter river, rising in the loneliest parts of the Liverpool Ranges, flows down into a region of prosperous farms and cattle-stations, thence to the district of the coal mines, from which coal is brought down to Newcastle to be loaded on board of numerous steamers at the mouth of the river.

Farther south the HAWKESBURY, famous for its scenery, gathers its waters by many branches from the deep and silent valleys of the Blue Mountains, and unites them on the plains into a noble current, which glides past farms and through meadow slopes, flowing northward till near the inlet of Broken Bay, where it turns eastward, and its banks become high and precipitous. Here stands the Hawkesbury Bridge (fig. 31), the finest railway bridge in Australia.

The SHOALHAVEN tumbles down from the mountains and runs north for 100 miles in a deep chasm which it has cut for itself in the table-land. Then turning east, it throws itself over many rocks and descends into a sandy lagoon-like mouth to mingle with the sea. The SNOWY RIVER rises near Mount Kosciusko in New South Wales, and flows southward into Victoria through country almost uninhabited; a wild jumble of ranges covered with dense forests of gum-trees tenanted by the kangaroo, the wallaby, and the gentle little animal called the "native bear." It is a rapid stream of crystal water which rushes through interesting scenery, but with too rapid a flow for navigation.

Among the rivers of Victoria the MITCHELL, MACALLISTER, and LATROBE flow through well-occupied lands, descending from the mountains to water plains which are mainly devoted to the fattening of cattle. The YARRA rises in a romantic forest of beech-trees at a height of nearly 4000 feet, and then rushes beneath forests of

FIG. 31.—BRIDGE OVER THE HAWKESBURY RIVER, 3000 FEET LONG.

gigantic gum-trees, and round the brown stems of numberless fern-trees, till it reaches the level land, where it flows through grassy meadows dotted with sheep and cattle, and under slopes planted with formal rows of vineyards. Then the river, still clear and pellucid, enters the suburbs of Melbourne, through which it winds in a course of 20 miles, though in a straight line the distance traversed is not more than 10 miles. The GLENELG rises in the Victorian Grampians and flows through grassy lands whereon are pastured millions of merino sheep, the owners of which live in spacious houses that stand on every pleasant slope. The limestone banks of this stream have been carved in places into fantastic caves, and in its silent reaches the platypus still **dives to** reach the entrance to its **underground home.**

These are all **short** rivers, their courses being **less than 500 miles in length.** The long rivers of Australia **take** their rise on the other side of the Dividing Ranges. Though the greater part of the rainfall **occurs** on the eastern side, yet enough rain falls to the west **to form the sources** of many **fine** rivers which all start off **westward into the interior.** But their progress **in that direction shows in a striking** manner the climatic differences between **the two sides of** the table-land. For instance in Queensland many of **these** streams join together to form the BARCOO **and the** THOMSON. But as these rivers advance into the **hot and level plains,** their currents become sluggish and **their water partly sinks into** the open soil, and partly is dried up **by the heat of the** sun. Hence when they unite to form COOPER'S CREEK their volume is greatly shrunk. This creek is for eleven months in the year only a long trench with grassy banks in which the water lies apparently as still as in a canal, although it is really moving at the rate of perhaps a mile or so in a **day into** LAKE EYRE, where it spreads out **into a great shallow expanse and is evaporated.** In the early summer this sheet of water is almost entirely dried up, and then appears as a wide **plain of mud** encrusted with salt. But in the later summer, when the tropical rains have fallen in Northern Queensland, Cooper's Creek spreads out into a vast stream 6 or 8 miles wide, rushing with impetuous flow into Lake Eyre, which then forms an expanse of water about the size of Wales. But this time of inundation **is soon over.** After flowing for **a month or so the river steadily shrinks and the lake continues for months to dry up until it wholly disappears.**

An immense number of mountain streams descend from the western side of the Dividing Range in Southern Queensland and **in the north of New South Wales** to form the rivers called the Warrego, Condamine, Gwydir, Nammoi, Castlereagh, Macquarie, and Bogan. But these rivers shrink steadily as they advance into the plains, and **for** the larger part of the year their lower courses are **absolutely dry,** though water may always be found in the centre of their beds by digging. But after heavy rains they flow with great speed and in large volume, carrying the stunted trees of the plains before them, until they unite to form the long river called the DARLING. This is a stream of strange vicissitudes. At the moment when this description is being written it is 10 miles broad and about 40 feet deep in the centre. This great body of water is rushing onward, too impetuous for navigation; but in a month or two it will have diminished to less than a mile wide, and will flow in a placid current 20 feet deep. Then will come the time for the river-steamers and barges to carry their cargoes of wool down to the southern seaports. But the river will still continue to fall until its current will cease to be perceptible. Then the water will fail altogether except in deeper places, where water-holes will remain, the last resource of the millions of sheep that nibble the grass or the salt bush of these mighty plains. Perhaps when next February comes at the close of the Australian summer, enough rain will fall to set the river flowing again. Perhaps this may not happen for two or three years, should seasons of drought occur.

The farther south we go the less intermittent do we find the streams. Thus the Lachlan, which gathers up the streamlets from the west side of the Blue Mountains, is not often dried up, though sometimes shrunk till it has scarcely any flow in it. But the MURRUMBIDGEE is a permanent stream, always with a good current, and generally rolling and eddying onward with a speed which frightens any but a very capable swimmer. Its headwaters flowing down great mountain valleys unite into the main stream, which is like a wide mountain torrent, its transparent and very cold water rippling over a pebbly bed. Out in the plains it glides as a dark and turbulent stream through grassy flats and clumps of gum-trees and cypress, past flocks of sheep and at long intervals the handsome dwellings of the squatters, receiving on its way the tributary waters of the Lachlan.

Farther south lies what must be regarded as the main river of Australia, the MURRAY, which along the greater part of its course divides the colonies of New South Wales and Victoria. Its waters, cold, clear, and bright, spring from the mountains round Mount Kosciusko, but soon losing their mountain vivacity settle down into a placid and commonplace river, dark in its surface, deep and mysterious-looking, with many a "snag," as the submerged trees are called that have been uprooted and borne down by bygone floods, to lie and ruffle the current, and to throw their arms up in sharp points, so dangerous to navigation.

The stream gliding on, over-arched by gum-trees and bright with wattle-trees (acacias) that look like dancing gold in the summer, widens out into a current 200 feet in breadth, and glides beneath the long railway bridge at Albury. From the southern side it receives the waters of perennial streams like itself, dark currents that flow deep in grassy banks, the Ovens, the Goulburn, the Campaspe, and the Loddon. It now becomes a wide river, which, having been from this point downwards cleared of "snags," bears many a river steamer with its attendant wool barges. From the north it receives the Murrumbidgee, and also the Darling when that stream happens to be flowing. Farther down it winds in a deep river valley, between cliffs which sometimes display great beds of oyster-shells that tell how different were the conditions in long past ages. In its lower part the river becomes a slow and sleepy current, broad but monotonous, at the bottom of a hot valley, and with little that is picturesque in its surroundings. At length it opens out into a broad lagoon called Lake Alexandrina, after our Queen, who when a princess was called Alexandrina-Victoria; a branch of this lake is called Lake Albert. They are both shallow, but somewhat pretty. On the margin of the water grow tall reeds, wherein wild ducks find plenty of food to keep them diving in busy flocks; while innumerable black swans dot the waters with their stately forms, contrasting well with the snow-white pelicans, which, in smaller flocks, here and there watch with sleepy-looking but really cunning eyes for the fish in the clear waters beneath them. Unfortunately the entrance from these lakes into the sea is blocked by a sand-bar, over which the waters flow in a shallow current, and as this bar is beaten by the breakers from the ocean, vessels cannot cross it; while the art of man has hitherto been powerless to keep a channel open through it. Hence goods have to be landed at Port Elliot and carried by railway over to the river steamers on the lake.

No other rivers traverse the south coast of Australia; along the west coast there are many, though none that are navigable. The Blackwood, the Swan river, the Murchison, the Gascoyne, and the Fortescue, are all streams of very variable volume, sometimes rushing torrents, sometimes so absolutely dry that travellers camped at the bottom of their beds have been afraid of perishing for want of water. Farther north, where more constant rains blow in from the Indian Ocean, the Victoria river, the Roper, the Albert, the Flinders, and the Mitchell are considerably more constant.

The LAKES of Australia are as uncertain as some of these rivers. Lake Eyre, Lake Torrens, Lake Gairdner, are marked as great lakes in the map of South Australia, but to see them we must visit the country a week or two after heavy rains have been falling on the Dividing Ranges, then, though shallow, they are indeed of great extent; at other times they are only immense areas of mud, baked and cracked and crusted with glittering salt.

Islands.—Close to the shores of Australia lie numerous small islands, none of them of great importance. KANGAROO ISLAND, already referred to, about 85 miles long and 30 broad, has not more than 400 inhabitants. Its hilly interior is densely wooded with small trees. The reason of its scanty population is doubtless to be found in the general poorness of its soil. In Bass Strait KING ISLAND blocks the entrance at one end, and FURNEAUX ISLAND at the other. They are both islands of somewhat miserable aspect, with high and forbidding shores, formerly the scene of many a shipwreck. Lighthouses have now made these rocky shores much less dangerous. King's Island is scarcely inhabited; but there are 500 or 600 persons living on Furneaux Island and the smaller islands round it. Many of these are half-castes, the children of seamen who in olden days deserted from their ships, and landed here to catch seals, when they carried off as wives black women from the shores of Tasmania. The people of Furneaux Island gain a living by sealing and catching a small kind of penguin, called mutton birds, which, when preserved, find a certain amount of sale on the mainland.

Off the coast of Queensland lie STRADBROKE, MORETON, and GREAT SANDY ISLANDS, all of them wide wastes of sandy soil, but here and there covered with grass, so that each island is occupied as a "sheep-run," and supports a small flock. The western shores of these islands are mostly lined with mangrove swamps; the eastern are fringed with sand-hills. The islands that line the coast farther north are more inviting, for they have rich soil, but they are small.

In the Gulf of Carpentaria the WELLESLEY ISLANDS and GROOTE EYLANDT are, for the most part, coral reefs, over which the sea has washed sand enough to raise them above the level of the waves. They are generally bare, but the north-west corner of Groote Eylandt presents higher ground clothed with small gum-trees. At the very north of Australia stand the two fine islands called MELVILLE ISLAND and BATHURST ISLAND. Their soil is good, and their regular heavy rains, added to the tropical heat which there prevails, have clothed them with a jungle of vegetation. The muddy shores are densely covered with mangrove-trees, through which it is generally impossible to find a passage. Inside this coast-belt of swamp the scenery is characteristically tropical—palms and gaudy tropical plants, with a profusion of gay creepers. There are no white men on the island, the population consisting of black and decidedly ferocious tribes.

The western side of Shark Bay, on the coast of Western Australia, is formed by a long low strip of sand called DIRK HARTOG ISLAND. Towards the Indian Ocean it presents a series of bold and jagged rocks, but everywhere else shows nothing but sand and a dry-looking species of grass.

But the most important island dependent on Australia is Tasmania, inhabited by 150,000 people. It is divided from the south of Australia by Bass Strait, a passage nearly 150 miles wide. The traveller who joined one of the excursion trips which start from time to time from Melbourne to sail round this pretty island, would skirt on the west coast a high and rocky shore. Cape Grim, a black headland, where the great rollers keep up an unending din, forms the north-western promontory of the island, succeeded southwards by great cliffs with lofty mountains behind them. Macquarie Harbour, a lonely and beautiful land-locked sheet of water, was famous in convict times as the place to which the worst prisoners were sent. After another 100 miles of wild precipitous coast the land turns eastward at South-West Cape and South Cape, the most southerly point of the island. Here the wind, always fresh, often enough blows in fierce hurricanes from the icy seas of the south. But to the eastward the coast is more sheltered. It is indented by Storm Bay, at the head of which the busy port of Hobart has been built at the foot of Mount Wellington.

Cape Pillar takes its name from the basalt of which it is formed, and which rises in black columns of varied lengths. The east coast presents a succession of pretty views—rocks, sandy bays, and lagoons covered with innumerable flocks of black swans, as far as Cape Portland in the north-east corner.

The north coast of Tasmania is comparatively tame. It has one important inlet called Port Dalrymple, a beautiful winding arm which branches among the wooded hills. A considerable amount of shipping is here to be seen, for the town of Launceston lies at the head of the inlet.

Tasmania is a mountainous island. The western half is entirely occupied by high ranges and narrow valleys, covered with unbroken forests, which, till recently, were left to the kangaroo and parrot; for all the black men have been exterminated, and until of late years there was no inducement for white men to dwell in that wild and unpromising country. But now when rich mines of tin and of gold are being discovered all over the district, the great expanse of forest is being cleared; and far in the heart of the ranges the solitudes are now marked by tall chimneys and staging and the cottages of the mining-labourers.

The mountains in the western half of Tasmania do not form definite ranges, but rise in confused swellings, the greatest altitude being about 5000 feet. The eastern half of Tasmania, though more level, consists only in part of plains, the most level part of the island being toward the centre. In the north-east corner the mountains predominate, and one singularly picturesque range, which rises 5000 feet high in bold columnar precipices, is called **Ben Lomond** by the settlers in affectionate remembrance of their Scottish homes. Along the east coast there are many lower ranges with scenery of great beauty.

Among the mountains lie the Great Lake, Lake Sorrell, Lake Echo, and Lake St. Clair. Their beaches of snow-white pebbles fringe broad mirrors of perfectly clear and limpid water, not so deep as to conceal the pebbly bed. Their surface is dotted with islets over-grown with cedar-trees; while from their shores rise softly-swelling hills covered with the unbroken foliage of undulating forests. From these lakes and from the mountain springs, many perennial streams descend to the sea. The largest river, the DERWENT, gathers its tributaries from all the lakes (though the main stream issues from Lake St. Clair), and after hurrying as a bright and rapid current for nearly 100 miles, reaches New Norfolk. It then becomes deep and placid, flowing between orchards and hop-plantations into a winding estuary fringed with hills, which make the panoramas here obtainable famous throughout Australia for their beauty. The SOUTH ESK rises near the east coast, but a range of mountains intervening between it and the sea deflects it inland, and enables it to water many a fertile meadow on its way to Port Dalrymple in the north.

Climate.—In no part of Australia is it ever disagreeably cold. Snow never falls on any part of the lowlands, although an occasional snow-shower occurs on the table-lands, where they are over 2000 feet high; and in the south snow regularly falls every winter on table-lands from 3000 to 5000 feet in height, where, in spite of the fine, clear, warm days which prevail even in winter, it lies on the shady side of the mountain-slopes for a couple of months or so.

But in every part of Australia it is occasionally disagreeably warm in the summer; though, as a rule, the dryness of the air, and the absence of any malarial vapours such as great heat develops where there is an excessive tropical vegetation, combine to make the summer healthy and as a rule pleasant. Most visitors regard the climate of Australia as the pleasantest to be found in all the world, except in small and favoured localities. But there are some who never forgive Australia for its hot **winds. These** blow in the summer time from the interior, and are so dry that they seem to absorb all the moisture in one's body; yet although giving rise to discomfort, they do no **harm; on the contrary** they are thought to dry up and **destroy various diseases.** They are often loaded with dust, which increases their powers of annoyance. But after all they **do not last** long. As is the case in **all dry climates,** that of Australia is liable to extreme variations. On the central plains, especially after a day of excessive heat, the night may be so cold that one has to make use of several blankets to keep warm in bed. But in any part of Australia, the greater part of the year consists of fine bright **days,** with a broad sky of unbroken blue, and a pleasant **breeze** blowing, followed by nights of cool and agreeable **freshness,** with stars twinkling in indescribable splendour **overhead,** in a perfectly cloudless sky. The average temperature of Sydney is 62°, of Melbourne **57°,** of Adelaide 64°.

Plants and Animals.—Throughout the whole of Australia the prevailing trees are EUCALYPTS, known generally as *gum-trees* on account of the gum which they secrete, and which may be seen standing like big translucent beads on their trunks and branches. There are "red gums," yielding a hard timber **that** makes excellent sleepers for railways; "blue gums," marked by a bluish-green foliage, and **giving** forth a pleasant odour from an **oil** which they **possess; and** "white gums," **whose stems,** the tallest in the **world, rise clear, smooth, and** white like marble pillars.

Next in frequency are ACACIAS of many sorts, the most
common being the wattle-trees, dear to every Australian
on account of the profusion of blossoms they bear in the
spring-time. Those with yellow blossoms, called "golden
wattles," line the banks of many of the rivers. In early
spring the whole country is scented with their fragrance.
A peculiar class of trees, called by the scientific name of
CASUARINA, is popularly known as oaks, "swamp oaks,"
"forest oaks," "she oaks," and so forth, although the trees
are not the least like oaks. They are melancholy-looking
trees, with no proper leaves, but only green rods, like
those of a pine-tree except that they are much longer and
hang like the branches of a weeping-willow. In the
northern parts of the east coast, fine cedars grow upon the
mountain ranges, and the cutting of their timber for
furniture-making forms a valuable trade. One district
near Brisbane yields the BUNYA-BUNYA, a handsome but
peculiar pine-tree, producing a kind of fruit much
appreciated by the natives. A common plant throughout
Australia is the BANKSIA, so called after Sir Joseph Banks,
the botanist who accompanied Captain Cook. It is called
the "honeysuckle" by the people of Australia, though it
has no resemblance to an English honeysuckle. Many of
the Banksias grow into stately trees of the size and somewhat of the shape of a horse-chestnut. In Queensland the
thickest forests are rendered gay by ORCHIDS which grow
suspended to the trunks and branches of trees. In the
south, the forests are enlivened by hollows and valleys
filled with the lovely TREE-FERN, which often reaches 30
or 40 feet in height, and spreads its immense fronds of
wavy green in a circle nearly 20 feet across.

But the most useful plants of Australia are all such as
have been brought from abroad. Vast quantities of wheat
and oats are now grown; fine plantations of sugar are
cultivated in the north, and hops in the south. Scarcely
any fruit found useful in any part of the world is not
grown, and does not thrive in Australia. The orangeries
and vineyards are especially notable.

Australia is distinguished by the peculiar character of
its native animals. Its quadrupeds are almost all *mar-*

supial, that is, the females are possessed of bags in front in which the **newly-born little** ones are carried by the mother. Her teats **are inside of the** bag, and the small creatures attach **their** mouths to them, and cling to them for a **month or** so, sucking the milk, and growing big, till they **are old** enough to leave the pouch. No animals of this kind are now found anywhere else in the world, except in parts of North America where the opossum abounds. Australia has eight different kinds of animals **of this class.** The KANGAROO and the WALLABY are much alike, except that the latter is considerably the smaller. They are **still** numerous,—so much so in some parts as to be troublesome. **But** the settlers slaughter them in great quantities, for they consume grass required for sheep. The kangaroo has become **scarce** in the south, but exists in abundance **in the middle and the** north wherever water and grass are plentiful. **Then there** are the Australian OPOSSUMS, **pretty creatures a little larger than** squirrels, but much more strikingly marked and coloured; and the BANDICOOTS, animals of the size of a rat, and, like it, lying concealed in holes or crevices or burrows during the day and coming out for food at night. In the south there is the KOALA, called by the settlers the "native bear," from its resemblance to a baby bear of a foot or eighteen inches in length. It is a quiet innocent creature, crawling about on the gum-tree branches and eating the **tenderest** leaves. The **WOMBAT,** found only in the far south, looks like a roll of wool about two feet long, from one end of which there projects a snout, and beneath which one can, by looking, detect the big claws of four feet. It makes its burrows beneath the surface roots of the **gum-trees, and** when evening has fallen emerges to feed on **softer roots which it** digs up in the forests.

All these animals use only vegetable matter for their **food. But** there are **three** sorts of marsupials which are carnivorous. The "Native Cats" are **not** true cats, though they resemble them in look and habits, for they sleep **by** day among the trees and descend **at** night to kill the settlers' chickens. They are smaller than an ordinary domestic cat, but have the same sort of fur, marked in

a similar way, though as a rule more prettily. Their
noses are pointed. These animals are found all over
Australia. The "Tasmanian Tiger" is of the size of a
shepherd's dog, a gaunt yellow creature, with black stripes
round the upper part of its body, and with an ugly snout.
Found nowhere but in Tasmania, and never numerous even
there, it is now slowly disappearing. The "Tasmanian
Devil" is an ugly-looking, misshapen, black creature, not
often met with in Tasmania, in which place alone it is
discovered. It is a stupid animal, wanders into houses in
its simplicity, and allows itself to be caught or knocked on
the head without difficulty.

Two very strange animals, quite peculiar to Australia,
are the PLATYPUS and the ECHIDNA. The former is
covered with fur like an otter, and has four webbed feet,
like those of a duck, and a black duck-like bill. It makes
a burrow in a river-bank, but with an opening below the
level of the water. It swims and dives in quiet shady
river-bends, and disappears on hearing the least noise.
The echidna is an animal about a foot or eighteen inches
long, covered with spines like a hedgehog. It lives chiefly
upon ants. With its bill, which is like a duck's but
narrower, it burrows into an ants' hill, and then with its
long whip-like sticky tongue draws the ants into its mouth
by the hundred. It passes a lazy existence for a while
after it finds a new ant-hill, lying rolling in the sand and
warming itself in the blazing sun. The only quadruped
native to Australia that is like anything found elsewhere
is the DINGO, a species of dog, generally of a light tawny
colour, but nearly white underneath. It is rather a pretty
animal, of about the size of a pointer, but it is much dis-
liked by the settlers, whose lambs it worries.

In regard to its birds, Australia is not so peculiar. The
EMU, a large running bird, with no wings, corresponds to
the ostrich of Africa and to the rhea of South America.
Its big bare legs, small head, wild eyes, and ragged dirty-
looking feathers give it rather a ludicrous aspect, and its
portentous powers of swallowing, from a pound of wire nails
to a gold watch, make it an awkward domestic pet. It is
now only met with in the unsettled districts of Australia.

T

The commonest birds of an Australian landscape are the COCKATOOS, which in great crowds form noisy colonies in thickets and on gum-trees. Those with white bodies and sulphur or rose coloured crests are the most usual. PARRAKEETS of astonishingly gay colours flit across the path as one traverses the bush. In the morning, everywhere throughout Australia, the ear is greeted with the mellow notes of the Australian magpie, which is extremely numerous. Hawks and sea-eagles are common enough and of many varieties. Owls are also numerous, the Mopoke's note being a familiar sound in the midnight darkness of the forest. Black Swans still exist in astounding numbers on lakes and quiet lagoons. Pelicans patiently fill their big bags with fish on the margin both of fresh and of sea water.

The beautiful Lyre-birds, of which the males have a most exquisitely-shaped tail, are shy creatures only found in the extreme south of Australia, and not to be seen save in the loneliest places. The Brush-turkeys, which are not really turkeys but birds of that size, build big mounds of decaying vegetable matter, lay their eggs on the top, cover them over with leaves, and leave the whole to rot, when the heat of the sun above and of the fermentation below, hatches the eggs and the young creep out to forage for themselves without ever knowing their parents.

Australia is well provided with smaller birds, mostly devoid of song, though many are brilliant in plumage. The most commonly noted is that wise-looking, big-headed bird called the Giant King-Fisher. It is slightly bigger than a starling, sits on the gum-trees and utters a note, so like a long and hearty laugh, that, noticing its absurdly solemn appearance immediately after, the settlers have called it the "Laughing Jack-ass."

In regard to reptiles, Australia is well supplied. Turtles are found in the seas to the north, and small ones frequent the streams and ponds of the warmer parts. Lizards abound of all sizes up to the IGUANA of four feet long, and the ALLIGATOR in Queensland, which is as much as twelve feet in length and is said to be occasionally more than twenty feet. There are plenty of Frogs, one of them of a brilliant emerald-green colour, living on the branches of trees, and therefore called the tree-frog.

Nearly sixty species of SNAKES inhabit Australia, and of these more than half are venomous. There are always twenty or thirty deaths every year in Australia from their bites, but these animals never meddle with people who do not meddle with them. They will always turn and glide rapidly away when they see a human being. But it is of course dangerous to tread upon one that may be lying in your path asleep, or to put your hand into holes in old trees, or into rabbit-burrows as Australian boys too often do.

But, after all, the most important animals are those which the white men have imported. Australia now has over a hundred and twenty million sheep, and immense numbers of cattle and horses; but a donkey is a great rarity. There are plenty of pigs and goats, as well as poultry of all kinds. Rabbits have become an absolute plague, and swarm in countless millions in some parts. Hares are abundant in the south. Deer are multiplying in some districts. Camels are increasing in the interior. Ostrich farms exist in South Australia. Buffaloes are numerous round Clarence Strait. Indeed there are very few of the animals useful to man which have not been introduced by the settlers into Australia.

Subdivisions and **Government.**—Australia is divided into five countries which are called colonies, because their inhabitants are colonists or the children of colonists who went out from England, Scotland, and Ireland in bygone years to make their homes in unsettled lands. These colonies are called New South Wales, Victoria, Queensland, South Australia, and West Australia, while the island of Tasmania forms a sixth colony of the Australian group. When these countries were first settled, the people formed what are known as "Crown colonies," ruled directly from the Government in London; the Governor sent out to preside in each being simply a British official bound only to carry out instructions sent to him from London. But as the people grew more numerous and prosperous and able to manage their own affairs, the British Government entered on a generous policy of which the world had previously had no experience in dealing with dependencies. Each of the colonies was promoted to the dignity of a self-governing community, with power to make its own laws and to manage its own affairs, subject only to the necessary restriction, that it should not pass laws or enter upon negotiations that would seriously embarrass or injure other portions of the British Empire.

Each colony is now governed by a Parliament consisting of an Upper and a Lower House, the latter being elected by the whole body of men above 21 years of age, and as an almost necessary consequence exercising the chief power in managing the affairs of the colony. In Victoria, South Australia, and Tasmania the Upper Houses are elected by a portion of the people, those who own at least a little property or who are householders. In New South Wales and Queensland the Upper Houses are nominated by the Governor, who is a gentleman sent out by the Queen's Government to represent Her Majesty in the colony. At present the question of a general confederation of the Australian colonies is under consideration.

One of the most uniform features throughout Australia is the prosperity of the people. A barefooted child is hardly ever to be seen on the streets, and no one is badly dressed except an occasional idler of tipsy habits. Villages, which are always called "townships," spring up suddenly round a railway station or beside some country inn; the State School soon appears wherever twelve or fifteen children can be gathered. Then comes a little church, and ere long another; then there is the local "School of Arts," or "Mechanics' Institute," or "Free Library," or whatever name the people choose for it. If the village is well situated it soon increases to two or three thousand people and will then boast several churches, half a dozen hotels, two or three schools, a Library, Court-house, Town-hall, Hospital, probably a Grammar School, a Newspaper, and before long a Gaswork, probably also Waterworks; and within ten years from the time when the first person settled on the site there may be a city in miniature with its business street occupied by two or three dozen good shops, and with Public Gardens, Annual Races, Annual Gathering for sports, Fire Brigade, and other institutions of the old world. All the eastern parts of Australia to a distance of from three hundred to five hundred miles back from the Pacific Ocean, are dotted over with progressive "townships" of this class, mostly all moving on to the dignity of "Boroughs," and with the proud hope of eventually being gazetted as "cities," which dignity a borough reaches when its annual revenue amounts to the sum of £26,000 per annum.

NEW SOUTH WALES

New South Wales is the senior colony and the only one which is a century old. Its great area of 309,000 square miles is inhabited by only 1,100,000 people, an average of less than four persons to the square mile; and of these by far the largest portion inhabit the plains between the mountains and the sea.

Upon the great inland plains there are forty millions of sheep, two millions of cattle, and nearly half a million of horses. But a comparatively small population is able to attend to these, and to send the wool, beef, and mutton to the seaports. On the table-land a good deal of wheat is grown, and fine cattle can be fattened there. On the coast plain, few sheep are to be seen; south of it, people keep cows, and make good butter and cheese; farther north they grow fruit, and export large quantities of oranges. In the most northern parts, maize, sugar, and bananas are cultivated. At Newcastle almost the whole population for 50 miles round is employed in raising and exporting coal.

Sydney, the capital of New South Wales, renowned for its charming situation, extends for 10 miles along the south side of Port Jackson, with little bays either running up into the centre of the city and lined with wharves, or surrounded by the gardens and houses of the suburbs. On the north shore of Port Jackson several large suburbs are

FIG. 32.—PITT STREET, SYDNEY.

divided from the city by a mile or two of green and sparkling salt water, over which small steamboats are continually plying. The harbour presents at night a fairy-like scene, when hundreds of these steamers with their red, white, blue, and green lights flit to and fro, and send long lines of quivering vibrations across the watery surface. Sydney is a city of rather narrow and generally crooked, but wonderfully busy streets. Many of the public buildings, such as the Post Office, Town Hall, Cathedral, University, Public Offices, Club Houses, and Banks, are handsome structures. The suburbs stretch away 6 miles to the Ocean Beach on one side, and 10 miles to Botany Bay on the other, a large extent of ground being occupied by the cottages of the working folks, who mostly possess their own dwellings. Sydney has now about 400,000 inhabitants, and it increases with great rapidity. It has suburbs which are now quite as large as it was itself thirty years ago.

Next in size is NEWCASTLE at the mouth of the Hunter river. A rocky islet standing off the shore has been connected with the mainland by a long breakwater so as partly to enclose the mouth of the river. This forms a spacious harbour in which a large fleet of steamers is always lying. The coal-fields of the neighbourhood furnish the supplies of coal which are here exported. The vessels come close into the wharves, where great cranes seize a whole truck loaded with coal, swing it into the air, let it down into the hold of the vessel, empty it there, and swing it up again and replace it on the railway. This operation, carried on simultaneously at a score of places, makes a great din, and gives rise to much black dust of coal. From the wharves steep streets ascend the side of a rocky hill; but one street that winds round the side of this hill is broad and busy, and dignified with some handsome buildings as befits the chief thoroughfare of a city of 20,000 inhabitants. All round Newcastle there lie at distances of from 2 to 15 miles, villages where from 500 to 2000 people have gathered round the large collieries, and the whole district is given over principally to coal-getting and coal-carrying.

Up the Hunter river, amidst prettier scenery, stand the

towns of MORPETH and MAITLAND. The latter is built in two separate portions. The Government selected for its site long ago a fine hill a mile or two away from the river, high enough to be safe from inundation, but the people chose to settle down on the river-banks and to take their chance of floods. Hence East Maitland stands upon the hill with pretty buildings and 2000 inhabitants, while West Maitland lies down on the flats with nearly 8000 inhabitants. This settlement owes its importance to the richness of the farms all along the river valley. On a market morning, the waggons rolling in from every side with stacks of gigantic melons, piles of grapes, black or white, with cases of oranges in great loads, with maize and potatoes, and immense mounds of lucerne made into fragrant hay, furnish striking proof how rich must be the soil and how genial the sun of this favoured district.

Farther north, on the Clarence river, lies the busy town of GRAFTON. Though it is 45 miles from the sea, yet the river is there more than half a mile wide, and large steamers sail up to the town and lie along its wharves, where they are loaded with maize, bananas, and other semi-tropical productions, but principally with sugar; for all the moist steaming flats along the river are well adapted to the sugar-cane, waving crops of which may be seen on every hand. The sugar is manufactured on the spot, and the smoky chimneys show from a distance the position of the sugar mills and refineries of which no less than 60 stand in the town and its neighbourhood.

The remaining important towns of New South Wales lie inland. PARAMATTA, 14 miles from Sydney, at the extreme end of Port Jackson, is now almost a suburb of the great city, the houses stretching nearly continuously from one to the other. Its inhabitants number about 12,000, and it has a prosperous appearance, but, being next to Sydney, the oldest town in Australia, its aspect differs a good deal from that of younger places; for it contains many buildings, walls, and avenues, that carry the mind back a hundred years to the foundation of the colony. A number of thriving towns are situated on the table-land. Chief of these is GOULBURN, south-west of

Sydney, with 8000 inhabitants, and possessing a dozen
churches, many schools, convents, and public buildings,
also factories, tanneries, mills, and three newspapers.
It is the busy centre of a prosperous farming district.
Farther north on the table-land stands BATHURST, a
pretty town of about 8000 inhabitants. Its spires, and
the dome of its fine suite of public buildings, rise from
amid abundance of trees, which give it a verdant aspect.
The surrounding country is partly used for pasturing sheep
and partly for farming. Hence bullock-drays, loaded with
wool or with sacks of corn, may be seen wending their way
from all sides, during the season, to the railway station in
the town, there to be placed in trucks and sent off to
Sydney over the mountains.

Out on the plains many thriving towns have been built.
WAGGA-WAGGA, with 4000 inhabitants, lies on the Murrumbidgee, which is here crossed by an enormous bridge
about 2 miles long. The river itself, only a furlong in
width in its usual condition, becomes a broad and raging
torrent in flood times, and its whole valley has to be
bridged. The town has one fine street, with lesser
thoroughfares branching to right and left. Nearly
2,000,000 sheep are grazed in the neighbourhood; large
flocks of them may be constantly seen passing out
and in, attended by men on horseback and their active
sheep dogs. A long way to the west, in the midst of
absolutely level plains, lies DENILIQUIN, which also has a
couple of million sheep in its neighbourhood to keep it
thriving. Here also shepherds, stockmen, and boundary
riders may be seen dashing up and down the streets,
with big boots and spurs, tight breeches, loose shirts, and
broad straw hats. Deniliquin has a number of good
buildings, and like all towns in Australia has its public
park, laid out with great care and at lavish expense. Still
farther out upon the plains to the north stands HAY, on
the banks of the Murrumbidgee, with a population of
3000 people almost all supplied with occupation by the
great flocks of sheep which browse upon the grass or
nibble the salt-bush over the vast extent of the surrounding plains. With wide streets, neat buildings, and plenty

of shady trees, it makes an attractive township. Away in
the plains to the north, the town of BOURKE with 4000
inhabitants stands on the river Darling. Three millions
of sheep are scattered over its district, the wool from
which is either shipped down the Darling when in flood,
or more generally is sent by railway to Sydney. Yet
farther out into the plains near the western edge of
the colony lies SILVERTON, a place of uncertain size,

FIG. 33.—BARK HUT IN AUSTRALIA, WITH ABORIGINALS.

with a population of nearly 20,000, which has sprung
up of late years round the silver mines of the Barrier
Ranges. Like similar mining settlements elsewhere it
has the appearance of having been run up in a hurry and
in a cheap style in the midst of a dreary waterless plain.
But on the neighbouring hills the mines are productive,
so that Silverton promises to become rich and permanent.

In a charming district to the south, close to the
boundary of Victoria, lies ALBURY, a pleasant town of
5000 inhabitants. The fine buildings in its handsome

streets look bright beneath the glow of the Australian
sky. All the surrounding district being well adapted for
vine-growing, the hill slopes have generally been planted
with vineyards.

VICTORIA

The colony of Victoria, though only one quarter of the
size of New South Wales, yet equals it in population, wealth,
and industry. The explanation of this remarkable activity
is to be found in the fact that its central part, among the
hills on the table-land, was thirty years ago the richest gold-
field in the world, and attracted crowds of energetic men
from all countries. The supply of gold, however, began to
fail, and the settlers betook themselves to other pursuits.
Finding the soil and climate exceptionally good, they
settled down to make a successful and prosperous community. The largest city is Melbourne, with about
480,000 inhabitants, but it covers five or six times as
much ground as a city of that population would occupy in
Europe, for its streets are so wide, its parks so abundant,
its houses so universally provided with gardens, that the
city extends to no less than 14 miles in length by about
10 in width. What is called the city proper, however, is
a compact mass, a mile long by three-quarters of a mile
wide, formed of straight streets that cut each other at right
angles. Long avenues of handsome buildings, many of
them rising to six, eight, ten, or even twelve stories, are
here and there interrupted by mean and paltry houses of
one or two stories which, as remnants of the first erections,
show how young the city is, and how rapid has been its
growth. It is less than sixty years since the blacks were
holding their *corrobborees* where the busiest streets now run,
and fifty years ago the site of the thoroughfare called Elizabeth Street, now thronged with carriages, cabs, vans, and
drays, and noisy with the bells of countless tramcars drawn
by invisible cables underground, was a streamlet overhung
with golden blossomed wattle-trees from which, at the first
stroke of man's hatchet, crowds of cockatoos rose screeching
into the air. The Post Office, and Town Hall, the Law

Courts, with their great dome lifted high above the smoke of the city; the Houses of Parliament, with their long rows of shining white pillars; and the Public Library, with its large collection of books and pictures, of statues and antiquities, afford striking evidence of the progress of the colony. Lines of tramway pass up and down the city in all directions, and into about twenty suburbs, four of which are on the shores of Port Phillip, two of them being the seaports of the city, while the other two consist of marine villas. Some of the suburbs are themselves cities of 40,000 inhabitants, and each of the twenty has its own Town Hall and Public Gardens, and manages its own affairs. Melbourne is the centre of trade for all Victoria, and the chief pleasure city of the Continent. Its five theatres and numerous concert-rooms and halls of entertainment attract large audiences every evening, and keep its streets thronged till past midnight.

The second city of Victoria is BALLARAT, distant 70 miles from Melbourne. It first sprang into existence as a camp of gold diggers on the banks of a small stream, but it is now a solid and substantial place of 40,000 inhabitants. Gold-mining is still largely followed. A short walk from the heart of the city will bring the visitor within sight of the "poppet-heads" or stagings of many a gold-mine. The miners descend in deep and narrow shafts a quarter of a mile into the earth, there to pick out the gold-bearing earth and quartz, and bring it up to have the gold taken out of it in these buildings near the top. But Ballarat has now much more business as the centre of an agricultural district; and it is chiefly the farmers who support the handsome banks and bustling shops. There are manufactures also in the city, among the most important of which are the great locomotive works. BENDIGO (a name adopted by popular vote in 1891 instead of SANDHURST) is of similar size. It also took its origin in gold-mining, and is still mainly a gold-producing place. The "poppet-heads," in a row, extending 7 or 8 miles, mark the line which the gold-bearing reefs follow underground. The Public Gardens are remarkable for their beauty, several acres of them having been turned into a forest of tree-ferns.

FIG. 34.—COLLINS STREET, MELBOURNE.

GEELONG, a city of 20,000 inhabitants, bends in a crescent round Corio Bay, one of the arms of Port Phillip. Its steeples and mansions rise pleasantly on the breezy shore, but behind these the ground is rather flat, till it slopes down again to the River Barwon, which, though only 2 miles away from Corio Bay, does not fall into it, but holds on its course to the open sea. Geelong is the port and business centre of a large district of Victoria, which is devoted to sheep-grazing, and produces large quantities of fine wool. On the western part of the coast of Victoria lie three promising seaport towns. The largest is WARRNAMBOOL, with 6000 inhabitants. The landing-place from the sea is too exposed to southerly gales, but immense and costly works are going forward to make the port secure. From the pier to the heart of the town is a distance of nearly a mile. Large churches, banks, schools, and business places denote the activity of the town, the chief industries being the growing of potatoes and wheat, and the raising of bacon. In the very heart of the pastoral region of Victoria the town of HAMILTON contains nearly 4000 inhabitants. The sheep districts of Victoria differ from those of New South Wales in being much more grassy and carrying many more sheep to the square mile. Hence the squatters round Hamilton are mostly men of great wealth. Their handsome mansions dot the country far around, and as they draw their supplies from the town, its long main street is lined with big shops and well-built banks. Fifty miles farther inland lies STAWELL, of 5000 inhabitants, a gold-producing town. The "rush" of diggers many years ago gave birth to this place, which grew to 10,000 people, but afterwards many left when the gold began to fail. But some rich mines are still worked there, one of them being more than half a mile deep. Another mining town not far from Ballarat is CLUNES. The roar of the "stampers," and the stream of milky water which flows from them, show the nature of the industry of the place. The quartz brought to the surface in cages, drawn by long ropes worked by steam-engines, is pounded by the stampers into dust, which is washed into the stream, while the fine gold is retained by reason of its weight. One mine alone has raised 2,000,000 pounds' worth of gold. To the north-east of Ballarat another mining town is called CASTLEMAINE, and contains 6000 inhabitants. It was built on the site of what were originally known as the Mount Alexander Diggings. There are still several thousands of miners at work in the district, though the yield of gold is now not very profitable. Seven or eight hundred Chinese may be seen laboriously rewashing the soil turned over by the early diggers, and getting out of it gold enough for their scanty livelihood. The town has some fine public buildings, as well as a brewery, the ale of which is well known throughout Australia.

The chief town on the Victorian side of the Murray is ECHUCA, with about 4000 people. Though the country around is flat, and by no means picturesque, the place has some features of interest, chief of which are the bridge over the Murray, a massive structure nearly half a mile long—the wharf where lie the river steamers that trade up and down the Murray, and a series of fine vineyards. Large quantities of wheat are grown in the district, and from the back country great loads of red gum timber are brought in by bullock-waggons to be sawn up into planks and railway sleepers at the five saw-mills which Echuca contains.

In the north-east of the colony stands the town of BEECHWORTH, where in bygone years 10,000 or 20,000 miners were congregated. Since then it has become a permanent town, with handsome streets, fine well-grown gardens, and large public buildings, all set in the midst of delightful mountain scenery. Beechworth is thus an attractive place, but as it is about 1800 feet above sea-level, it is rather cold in winter, while the district around it is too hilly to be of much use for agriculture. It still depends upon gold-mining as its staple industry, about 2000 English and 1000 Chinese miners being at work in the neighbourhood. The Chinese bring with them the manners and customs of their own country. Their houses are poorly made and generally dilapidated; but the Joss-houses here and there, with the smell of incense and of roast pork which proceeds from them, and the blue-jacketed, pig-tailed worshippers who pass in and out, at once arrest the attention of a stranger. Lastly, away in the east, in the rich district known as Gippsland, the town of SALE, with a population of 4000, stands on a wide and grassy plain at the head of Lake Wellington. Built on perfectly flat ground, it consists of well-made streets, and contains many good buildings. Its inhabitants are engaged in the trade that arises in a busy cattle-rearing district. There are 20,000 people on the farms of the neighbourhood, and as these are highly prosperous the city also flourishes. Not far from Sale is one of the three aboriginal stations, where the Victorian Government provides for the small remnant that is left of the original black inhabitants. These were never very numerous; the whole black population of the colony having been originally much under 10,000. The blacks, from their feuds with one another, their intemperance, and the havocs made by contagious diseases, have dwindled down to a couple of hundred, with about 300 or 400 half-castes, who are well housed and well cared for.

The extreme east of Victoria is a wild country of giant timber and forests of tree-ferns, upon which settlers have as yet encroached but little. The plains of Gippsland are occupied by settlers who have felled the mighty trees of 200 and 300 feet in height, and have cleared away the dense undergrowth. The rich soil now provides good crops, but especially excellent grass, which fattens immense numbers of cattle. The whole central part of the colony is devoted to wheat-growing, and in especial the valley of the Goulburn, which is one unbroken succession of "free selections," as the farms are called which have been bought from the Government on easy terms. The western part of the colony is of two kinds. In the south the great grassy undulations, lightly timbered like an English park, support many millions of merino sheep, whose wool is esteemed the best in the world. But the northern part, known as "the Wimmera," stretches as a vast waterless plain, of which no use was made until recently, when, by the aid of irrigation, this land was found to be peculiarly rich for wheat-growing, and it is now being rapidly occupied for that purpose.

SOUTH AUSTRALIA

The name South Australia is given to a colony which, strange to say, is not the most southern in Australia. The area of this colony is so vast as to surpass that of any country in Europe except Russia, and it has in addition an immense tract called the Northern Territory added to it at least for the present, the whole being 900,000 square miles, almost a third part of Australia. A large portion of this land is not attractive, and yet the colonists, by means of care and enterprise, are steadily making it useful, for its only defect is the want of water. On the dry plains they build their homes, make tanks and dams to retain the water when it does fall, and let the sheep run over the level tracts, which, bare as they may seem, yield in the dry seasons bushes and grassy tufts sufficient to keep the animals alive till the rainy season comes, when a short sweet grass everywhere springs up in a few days. The great problem is to provide water for the sheep during the dry season, and skill and capital are steadily overcoming that difficulty. Hence places which the explorers named Mount Hopeless and the "Never Never Land" and so forth are now occupied by prosperous sheep-stations. Yet more than half of the colony is as yet quite uninhabited; and of the part that is inhabited the great bulk is but slightly peopled. The population is mostly gathered in the south-eastern corner, where the soil is in many places excellent, and the rainfall reliable. There, especially among the Mount Lofty Ranges, and in the neighbourhood, fine farms and orchards have been formed. South Australia produces excellent wheat, good oranges, and well-flavoured grapes. But indeed there is very little in the way of fruit or grain that it cannot be made to yield, so that its progress is certain.

At present South Australia has only 350,000 people

for her vast territory. Of these 120,000 are gathered in Adelaide, which stands on a plain 10 miles wide between the Mount Lofty Ranges and the Gulf of St. Vincent. With the rolling sea in front, and the blue hills rising tier after tier behind, the city is charmingly placed. Seen from a distance it first presents two towers, those of its Post Office and Town Hall rising out of the plain, and surrounded by a wide level of houses, over which hangs a slight smoke amid the general brightness and sunniness of the Australian atmosphere. It is surrounded by pleasant suburbs of villas and cottages with gardens and tree-covered reserves. The central city—encircled with the park lands as a broad belt of verdure—can boast of handsome streets, one of which, King William Street, broad, with fine buildings and plenty of trees, presents a remarkably striking vista. And across it run many lines of busy thoroughfares. In the northern side of the rectangle made by the park lands, stand the Governor's Residence, Parliament House, Public Library, University, and other buildings. Adelaide is at present an attractive city, but is rapidly developing many manufactures, which may eventually make it less so.

South Australia possesses no other town of much importance. The largest are those which have gathered round the rich copper mines of the colony. MOONTA and WALLAROO, which lie close together upon the eastern shores of Spencer Gulf, have each only 1500 people within their municipal boundaries, but each has 3000 or 4000 miners not far away. These miners live in cottages a little inland round the various copper mines, but the towns themselves lie on the sea-shore, and are kept busy in exporting the copper and importing the various necessities of the miners. KAPUNDA, on the contrary, stands remote from the sea, at a place about 50 miles north of Adelaide. Near it some copper mines, once immensely rich, are now almost worked out. The surrounding land, however, in spite of the dangers of seasons of drought, is largely tilled for wheat-growing, so that Kapunda will still probably exist when the copper is all gone. KOORINGA, 50 miles still farther north, has grown up around

FIG. 35.—KING WILLIAM STREET, ADELAIDE.

some famous copper mines, which in their day yielded
£4,000,000 worth of copper, though the yield from
them is now greatly fallen off. GAWLER, 25 miles
from Adelaide, is the centre of a large agricultural
district, where much wheat is grown. But good wine is
also made here, and the town has some foundries and
large saw-mills. MOUNT GAMBIER TOWN, in the south-
eastern corner of the colony, stands on the slope of the
extinct volcano called Mount Gambier. All the district
around it is composed of rich volcanic soil, on which
wheat, oats, barley, and potatoes grow luxuriantly. It
has about 3000 inhabitants, but the surrounding country
is populous with farmers.

The **Northern Territory** is a vast area, whose resources
have been as yet scarcely touched. It has one town
called PALMERSTON on the shores of Port Darwin, with
a population of 600. A number of small villages lie here
and there, either on the coast or around the silver mines,
or in the gold-fields which have been discovered inland,
but their inhabitants only form a fringe of population
round a great uninhabited district, into which, however,
settlers are advancing with cattle. There is plenty of fine
grassy land and no want of water. The only drawbacks
are that the climate is rather warm, and that the wild
blacks, with their spears and clubs, are ferocious and
treacherous neighbours.

QUEENSLAND

The north-east of Australia is occupied by another
colony of wide extent, called Queensland. The area of
this region amounts to 668,000 square miles, and is
therefore more than three times the size of the German
Empire. Its most northerly point, Cape York, lies
within 11° of the Equator, and the settlers who are
engaged in pearl-fishing among the islands round that cape
have to endure a climate of severely tropical character.
The south of the colony, on the other hand, lies hundreds
of miles outside of the tropics, and its inhabitants enjoy a

mild and equable climate. As in New South Wales **a coast-plain intervenes between the table-land and the sea.** In Queensland, however, this plain is generally hot and moist, so that vegetation grows luxuriantly upon it. The **forests** are magnificent, and much profit arises from cutting cedar and other timber for exportation. Maize and arrowroot are grown in the fertile **river-valleys,** and sugar-canes wave their green **blades over some 60,000 or 70,000** acres, supplying for export 60,000 **tons of** refined sugar and nearly 2,000,000 gallons of treacle.

The table-lands **are much** cooler in **climate,** and there **the oats and** potatoes required **for** the colony **are grown. Large** districts of this elevated **ground consist of open "downs,"** or grassy undulating **land, whereon immense herds** of cattle are kept to be gathered for sale in Brisbane, **Sydney, and** Melbourne. But by far the largest portion of the colony consists of the great plains of the interior, which, in the south, suffer from periods of drought **like** the plains of New South Wales, of which indeed they form **only a** continuation. In the north, however, **these plains are watered by periodical tropical rains,** and **offer a fine field of enterprise for those who can endure the heat of the climate.** Though **the sheep and cattle now on these plains** may be numbered **by** millions, much more **than half of the** country is still unoccupied. Settlement, **however, is** steadily advancing into the lonely places.

This vast colony is inhabited by less than 400,000 persons, of whom about 350,000 are white people, about 10,000 **are Chinese, and** nearly 20,000 are aborigines who **wander from place to place** through the unsettled or thinly-**settled parts of the** colony. There used **to** be large **numbers of Kanakas or** South Sea Islanders on the sugar-plantations. **These** were brought over in ships from the islands to provide **cheap** labour, as nothing could be done with the **Australian natives,** who will not work. But the Queensland Parliament **has** forbidden its people to bring **over** any more of these dusky labourers, as it was found difficult to prevent them from sinking into a kind of **slavery.**

The chief city, **Brisbane,** with about 80,000 inhabitants, stands on the river Brisbane about 25 miles from its mouth. This stream winds as a deep smooth current, with green and park-like banks. In approaching the town by water the traveller first sails past far-stretching suburbs of villas and gardens, and at last finds the city built on either side of the river. On the right, long wharves line the banks, where many steamers and sailing-ships, loading or unloading, keep the steam-cranes employed. Behind these the streets form a populous level, broken by the steeples and towers of many churches, and the pillared fronts of public buildings. Farther up the river the houses are crowded quite as thickly on the left-hand side, but they cease altogether on the right, where the Botanic Gardens begin, of which the Brisbane people are so justly proud. Gorgeous flower-beds, clumps of palms, and feathery clusters of bamboos are here backed by the Governor's house, which stands beside them, and the Houses of Parliament, which raise their long rows of windows behind. Beyond this green and pretty part the river again bends, and the visitor finds himself face to face with houses once more, thick on either hand. At last he reaches a large and handsome iron bridge, which spans the river in a line with the finest street and chief business thoroughfare of Brisbane. Here are the great Public Offices, the Town Hall, banks, two theatres, churches, a great many newspaper offices, and handsome rows of shops. Brisbane, as the chief port of so large and so prosperous a territory, has a great amount of traffic, which increases from year to year at a marvellous rate.

But as Queensland has an immense coast-line, other ports have naturally been required to provide more convenient shipping-places for the people of the northern parts. The most important of these ports, ROCKHAMPTON, with 12,000 people, stands nearly 30 miles up the broad river Fitzroy, which is crossed by a fine suspension bridge resting on five heavy piers. It is a busy place, with manufactures and plenty of trade, and supports two rival newspapers. The chief thoroughfare of the town runs parallel to the river, with several good buildings in it. All the streets are broad and abundantly planted with

trees. The district round the town is famous for gold
and copper mines. Mount Morgan, the richest gold-mine
in the world, lies only a short distance away. This hill,
which some years ago was sold for £320, being considered
a worthless mass of rocks, is now valued at £8,000,000,
seeing that it is known to be wholly composed of rich
gold-bearing quartz.

Half-way between Brisbane and Rockhampton, MARY-
BOROUGH, with 9000 inhabitants, is situated about 25
miles up the river Mary. Its buildings are mostly of one
story, many of them being made of wood with iron roofs.
The foliage is wonderfully luxuriant, and the back-yards
of the poorest cottages are gay with the hibiscus and
many another bright tropical flower. The river-flats
support numerous sugar-plantations, which give work to
thirty-three sugar-mills. A little way inland, towards the
hill-ranges, forests of cedar furnish large red logs, which
are exported. There are breweries and factories, two
foundries, and a shipbuilding yard, so that Maryborough
is a busy place, to which many large steamers ascend
from the sea. Besides enjoying the traffic from its own
industries it is the seaport of GYMPIE, a gold-producing
town of about 8000 people, some 60 miles farther up the
Mary river. About twenty-five years ago the district was
quite lonely when a miner, who was "prospecting," found
gold-bearing quartz in it. Since then some £5,000,000
or £6,000,000 worth of gold have been raised from the
mines, while the surrounding lands have been turned into
cattle-stations.

If we proceed northward along the coast of Queensland
we meet a multitude of thriving towns, which will most
certainly be large places in another generation. BUNDA-
BERG, on the river Burnett, with a population of 3000,
is surrounded by rich flats of sugar-cane. To the north
of Rockhampton the town of MACKAY, with 5000 inhabitants, is surrounded by nearly 20,000 acres of sugar-cane,
which produce each year about the same number of tons
of sugar, while the town is also the seaport of a copper-
mining district and a gold-field which lies inland. TOWNS-
VILLE, being only 19° from the Equator, is one of the

hottest places in Australia. Its inhabitants number 9000. It lies along a shining beach, and climbs half-way up a hill. As the port for the vast cattle-stations of North Queensland, and likewise for CHARTERS TOWERS, an important gold-field town 80 miles to the south-west, it enjoys a large and increasing trade.

Still farther north, in a still more oppressively hot climate, stands COOKTOWN, with a population of nearly

FIG. 36.—QUEENSLAND—PROSPECTORS' CAMP.

3000 white persons and some 600 or 800 Chinese, who are employed to do all the hard work. Cooktown faces a small estuary, upon the sandy shores of which Captain Cook beached his famous ship the *Endeavour* more than a century ago. Behind it rises the bold eminence of Mount Cook. The main street of the town runs along the water's edge, but the houses rise up the lower spurs of the mountains, and as they are all wooden cottages painted white, they look bright and clean when set in their framework of dark tropical foliage.

All over the settled portions of Queensland there are little pastoral townships, each acting as the centre of a district busy with cattle. These places have a wonderful rate of growth, for in ten years a cluster of half a dozen houses (Fig. 36) grows into a town with eight or ten miles of streets, lighted with gas and supplied with a water system. But the largest of these inland towns are of greater age. The first is IPSWICH, of 8000 inhabitants. It is 24 miles west of Brisbane, pleasantly situated on the slopes of three gentle wooded hills which dip into a river-valley. Its main street is bright and well kept, with many handsome buildings. TOOWOOMBA lies 100 miles west of Brisbane, on top of the table-land, 2000 feet above sea-level. It is therefore cool and invigorating in its climate, and the neighbourhood is rich with luxuriant orchards where the orange grows in profusion. The town is kept busy by being the centre of the Darling Downs District, on which are depastured 1,000,000 sheep, and great herds of cattle. In Toowoomba out of 6000 inhabitants 1000 are Germans who own vineyards in the neighbourhood and are largely employed in wine-making.

WESTERN AUSTRALIA

More than a third of Australia is included in the territory of the colony called **Western** Australia. But at present it is the mere skeleton of a colony. The population is almost all gathered in the south-western corner; but as the whole of it is under 50,000 persons, it forms but a scanty sprinkling for an area of 1,000,000 square miles. As a matter of fact, at least three-quarters of that area are quite unsettled. The region has with much danger been crossed by explorers. Small tribes of native blacks at intervals of hundreds of miles from each other contrive somehow to exist in these waste places; but the only civilised population has planted itself along the coast, chiefly around the Swan river.

Western Australia was not settled until the year 1829, and was the last of the Australian colonies to receive responsible government. Its progress at first was comparatively slow, but it is now advancing more rapidly. In 1889 it had 500 miles of railways and nearly 3000 miles of telegraph lines. Its chief exports are wool, pearls and shells obtained from the neighbouring sea, timber, and skins. Gold is known to occur in the interior.

The capital, **Perth**, is situated on a broad lake-like reach of the **river**. Though inhabited by 10,000 people this town shows little of the feverish bustle so characteristic of most Australian towns of similar size. It has no manufactures, and not much commerce; it is a steady-going seat of Government, with a number of pretty and indeed handsome buildings but none of the big stores and noisy wharves that might be expected. FREMANTLE, inhabited by nearly 4000 persons, lies at the mouth of the Swan river, some of its houses fronting the ocean beach and some the placid waters of the river. It is the chief port of the colony, yet is not a place of great bustle; a quiet feeling of contented comfort appears in the cottages and villas which mostly stand well back from the street buried in masses of garden foliage. ALBANY, on the shores of King George's Sound on the extreme southern coast, comes next in importance, though it contains little more than 1000 inhabitants. Its harbour is so fine that Albany has become a favourite calling-place for steamers; coal is carried thither in sailing vessels, and is kept for the use of steamers as they pass. Round Albany there is a fairly good sheep-district. North of the Murchison river the population is extremely scanty and scattered.

TASMANIA

Tasmania forms the sixth colony, with 146,000 inhabitants; its area is about 26,000 square miles, so that it is a little smaller than Ireland. The main industries are the rearing of sheep (which number nearly 2,000,000), cattle-breeding and agriculture—wheat and oats are cultivated; but a characteristic occupation is the growing of fruit and

its conversion into jam, of which about 3000 tons are
exported every year. Mining also has of late years
become a busy industry, especially at the tin mines among
the mountains of the north-west corner. Gold is also
eagerly sought and successfully worked to a moderate
extent in many places.

The chief town, Hobart, contains about 30,000 inhabitants. Behind it Mount Wellington rises in bold slopes,
clad in giant timber, its head wrapped in cloud 4000 feet
above sea-level; while the lowest spurs of the mountain
descend to the edge of the bays into which the estuary of
the Derwent opens. Round one of these bays stretch the
old wooden wharves of Hobart with numerous steamers
and sailing craft; round two or three other bays the
shining sands are lined with pleasant suburbs; and the
houses mount up the spurs and lower slopes 1000 feet
above sea-level, with the sombre crest of the vast mountain
standing high above them. There are seven jam factories
by the wharves, whence in the various fruit seasons a scent
of raspberry, strawberry, quince or plum jam pervades the
whole town. In the summer the place is thronged with
visitors from Australia who escape from the heat to pass
the Christmas weather in the cool and delightful climate
of this attractive island.

In the north of the island LAUNCESTON contains 20,000
inhabitants, and stands in a hollow like a great punch-bowl,
at the head of the Tamar river, which is really the estuary
of the North Esk and South Esk rivers. These streams
tumble down from the surrounding hills in the most
picturesque falls and cataracts amid delightful scenery, to
join in a broad current upon which the tide rises and falls
to such an extent that ships which are floating at one time
beside the wharves with 20 feet of water below them, will,
six hours later, be lying on the mud half a mile away from
the water's edge. Launceston lies just below the place
where these rivers fall down into the estuary. It is a
bustling town, its chief street being filled with fine shops,
and thronged with cabs and resounding with people passing
to and fro as if it were a thoroughfare in some vast city.
Tasmania has no other town of much size, although there

are pretty places such **as** LATROBE, NEW NORFOLK, **and** CAMPBELLTOWN, which are thriving **as** well as **attractive. Near the** latter town there is a district in which stud-sheep **of the highest** quality **are** reared. Every year the best rams from **these** splendid flocks fetch **as** high a price as a **thousand** guineas each among the great wool-growing magnates **of** Australia.

XIV.—NEW ZEALAND

Geographical Position.—About 1000 miles to the east of Australia lie the islands of New Zealand, which are very nearly the antipodes of England. A little island to the south of them is called Antipodes Island, because it is the other end of that diameter of the earth which passes through London. The parallel of 40° south latitude and the meridian of 176° east longitude intersect in the northern of the islands.

Size, Configuration, and Coast-Line.—New Zealand consists of three islands, whose area amounts to a little more than 100,000 square miles, the greatest length being nearly 1000 miles. The islands are variously named, but the names used officially in the colony are North Island, South Island, and Stewart Island. A good view of the coast scenery of New Zealand can now be easily obtained, as steamers carry excursionists from Australia during the summer round the magnificent shores of these islands. Let us, in imagination, take part in one of these pleasure-trips and mark the varying outer aspect of the country. We head for the west coast of the South Island, and while yet many miles away, see the long line of snow-clad mountains rising to north and to south in majestic grandeur. On nearer approach the mountains are seen to end at the sea-level in lofty cliffs, the base of which is continually chafed by the waves. Reaching the coast at WEST CAPE we turn northwards, and in the dark sea-wall we notice every few miles the entrance to deep narrow inlets such as are called in Norway "fiords," filled with still water on which are thrown the shadows of the towering crags that surround them. The ledges of the precipices are hung

Fig. 37.—Pembroke Mountains, Milford Sound, New Zealand.

with ferns which flourish luxuriantly in the moist air.
Here and there from the summit of these cliffs, many
hundred feet above the placid sea-water, a river escaping
from the melting ice and snow of the interior, throws itself
in a white cascade that shoots down into the sea. Some
of these falls make an everlasting roar louder than the
noise of thunder. At the head of one of these recesses,
though still on the sea, we are deep in the bosom of the
mountains, and we can catch a glimpse of the far higher

FIG. 38.—HALL'S ARM, SMITH SOUND, NEW ZEALAND.

peaks and the chilly glitter of their sloping glaciers. No
one has ever crossed that mountain range hereabouts. Its
white summits and fern-covered valleys are equally
untrodden by man.

The coast, though still interesting, grows less impressive farther north, seeing that the mountains steadily
recede from the shore. But the scenery improves again
towards the northern end of the island as we reach what
Captain Cook called Cape Farewell when he said good-bye
to the shores of New Zealand. The strait which separates
the two large islands is appropriately called Cook Strait;

for Captain Cook, though not the first discoverer of these islands, was the first to give much information about them. On the south it opens into Tasman Bay, so called after the brave Dutchman who was actually the first discoverer of New Zealand, and into Massacre Bay, so called because a boat's crew of Tasman's Dutchmen were there massacred by the natives.

Having reached the end of the strait, which takes a voyage of nearly a day, let us round the lofty promontory of Cape Palliser and follow the east coast of the North Island. It is a pretty coast, though not nearly so grand as that on the west side of the South Island. Hawke Bay is fringed with a long sweep of sandy beach, backed by a forest of wild luxuriance, behind which the blue outlines of lofty hills close in a region hardly fit for any settlement, except where two or three small villages break the line of the beach, with their houses and clustered vegetation. Still farther north the coast becomes wilder, till it ends in a cape of white cliffs, bare, naked, and rugged, but backed by a wonderful panorama of mountains. Five noble ranges run inland, with their ends presented towards the sea, and for a large part of the year their summits are capped with snow. Rounding this, which is called the East Cape, we enter the Bay of Plenty, an open curve of the coast, still backed by forests out of which rise many mountains some of which are old volcanoes. In the bay lie many small islands which are really the tops of partially submerged volcanoes. Hauraki Gulf is similarly studded with volcanic islands; one of these is the wild-looking crater Rangitoto, a great black bowl with sides 1000 feet high. Never-failing interest attends the voyage along these cliffy shores, broken into many bays by the action of the Pacific rollers which have likewise carved out many little islands, some of which are loaded with verdure. The northern part of the North Island runs out into a long peninsula that ends in North Cape and Cape Maria Van Diemen. As we sail southward along the west coast of it, we pass Kaipara Harbour, and Manukau Harbour, which runs into the land so as almost to meet the Hauraki Gulf, leaving but a very narrow neck of land to be cut through to make all this long peninsula an island.

The most notable feature on the west side of the **North Island** is the high mountain called Egmont, which projects as a great headland into the Pacific Ocean. It was once an active volcano, and the vast masses of ashes and molten lava which it poured forth have built up a cone over 8000 feet high, and 40 miles wide at its base. The seaward base of this cone has been carved by the waves into a vast semicircle of cliffs, the outermost projection of which is called **Cape Egmont**. It is a dangerous coast, and the hulls of two or three shattered vessels which may chance to be visible among the rocks tell their tale of the disasters that from time to time happen there.

Again threading the passage of Cook Strait let us imagine ourselves to round Cape Campbell, and sail southward along the eastern shore of the South Island, which presents a singular contrast to its western coast. Small towns lie on the shores at distances of about 10 miles, as far as the rocky mountainous mass called Banks Peninsula, which juts out from the coast. Here a stream of steamers and ships may be seen moving north or south along the shores on their voyage to and from the numerous busy ports of this coast. Far to the south, Foveaux Strait, a deep passage, but stormy and dangerous because of its sweeping tides and its many islands, separates the South Island from Stewart Island. The latter, formed of a mass of hills covered with dense forests, is little inhabited, the 200 people it contains being mostly engaged in gathering the large oysters that are found on its shores. The most southerly point of New Zealand is South Cape, that projection of Stewart Island which faces the wild blasts from the Antarctic Ocean.

New Zealand is a most mountainous country. It has only one piece of level ground of any important extent; this lies in the South Island, where it occupies the eastern half of the province of Canterbury, and is called the **Canterbury Plain**. Its broad meadows of fresh green grass and well-cultivated farms are traversed by streams of clear cold water from the mountains. With its fine

x

soil and its excellent climate this plain is a favourite place for the farmer. The South Island is traversed along its western coast by the magnificent mountain range already referred to. These snow-clad peaks, called the **Southern Alps,** extend 200 miles in length. They culminate in MOUNT COOK, the highest peak of New Zealand, which attains a height of more than 12,000 feet. No one has ever been actually on the top of it, though an Englishman who went to New Zealand for the purpose, taking two Swiss guides with him, got close to the summit after a fortnight of extremely dangerous labour. There are also many peaks of from 8000 to 11,000 feet in height, whose snowy summits no one has yet attempted to climb. From the snow-fields that gather among those mountains, glaciers creep down into the valleys. The largest is the Tasman glacier, an immense river of ice, with branches descending from Mount Cook and the neighbouring giants, and supplying the streams that water the Canterbury Plains. In the south the ranges spread out over the whole width of the island, with endless prospects of fine scenery, but no great extent of land level enough for cultivation. In the north of the island also the Southern Alps spread out into nearly a dozen ranges, some of the snow-clad peaks of which rise to 5000 and 6000 feet in height. These uplands, separated by longitudinal valleys, extend up to Cook Strait.

The North Island is hardly less mountainous, though none of its peaks are so high. The island is filled with ranges running north and south. One of those begins with the immense cone of Mount Egmont above noticed. Then there is the range called the Ruahine and another the Tararua, with smaller companion ridges all running the same way. But the most interesting are the volcanic peaks which rise in the centre. Ruapehu is over 9000 feet high, and Tongariro over 7000 feet. These are feebly active volcanoes from whose summit a lurid glow at times lights up the midnight clouds. All over the North Island many peaks which have been once volcanic are now believed to be extinct. But how little reliance is to be placed sometimes on such beliefs was

shown by the sudden and unexpected eruption of TARA-
WERA, one of those so-called extinct craters. It had
always been famous for its hot springs and its fountains
of boiling water. This water in its passage underground
dissolves out some of the substances of which the rocks
are made, and deposits these on the surface as it cools.
By this means terraces and steps have been formed which
look like transparent marble. There used to be two fine
sights of this sort—the Pink and the White Terrace.
Mount Tarawera, which though recognised as a volcano
had been quiet ever since white men settled in New
Zealand, and was thought to be extinct, in 1886 suddenly
began to shoot forth stones, pumice, and clouds of fine
dust. The terraces were overwhelmed as well as one of
the little hot-water lakes lying at their feet, and the
whole country for many miles around was buried under
a thick deposit of volcanic mud and dust.

Like most mountainous countries New Zealand is
dotted over with great numbers of lakes. The largest,
called Lake Taupo, in the centre of the North Island,
measures about 25 miles in length and breadth, and lies
enclosed among barren cliffs, behind which mountain peaks
rise on every side, clothed in dense vegetation to their
summits, except, as in the case of Tongariro, where they rise
above the line of perpetual snow. This sheet of water is
subject to sudden storms which sweep down from the
mountain gorges. Its waters pour out at the northern
end in a river called the Waikato, the finest stream in
New Zealand. It emerges from the lake in a deep, smooth,
and swift current 300 yards wide, which where the channel
contracts farther down becomes a rushing torrent, filling
the valley with a never-ending roar. Soon afterwards it is
joined by a river of hot water, and then once more assumes
the character of a quiet, broad, and deep stream, though
too rapid to be of much use for navigation, till at length
it falls into the sea.

The river of hot water just alluded to comes from the
hot lakes, Rotorua, Rotoiti, Rotoma, and Tarawera, which
lie all together near Mount Tarawera. The whole district
around these waters is hot under foot; steam escapes from

the ground on all sides, and sulphurous vapours hang in the valleys or are emitted from the hill-slopes. The shores of these lakes are formed of cakes of hot mud with boiling mud below; cases have been known in which the thin crust of dried mud has given way, and the incautious visitor has been engulfed in the cauldron underneath.

Though the South Island possesses none of these volcanic wonders, it can boast of lakes that are famous for the beauty of their scenery. The largest of these is the Te Anau, a long deep lake of glacier water, lying between the mountain ranges near the west coast. Lake Manipori to the south, and Lakes Wanaka and Hawea to the north, are of the same character; but the most noted of them all is Lake Wakatipu, a long sheet of water winding among magnificent ranges, which terminate in precipices or in rugged slopes, beyond which may be seen the great snow-fields and the glaciers that issue from them. Mount Earnslaw, which fronts the last reach of the lake, is more than 9000 feet high, its sides clad in forests of white and black birch-trees, and its summit gleaming with everlasting snow and ice.

The streams that escape from Lakes Wakatipu, Hawea, and Wanaka unite to form the river Clutha, which is the longest river of New Zealand. Descending through picturesque country, this river becomes a broad, deep, and swift but smooth current almost level with the green banks, which it has cut for itself out of the clay and loam of a fertile district. The **Waitaki** and the Waiau are other important streams of the South Island.

Climate.—Judging by its exceptionally low death-rate, New Zealand has one of the most healthy climates in the world. Visitors sometimes complain that it is excessively breezy, the prevailing winds blowing strongly from the south-west and north-west. But to healthy people this only makes it all the fresher and more enjoyable. No part of New Zealand is quite so cold as the south of England, although in Stewart Island the average temperature is nearly the same. The extreme north of New Zealand is like the south of Italy in climate. But the average climate of the colony may be regarded as about the same

as that of Venice; no month averages lower than 36°
Fahr., or more than 82°. Snow never falls in the very
north, but in the south there are from five to fifteen snowy
days in the year.

Plants and Animals.—New Zealand differs widely not
only from all the rest of the world, but even from its neigh-
bour Australia, in regard to its plants. A distinguished
botanist declares that two-thirds of the species are not
known in any other part of the world, and it has many
genera all to itself. There are no gum-trees in New
Zealand except those which the settlers are now planting
in great numbers. But New Zealand has dense forests
of ever-green trees, such as the Kauri pine, whose fine
white close-grained timber is much prized all over the
civilised world. Many species of beech and yew grow
densely in the forests, and altogether over a hundred different kinds of good timber-trees are known in New
Zealand. These are laced together by creepers called
supplejacks, which twine and twist for hundreds of yards,
with stems as thick as a man's wrist, so as to make the
forests impassable except with axes and immense labour.
A great feature in the New Zealand forests consists in
the tree-ferns, of which 130 species are known. But one
of the most useful plants is the phormium or New Zealand
flax, which is much used for making strong ropes.

There are scarcely any animals indigenous to New
Zealand. A kind of dog, two kinds of rats, some bats,
and some lizards are the only animals except birds that
are native to these islands. There are no snakes of any
sort. The country, however, was once rich in birds—the
moa, a bird of the running class like the ostrich, being, so
far as we know, the largest that ever inhabited the earth.
It has been long extinct, but its bones show that it sometimes reached a height of 10 or 12 feet. New Zealand
still has 120 species of birds, chiefly pigeons, ducks, hawks,
and parrots.

But, as in Australia, the imported animals are far more
numerous than those that are indigenous. New Zealand
has 20,000,000 sheep—not so good for wool as those of
Australia, but much better for mutton; and the people of

New Zealand now send much frozen mutton to England. They have over a million cattle, and a quarter of a million of horses. They have plenty of poultry, and too many rabbits and hares. Besides these, quails and pheasants and partridges have been introduced, and are abundant in some parts. Wheat, oats, barley, potatoes, turnips, etc., grow well, and cover a million and a quarter of acres.

Native Race.—New Zealand, when first discovered by white men, was inhabited by a race much akin to the South Sea Islanders. These are called by their own name, Maori. Their traditions seem to be true, that their ancestors came some centuries ago from islands in the direction of the Sandwich Islands, and that they multiplied and spread over the North Island till they numbered over 100,000. Strange to say, the South Island, though the larger, never had many Maoris. There are now about 40,000 survivors of the race, but they are steadily diminishing in numbers. They copy the drinking customs of the white men, and are attacked by lung diseases. They are a finely-built race of powerful frames—tall, straight, and active; brown in colour, with faces tattooed in handsome patterns.

Discovery and Settlement.—The Maoris formed petty sovereignties which fought desperately with one another, knowing nothing of the world outside of their own islands until Tasman came to them in 1642, and made known to Europeans that such islands existed. No other visitor approached them till Captain Cook in 1770 sailed round these islands, and mapped out their coasts with as much care as time permitted. In 1814 missionaries landed, and were the first white men resident in New Zealand. The first colonisation, however, did not take place till 1839, and the first Governor was sent to take charge in 1840. Since that time Englishmen, Irishmen, and especially Scotchmen, have landed in the country by thousands.

The Maoris at first offered no great resistance, but when they realised that their country was going to be wholly occupied by strangers, they rose in opposition and fought stoutly from 1861 to 1865. Much courage, though also much cruelty, was displayed, but after a prolonged struggle the country was pacified for two or three years. Several patriot chiefs, however, wandered among the hills, refusing to submit, and continued to gather their forces whenever a chance was offered to sweep down upon the homes of the colonists. It was not till 1881 that all such

Fig. 39.—A Maori.

troubles were brought to an end. In the New Zealand Parliament two Maori members sit in the Upper House and four in the Lower House. Many of the Maoris are becoming indistinguishable from Englishmen save by the colour of their skin.

Population.—The total population, including Maoris

is now over 600,000, of whom more than half have been born in the colony, while nearly the whole of the other half came originally from the British Islands.

Products, Industries, and Commerce.—The people in New Zealand are mostly engaged on the land. They export three or four million pounds' worth of wool each year, and about 1,000,000 carcases of mutton, for which they receive more than half a million pounds. What with timber, wheat, oats, hides, tallow, and butter, together with a fair amount of gold and coal, their exports amount altogether to about seven million pounds per annum.

Subdivisions and Government.—There was a time when New Zealand formed eight separate colonies, but they have all united into one, of which the former colonies are now the provinces. The largest cities are Auckland, Christchurch, and Dunedin; but when federation took place, Wellington was chosen to be the capital on account of its central situation.

The most northern province, called **Auckland**, has an area about half that of England. Its long northern peninsula is the part most occupied by the white settlers, all the southern part of the province having been till lately almost entirely inhabited by Maoris. The southern parts of the province of Auckland are thinly inhabited, being a lonely region of forests of the Kauri and other sorts of pine, broken by lakes and volcanoes, and desert patches filled with hot springs and fumaroles. The northern part of the province is well peopled, and many thousands of farms are scattered through districts of rich soil, formed from the decay of the volcanic products. There the settlers grow wheat, oats, and potatoes, and find lucrative employment in cutting various sorts of timber, especially the Kauri pine. The population of the province is about 130,000, of whom nearly a half, that is about 60,000, are gathered in the city of AUCKLAND, which stands on a narrow neck 6 miles broad between two large harbours. Long wharves have been built in the eastern harbour. But shipping may also lie at a suburb less than 6 miles away in the western harbour. All round the city there rise numerous volcanic hills.

One of these, named Mount Eden, a mile distant, has on its top a vast bowl-shaped crater strewn with cinders. In bygone years the Maoris must have used it as a fort, for the places most easy of access have been defended by earthen mounds. From the summit of this now silent volcano a noble panorama of land and water may be seen,— the broad harbours with their bays, islands, and shipping; the black crests of other extinct craters dotting the country, intermingled with woods and farms; and immediately below, the busy city, with its tramcars, railways, and wharves.

Three smaller provinces lie south of Auckland in the North Island. Of these the westernmost is **Taranaki**, so called after the native name of Mount Egmont, which occupies a large part of the province. More than two-thirds of this district are covered with forests, still practically unexplored. Plentiful rains, a warm climate, and rich volcanic soil, make the place exceedingly fertile; but it costs too much for the settler to clear away those huge trees, and all those dense bushes interwoven with the giant vines called "supplejacks." But there are some districts of fern lands where nothing but a luxuriant growth of ferns has had to be cleared away, and on these there are more than 2000 farms, and a prosperous population of about 22,000 persons. Three thousand inhabitants occupy the town of NEW PLYMOUTH, a picturesque and quiet place on the west coast.

Of the province of Wellington the northern half is also mountainous, and covered with vast and sombre forests. But the southern portions are fairly level, and well watered. Here fine grassy plains support nearly 3,000,000 sheep, the wool of which supplies the chief income of the province. But there are also many cattle, and a considerable amount of land is under crops of wheat and oats. The population is about 97,000, but in addition there are still many thousands of Maoris who live their old primitive life in the spacious forests of the north. The chief town is WELLINGTON, of nearly 30,000 inhabitants. The buildings there are mostly constructed of wood, as the place has in the past been visited by earthquakes, which have proved disastrous to stone or brick erections. The city lies along the beach of Port Nicholson, a harbour so completely land-locked as to look like a lake. The hills rise sharply behind it, and the houses consequently run in a long narrow line between the water and the slopes. Among them may be seen the immense wooden building used for Government offices, and the handsome pile of the Parliament Houses; for, as already stated, Wellington was made the capital of New Zealand, when the provinces united to form a single colony.

The province of **Hawke's Bay** occupies a large part of the east coast of the North Island. Its chief town is Napier, a quiet place of 8000 inhabitants. The small harbour called Port Napier has for one of its horns a peninsula which terminates in a hill. On the flat part of the peninsula stands the business part of the town. The suburbs cannot spread eastwards, for there lies the shingly beach of the ocean; nor westwards, for there are the waters of the harbour. Hence the residences of the people climb the steep hillsides with terraced gardens, while many villas crown the summit. To the south of Napier plains of singularly fertile land yield large crops, principally of oats and barley. Behind these plains a wide pastoral district affords food for nearly 3,000,000 sheep, while beyond rise the mountain ranges, clothed with forests of valuable timber, in which dwell the wood-cutters and sawyers, and also nearly 4000 Maoris.

In the South Island the most northerly province is **Nelson**, a district more remarkable for its impressive scenery than for its suitability to settlement. It is marked by lofty mountain ranges, with peaks from 5000 to 10,000 feet in height. Their lower slopes are clothed in impenetrable forests, while their summits are capped with snow. Deep in the valleys between the ridges the air is warm and moist, and in these sheltered hollows, where the soil is exceedingly rich, a profusion is found of ferns and mosses such as the world nowhere else contains. Yet here and there small districts are suitable for the growth of wheat, oats, barley, and potatoes. A large area is utilised by the settlers for sheep and cattle, but

the total population of the province is only 34,000. The chief town, NELSON, with 7500 inhabitants, is charmingly situated on a bay, with a complete semicircle of **lofty** hills surrounding it.

Marlborough is a province of the same character, occupying, side by side with Nelson, the northern part of South Island. Long and rugged mountain **ranges,** deep fern-clad valleys, and bold **coast scenery make the region** one of remarkable picturesqueness, but **leave little room for agriculture.** The people, **who are only** 12,000 **in number,** have nearly 1,000,000 sheep depastured on the **more open parts,** chiefly **around** the capital, which is called BLENHEIM, a small **town** which makes **only slow progress, having no** harbour and being enclosed by so **hilly a country.**

South of Nelson and Marlborough there are **two other** provinces which, side by side, occupy the full width **of the** island. They are separated by the Southern Alps. That to the west, called **Westland, is a long strip about** 30 miles **in width, and** occupied **so entirely by the mountains** and their spurs **that** little space is **left either for agriculture or for pastoral** pursuits. **Yet it has a varying** population of **from** 16,000 **to** 25,000 **persons.** These find their subsistence chiefly **in** gold-mining; for the precious metal is plentiful all along **these** coasts, chiefly at HOKITIKA **and** GREYMOUTH, from each of which considerable quantities of **it have in bygone** years been exported. But gold-mining being subject to many **changes of fortune, the populations of** these places are **fluctuating.** Greymouth, however, is surrounded by beds **of coal, and the** opening of four collieries will tend to make its prosperity more steady.

The eastern province is called **Canterbury.** There is only one route into it **from** Westland, **namely by the road** from Hokitika to Christchurch, which passes over the mountains by wildly picturesque gorges, beneath immense precipices, or **along** the edges of chasms, by the side of rushing streams, **and** past many waterfalls. The hillsides on **the** west are covered with cedar-trees and white pines, while an indescribable profusion of ferns and small vegetation **covers the** country. The eastern side of the mountain range affords a striking contrast of scenery, for it is destitute of trees and ferns, and presents a barren wildness on every hand. For as the prevailing winds blow the clouds from the west, and the mountain barrier intercepts the moisture, the air-currents pass over to the eastern side desiccated and cloudless. The eastern slopes are consequently dry and barren. Far beyond them, along the sea-board, lie the spacious Canterbury plains, whereon there were originally no trees; but the soil being good, the settlers have remedied that defect by planting the district. Having to choose trees that would grow with little rain they selected the blue-gum of Australia, for there are no gum-trees native to New Zealand. These wide plains are now diversified with groves and clumps of trees which shelter their 5,000,000 sheep from the icy winds that descend from the mountains. For the prevailing westerly winds, though they leave their moisture on the Westland side, themselves cross the ridges, and descend upon the plain, cold, dry, and penetrating. Of late years the settlers have given the preference to certain sorts of pines for shelter-trees, and have planted them extensively.

CHRISTCHURCH, the capital of the province of Canterbury, stands in the midst of green plains well shaded with trees, and containing 35,000 inhabitants. The ground on which it is built is quite flat, a square mile in extent. The streets and houses have a neat and comfortable appearance, but there is no very noticeable bustle of trade. The central city is encircled by a complete belt of parks, outside of which lie many pretty suburbs. Christchurch is 8 miles from the sea, from which it is separated by a high range of hills. Its port, called LYTTELTON, a busy place of 4000 persons, lies round a little harbour, where it seems to have been squeezed between precipitous mountains and the sea. In order to connect it with Christchurch a tunnel nearly 2 miles long has been cut through the mountains, and through this opening a large traffic is carried on by railway between the harbour and the populous plains round Christchurch. The whole province of Canterbury has 128,000 persons, who possess

immense numbers of sheep and cattle, and own a great
number of farms, which yield from 8,000,000 to
10,000,000 bushels of wheat and oats every year. Coal
is abundant throughout the province, which seems to
have every element of prosperity. Fruit of excellent
quality is grown near the coast, and an important trade
is now being carried on in the freezing of meat for
exportation to England.

The southern part of the South Island forms the
province of **Otago**. Its western half abounds in magnificent scenery, with great mountain ridges, deeply cut into by
fiords (Fig. 40), with lakes, glaciers, and torrents, and with
sombre forests and deep fern-filled valleys. This is no land
for human enterprise; but in the middle of the province,
where the mountain ridges are much lower and not buried
under such heavy forests, they enclose many a well-watered
grassy valley, adapted for grazing sheep, of which the
province possesses about 5,000,000. In the eastern part
the hills are still lower, and being rounded in shape are
suitable for sheep pasture to their very summit, while the
valleys and the plains that skirt the larger rivers are
wonderfully fertile, so that the farmers, whose comfortable
cottages dot the land, can export each year 10,000,000 or
12,000,000 bushels of wheat and oats and 40,000 or
50,000 tons of potatoes. Moreover Otago boasts considerable mineral wealth. Gold is scattered here and there in
many parts of the colony, and is exported to the value of
about half a million pounds per annum. The population
of the province numbers upwards of 150,000.

The chief city of Otago is DUNEDIN, a bright, lively,
and prosperous place of 50,000 inhabitants. It stands at
the head of a long, narrow harbour, from which the streets
rise rather steeply up the hillside. But the cross streets
are level, broad, and busy. They present on the whole
the finest avenues of buildings to be found in New Zealand.
Nine miles farther down the long harbour, and only six
miles from its mouth, lies Port Chalmers, which receives
such of the larger ships as are unable for want of depth to
sail as far as Dunedin. Farther north on the east coast
stands Oamaru, with a population of 6000; it is some-

times called the White City for the reason that it is wholly built of a brilliant white stone of beautiful texture. The quarries of this stone round about are a source of profit to the town as the material is exported to many parts of Australia. But Oamaru is also surrounded by a fine agricultural region yielding some 3,000,000 or 4,000,000 bushels of grain every year. The export of so much grain, and of the stone, and the wool which the neighbourhood produces, attracts a great deal of shipping to the place, which would find no shelter there from the hurricanes of the ocean, but that a magnificent artificial harbour has been formed, with breakwaters half a mile long, 36 feet broad, and 32 feet high, strong enough to defy the wintry tempests of the Pacific. Within their shelter a fleet can anchor in perfect safety.

The most southern part of the South Island used to form the province of Southland but is now incorporated with Otago. Its chief town is INVERCARGILL, the most southerly town in the world, until Punta Arenas on Magellan's Strait shall wake up and become really a town. Invercargill has about 9000 inhabitants, who are engaged in providing for a rich pastoral district lying round the south-eastern part of the island.

Several small groups of islands lie round New Zealand, near enough to be considered with it. The Chatham Islands lie 360 miles to the east. The largest of them is about 40 miles long. They are all low, and somewhat bare, forming mostly a succession of moorlands mixed with bogs and lakes. These waters are frequented by immense quantities of wild fowl, and they are also visited by sea-birds which in the season come to breed in prodigious numbers. There are about 200 people on the island, partly whites and partly half-castes, who make a living by supplying beef and other provisions to the crews of whaling ships which frequent the surrounding seas.

Away to the south of New Zealand lie the Auckland Islands, which are uninhabited. No one would care to dwell on those remote and inaccessible shores. The largest of the group is about 30 miles long, and has mountains running up to the height of 2000 feet. These

Fig. 40.—Portobello, Otago Harbour.

heights, and indeed all the islands, are covered with forests of low bushes, stunted and distorted by the icy gales that blow up from Antarctic Seas. The shores present an inhospitable aspect, and have been the scene of many calamitous shipwrecks. So frequent, indeed, have these wrecks become that a supply of provisions has been placed under a big cairn for the use of such few survivors as may chance to get ashore when a vessel strikes these angry rocks. Of late years these provisions have been of frequent use.

Lonelier still are Campbell Island, and far away into the mists of the south Macquarie Island—the chosen home in the breeding season of vast flocks of albatrosses, which then desist from their flight over the dark waters, and, for one month in the year, remain on land beside the pair of white eggs which they lay.

North-east of New Zealand there is a group called the Kermadec Islands, which are all small, with black basaltic cliffs, rising into peaks well clad with vegetation; but they are as yet uninhabited, though formally annexed to New Zealand in 1887.

MEANS OF COMMUNICATION IN AUSTRALASIA

All the colonies except West Australia are well supplied with railways. A traveller can now go by rail from Adelaide to Melbourne, from Melbourne to Sydney, from Sydney to Brisbane. From Adelaide he can travel by six branch lines to all the townships of South Australia; and one of the lines is now pushing far out into the desert where there is little in the way of habitation; for the people of South Australia intend to carry a railway completely across Australia to the north, and they have already made a good beginning. Victoria is traversed by a network of railways; no less than fifty lines make its fertile lands valuable by rendering them accessible. New South Wales has a still greater length of railways, though they do not nearly so well ramify through the country. Besides the lines that join Sydney to Melbourne and Adelaide, others run inland, one to Bourke, and the other to Hay, with branches here and there to supply the needs of the pastoral districts. Queensland possesses so long a coast, and so many seaports, that she has had to form six independent centres for her railways. One line goes 700 miles inland from Brisbane; another system branches out in different directions from Maryborough; another extends 400 miles inland from Rockhampton; the fourth in a short line which starts from Mackay; the fifth has several branches with Townsville for their centre; while the sixth runs inland from Cooktown for 60 miles.

In Tasmania a main line runs north and south, from Launceston to Hobart, giving off several branches to right and to left. A larger branch starting from Launceston reaches the north coast at the river Mersey. West Australia possesses a line about 40 miles in length which extends from Perth eastward into the interior. Another line connects Perth with Albany. In New Zealand numerous separate systems of railways have been formed. The most complete among them runs from Invercargill along the coast through Dunedin to Christchurch. Its numerous branches are confined to the eastern half of the island. A short line runs inland from Blenheim, and one of still smaller dimensions from Nelson. In the North Island, a line connects Wellington with Auckland, another joins Wellington to Napier, and a third runs from Wellington to New Plymouth. These lines mostly follow the coast, but in addition there are short branches which penetrate the interior.

Australia is provided with such an abundance of telegraph lines that each village of 100 inhabitants is placed in communication with every part of Australasia. A cable joins Australia to Tasmania, and another to New Zealand. In addition the colonies are all joined with England by a line that runs across Australia from Adelaide to Port Darwin, thence by cable to the island of Java, and so to India.

All the coast cities and towns of Australia keep up a communication among themselves by fleets of intercolonial steamers, ranging from 500 to 3000 tons burthen. They are also linked with England by no less than seven lines of mail steamers. The Peninsular and Oriental Company sends a vessel once a fortnight from Southampton by the Straits of Gibraltar, Suez Canal, and Red Sea, to Ceylon; thence to Albany, Adelaide, Melbourne, and Sydney. Once a fortnight, in alternate weeks, the Orient Company sends a steamer by the same route. These are both British lines. But the French despatch, once a month, a steamer from Marseilles through the Suez Canal to Sydney and Melbourne, and the Germans send one once a month from Hamburg by the same route to the same ports. The vessels of these four lines are magnificent steamers of from 4000 to 8000 tons burthen. The three remaining lines, all owned by British companies, are supplied with smaller vessels. One of them, called the Union line, sends a steamer once a month from England to Hobart, and thence to New Zealand. The other two lines reach England only indirectly. The vessels of one of them—the Pacific Navigation Company—sail from Sydney across the Pacific Ocean to the Sandwich Islands, and then to San Francisco, whence the journey is continued by rail across North America to New York, where another steamer is taken for the voyage across the Atlantic to England. The steamships of the last of the seven lines begin their voyage once a fortnight from Brisbane, call at all the Queensland ports, sail through Torres Straits to Java, then round the Indian Peninsula, and through the Suez Canal to London. By means of all these services three large steamers arrive every week in Australasia from Europe, making the intercourse frequent and easy, and as the vessels usually complete their journey in about five weeks, the transit may be said to be rapid.

XV.—PACIFIC ISLANDS

BRITAIN has taken possession of numerous groups of islands scattered over the vast Pacific Ocean. Many of these are of little value in themselves, but may become of great importance in the future as coaling-stations, or as points for submarine lines of telegraph.

Nearly 2000 miles to the east of Australia lie the **Fiji Islands**, one of the most recent of the British Colonies. They were discovered 250 years ago by the Dutchman Tasman, but were left undisturbed by white men till about half a century ago, when, in spite of the fierce habits of the natives, European traders began to settle for trade or other purposes along the shores. The firearms of the strangers gave them a great ascendency, and as visitors and settlers became more and more numerous, the natives, about thirty years ago, offered to add their islands to the Empire of the Queen of Great Britain. This proposal was at that time declined; but in 1874, when it was renewed, Fiji was admitted as a colony of the British Empire.

There are about 250 islands or islets in the group, of which 100 are large enough to be inhabited. They are really the tops of extinct volcanoes, which rise on a plateau from the bed of the Pacific Ocean. From this submerged plateau these islands raise their mountain-tops, covered with rich forests, to 3000, and in the largest island to 5000, feet above the sea-level. They are fringed with coral-reefs, which run round them all, close to the shore, raising their surfaces here and there, but leaving them generally awash with the Pacific rollers, and enclosing between them and the shore basins of pale green or delicate pink water, wherein swim strangely beautiful fish. Behind the shores, with their sandy beaches, rise bold cliffs, beyond which dark trees and waving jungle sweep far aloft into a clear blue sky. Cool streams tumble through the rocky gorges, to spread out here and there upon alluvial flats, whereon the sugar-cane is cultivated in broad plantations, while long avenues of banana-trees show their large pale-green fleshy leaves and yellow clumps of fruit.

The largest island is VITI LEVU, the second in size is VANUA LEVU; both about 90 miles long, but the former broad and the latter narrow. Each of them presents a hilly centre, but both have on their shores fertile flats, in which coffee, maize, pea-nuts, and cotton, but especially bananas and sugar, are grown. Along the coasts plantations of cocoa-nut palms add greatly to the picturesqueness of the scenery, besides providing each year £60,000 worth of nuts for export.

The chief town is Suva, on the southern shores of Viti Levu. Here the Governor resides, and the Legislative Council meets which manages the affairs of the colony. This council consists only of white men, although the white people of Fiji number not more than 4000, while the native races are at least 120,000. Suva has one broad street nearly a mile long, in which stand three churches, four hotels, and a considerable number of shops; a post-office, a hospital, a mechanics' institute, and a school. The town has only 1000 white people, but it contains a large number of Fijians, who nowadays are mostly clad in European style, and live, as well as they can, after the European model. But a little way inland they may still be seen more nearly in their original state—strong, active, well-knit men, with smooth and shining copper-coloured skins, clad in light garments, sometimes of their own primitive weaving, but now more often light shirts and robes of English manufacture. In bygone days they were inveterate cannibals, and their wars with one another were interminable and ferocious. Now they are peaceful enough, and in outward appearances, at least, are immensely improved.

Levuka, the second town, stands on a small island not far from Suva. It is enchantingly situated, the villas of the residents rising on the hillside amidst a profusion of fig-trees and palms, while its chief street fronts the beach, the public offices, churches, school, town hall, and other buildings looking out on the coral-studded harbour.

FIG. 41.—GROUP OF FIJI MEN.

Fiji has a delightful climate for nine months of the year, but, though in summer not oppressively warm, it is found to be rather unhealthy for Europeans.

New Guinea.—To the north of Australia lies a large island called Papua or New Guinea. It is 1500 miles long and from 200 to 400 miles broad. Its area amounts to 250,000 square miles, or more than that of Spain and Portugal together. Three nations claim a share in this island. The Dutch profess to hold all the western half, but as there are no Dutchmen there, their colony is more a name than a reality. The eastern half is divided between the Germans and the British—the Germans having the northern, the British the southern part. The British

FIG. 42.—PEACE ORNAMENTS OF NEW GUINEA.
1. Spearing fish among the coral.   2. Canoe paddles.
3. Fishing-spears.   4. Grass petticoats, or ramna.   5. Fishing-net.

portion contains about 85,000 square miles, and is therefore equal in area to Great Britain. It is a fertile land, but with too hot a climate, and too oppressively dense a vegetation, to make it a suitable home for Europeans. The coast of the British part of the island curves up in a great bay called the Gulf of Papua, of which the western shores are low, while the eastern are high and bold. The western shores are formed by great flat mud islands, which have gathered at the mouth of the

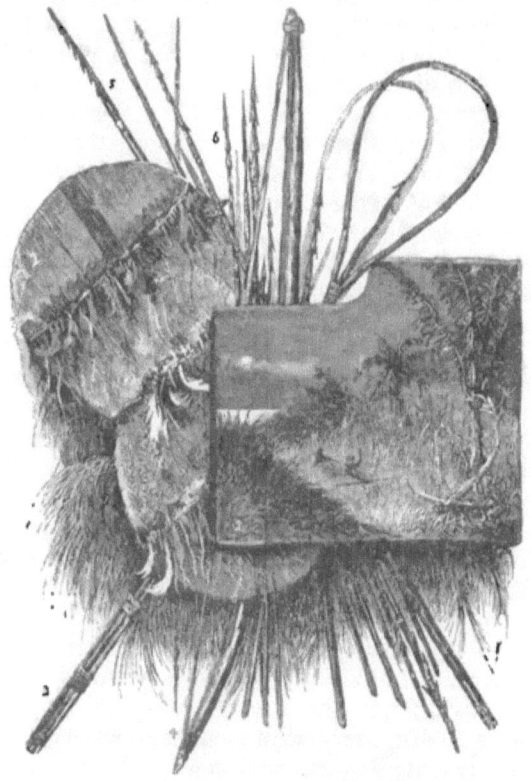

Fig. 43.—Weapons of New Guinea.
1. Shield.   2. Man-trapping at Yule Island.   3. A man-trap.
4. Bow.   5. Spears.   6. Arrows.

Fly river. Up this river various expeditions have of late years gone in steamers, and penetrated near to its sources in the lofty mountains of the interior. Hence this river is well mapped. The interior of the island is otherwise almost unknown. It seems to consist of one vast forest, unbroken except in a few places where grassy plains occur. The eastern shores of the Gulf of Papua run out into a long peninsula, which is better explored. It is filled by the Owen Stanley Mountains, whose highest peak, generally snow-clad though so close to the Equator, is 13,000 feet above sea-level; and a long line of peaks, almost as lofty, runs out to the extremity of the peninsula. From the shores up to almost the summits of these ranges the whole country is covered with forests, in which grow the camphor-tree, the sago-palm, and the nutmeg-tree. Courageous explorers have reached the tops of many of these peaks, and report that they looked down on a silent ocean of verdure, but that the valleys were indescribably beautiful with their stately tree-ferns and palm-trees rising boldly up from the limitless extent of vegetation.

The whole of New Guinea is estimated to contain about 1,000,000 natives, who are by no means in the lowest scale of savagery. They make neat huts, often on piles over the water, sometimes among the branches of trees. But generally their huts are ranged in regular streets, wherein naked children may be seen tumbling about among fat pigs. They make ropes and pottery, build neat little bridges, and carve good canoes. But they fight a great deal among themselves, and, on the whole, have proved hostile to the settlement of white men.

This opposition, however, would matter little if white men wished to settle there, for they would go in spite of the natives; but the hot climate, and the fever which attacks almost every white man who sleeps in the island, have prevented much settlement. A little village called Granville has been formed at Port Moresby, on the eastern side of the Gulf of Papua; but it has only a handful of white men in it, and about 200 native huts gathered round the residence of the Queen's Commissioner, who acts as a sort of governor. New Guinea has so many possibilities in the way of trade—in sago, nutmegs, camphor, sugar, cocoa-nuts, flax, in the cutting of cedar timber, which is abundant, as well as in the production of india-rubber from the juice of the caoutchouc-tree—that it may

FIG. 44.—A LOOK INTO THE INTERIOR OF NEW GUINEA.

perhaps, in spite of the climate, become eventually a valuable part of the British Empire.

The animals of New Guinea are closely allied to those of Australia. Nearly all the mammals are marsupial, chiefly kangaroos, of which the most remarkable is the tree kangaroo. The island is rich in birds, among which are found the beautiful birds of paradise, crowned pigeons, and jet black cockatoos.

Among the numerous minor islands and groups of islands in the Pacific Ocean which have been annexed to the British Empire, the following are the chief :—

The Cook **Islands** lie to the east of Fiji. They consist of eleven volcanic islets, fertile, and well peopled by a fine-looking brown-red race.

Starbuck, **Malden**, and Fanning are three small islands lying to the north of Cook Island. Norfolk Island and **Lord Howe** Island are also very small. They lie to the east of Australia, and are politically attached to New South Wales.

THE END

Printed by R. & R. CLARK, *Edinburgh*.

MACMILLAN'S GEOGRAPHICAL SERIES.

Edited by SIR ARCHIBALD GEIKIE, F.R.S.,
Director-General of the Geological Survey of the United Kingdom.

The Teaching of Geography. A Practical Handbook for the use of Teachers. By Sir ARCHIBALD GEIKIE, F.R.S. Globe 8vo. 2s.

The *Times* says:—"The book is written with Mr. Geikie's well-known fluency and eloquence, and will be read with profit and pleasure by any one. Nothing, in our estimation, could be more satisfactory, or calculated to lead to more profitable results, than the suggestions contained in the introductory chapters for the elementary teaching of the subject. . . . Mr. Geikie's volume, as a whole, lifts geography into a new atmosphere. If his suggestions are faithfully followed in all our schools the result could not but be of the highest benefit to education all round. . . . It ought to be welcomed with open arms by all friends of real education."

The *Journal of Education* says:—"This simple and unpretentious handbook for teachers serves as a fitting introduction to a new geographical series projected and edited by the same author. Such a series, the scope of which is indirectly indicated in this volume, is greatly needed—something less arid and formal than the tabular statements of the old-fashioned geographies, and more methodical and systematic than the modern geographical Readers. And no fitter editor for such a series could have been chosen. Not only has Dr. Geikie a wide and profound knowledge of his subject, but he has grasped the first principle of pedagogics,—that knowledge profiteth little or nothing unless it is gained in the right way, by observation and induction, and so becomes a living germ of future growth, not a store of raw material. This principle is the keynote of the handbook, and its various applications are admirably worked out, especially in the earlier stages."

The Elementary School Atlas. With 24 Maps in Colours, specially designed to illustrate all Elementary Text-Books of Geography. By JOHN BARTHOLOMEW, F.R.G.S. 4to. 1s.

The *Guardian* says:—"The shilling *Elementary School Atlas*, which we have received from Messrs. Macmillan and Co., is almost a model of judicious selection and arrangement. Of the twenty-four plates which it contains, six are devoted to the continents and Australasia, as many double-page maps of the British Isles, and the remainder to useful diagrams and physiological charts. This is as it should be. With the exception of the chart showing zones of climate, the plates are well coloured, the names throughout are distinctly printed, and above all there are not too many of them."

Geography of the British Isles. By Sir ARCHIBALD GEIKIE, F.R.S. 18mo. 1s.

The *Athenæum* says:—"A favourable specimen of what a book of this type should be. It is surprising how large an amount of information and what variety of matter the author has succeeded in crowding into 127 very small pages without rendering his little book repellent."

The *Literary World* says:—"Dr. A. Geikie is so well known by his able and lucid treatises on geology that those who believe in combining some instruction in that branch of science with the teaching of geography will welcome a work like the *Elementary Geography of the British Isles*, issued in 'Macmillan's Geographical Series.' We have rarely met with a school book at once so delightful and so valuable."

An Elementary Class Book of General Geography. By HUGH ROBERT MILL, D.Sc., F.R.S.E., Lecturer on Physiography and on Commercial Geography in the Heriot-Watt College, Edinburgh. With Illustrations. Crown 8vo. 3s. 6d.

The *Journal of Education* says:—"We can recommend it to teachers as a valuable help . . . for the book has many excellences. The description, for example, of the geographical position of Africa (section 513), is admirable both as a summary and as an aid to the memory. The work also abounds in vivid and interesting descriptions of landscapes and scenes, in numerous statistical tables of much value, and in beautiful characteristic illustrations, from the Selvas of the Amazon to Antarctic icewalls and icebergs, from a busy thoroughfare in London or Cairo to the solitude of an oasis in the Sahara, from the sleepy canals of flat Holland to the awe-inspiring passes of the Himalayan mountains; all well calculated to stimulate the young imagination. A full index concludes the work."

The *Guardian* says:—"The descriptive portions of the work are excellently written and arranged, and give a better idea of the configuration of the continents, and of the history, political divisions, industries, customs, and habits of the peoples who inhabit them, than any other school text-book which has come beneath our notice."

An Elementary Geography of India, Burma, and Ceylon. By H. F. BLANFORD, F.R.S. With Illustrations. Globe 8vo. 2s. 6d.

The *Academy* says:—"The first portion of the book, treating of India generally, is a model of clear exposition, and is made as interesting as the character of the subject permits."

The *Speaker* says:—"The book is at once simple and scientific, and it is not merely well written, but admirably arranged. No aspect of the subject appears to have been overlooked, and we are not aware of any text-book which gives in similar compass as vivid and interesting a summary of the whole field of inquiry. The volume is well illustrated."

The *Saturday Review* says:—"Mr. Blanford's *Elementary Geography of India, Burma, and Ceylon,* is a valuable addition to 'Macmillan's Geographical Series.' In method and arrangement it is a model of clearness and conciseness. The woodcuts are good, and the statistical information, admirably tabulated, is neither more nor less than is necessary."

Maps and Map Drawing. By WILLIAM A. ELDERTON. 18mo. 1s.

The *Morning Post* says:—"May be recommended as a useful book to those students who have an elementary knowledge of geometry, and the use of the more common mathematical instruments. . . . A careful perusal of Mr. Elderton's book will remove many of the difficulties experienced by beginners and help them to retain in their memories the form of the countries they have to delineate."

Geography of Europe. By JAMES SIME, M.A. With Illustrations. Globe 8vo. 3s.

The *Glasgow Herald* says:—"It contains a vast amount of remarkably well-arranged information, and numerous illustrations are given both of the more striking European cities and of natural phenomena."

The *University Correspondent* says:—"Mr. Sime's book is worthy of its place in this admirable series. . . . The whole treatment is fresh and suggestive; in particular, the stress laid on the peculiarities of the inland seas, and on the relation of race and language, and the classification of valleys as 'longitudinal' and 'transverse,' call for praise."

Geography of the British Colonies. By G. M. DAWSON and A. SUTHERLAND.

Physical and Political School Atlas. Consisting of 80 Maps and complete Index. Prepared for the use of Senior Pupils. By J. G. BARTHOLOMEW, F.R.G.S. Royal 4to. 8s. 6d. Half morocco. 10s. 6d.

MACMILLAN AND CO., LONDON.

April 1892

A Catalogue

OF

Educational Books

PUBLISHED BY

Macmillan & Co.

BEDFORD STREET, STRAND, LONDON

For books of a less educational character on the subjects named below, see Macmillan and Co.'s Classified Catalogue of Books in General Literature.

CONTENTS

	PAGE
GREEK AND LATIN CLASSICS—	
ELEMENTARY CLASSICS	2
CLASSICAL SERIES	4
CLASSICAL LIBRARY; Texts, Commentaries, Translations	6
GRAMMAR, COMPOSITION, AND PHILOLOGY	8
ANTIQUITIES, ANCIENT HISTORY, AND PHILOSOPHY	11
MODERN LANGUAGES AND LITERATURE—	
ENGLISH	13
FRENCH	17
GERMAN	19
MODERN GREEK	20
ITALIAN	20
SPANISH	20
MATHEMATICS—	
ARITHMETIC	20
BOOK-KEEPING	21
ALGEBRA	22
EUCLID AND PURE GEOMETRY	22
GEOMETRICAL DRAWING	23
MENSURATION	23
TRIGONOMETRY	23
ANALYTICAL GEOMETRY	24
PROBLEMS AND QUESTIONS IN MATHEMATICS	25
HIGHER PURE MATHEMATICS	25
MECHANICS	26
PHYSICS	27
ASTRONOMY	29
HISTORICAL	30
NATURAL SCIENCES—	
CHEMISTRY	30
PHYSICAL GEOGRAPHY, GEOLOGY, AND MINERALOGY	32
BIOLOGY	32
MEDICINE	34
HUMAN SCIENCES—	
MENTAL AND MORAL PHILOSOPHY	35
POLITICAL ECONOMY	36
LAW AND POLITICS	37
ANTHROPOLOGY	38
EDUCATION	38
TECHNICAL KNOWLEDGE—	
CIVIL AND MECHANICAL ENGINEERING	38
MILITARY AND NAVAL SCIENCE	39
AGRICULTURE AND FORESTRY	39
DOMESTIC ECONOMY	40
COMMERCE	40
GEOGRAPHY	40
HISTORY	41
ART	43
DIVINITY	44

THE GREEK ELEGIAC POETS.—FROM CALLINUS TO CALLIMACHUS. Selected by Rev. HERBERT KYNASTON, D.D.
THUCYDIDES.—BOOK IV. CHS. 1-41. THE CAPTURE OF SPHACTERIA. By C. E. GRAVES, M.A.

CLASSICAL SERIES
FOR COLLEGES AND SCHOOLS.
Fcap. 8vo.

ÆSCHINES.—IN CTESIPHONTA. By Rev. T. GWATKIN, M.A., and E. S. SHUCKBURGH, M.A. 5s.
ÆSCHYLUS.—PERSÆ. By A. O. PRICKARD, M.A., Fellow and Tutor of New College, Oxford. With Map. 2s. 6d.
  SEVEN AGAINST THEBES. SCHOOL EDITION. By A. W. VERRALL, Litt.D., and M. A. BAYFIELD, M.A. 2s. 6d.
ANDOCIDES.—DE MYSTERIIS. By W. J. HICKIE, M.A. 2s. 6d.
ATTIC ORATORS.—Selections from ANTIPHON, ANDOCIDES, LYSIAS, ISOCRATES, and ISAEUS. By R. C. JEBB, Litt.D., Regius Professor of Greek in the University of Cambridge. 5s.
*CÆSAR.—THE GALLIC WAR. By Rev. JOHN BOND, M.A., and Rev. A. S. WALPOLE, M.A. With Maps. 4s. 6d.
CATULLUS.—SELECT POEMS. By F. P. SIMPSON, B.A. 3s. 6d. The Text of this Edition is carefully expurgated for School use.
*CICERO.—THE CATILINE ORATIONS. By A. S. WILKINS, Litt.D., Professor of Latin, Owens College, Manchester. 2s. 6d.
  PRO LEGE MANILIA. By Prof. A. S. WILKINS, Litt.D. 2s. 6d.
  THE SECOND PHILIPPIC ORATION. By JOHN E. B. MAYOR, M.A., Professor of Latin in the University of Cambridge. 3s. 6d.
  PRO ROSCIO AMERINO. By E. H. DONKIN, M.A. 2s. 6d.
  PRO P. SESTIO. By Rev. H. A. HOLDEN, Litt.D. 3s. 6d.
  SELECT LETTERS. By R. Y. TYRRELL, M.A. 4s. 6d.
DEMOSTHENES.—DE CORONA. By B. DRAKE, M.A. 7th Edition, revised by E. S. SHUCKBURGH, M.A. 3s. 6d.
  ADVERSUS LEPTINEM. By Rev. J. R. KING, M.A., Fellow and Tutor of Oriel College, Oxford. 2s. 6d.
  THE FIRST PHILIPPIC. By Rev. T. GWATKIN, M.A. 2s. 6d.
  IN MIDIAM. By Prof. A. S. WILKINS, Litt.D., and HERMAN HAGER, Ph.D., the Owens College, Victoria University, Manchester. [In preparation.
EURIPIDES.—HIPPOLYTUS. By Rev. J. P. MAHAFFY, D.D., Fellow of Trinity College, and Professor of Ancient History in the University of Dublin, and J B. BURY, M.A., Fellow of Trinity College, Dublin. 2s. 6d.
  MEDEA. By A. W. VERRALL, Litt.D., Fellow of Trinity College, Cambridge. 2s. 6d.
  IPHIGENIA IN TAURIS. By E. B. ENGLAND, M.A. 3s.
  ION. By M. A. BAYFIELD, M.A., Headmaster of Christ's College, Brecon. 2s. 6d.
  BACCHAE. By R. Y. TYRRELL, M.A., Regius Professor of Greek in the University of Dublin. [In preparation.
HERODOTUS.—BOOK III. By G. C. MACAULAY, M.A. 2s. 6d.
  BOOK V. By J. STRACHAN, M.A., Professor of Greek, Owens College, Manchester. [In preparation.
  BOOK VI. By the same. 3s. 6d.
  BOOK VII. By Mrs. MONTAGU BUTLER. 3s. 6d.
HOMER.—ILIAD. BOOKS I., IX., XI., XVI.-XXIV. THE STORY OF ACHILLES. By the late J. H. PRATT, M.A., and WALTER LEAF, Litt.D., Fellows of Trinity College, Cambridge. 5s.
  ODYSSEY. BOOK IX. By Prof. JOHN E. B. MAYOR. 2s. 6d.
  ODYSSEY. BOOKS XXI.-XXIV. THE TRIUMPH OF ODYSSEUS. By S. G. HAMILTON, M.A., Fellow of Hertford College, Oxford. 2s. 6d.

CLASSICAL SERIES

HORACE.—*THE ODES. By T. E. Page, M.A., Assistant Master at the Charterhouse. 5s. (BOOKS I., II., and IV. separately, 2s. each.)
   THE SATIRES. By Arthur Palmer, M.A., Professor of Latin in the University of Dublin. 5s.
   THE EPISTLES AND ARS POETICA. By Prof. A. S. Wilkins, Litt.D. 5s.
ISAEOS.—THE ORATIONS. By William Ridgeway, M.A., Professor of Greek, Queen's College, Cork.   *[In preparation.*
JUVENAL.—*THIRTEEN SATIRES. By E. G. Hardy, M.A. 5s. The Text is carefully expurgated for School use.
   SELECT SATIRES. By Prof. John E. B. Mayor. X. and XI. 3s. 6d. XII.-XVI. 4s. 6d.
LIVY.—*BOOKS II. and III. By Rev. H. M. Stephenson, M.A. 3s. 6d.
   *BOOKS XXI. and XXII. By Rev. W. W. Capes, M.A. With Maps. 4s. 6d.
   *BOOKS XXIII. and XXIV. By G. C. Macaulay, M.A. With Maps. 3s. 6d.
   *THE LAST TWO KINGS OF MACEDON. EXTRACTS FROM THE FOURTH AND FIFTH DECADES OF LIVY. By F. H. Rawlins, M.A., Assistant Master at Eton. With Maps. 2s. 6d.
   THE SUBJUGATION OF ITALY. SELECTIONS FROM THE FIRST DECADE. By G. E. Marindin, M.A.   *[In preparation.*
LUCRETIUS.—BOOKS I.-III. By J. H. Warburton Lee, M.A., late Assistant Master at Rossall. 3s. 6d.
LYSIAS.—SELECT ORATIONS. By E. S. Shuckburgh, M.A. 5s.
MARTIAL.—SELECT EPIGRAMS. By Rev. H. M. Stephenson, M.A. 5s.
*OVID.—FASTI. By G. H. Hallam, M.A., Assistant Master at Harrow. 3s. 6d.
*HEROIDUM EPISTULÆ XIII. By E. S. Shuckburgh, M.A. 3s. 6d.
   METAMORPHOSES. BOOKS I.-III. By C. Simmons, M.A. *[In preparation.*
   BOOKS XIII. and XIV. By the same. 3s. 6d.
PLATO.—LACHES. By M. T. Tatham, M.A. 2s. 6d.
   THE REPUBLIC. BOOKS I.-V. By T. H. Warren, M.A., President of Magdalen College, Oxford. 5s.
PLAUTUS.—MILES GLORIOSUS. By R. Y. Tyrrell, M.A., Regius Professor of Greek in the University of Dublin. 2d Ed., revised. 3s. 6d.
   AMPHITRUO. By Prof. Arthur Palmer, M.A. 3s. 6d.
   CAPTIVI. By A. R. S. Hallidie, M.A. 3s. 6d.
PLINY.—LETTERS. BOOKS I. and II. By J. Cowan, M.A., Assistant Master at the Manchester Grammar School. 3s.
   LETTERS. BOOK III. By Prof. John E. B. Mayor. With Life of Pliny by G. H. Rendall, M.A. 3s. 6d.
PLUTARCH.—LIFE OF THEMISTOKLES. By Rev. H. A. Holden, Litt.D. 3s. 6d.
   LIVES OF GALBA AND OTHO. By E. G. Hardy, M.A. 5s.
POLYBIUS.—THE HISTORY OF THE ACHÆAN LEAGUE AS CONTAINED IN THE REMAINS OF POLYBIUS. By Rev. W. W. Capes, M.A. 5s.
PROPERTIUS.—SELECT POEMS. By Prof. J. P. Postgate, Litt.D., Fellow of Trinity College, Cambridge. 2d Ed., revised. 5s.
SALLUST.—*CATILINA and JUGURTHA. By C. Merivale, D.D., Dean of Ely. 3s. 6d. Or separately, 2s. each.
   *BELLUM CATULINÆ. By A. M. Cook, M.A., Assistant Master at St. Paul's School. 2s. 6d.
   JUGURTHA. By the same.   *[In preparation.*
TACITUS.—THE ANNALS. BOOKS I. and II. By J. S. Reid, Litt.D. *[In prep.*
   BOOK VI. By A. J. Church, M.A., and W. J. Brodribb, M.A. 2s.
   THE HISTORIES. BOOKS I. and II. By A. D. Godley, M.A., Fellow of Magdalen College, Oxford. 3s. 6d.
   BOOKS III.-V. By the same. 3s. 6d.
   AGRICOLA and GERMANIA. By A. J. Church, M.A., and W. J. Brodribb, M.A. 3s. 6d. Or separately, 2s. each.
TERENCE.—HAUTON TIMORUMENOS. By E. S. Shuckburgh, M.A. 2s. 6d. With Translation. 3s. 6d.
   PHORMIO. By Rev. John Bond, M.A., and Rev. A. S. Walpole, M.A. 2s. 6d.

GREEK AND LATIN CLASSICS

THUCYDIDES.—BOOK I. By CLEMENT BRYANS, M.A. [*In preparation.*
   BOOK II. By E. C. MARCHANT, M.A., Fellow of St. Peter's Coll., Cam. 3s. 6d.
   BOOK III. By the same. [*In preparation.*
   BOOK IV. By C. E. GRAVES, M.A., Classical Lecturer at St. John's College, Cambridge. 3s. 6d.
   BOOK V. By the same. 3s. 6d.
   BOOKS VI. AND VII. By Rev. PERCIVAL FROST, M.A. With Map. 3s. 6d.
   BOOKS VI. AND VII. (separately). By E. C. MARCHANT, M.A. [*In preparation.*
   BOOK VIII. By Prof. T. G. TUCKER, Litt.D. [*In the Press.*
TIBULLUS.—SELECT POEMS. By Prof. J. P. POSTGATE, Litt.D. [*In preparation.*
VIRGIL.—ÆNEID. BOOKS II. AND III. THE NARRATIVE OF ÆNEAS. By E. W. HOWSON, M.A., Assistant Master at Harrow. 2s.
XENOPHON.—THE ANABASIS. BOOKS I.-IV. By Profs. W. W. GOODWIN and J. W. WHITE. Adapted to Goodwin's Greek Grammar. With Map. 3s. 6d.
   HELLENICA. BOOKS I. AND II. By H. HAILSTONE, B.A. With Map. 2s. 6d.
   CYROPÆDIA. BOOKS VII. AND VIII. By A. GOODWIN, M.A., Professor of Classics in University College, London. 2s. 6d.
   MEMORABILIA SOCRATIS. By A. R. CLUER, B.A., Balliol College, Oxford. 5s.
   HIERO. By Rev. H. A. HOLDEN, Litt.D. 2s. 6d.
   OECONOMICUS. By the same. With Lexicon. 5s.

CLASSICAL LIBRARY.

Texts, Edited with Introductions and Notes, for the use of Advanced Students; Commentaries and Translations.

ÆSCHYLUS.—THE SUPPLICES. A Revised Text, with Translation. By T. G TUCKER, Litt.D., Professor of Classical Philology in the University of Melbourne. 8vo. 10s. 6d.
   THE SEVEN AGAINST THEBES. With Translation. By A. W. VERRALL, Litt.D., Fellow of Trinity College, Cambridge. 8vo. 7s. 6d.
   AGAMEMNON. With Translation. By A. W. VERRALL, Litt.D. 8vo. 12s.
   AGAMEMNON, CHOEPHOROE, AND EUMENIDES. By A. O. PRICKARD, M.A., Fellow and Tutor of New College, Oxford. 8vo. [*In preparation.*
   THE EUMENIDES. With Verse Translation. By BERNARD DRAKE, M.A. 8vo. 5s.
ANTONINUS, MARCUS AURELIUS.—BOOK IV. OF THE MEDITATIONS. With Translation. By HASTINGS CROSSLEY, M.A. 8vo. 6s.
ARISTOPHANES.—THE BIRDS. Translated into English Verse. By B. H. KENNEDY, D.D. Cr. 8vo. 6s. Help Notes to the Same, for the Use of Students. 1s. 6d.
   SCHOLIA ARISTOPHANICA; being such Comments adscript to the text of Aristophanes as are preserved in the Codex Ravennas, arranged, emended, and translated. By Rev. W. G. RUTHERFORD, M.A., LL.D. 8vo. [*In the Press.*
ARISTOTLE.—THE METAPHYSICS. BOOK I. Translated by a Cambridge Graduate. 8vo. 5s.
   THE POLITICS. By R. D. HICKS, M.A., Fellow of Trinity College, Cambridge. 8vo. [*In the Press.*
   THE POLITICS. Translated by Rev. J. E. C. WELLDON, M.A., Headmaster of Harrow. Cr. 8vo. 10s. 6d.
   THE RHETORIC. Translated by the same. Cr. 8vo. 7s. 6d.
   AN INTRODUCTION TO ARISTOTLE'S RHETORIC. With Analysis, Notes, and Appendices. By E. M. COPE, Fellow and late Tutor of Trinity College, Cambridge. 8vo. 14s.
   THE ETHICS. Translated by Rev. J. E. C. WELLDON, M.A. Cr. 8vo. [*In prep.*
   THE SOPHISTICI ELENCHI. With Translation. By E. POSTE, M.A., Fellow of Oriel College, Oxford. 8vo. 8s. 6d.
   ON THE CONSTITUTION OF ATHENS. By J. E. SANDYS, Litt.D. [*In prep.*
   ON THE CONSTITUTION OF ATHENS. Translated by E. POSTE, M.A. Cr. 8vo. 3s. 6d.
   ON THE ART OF POETRY. A Lecture. By A. O. PRICKARD, M.A., Fellow and Tutor of New College, Oxford. Cr. 8vo. 3s. 6d.

ATTIC ORATORS.—FROM ANTIPHON TO ISAEOS. By R. C. JEBB, Litt.D., Regius Professor of Greek in the University of Cambridge. 2 vols. 8vo. 25s.
BABRIUS.—With Lexicon. By Rev. W. G. RUTHERFORD, M.A., LL.D., Headmaster of Westminster. 8vo. 12s. 6d.
CICERO.—THE ACADEMICA. By J. S. REID, Litt.D., Fellow of Caius College, Cambridge. 8vo. 15s.
THE ACADEMICS. Translated by the same. 8vo. 5s. 6d.
SELECT LETTERS. After the Edition of ALBERT WATSON, M.A. **Translated** by G. E. JEANS, M.A., Fellow of Hertford College, Oxford. Cr. 8vo. **10s. 6d.**
EURIPIDES.—MEDEA. By A. W. VERRALL, Litt.D. 8vo. 7s. 6d.
IPHIGENEIA AT AULIS. By E. B. ENGLAND, M.A. 8vo. 7s. 6d.
*INTRODUCTION TO THE STUDY OF EURIPIDES. By Professor J. P. MAHAFFY. Fcap. 8vo. 1s. 6d. (*Classical Writers.*)
HERODOTUS.—BOOKS I.-III. THE ANCIENT EMPIRES OF THE EAST. By A. H. SAYCE, Deputy-Professor of Comparative Philology in the University of Oxford. 8vo. 16s.
BOOKS IV.-IX. By R. W. MACAN, M.A., Reader in Ancient History in the University of Oxford. 8vo. [*In preparation.*
THE HISTORY. Translated by **G. C. MACAULAY, M.A.** 2 vols. Cr. 8vo. 18s.
HOMER.—THE ILIAD. By **WALTER LEAF, Litt.D.** 8vo. Books I.-XII. 14s. Books XIII.-XXIV. 14s.
THE ILIAD.—Translated into English Prose by ANDREW LANG, M.A., WALTER LEAF, Litt.D., and ERNEST MYERS, M.A. Cr. 8vo. 12s. 6d.
THE ODYSSEY. Done into English by S. H. BUTCHER, M.A., Professor of Greek in the University of Edinburgh, and ANDREW LANG, M.A. Cr. 8vo. 6s.
*INTRODUCTION TO THE STUDY OF HOMER. By the Right Hon. W. E. GLADSTONE. 18mo. 1s. (*Literature Primers.*)
HOMERIC DICTIONARY. Translated from the German of Dr. G. AUTENRIETH by R. P. KEEP, Ph.D. Illustrated. Cr. 8vo. 6s.
HORACE.—Translated by J. LONSDALE, M.A., and S. LEE, M.A. Gl. 8vo. 3s. 6d.
STUDIES, LITERARY AND HISTORICAL, IN THE ODES OF HORACE. By A. W. VERRALL, Litt.D. 8vo. 8s. 6d.
JUVENAL.—THIRTEEN SATIRES OF JUVENAL. By JOHN E. B. MAYOR, M.A., Professor of Latin in the University of Cambridge. Cr. 8vo. 2 vols. 10s. 6d. each.
THIRTEEN SATIRES. Translated by ALEX. LEEPER, M.A., LL.D., Warden of Trinity College, Melbourne. Revised Ed. Cr. 8vo. 3s. 6d.
KTESIAS.—THE FRAGMENTS OF THE PERSIKA OF KTESIAS. By JOHN GILMORE, M.A. 8vo. 8s. 6d.
LIVY.—BOOKS I.-IV. Translated by Rev. H. M. STEPHENSON, M.A. [*In prep.*
BOOKS XXI.-XXV. Translated by A. J. CHURCH, M.A., and W. J. BRODRIBB, M.A. Cr. 8vo. 7s. 6d.
*INTRODUCTION TO THE STUDY OF LIVY. By Rev. **W. W.** CAPES, M.A. Fcap. 8vo. 1s. 6d. (*Classical Writers.*)
LONGINUS.—ON THE SUBLIME. Translated by H. L. HAVELL, B.A. With Introduction by ANDREW LANG. Cr. 8vo. 4s. 6d.
MARTIAL.—BOOKS I. AND II. OF THE EPIGRAMS. By Prof. JOHN E. B. MAYOR, M.A. 8vo. [*In the Press.*
MELEAGER.—FIFTY POEMS OF MELEAGER. Translated by WALTER HEADLAM. Fcap. 4to. 7s. 6d.
PAUSANIAS.—DESCRIPTION OF GREECE. Translated with Commentary by J. G. FRAZER, M.A., Fellow of Trinity College, Cambridge. [*In prep.*
PHRYNICHUS.—THE NEW PHRYNICHUS; being a Revised Text of the Ecloga **of the Grammarian** Phrynichus. With Introduction and Commentary by **Rev.** W. G. RUTHERFORD, M.A., LL.D., Headmaster of Westminster. 8vo. 18s.
PINDAR.—THE EXTANT ODES OF PINDAR. Translated by ERNEST MYERS, M.A. Cr. 8vo. 5s.
THE OLYMPIAN AND PYTHIAN ODES. Edited, with an Introductory Essay, by BASIL GILDERSLEEVE, Professor of Greek in the Johns Hopkins University, U.S.A. Cr. 8vo. 7s. 6d.

GREEK AND LATIN CLASSICS

THE NEMEAN ODES. By J. B. BURY, M.A., Fellow of Trinity College, Dublin. 8vo. 12s.

THE ISTHMIAN ODES. By the same Editor. 12s.

PLATO.—PHÆDO. By R. D. ARCHER-HIND, M.A., Fellow of Trinity College, Cambridge. 8vo. 8s. 6d.

PHÆDO. By W. D. GEDDES, LL.D., Principal of the University of Aberdeen. 8vo. 8s. 6d.

TIMAEUS. With Translation. By R. D. ARCHER-HIND, M.A. 8vo. 16s.

THE REPUBLIC OF PLATO. Translated by J. LL. DAVIES, M.A., and D. J. VAUGHAN, M.A. 18mo. 4s. 6d.

EUTHYPHRO, APOLOGY, CRITO, AND PHÆDO. Translated by F. J. CHURCH. 18mo. 2s. 6d. net.

PHÆDRUS, LYSIS, AND PROTAGORAS. Translated by J. WRIGHT, M.A. 18mo. 4s. 6d.

PLAUTUS.—THE MOSTELLARIA. By WILLIAM RAMSAY, M.A. Ed. by G. G. RAMSAY, M.A., Professor of Humanity, University of Glasgow. 8vo. 14s.

PLINY.—CORRESPONDENCE WITH TRAJAN. C. Plinii Caecilii Secundi Epistulæ ad Traianum Imperatorem cum Eiusdem Responsis. By E. G. HARDY, M.A. 8vo. 10s. 6d.

POLYBIUS.—THE HISTORIES OF POLYBIUS. Translated by E. S. SHUCK-BURGH, M.A. 2 vols. Cr. 8vo. 24s.

SALLUST.—CATILINE AND JUGURTHA. Translated by A. W. POLLARD, B.A. Cr. 8vo. 6s. THE CATILINE (separately). 3s.

SOPHOCLES.—ŒDIPUS THE KING. Translated into English Verse by E. D. A. MORSHEAD, M.A., Assistant Master at Winchester. Fcap. 8vo. 3s. 6d.

TACITUS.—THE ANNALS. By G. O. HOLBROOKE, M.A., Professor of Latin in Trinity College, Hartford, U.S.A. With Maps. 8vo. 16s.

THE ANNALS. Translated by A. J. CHURCH, M.A., and W. J. BRODRIBB, M.A. With Maps. Cr. 8vo. 7s. 6d.

THE HISTORIES. By Rev. W. A. SPOONER, M.A., Fellow and Tutor of New College, Oxford. 8vo. 16s.

THE HISTORY. Translated by A. J. CHURCH, M.A., and W. J. BRODRIBB, M.A. With Map. Cr. 8vo. 6s.

THE AGRICOLA AND GERMANY, WITH THE DIALOGUE ON ORATORY. Translated by the same. With Maps. Cr. 8vo. 4s. 6d.

*INTRODUCTION TO THE STUDY OF TACITUS. By A. J. CHURCH, M.A., and W. J. BRODRIBB, M.A. Fcap. 8vo. 1s. 6d. (*Classical Writers.*)

THEOCRITUS, BION, AND MOSCHUS. Translated by A. LANG, M.A. 18mo. 4s. 6d. Also an Edition on Large Paper. Cr. 8vo. 9s.

THUCYDIDES.—BOOK IV. A Revision of the Text, Illustrating the Principal Causes of Corruption in the Manuscripts of this Author. By Rev. W. G. RUTHERFORD, M.A., LL.D., Headmaster of Westminster. 8vo. 7s. 6d.

BOOK VIII. By H. C. GOODHART, M.A., Professor of Latin in the University of Edinburgh. [*In the Press.*

VIRGIL.—Translated by J. LONSDALE, M.A., and S. LEE, M.A. Gl. 8vo. 3s. 6d.

THE ÆNEID. Translated by J. W. MACKAIL, M.A., Fellow of Balliol College, Oxford. Cr. 8vo. 7s. 6d.

XENOPHON.—Translated by H. G. DAKYNS, M.A. In four vols. Cr. 8vo. Vol. I. "The Anabasis" and "The Hellenica I. and II." 10s. 6d. Vol. II. "Hellenica" III.-VII., and the two Polities—"Athenian" and "Laconian," the "Agesilaus," and the tract on "Revenues." With Maps and Plans. [*In the Press.*

GRAMMAR, COMPOSITION, & PHILOLOGY.
Latin.

*BELCHER.—SHORT EXERCISES IN LATIN PROSE COMPOSITION AND EXAMINATION PAPERS IN LATIN GRAMMAR. Part I. By Rev. H. BELCHER, LL.D., Rector of the High School, Dunedin, N.Z. 18mo. 1s. 6d. KEY, for Teachers only. 18mo. 3s. 6d.

*Part II., On the Syntax of Sentences, with an Appendix, including EXERCISES IN LATIN IDIOMS, etc. 18mo. 2s. KEY, for Teachers only. 18mo. 3s.

GRAMMAR, COMPOSITION, AND PHILOLOGY

*BRYANS.—LATIN PROSE EXERCISES BASED UPON CÆSAR'S GALLIC WAR. With a Classification of Cæsar's Chief Phrases and Grammatical Notes on Cæsar's Usages. By CLEMENT BRYANS, M.A., Assistant Master at Dulwich College. Ex. fcap. 8vo. 2s. 6d. KEY, for Teachers only. 4s. 6d.

COOKSON.—A LATIN SYNTAX. By CHRISTOPHER COOKSON, M.A., Assistant Master at St. Paul's School. 8vo. [*In preparation.*

CORNELL UNIVERSITY STUDIES IN CLASSICAL PHILOLOGY. Edited by I. FLAGG, W. G. HALE, and B. I. WHEELER. I. The *CUM*-Constructions: their History and Functions. By W. G. HALE. Part 1. Critical. 1s. 8d. net. Part 2. Constructive. 3s. 4d. net. II. Analogy and the Scope of its Application in Language. By B. I. WHEELER. 1s. 3d. net.

*EICKE.—FIRST LESSONS IN LATIN. By K. M. EICKE, B.A., Assistant Master at Oundle School. Gl. 8vo. 2s. 6d.

*ENGLAND.—EXERCISES ON LATIN SYNTAX AND IDIOM. ARRANGED WITH REFERENCE TO ROBY'S SCHOOL LATIN GRAMMAR. By E. B. ENGLAND, Assistant Lecturer at the Owens College, Manchester. Cr. 8vo. 2s. 6d. KEY, for Teachers only. 2s. 6d.

GILES.—A SHORT MANUAL OF PHILOLOGY FOR CLASSICAL STUDENTS. By P. GILES, M.A., Reader in Comparative Philology in the University of Cambridge. Cr. 8vo. [*In the Press.*

HADLEY.—ESSAYS, PHILOLOGICAL AND CRITICAL. By JAMES HADLEY, late Professor in Yale College. 8vo. 16s.

HODGSON.—MYTHOLOGY FOR LATIN VERSIFICATION. Fables for rendering into **Latin Verse.** By F. HODGSON, B.D., late Provost of Eton. New Ed., revised by F. C. HODGSON, M.A. 18mo. 3s.

LUPTON.—*AN INTRODUCTION TO LATIN ELEGIAC VERSE COMPOSITION. By J. H. LUPTON, Sur-Master of St. Paul's School. Gl. 8vo. 2s. 6d. KEY TO PART II. (XXV.-C.) Gl. 8vo. 3s. 6d.

*AN INTRODUCTION TO LATIN LYRIC VERSE COMPOSITION. By the same. Gl. 8vo. 3s. KEY, for Teachers only. Gl. 8vo. 4s. 6d.

*MACMILLAN.—FIRST LATIN GRAMMAR. By M. C. MACMILLAN, M.A. Fcap. 8vo. 1s. 6d.

MACMILLAN'S LATIN COURSE.—By A. M. COOK, M.A., Assistant Master at St. Paul's School.
  *FIRST PART. Gl. 8vo. 3s. 6d.
  *SECOND PART. 2s. 6d. [*Third Part in preparation.*

*MACMILLAN'S SHORTER LATIN COURSE.—By A. M. COOK, M.A. Abridgment of "Macmillan's Latin Course," First Part. Gl. 8vo. 1s. 6d. KEY, for Teachers only. 4s. 6d.

*MACMILLAN'S LATIN READER.—A LATIN READER FOR THE LOWER FORMS IN SCHOOLS. By H. J. HARDY, M.A., Assistant Master at Winchester. Gl. 8vo. 2s. 6d.

NIXON.—PARALLEL EXTRACTS, Arranged for Translation into English and Latin, with Notes on Idioms. By J. E. NIXON, M.A., Fellow and Classical Lecturer, King's College, Cambridge. Part I.—Historical and Epistolary. Cr. 8vo. 3s. 6d.

  PROSE EXTRACTS, Arranged for Translation into English and Latin, with General and Special Prefaces on Style and Idiom. By the same. I. Oratorical. II. Historical. III. Philosophical. IV. Anecdotes and Letters. 2d Ed., enlarged to 280 pp. Cr. 8vo. 4s. 6d. SELECTIONS FROM THE SAME. 3s. Translations of about 70 Extracts can be supplied to Schoolmasters (2s. 6d.), on application to the Author: and about 40 similarly of "Parallel Extracts." 1s. 6d. post free.

*PANTIN.—A FIRST **LATIN VERSE** BOOK. By W. E. P. PANTIN, M.A., Assistant Master at St. Paul's School. Gl. 8vo. 1s. 6d. [KEY, *in Prep.*

*PEILE.—A PRIMER OF PHILOLOGY. By J. PEILE, Litt.D., Master of Christ's College, Cambridge. 18mo. 1s.

*POSTGATE.—SERMO LATINUS. A short Guide to Latin Prose Composition. By Prof. J. P. POSTGATE, Litt.D., Fellow of Trinity College, Cambridge. Gl. 8vo. 2s. **6d.** KEY to "Selected Passages." Gl. 8vo. 3s. 6d.

POTTS.—*HINTS TOWARDS LATIN PROSE COMPOSITION. By A. W. POTTS, M.A., LL.D., late Fellow of St. John's College, Cambridge. Ex. fcap. 8vo. 3s.
*PASSAGES FOR TRANSLATION INTO LATIN PROSE. Edited with Notes and References to the above. Ex. fcap. 8vo. 2s. 6d. KEY, for Teachers only. 2s. 6d.
*PRESTON.—EXERCISES IN LATIN VERSE OF VARIOUS KINDS. By Rev. G. PRESTON. Gl. 8vo. 2s. 6d. KEY, for Teachers only. Gl. 8vo. 5s.
REID.—A GRAMMAR OF TACITUS. By J. S. REID, Litt.D., Fellow of Caius College, Cambridge. [In the Press.
A GRAMMAR OF VIRGIL. By the same. [In preparation.
ROBY.—Works by H. J. ROBY, M.A., late Fellow of St. John's College, Cambridge.
A GRAMMAR OF THE LATIN LANGUAGE, from Plautus to Suetonius. Part I. Sounds, Inflexions, Word-formation, Appendices. Cr. 8vo. 9s. Part II. Syntax, Prepositions, etc. 10s. 6d.
*SCHOOL LATIN GRAMMAR. Cr. 8vo. 5s.
ROBY and WILKINS. AN ELEMENTARY LATIN GRAMMAR. By H. J. ROBY, M.A. and Prof. A. S. WILKINS. [In the Press.
*RUSH.—SYNTHETIC LATIN DELECTUS. With Notes and Vocabulary. By E. RUSH, B.A. Ex. fcap. 8vo. 2s. 6d.
*RUST.—FIRST STEPS TO LATIN PROSE COMPOSITION. By Rev. G. RUST, M.A. 18mo. 1s. 6d. KEY, for Teachers only. By W. M. YATES. 18mo. 3s. 6d.
SHUCKBURGH.—PASSAGES FROM LATIN AUTHORS FOR TRANSLATION INTO ENGLISH. Selected with a view to the needs of Candidates for the Cambridge Local, and Public Schools' Examinations. By E. S. SHUCKBURGH, M.A. Cr. 8vo. 2s.
*SIMPSON.—LATIN PROSE AFTER THE BEST AUTHORS : Cæsarian Prose. By F. P. SIMPSON, B.A. Ex. fcap. 8vo. 2s. 6d. KEY, for Teachers only. 5s.
STRACHAN and WILKINS.—ANALECTA. Selected Passages for Translation. By J. S. STRACHAN, M.A., Professor of Greek, and A. S. WILKINS, Litt.D., Professor of Latin, Owens College, Manchester. Cr. 8vo. 5s. KEY to Latin Passages. Cr. 8vo. Sewed, 6d. KEY to Greek Passages. Sewed, 6d.
THRING.—A LATIN GRADUAL. By the Rev. E. THRING, M.A., late Headmaster of Uppingham. A First Latin Construing Book. Fcap. 8vo. 2s. 6d.
A MANUAL OF MOOD CONSTRUCTIONS. Fcap. 8vo. 1s. 6d.
*WELCH and DUFFIELD.—LATIN ACCIDENCE AND EXERCISES ARRANGED FOR BEGINNERS. By W. WELCH and C. G. DUFFIELD. 18mo. 1s. 6d.
WRIGHT.—Works by J. WRIGHT, M.A., late Headmaster of Sutton Coldfield School.
A HELP TO LATIN GRAMMAR; or, the Form and Use of Words in Latin, with Progressive Exercises. Cr. 8vo. 4s. 6d.
THE SEVEN KINGS OF ROME. An Easy Narrative, abridged from the First Book of Livy by the omission of Difficult Passages; being a First Latin Reading Book, with Grammatical Notes and Vocabulary. Fcap. 8vo. 3s. 6d.
FIRST LATIN STEPS; OR, AN INTRODUCTION BY A SERIES OF EXAMPLES TO THE STUDY OF THE LATIN LANGUAGE. Cr. 8vo. 3s.
A COMPLETE LATIN COURSE, comprising Rules with Examples, Exercises, both Latin and English, on each Rule, and Vocabularies. Cr. 8vo. 2s. 6d.

Greek.

BLACKIE.—GREEK AND ENGLISH DIALOGUES FOR USE IN SCHOOLS AND COLLEGES. By JOHN STUART BLACKIE, Emeritus Professor of Greek in the University of Edinburgh. New Edition. Fcap. 8vo. 2s. 6d.
A GREEK PRIMER, COLLOQUIAL AND CONSTRUCTIVE. Cr. 8vo. 2s. 6d.
BRYANS.—GREEK PROSE EXERCISES based upon Thucydides. By C. BRYANS, M.A. [In preparation.
GILES.—See under Latin.
GOODWIN.—Works by W. W. GOODWIN, LL.D., D.C.L., Professor of Greek in Harvard University.
SYNTAX OF THE MOODS AND TENSES OF THE GREEK VERB. New Ed., revised and enlarged. 8vo. 14s.
*A GREEK GRAMMAR. Cr. 8vo. 6s.
*A GREEK GRAMMAR FOR SCHOOLS. Cr. 8vo. 3s. 6d.

GRAMMAR, COMPOSITION, AND PHILOLOGY 11

HADLEY.—See under Latin.
HADLEY—ALLEN.—A GREEK GRAMMAR FOR SCHOOLS AND COLLEGES. By JAMES HADLEY, late Professor in Yale College. Revised by F. DE F. ALLEN, Professor in Harvard College. Cr. 8vo. 6s.

*JACKSON.—FIRST STEPS TO GREEK PROSE COMPOSITION. By BLOMFIELD JACKSON, M.A. 18mo. 1s. 6d. KEY, for Teachers only. 18mo. 3s. 6d.

*SECOND STEPS TO GREEK PROSE COMPOSITION, with Examination Papers. By the same. 18mo. 2s. 6d. KEY, for Teachers only. 18mo. 3s. 6d.

KYNASTON.—EXERCISES IN THE COMPOSITION OF GREEK IAMBIC VERSE. By Rev. H. KYNASTON, D.D., Professor of Classics in the University of Durham. With Vocabulary. Ex. fcap. 8vo. 5s. KEY, for Teachers only. Ex. fcap. 8vo. 4s. 6d.

MACKIE.—PARALLEL PASSAGES FOR TRANSLATION INTO GREEK AND ENGLISH. With Indexes. By Rev. E. C. MACKIE, M.A., Classical Master at Heversham Grammar School. Gl. 8vo. 4s. 6d.

MACMILLAN'S GREEK COURSE.—Edited by Rev. W. G. RUTHERFORD, M.A., LL.D., Headmaster of Westminster. Gl. 8vo.
 *FIRST GREEK GRAMMAR—ACCIDENCE. By the Editor. 2s.
 *FIRST GREEK GRAMMAR—SYNTAX. By the same. 2s.
 ACCIDENCE AND SYNTAX. In one volume. 3s. 6d.
 *EASY EXERCISES IN GREEK ACCIDENCE. By H. G. UNDERHILL, M.A., Assistant Master at St. Paul's Preparatory School. 2s.
 *A SECOND GREEK EXERCISE BOOK. By Rev. W. A. HEARD, M.A., Headmaster of Fettes College, Edinburgh. 2s. 6d.
 EASY EXERCISES IN GREEK SYNTAX. By Rev. G. H. NALL, M.A., Assistant Master at Westminster School. 2s. 6d.
 MANUAL OF GREEK ACCIDENCE. By the Editor. [In preparation.
 MANUAL OF GREEK SYNTAX. By the Editor. [In preparation.
 ELEMENTARY GREEK COMPOSITION. By the Editor. [In preparation.

*MACMILLAN'S GREEK READER.—STORIES AND LEGENDS. A First Greek Reader, with Notes, Vocabulary, and Exercises. By F. H. COLSON, M.A., Headmaster of Plymouth College. Gl. 8vo. 3s.

*MARSHALL.—A TABLE OF IRREGULAR GREEK VERBS, classified according to the arrangement of Curtius's Greek Grammar. By J. M. MARSHALL, M.A., Headmaster of the Grammar School, Durham. 8vo. 1s.

MAYOR.—FIRST GREEK READER. By Prof. JOHN E. B. MAYOR, M.A., Fellow of St. John's College, Cambridge. Fcap. 8vo. 4s. 6d.

MAYOR.—GREEK FOR BEGINNERS. By Rev. J. B. MAYOR, M.A., late Professor of Classical Literature in King's College, London. Part I., with Vocabulary, 1s. 6d. Parts II. and III., with Vocabulary and Index. Fcap. 8vo. 3s. 6d. Complete in one Vol. 4s. 6d.

PEILE.—See under Latin.

RUTHERFORD.—THE NEW PHRYNICHUS; being a Revised Text of the Ecloga of the Grammarian Phrynichus. With Introduction and Commentary. By the Rev. W. G. RUTHERFORD, M.A., LL.D., Headmaster of Westminster. 8vo. 18s.

STRACHAN—WILKINS.—See under Latin.

WHITE.—FIRST LESSONS IN GREEK. Adapted to GOODWIN'S GREEK GRAMMAR, and designed as an introduction to the ANABASIS OF XENOPHON. By JOHN WILLIAMS WHITE, Assistant Professor of Greek in Harvard University, U.S.A. Cr. 8vo. 3s. 6d.

WRIGHT.—ATTIC PRIMER. Arranged for the Use of Beginners. By J. WRIGHT M.A. Ex. fcap. 8vo. 2s. 6d.

ANTIQUITIES, ANCIENT HISTORY, AND PHILOSOPHY.

ARNOLD.—A HISTORY OF THE EARLY ROMAN EMPIRE. By W. T. ARNOLD, M.A. [In preparation.

GREEK AND LATIN CLASSICS

ARNOLD.—THE SECOND PUNIC WAR. Being Chapters from THE HISTORY OF ROME by the late THOMAS ARNOLD, D.D., Headmaster of Rugby. Edited, with Notes, by W. T. ARNOLD, M.A. With 8 Maps. Cr. 8vo. 5s.

*BEESLY.—STORIES FROM THE HISTORY OF ROME. By Mrs. BEESLY. Fcap. 8vo. 2s. 6d.

BLACKIE.—HORÆ HELLENICÆ. By JOHN STUART BLACKIE, Emeritus Professor of Greek in the University of Edinburgh. 8vo. 12s.

BURN.—ROMAN LITERATURE IN RELATION TO ROMAN ART. By Rev. ROBERT BURN, M.A., late Fellow of Trinity College, Cambridge. Illustrated. Ex. cr. 8vo. 14s.

BURY.—A HISTORY OF THE LATER ROMAN EMPIRE FROM ARCADIUS TO IRENE, A.D. 395-800. By J. B. BURY, M.A., Fellow of Trinity College, Dublin. 2 vols. 8vo. 32s.

BUTCHER.—SOME ASPECTS OF THE GREEK GENIUS. By S. H. BUTCHER, M.A., Professor of Greek, Edinburgh. Cr. 8vo. 7s. 6d. net.

*CLASSICAL WRITERS.—Edited by JOHN RICHARD GREEN, M.A., LL.D. Fcap. 8vo. 1s. 6d. each.
  SOPHOCLES. By Prof. L. CAMPBELL, M.A.
  EURIPIDES. By Prof. MAHAFFY, D.D.
  DEMOSTHENES. By Prof. S. H. BUTCHER, M.A.
  VIRGIL. By Prof. NETTLESHIP, M.A.
  LIVY. By Rev. W. W. CAPES, M.A.
  TACITUS. By A. J. CHURCH, M.A., and W. J. BRODRIBB, M.A.
  MILTON. By Rev. STOPFORD A. BROOKE, M.A.

DYER.—STUDIES OF THE GODS IN GREECE AT CERTAIN SANCTUARIES RECENTLY EXCAVATED. By LOUIS DYER, B.A. Ex. Cr. 8vo. 8s. 6d. net.

FREEMAN.—HISTORICAL ESSAYS. By EDWARD A. FREEMAN, D.C.L., LL.D., late Regius Professor of Modern History in the University of Oxford. Second Series. [Greek and Roman History.] 8vo. 10s. 6d.

GARDNER.—SAMOS AND SAMIAN COINS. An Essay. By PERCY GARDNER, Litt.D., Professor of Archæology in the University of Oxford. 8vo. 7s. 6d.

GEDDES.—THE PROBLEM OF THE HOMERIC POEMS. By W. D. GEDDES, Principal of the University of Aberdeen. 8vo. 14s.

GLADSTONE.—Works by the Rt. Hon. W. E. GLADSTONE, M.P.
  THE TIME AND PLACE OF HOMER. Cr. 8vo. 6s. 6d.
  LANDMARKS OF HOMERIC STUDY. Cr. 8vo. 2s. 6d.
  *A PRIMER OF HOMER. 18mo. 1s.

GOW.—A COMPANION TO SCHOOL CLASSICS. By JAMES Gow, Litt.D., Head Master of the High School, Nottingham. Illustrated. Cr. 8vo. 6s.

HARRISON and VERRALL.—MYTHOLOGY AND MONUMENTS OF ANCIENT ATHENS. Translation of a portion of the "Attica" of Pausanias. By MARGARET DE G. VERRALL. With Introductory Essay and Archæological Commentary by JANE E. HARRISON. With Illustrations and Plans. Cr. 8vo. 16s.

JEBB.—Works by R. C. JEBB, Litt.D., Professor of Greek in the University of Cambridge.
  THE ATTIC ORATORS FROM ANTIPHON TO ISAEOS. 2 vols. 8vo. 25s.
  *A PRIMER OF GREEK LITERATURE. 18mo. 1s.

KIEPERT.—MANUAL OF ANCIENT GEOGRAPHY. By Dr. H. KIEPERT. Cr. 8vo. 5s.

LANCIANI.—ANCIENT ROME IN THE LIGHT OF RECENT DISCOVERIES. By RODOLFO LANCIANI, Professor of Archæology in the University of Rome. Illustrated. 4to. 24s.

LEAF.—INTRODUCTION TO THE ILIAD FOR ENGLISH READERS. By WALTER LEAF, Litt.D. [In the Press.

MAHAFFY.—Works by J. P. MAHAFFY, D.D., Fellow of Trinity College, Dublin, and Professor of Ancient History in the University of Dublin.
  SOCIAL LIFE IN GREECE; from Homer to Menander. Cr. 8vo. 9s.
  GREEK LIFE AND THOUGHT; from the Age of Alexander to the Roman Conquest. Cr. 8vo. 12s. 6d.

ANCIENT HISTORY AND PHILOSOPHY

THE GREEK WORLD UNDER ROMAN SWAY. From Plutarch to Polybius. Cr. 8vo. 10s. 6d.
PROBLEMS IN GREEK HISTORY. Cr. 8vo. 7s. 6d.
RAMBLES AND STUDIES IN GREECE. Illustrated. Cr. 8vo. 10s. 6d.
A HISTORY OF CLASSICAL GREEK LITERATURE. Cr. 8vo. Vol. I. The Poets. Part I. Epic and Lyric. Part II. Dramatic. Vol. II. Prose Writers. Part I. Herodotus to Plato. Part II. Isocrates to Aristotle. 4s. 6d. each.
*A PRIMER OF GREEK ANTIQUITIES. With Illustrations. 18mo. 1s.
*EURIPIDES. 18mo. 1s. 6d. (*Classical Writers*.)
MAYOR.—BIBLIOGRAPHICAL CLUE TO LATIN LITERATURE. Edited after HÜBNER. By Prof. JOHN E. B. MAYOR. Cr. 8vo. 10s. 6d.
NEWTON.—ESSAYS ON ART AND ARCHÆOLOGY. By Sir CHARLES NEWTON, K.C.B., D.C.L. 8vo. 12s. 6d.
PHILOLOGY.—THE JOURNAL OF PHILOLOGY. Edited by W. A. WRIGHT, M.A., I. BYWATER, M.A., and H. JACKSON, Litt.D. 4s. 6d. each (half-yearly).
SAYCE.—THE ANCIENT EMPIRES OF THE EAST. By A. H. SAYCE, M.A., Deputy-Professor of Comparative Philology, Oxford. Cr. 8vo. 6s.
SCHMIDT and WHITE. AN INTRODUCTION TO THE RHYTHMIC AND METRIC OF THE CLASSICAL LANGUAGES. By Dr. J. H. H. SCHMIDT. Translated by JOHN WILLIAMS WHITE, Ph.D. 8vo. 10s. 6d.
SHUCHHARDT.—DR. SCHLIEMANN'S EXCAVATIONS AT TROY, TIRYNS, MYCENÆ, ORCHOMENOS, ITHACA, presented in the light of recent knowledge. By Dr. CARL SHUCHHARDT. Translated by EUGENIE SELLERS. Introduction by WALTER LEAF, Litt.D. Illustrated. 8vo. 18s. net.
SHUCKBURGH.—A SCHOOL HISTORY OF ROME. By E. S. SHUCKBURGH, M.A. Cr. 8vo. [*In preparation.*
*STEWART.—THE TALE OF TROY. Done into English by AUBREY STEWART. Gl. 8vo. 3s. 6d.
*TOZER.—A PRIMER OF CLASSICAL GEOGRAPHY. By H. F. TOZER, M.A. 18mo. 1s.
WALDSTEIN.—CATALOGUE OF CASTS IN THE MUSEUM OF CLASSICAL ARCHÆOLOGY, CAMBRIDGE. By CHARLES WALDSTEIN, University Reader in Classical Archæology. Cr. 8vo. 1s. 6d. Large Paper Edition, small 4to. 5s.
WILKINS.—Works by Prof. WILKINS, Litt.D., LL.D.
*A PRIMER OF ROMAN ANTIQUITIES. Illustrated. 18mo. 1s.
*A PRIMER OF ROMAN LITERATURE. 18mo. 1s.
WILKINS and ARNOLD.—A MANUAL OF ROMAN ANTIQUITIES. By Prof. A. S. WILKINS, Litt.D., and W. T. ARNOLD, M.A. Cr. 8vo. [*In prep.*

MODERN LANGUAGES AND LITERATURE.

English; French; German; Modern Greek; Italian; Spanish.

ENGLISH.

*ABBOTT.—A SHAKESPEARIAN GRAMMAR. An Attempt to Illustrate some of the Differences between Elizabethan and Modern English. By the Rev. E. A. ABBOTT, D.D., formerly Headmaster of the City of London School. Ex. fcap. 8vo. 6s.
ADDISON.—SELECTIONS. With Introduction and Notes, by K. DEIGHTON. [*In the Press.*
*BACON.—ESSAYS. With Introduction and Notes, by F. G. SELBY, M.A., Principal and Professor of Logic and Moral Philosophy, Deccan College, Poona. Gl. 8vo. 3s.; sewed, 2s. 6d.
THE ADVANCEMENT OF LEARNING. By the same. [*In the Press.*

MODERN LANGUAGES AND LITERATURE

BROOKE.—EARLY ENGLISH LITERATURE. By Rev. STOPFORD A. BROOKE, M.A. 2 vols. 8vo. [*Vol. I. In the Press.*
BROWNING.—A PRIMER ON BROWNING. By F. M. WILSON. Gl. 8vo. 2s. 6d.
*BURKE.—REFLECTIONS ON THE FRENCH REVOLUTION. By F. G. SELBY, M.A. Gl. 8vo. 5s.
BUTLER.—HUDIBRAS. With Introduction and Notes, by ALFRED MILNES, M.A. Ex. fcap. **8vo.** Part I. 3s. 6d. Parts II. and III. 4s. 6d.
CAMPBELL.—SELECTIONS. With Introduction and Notes, by **CECIL M.** BARROW, M.A., Principal of Victoria College, Palghât. Gl. 8vo. [*In preparation.*
COLLINS.—THE STUDY OF ENGLISH LITERATURE: A Plea for its Recognition at the Universities. By J. CHURTON COLLINS, M.A. Cr. 8vo. 4s. 6d.
COWPER.—*THE TASK: an Epistle to Joseph Hill, Esq.; TIROCINIUM, or a Review of the Schools; and THE HISTORY OF JOHN GILPIN. **Edited**, with Notes, by W. BENHAM, B.D. Gl. 8vo. 1s.
   THE TASK. With Introduction and Notes, by F. J. ROWE, **M.A.**, and W. T. WEBB, M.A., Professors of English Literature, Presidency College, Calcutta. [*In preparation.*
DRYDEN.—SELECT PROSE WORKS. Edited, with Introduction and **Notes, by** Prof. C. D. YONGE. Fcap. 8vo. 2s. 6d.
*GLOBE READERS. For Standards I.-VI. Edited by A. F. MURISON. Illustrated. Gl. 8vo.

   Primer I. (48 pp.)   3d. | Book III. (282 pp.)   1s. 3d.
   Primer II. (48 pp.)   3d. | Book IV. (328 pp.)   1s. 9d.
   Book I. (132 pp.)   6d. | Book V. (408 pp.)   2s.
   Book II. (136 pp.)   9d. | Book VI. (430 pp.)   2s. 6d.

*THE SHORTER GLOBE READERS.—Illustrated. Gl. 8vo.

   Primer I. (48 pp.)   3d. | Standard III. (178 pp.)   1s.
   Primer II. (48 pp.)   3d. | Standard IV. (182 pp.)   1s.
   Standard I. (90 pp.)   6d. | Standard V. (216 pp.)   1s. 3d.
   Standard II. (124 pp.)   9d. | Standard VI. (228 pp.)   1s. **6d.**

*GOLDSMITH.—THE TRAVELLER, or a Prospect of Society; and THE DESERTED VILLAGE. With Notes, Philological and Explanatory, by J. W. HALES, M.A. Cr. 8vo. 6d.
   *THE TRAVELLER AND THE DESERTED VILLAGE. With Introduction and Notes, by A. BARRETT, B.A., Professor of English Literature, Elphinstone College, Bombay. Gl. 8vo. 1s. 9d.; sewed, 1s. 6d. The Traveller (separately), 1s., sewed.
*THE VICAR OF WAKEFIELD. With a Memoir of Goldsmith, by Prof. MASSON. Gl. 8vo. 1s.
   SELECT ESSAYS. With Introduction and Notes, by Prof. C. D. YONGE. Fcap. 8vo. 2s. 6d.
*GRAY.—POEMS. With Introduction and Notes, by JOHN BRADSHAW, LL.D. Gl. 8vo. 1s. 9d.; sewed, 1s. 6d.
*HALES.—LONGER ENGLISH POEMS. With Notes, Philological and Explanatory, and an Introduction on the Teaching of English, by J. W. HALES, M.A., Professor of English Literature at King's College, London. Ex. fcap. 8vo. 4s. 6d.
*HELPS.—ESSAYS WRITTEN IN THE INTERVALS OF BUSINESS. With Introduction and Notes, by F. J. ROWE, M.A., and W. T. WEBB, M.A. Gl. 8vo. 1s. 9d.; sewed, 1s. 6d.
*JOHNSON.—LIVES OF THE POETS. The Six Chief Lives (Milton, Dryden, Swift, Addison, Pope, Gray), with Macaulay's "Life of Johnson." With Preface and Notes by MATTHEW ARNOLD. Cr. 8vo. 4s. 6d.
   LIFE OF MILTON. With Introduction and Notes, by K. DEIGHTON.
[*In the Press.*
KELLNER.—HISTORICAL OUTLINES OF ENGLISH SYNTAX. By L. KELLNER, Ph.D. Globe 8vo. [*In the Press.*
*LITERATURE PRIMERS.—Edited by J. R. GREEN, LL.D. 18mo. 1s. each.
   ENGLISH GRAMMAR. By Rev. R. MORRIS, LL.D.
   ENGLISH GRAMMAR EXERCISES. By R. MORRIS, LL.D., and H. C. BOWEN, **M.A.**

EXERCISES ON MORRIS'S PRIMER OF ENGLISH GRAMMAR. By J. WETHERELL, M.A.
ENGLISH COMPOSITION. By Professor NICHOL.
QUESTIONS AND EXERCISES ON ENGLISH COMPOSITION. By Prof. NICHOL and W. S. M'CORMICK.
ENGLISH LITERATURE. By STOPFORD BROOKE, M.A.
SHAKSPERE. By Professor DOWDEN.
THE CHILDREN'S TREASURY OF LYRICAL POETRY. Selected and arranged with Notes by FRANCIS TURNER PALGRAVE. In Two Parts. 1s. each.
PHILOLOGY. By J. PEILE, Litt.D.
ROMAN LITERATURE. By Prof. A. S. WILKINS, Litt.D.
GREEK LITERATURE. By Prof. JEBB, Litt.D.
HOMER. By the Rt. Hon. W. E. GLADSTONE, M.P.

A HISTORY OF ENGLISH LITERATURE IN FOUR VOLUMES. Cr. 8vo.
EARLY ENGLISH LITERATURE. By STOPFORD BROOKE, M.A. [*In preparation.*
ELIZABETHAN LITERATURE. (1560-1665.) By GEORGE SAINTSBURY. 7s. 6d.
EIGHTEENTH CENTURY LITERATURE. (1660-1780.) By EDMUND GOSSE, M.A. 7s. 6d.
THE MODERN PERIOD. By Prof. DOWDEN. [*In preparation.*

MACMILLAN'S HISTORY READERS. (*See* History, p. 43.)

*MACMILLAN'S READING BOOKS.
PRIMER. 18mo. (48 pp.) 2d.
BOOK I. (96 pp.) 4d.
BOOK II. (144 pp.) 5d.
BOOK III. (160 pp.) 6d.
BOOK IV. (176 pp.) 8d.
BOOK V. (380 pp.) 1s.
BOOK VI. Cr. 8vo. (430 pp.) 2s.
Book VI. is fitted for Higher Classes, and as an Introduction to English Literature.

*MACMILLAN'S COPY BOOKS.—1. Large Post 4to. Price 4d. each. 2. Post Oblong. Price 2d. each.
 1. INITIATORY EXERCISES AND SHORT LETTERS.
 2. WORDS OF SHORT LETTERS.
 3. LONG LETTERS. With Words containing Long Letters—Figures.
 4. WORDS CONTAINING LONG LETTERS.
 4a. PRACTISING AND REVISING COPY-BOOK. For Nos. 1 to 4.
 5. CAPITALS AND SHORT HALF-TEXT. Words beginning with a Capital.
 6. HALF-TEXT WORDS beginning with Capitals—Figures.
 7. SMALL-HAND AND HALF-TEXT. With Capitals and Figures.
 8. SMALL-HAND AND HALF-TEXT. With Capitals and Figures.
 8a. PRACTISING AND REVISING COPY-BOOK. For Nos. 5 to 8.
 9. SMALL-HAND SINGLE HEADLINES—Figures.
 10. SMALL-HAND SINGLE HEADLINES—Figures.
 11. SMALL-HAND DOUBLE HEADLINES—Figures.
 12. COMMERCIAL AND ARITHMETICAL EXAMPLES, &c.
 12a. PRACTISING AND REVISING COPY-BOOK. For Nos. 8 to 12.
 Nos. 3, 4, 5, 6, 7, 8, 9 *may be had with Goodman's Patent Sliding Copies.* Large Post 4to. Price 6d. each.

MARTIN.—*THE POET'S HOUR: Poetry selected for Children. By FRANCES MARTIN. 18mo. 2s. 6d.
*SPRING-TIME WITH THE POETS. By the same. 18mo. 3s. 6d.
*MILTON.—PARADISE LOST. Books I. and II. With Introduction and Notes, by MICHAEL MACMILLAN, B.A., Professor of Logic and Moral Philosophy, Elphinstone College, Bombay. Gl. 8vo. 1s. 9d.; sewed, 1s. 6d. Or separately, 1s. 3d.; sewed, 1s. each.
*L'ALLEGRO, IL PENSEROSO, LYCIDAS, ARCADES, SONNETS, &c. With Introduction and Notes, by W. BELL, M.A., Professor of Philosophy and Logic, Government College, Lahore. Gl. 8vo. 1s. 9d.; sewed, 1s. 6d.
*COMUS. By the same. Gl. 8vo. 1s. 3d.; sewed, 1s.
*SAMSON AGONISTES. By H. M. PERCIVAL, M.A., Professor of English Literature, Presidency College, Calcutta. Gl. 8vo. 2s.; sewed, 1s. 9d.
*INTRODUCTION TO THE STUDY OF MILTON. By STOPFORD BROOKE, M.A. Fcap. 8vo. 1s. 6d. (*Classical Writers.*)

16   MODERN LANGUAGES AND LITERATURE

MORRIS.—Works by the Rev. R. Morris, LL.D.
*A PRIMER OF ENGLISH GRAMMAR. 18mo. 1s.
*ELEMENTARY LESSONS IN HISTORICAL ENGLISH GRAMMAR, containing Accidence and Word-Formation. 18mo. 2s. 6d.
*HISTORICAL OUTLINES OF ENGLISH ACCIDENCE, with Chapters on the Development of the Language, and on Word-Formation. Ex. fcap. 8vo. 6s.
NICHOL and M'CORMICK.—A SHORT HISTORY OF ENGLISH LITERATURE. By Prof. John Nichol and Prof. W. S. M'Cormick. [*In preparation.*]
OLIPHANT.—THE LITERARY HISTORY OF ENGLAND, 1790–1825. By Mrs. Oliphant. 3 vols. 8vo. 21s.
OLIPHANT.—THE OLD AND MIDDLE ENGLISH. By T. L. Kington Oliphant. 2d Ed. Gl. 8vo. 9s.
THE NEW ENGLISH. By the same. 2 vols. Cr. 8vo. 21s.
PALGRAVE.—THE GOLDEN TREASURY OF SONGS AND LYRICS. Selected by F. T. Palgrave. 18mo. 2s. 6d. net.
*THE CHILDREN'S TREASURY OF LYRICAL POETRY. Selected by the same. 18mo. 2s. 6d. Also in Two Parts. 1s. each.
PATMORE.—THE CHILDREN'S GARLAND FROM THE BEST POETS. Selected by Coventry Patmore. Gl. 8vo. 2s. 18mo. 2s. 6d. net.
PLUTARCH.—Being a Selection from the Lives which illustrate Shakespeare. North's Translation. Edited by Prof. W. W. Skeat, Litt.D. Cr. 8vo. 6s.
*RANSOME.—SHORT STUDIES OF SHAKESPEARE'S PLOTS. By Cyril Ransome, M.A., Professor of Modern History and Literature, Yorkshire College, Leeds. Cr. 8vo. 3s. 6d.
*RYLAND.—CHRONOLOGICAL OUTLINES OF ENGLISH LITERATURE. By F. Ryland, M.A. Cr. 8vo. 6s.
SCOTT.—*LAY OF THE LAST MINSTREL, and THE LADY OF THE LAKE. Edited by Francis Turner Palgrave. Gl. 8vo. 1s.
*THE LAY OF THE LAST MINSTREL. With Introduction and Notes, by G. H. Stuart, M.A., Principal of Kumbakonam College, and E. H. Elliot, B.A. Gl. 8vo. 2s.; sewed, 1s. 9d. Canto I. 9d. Cantos I. to III. and IV. to VI. 1s. 3d. each; sewed, 1s. each.
*MARMION, and THE LORD OF THE ISLES. By F. T. Palgrave. Gl. 8vo. 1s.
*MARMION. With Introduction and Notes, by Michael Macmillan, B.A. Gl. 8vo. 3s.; sewed, 2s. 6d.
*THE LADY OF THE LAKE. By G. H. Stuart, M.A. **Gl. 8vo.** 2s. 6d.; sewed, 2s.
*ROKEBY. With Introduction and Notes, by Michael Macmillan, B.A. Gl. 8vo. 3s.; sewed, 2s. 6d.
SHAKESPEARE.—*A SHAKESPEARIAN GRAMMAR. By Rev. E. A. Abbott, D.D. Gl. 8vo. 6s.
*A PRIMER OF SHAKESPERE. By Prof. Dowden. 18mo. 1s.
*SHORT STUDIES OF SHAKESPEARE'S PLOTS. By Cyril Ransome, M.A. Cr. 8vo. 3s. 6d.
*THE TEMPEST. With Introduction and Notes, by K. Deighton. Gl. 8vo. 1s. 9d.; sewed, 1s. 6d.
*MUCH ADO ABOUT NOTHING. By the same. 2s.; sewed, 1s. 9d.
*A MIDSUMMER NIGHT'S DREAM. By the same. 1s. 9d.; sewed, 1s. 6d.
*THE MERCHANT OF VENICE. By the same. 1s. 9d.; sewed, 1s. 6d.
*AS YOU LIKE IT. By the same. 1s. 9d.; sewed, 1s. 6d.
*TWELFTH NIGHT. By the same. 1s. 9d.; sewed, 1s. 6d.
*THE WINTER'S TALE. By the same. 2s.; sewed, 1s. 9d.
*KING JOHN. By the same. 1s. 9d.; sewed, 1s. 6d.
*RICHARD II. By the same. 1s. 9d.; sewed, 1s. 6d.
*HENRY V. By the same. 1s. 9d.; sewed, 1s. 6d.
*RICHARD III. By C. H. Tawney, M.A., Principal and Professor of English Literature, Presidency College, Calcutta. 2s. 6d.; sewed, 2s.
*CORIOLANUS. By K. Deighton. 2s. 6d.; sewed, 2s.
*JULIUS CÆSAR. By the same. 1s. 9d.; sewed, 1s. 6d.
*MACBETH. By the same. 1s. 9d.; sewed, 1s. 6d.
*HAMLET. **By** the same. 2s. 6d.; sewed, 2s.

*KING LEAR. By the same. 1s. 9d. ; sewed, 1s. 6d.
*OTHELLO. By the same. 2s. ; sewed, 1s. 9d.
*ANTONY AND CLEOPATRA. By the same. 2s. 6d. ; sewed, 2s.
*CYMBELINE. By the same. 2s. 6d. ; sewed, 2s.
*SONNENSCHEIN and MEIKLEJOHN.—THE ENGLISH METHOD OF TEACHING TO READ. By A. SONNENSCHEIN and J. M. D. MEIKLEJOHN, M.A. Fcap. 8vo.
  THE NURSERY BOOK, containing all the Two-Letter Words in the Language. 1d. (Also in Large Type on Sheets for School Walls. 5s.)
  THE FIRST COURSE, consisting of Short Vowels with Single Consonants. 7d.
  THE SECOND COURSE, with Combinations and Bridges, consisting of Short Vowels with Double Consonants. 7d.
  THE THIRD AND FOURTH COURSES, consisting of Long Vowels, and all the Double Vowels in the Language. 7d.
*SOUTHEY.—LIFE OF NELSON. With Introduction and Notes, by MICHAEL MACMILLAN, B.A. Gl. 8vo. 3s. ; sewed, 2s. 6d.
SPENSER.—THE FAIRY QUEEN. BOOK I. With Introduction and Notes, by H. M. PERCIVAL, M.A. [*In the Press.*
TAYLOR.—WORDS AND PLACES; or, Etymological Illustrations of History, Ethnology, and Geography. By Rev. ISAAC TAYLOR, Litt.D. Gl. 8vo. 6s.
TENNYSON.—THE COLLECTED WORKS OF LORD TENNYSON. An Edition for Schools. In Four Parts. Cr. 8vo. 2s. 6d. each.
  TENNYSON FOR THE YOUNG. Edited, with Notes for the Use of Schools, by the Rev. ALFRED AINGER, LL.D., Canon of Bristol. 18mo. 1s. net.
*SELECTIONS FROM TENNYSON. With Introduction and Notes, by F. J. ROWE, M.A., and W. T. WEBB, M.A. New Ed., enlarged. Gl. 8vo. 3s. 6d.
  This selection contains :—Recollections of the Arabian Nights, The Lady of Shalott, Œnone, The Lotos Eaters, Ulysses, Tithonus, Morte d'Arthur, Sir Galahad, Dora, Ode on the Death of the Duke of Wellington, The Revenge, The Palace of Art, The Voyage, The Brook, Demeter and Persephone.
*ENOCH ARDEN. By W. T. WEBB, M.A. Gl. 8vo. 2s.
*AYLMER'S FIELD. By W. T. WEBB, M.A. 2s.
*THE PRINCESS; A MEDLEY. By P. M. WALLACE, B.A. 3s. 6d.
*THE COMING OF ARTHUR, and THE PASSING OF ARTHUR. By F. J. ROWE, M.A. Gl. 8vo. 2s.
THRING.—THE ELEMENTS OF GRAMMAR TAUGHT IN ENGLISH. By EDWARD THRING, M.A. With Questions. 4th Ed. 18mo. 2s.
*VAUGHAN.—WORDS FROM THE POETS. By C. M. VAUGHAN. 18mo. 1s.
WARD.—THE ENGLISH POETS. Selections, with Critical Introductions by various Writers and a General Introduction by MATTHEW ARNOLD. Edited by T. H. WARD, M.A. 4 Vols. Vol. I. CHAUCER TO DONNE.—Vol. II. BEN JONSON TO DRYDEN.—Vol. III. ADDISON TO BLAKE.—Vol. IV. WORDSWORTH TO ROSSETTI. 2d Ed. Cr. 8vo. 7s. 6d. each.
WARD.—A HISTORY OF ENGLISH DRAMATIC LITERATURE, TO THE DEATH OF QUEEN ANNE. By A. W. WARD, Litt.D., Principal of Owens College, Manchester. 2 Vols. 8vo. [New Ed. *in preparation.*
WOODS.—*A FIRST POETRY BOOK. By M. A. WOODS. Fcap. 8vo. 2s. 6d.
*A SECOND POETRY BOOK. By the same. 4s. 6d.; or, Two Parts. 2s. 6d. each.
*A THIRD POETRY BOOK. By the same. 4s. 6d.
  HYMNS FOR SCHOOL WORSHIP. By the same. 18mo. 1s. 6d.
WORDSWORTH.—SELECTIONS. With Introduction and Notes, by F. J. ROWE, M.A., and W. T. WEBB, M.A. Gl. 8vo. [*In preparation.*
YONGE.—*A BOOK OF GOLDEN DEEDS. By CHARLOTTE M. YONGE. Gl. 8vo. 2s.
*THE ABRIDGED BOOK OF GOLDEN DEEDS. 18mo. 1s.

FRENCH.

BEAUMARCHAIS.—LE BARBIER DE SEVILLE. With Introduction and Notes, by L. P. BLOUET. Fcap. 8vo. 3s. 6d.

MODERN LANGUAGES AND LITERATURE

*BOWEN.—FIRST LESSONS IN FRENCH. By H. COURTHOPE BOWEN, M.A. Ex. fcap. 8vo. 1s.

BREYMANN.—FIRST FRENCH EXERCISE BOOK. By HERMANN BREYMANN, Ph.D., Professor of Philology in the University of Munich. Ex. fcap. 8vo. 4s. 6d.
SECOND FRENCH EXERCISE BOOK. By the same. Ex. fcap. 8vo. 2s. 6d.

FASNACHT.—Works by G. E. FASNACHT, late Assistant Master at Westminster.
THE ORGANIC METHOD OF STUDYING LANGUAGES. Ex. fcap. 8vo. I. French. 3s. 6d.
A FRENCH GRAMMAR FOR SCHOOLS. Cr. 8vo. 3s. 6d.
GRAMMAR AND GLOSSARY OF THE FRENCH LANGUAGE OF THE SEVENTEENTH CENTURY. Cr. 8vo. [In preparation.

MACMILLAN'S PRIMARY SERIES OF FRENCH READING BOOKS.—Edited by G. E. FASNACHT. Illustrations, Notes, Vocabularies, and Exercises. Gl. 8vo.
*FRENCH READINGS FOR CHILDREN. By G. E. FASNACHT. 1s. 6d.
*CORNAZ—NOS ENFANTS ET LEURS AMIS. By EDITH HARVEY. 1s. 6d.
*DE MAISTRE—LA JEUNE SIBÉRIENNE ET LE LÉPREUX DE LA CITÉ D'AOSTE. By STEPHANE BARLET, B.Sc. 1s. 6d.
*FLORIAN—FABLES. By Rev. CHARLES YELD, M.A., Headmaster of University School, Nottingham. 1s. 6d.
*LA FONTAINE—A SELECTION OF FABLES. By L. M. MORIARTY, B.A., Assistant Master at Harrow. 2s. 6d.
*MOLESWORTH—FRENCH LIFE IN LETTERS. By Mrs. MOLESWORTH. 1s. 6d.
*PERRAULT—CONTES DE FÉES. By G. E. FASNACHT. 1s. 6d.

MACMILLAN'S PROGRESSIVE FRENCH COURSE.—By G. E. FASNACHT. Ex. fcap. 8vo.
*FIRST YEAR, Easy Lessons on the Regular Accidence. 1s.
*SECOND YEAR, an Elementary Grammar with Exercises, Notes, and Vocabularies. 2s.
*THIRD YEAR, a Systematic Syntax, and Lessons in Composition. 2s. 6d.
THE TEACHER'S COMPANION TO THE ABOVE. With Copious Notes, Hints for Different Renderings, Synonyms, Philological Remarks, etc. By G. E. FASNACHT. Ex. fcap. 8vo. Each Year 4s. 6d.

*MACMILLAN'S FRENCH COMPOSITION.—By G. E. FASNACHT. Ex. fcap. 8vo. Part I. Elementary. 2s. 6d. [Part II. Advanced, in the Press.
THE TEACHER'S COMPANION TO MACMILLAN'S COURSE OF FRENCH COMPOSITION. By G. E. FASNACHT. Part I. Ex. fcap. 8vo. 4s. 6d.

MACMILLAN'S PROGRESSIVE FRENCH READERS. By G. E. FASNACHT. Ex. fcap. 8vo.
*FIRST YEAR, containing Tales, Historical Extracts, Letters, Dialogues, Ballads, Nursery Songs, etc., with Two Vocabularies: (1) in the order of subjects; (2) in alphabetical order. With Imitative Exercises. 2s. 6d.
*SECOND YEAR, containing Fiction in Prose and Verse, Historical and Descriptive Extracts, Essays, Letters, Dialogues, etc. With Imitative Exercises. 2s. 6d.

MACMILLAN'S FOREIGN SCHOOL CLASSICS. Ed. by G. E. FASNACHT. 18mo.
*CORNEILLE—LE CID. By G. E. FASNACHT. 1s.
*DUMAS—LES DEMOISELLES DE ST. CYR. By VICTOR OGER, Lecturer at University College, Liverpool. 1s. 6d.
LA FONTAINE'S FABLES. By L. M. MORIARTY, B.A. [In preparation.
*MOLIÈRE—L'AVARE. By the same. 1s.
*MOLIÈRE—LE BOURGEOIS GENTILHOMME. By the same. 1s. 6d.
*MOLIÈRE—LES FEMMES SAVANTES. By G. E. FASNACHT. 1s.
*MOLIÈRE—LE MISANTHROPE. By the same. 1s.
*MOLIÈRE—LE MÉDECIN MALGRÉ LUI. By the same. 1s.
*MOLIÈRE—LES PRÉCIEUSES RIDICULES. By the same. 1s.
*RACINE—BRITANNICUS. By E. PELLISSIER, M.A. 2s.
*FRENCH READINGS FROM ROMAN HISTORY. Selected from various Authors, by C. COLBECK, M.A., Assistant Master at Harrow. 4s. 6d.
*SAND, GEORGE—LA MARE AU DIABLE. By W. E. RUSSELL, M.A. Assistant Master at Haileybury. 1s.

FRENCH—GERMAN

*SANDEAU, JULES—MADEMOISELLE DE LA SEIGLIÈRE. By H. C. STEEL, Assistant Master at Winchester. 1s. 6d.
*VOLTAIRE—CHARLES XII. By G. E. FASNACHT. 3s. 6d.
*MASSON.—A COMPENDIOUS DICTIONARY OF THE FRENCH LANGUAGE. Adapted from the Dictionaries of Professor A. ELWALL. By GUSTAVE MASSON. Cr. 8vo. 3s. 6d.
MOLIÈRE.—LE MALADE IMAGINAIRE. With Introduction and Notes, by F. TARVER, M.A., Assistant Master at Eton. Fcap. 8vo. 2s. 6d.
*PELLISSIER.—FRENCH ROOTS AND THEIR FAMILIES. A Synthetic Vocabulary, based upon Derivations. By E. PELLISSIER, M.A., Assistant Master at Clifton College. Gl. 8vo. 6s.

GERMAN.

*BEHAGHEL.—A SHORT HISTORICAL GRAMMAR OF THE GERMAN LANGUAGE. By Dr. OTTO BEHAGHEL. Translated by EMIL TRECHMANN, M.A., Ph.D., University of Sydney. Gl. 8vo. 3s. 6d.
BUCHHEIM.—DEUTSCHE LYRIK. The Golden Treasury of the best German Lyrical Poems. Selected by Dr. BUCHHEIM. 18mo. 4s. 6d.
BALLADEN UND ROMANZEN. Selection of the best German Ballads and Romances. By the same. 18mo. 4s. 6d.
HUSS.—A SYSTEM OF ORAL INSTRUCTION IN GERMAN, by means of Progressive Illustrations and Applications of the leading Rules of Grammar. By H. C. O. HUSS, Ph.D. Cr. 8vo. 5s.
MACMILLAN'S PRIMARY SERIES OF GERMAN READING BOOKS. Edited by G. E. FASNACHT. With Notes, Vocabularies, and Exercises. Gl. 8vo.
*GRIMM—KINDER UND HAUSMÄRCHEN. By G. E. FASNACHT. 2s. 6d.
*HAUFF—DIE KARAVANE. By HERMAN HAGER, Ph.D. 3s.
*SCHMID, CHR. VON—H. VON EICHENFELS. By G. E. FASNACHT. 2s. 6d.
MACMILLAN'S PROGRESSIVE GERMAN COURSE. By G. E. FASNACHT. Ex. fcap. 8vo.
*FIRST YEAR. Easy Lessons and Rules on the Regular Accidence. 1s. 6d.
*SECOND YEAR. Conversational Lessons in Systematic Accidence and Elementary Syntax. With Philological Illustrations and Vocabulary. 3s. 6d.
[THIRD YEAR *In the Press.*
THE TEACHER'S COMPANION TO THE ABOVE. With copious Notes, Hints for Different Renderings, Synonyms, Philological Remarks, etc. By G. E. FASNACHT. Ex. fcap. 8vo. Each Year. 4s. 6d.
MACMILLAN'S GERMAN COMPOSITION. By G. E. FASNACHT. Ex. fcap. 8vo.
*I. FIRST COURSE. Parallel German-English Extracts and Parallel English-German Syntax. 2s. 6d.
THE TEACHER'S COMPANION TO THE ABOVE. By G. E. FASNACHT. FIRST COURSE. Gl. 8vo. 4s. 6d.
MACMILLAN'S PROGRESSIVE GERMAN READERS. By G. E. FASNACHT. Ex. fcap. 8vo.
*FIRST YEAR, containing an Introduction to the German order of Words, with Copious Examples, extracts from German Authors in Prose and Poetry; Notes, and Vocabularies. 2s. 6d.
MACMILLAN'S FOREIGN SCHOOL CLASSICS.—Edited by G. E. FASNACHT. 18mo.
*GOETHE—GÖTZ VON BERLICHINGEN, By H. A. BULL, M.A. 2s.
*GOETHE—FAUST. PART I., followed by an Appendix on PART II. By JANE LEE, Lecturer in German Literature at Newnham College, Cambridge. 4s. 6d.
*HEINE—SELECTIONS FROM THE REISEBILDER AND OTHER PROSE WORKS. By C. COLBECK, M.A., Assistant Master at Harrow. 2s. 6d.
*SCHILLER—SELECTIONS FROM SCHILLER'S LYRICAL POEMS. With a Memoir. By E. J. TURNER, B.A., and E. D. A. MORSHEAD, M.A., Assistant Masters at Winchester. 2s. 6d.
*SCHILLER—DIE JUNGFRAU VON ORLEANS. By JOSEPH GOSTWICK. 2s. 6d.
*SCHILLER—MARIA STUART. By C. SHELDON, D.Litt., of the Royal Academical Institution, Belfast. 2s. 6d.
*SCHILLER—WILHELM TELL. By G. E. FASNACHT. 2s. 6d.

*SCHILLER—WALLENSTEIN, DAS LAGER. By H. B. COTTERILL, M.A. 2s.
*UHLAND—SELECT BALLADS. Adapted for Beginners. With Vocabulary. By G. E. FASNACHT. 1s.
*PYLODET.—NEW GUIDE TO GERMAN CONVERSATION; containing an Alphabetical List of nearly 800 Familiar Words; followed by Exercises, Vocabulary, Familiar Phrases and Dialogues. By L. PYLODET. 18mo. 2s. 6d.
SMITH.—COMMERCIAL GERMAN. By F. C. SMITH, M.A. 2s. 6d.
WHITNEY.—A COMPENDIOUS GERMAN GRAMMAR. By W D. WHITNEY, Professor of Sanskrit and Instructor in Modern Languages in Yale College. Cr. 8vo. 4s. 6d.
A GERMAN READER IN PROSE AND VERSE. By the same. With Notes and Vocabulary. Cr. 8vo. 5s.
*WHITNEY and EDGREN.—A COMPENDIOUS GERMAN AND ENGLISH DICTIONARY. By Prof. W. D. WHITNEY and A. H. EDGREN. Cr. 8vo. 5s.
THE GERMAN-ENGLISH PART, separately, 3s. 6d.

MODERN GREEK.

VINCENT and DICKSON.—HANDBOOK TO MODERN GREEK. By Sir EDGAR VINCENT, K.C.M.G., and T. G. DICKSON, M.A. With Appendix on the relation of Modern and Classical Greek by Prof. JEBB. Cr. 8vo. 6s.

ITALIAN.

DANTE.—With Translation and Notes, by A. J. BUTLER, M.A.
 THE HELL. Cr. 8vo. 12s. 6d.
 THE PURGATORY. Cr. 8vo. 12s. 6d.
 THE PARADISE. 2d Ed. Cr. 8vo. 12s. 6d.
 READINGS ON THE PURGATORIO OF DANTE. Chiefly based on the Commentary of Benvenuto Da Imola. By Hon. W. WARREN VERNON, M.A. With Introduction by DEAN CHURCH. 2 vols. Cr. 8vo. 24s.
 THE DIVINE COMEDY. Transl. by C. E. NORTON. Cr. 8vo. 6s. each. I. HELL. II. PURGATORY.

SPANISH.

CALDERON.—FOUR PLAYS OF CALDERON. *El Principe Constante, La Vida es Sueno, El Alcalde de Zalamea,* and *El Escondido y La Tapada.* With Introduction and Notes. By NORMAN MACCOLL, M.A. Cr. 8vo. 14s.

MATHEMATICS.

Arithmetic, Book-keeping, Algebra, Euclid and Pure Geometry, Geometrical Drawing, Mensuration, Trigonometry, Analytical Geometry (Plane and Solid), Problems and Questions in Mathematics, Higher Pure Mathematics, Mechanics (Statics, Dynamics, Hydrostatics, Hydrodynamics: see also Physics), Physics (Sound, Light, Heat, Electricity, Elasticity, Attractions, &c.), Astronomy, Historical.

ARITHMETIC.

*ALDIS.—THE GREAT GIANT ARITHMOS. A most Elementary Arithmetic for Children. By MARY STEADMAN ALDIS. Illustrated. Gl. 8vo. 2s. 6d.
*BRADSHAW.—A COURSE OF EASY ARITHMETICAL EXAMPLES FOR BEGINNERS. By J. G. BRADSHAW, B.A., Assistant Master at Clifton College. Gl. 8vo. 2s. With Answers, 2s. 6d.
*BROOKSMITH.—ARITHMETIC IN THEORY AND PRACTICE. By J. BROOKSMITH, M.A. Cr. 8vo. 4s. 6d. KEY. Crown 8vo. 10s. 6d.
*BROOKSMITH.—ARITHMETIC FOR BEGINNERS. By J. and E. J. BROOKSMITH. Gl. 8vo. 1s. 6d. KEY.

ARITHMETIC—BOOK-KEEPING

CANDLER.—HELP TO ARITHMETIC. For the use of Schools. By H. CANDLER, Mathematical Master of Uppingham School. 2d Ed. Ex. fcap. 8vo. 2s. 6d.

COLLAR.—NOTES ON THE METRIC SYSTEM. By GEO. COLLAR, B.A., B.Sc. Gl. 8vo. 3d.

*DALTON.—RULES AND EXAMPLES IN ARITHMETIC. By Rev. T. DALTON, M.A., Senior Mathematical Master at Eton. With Answers. 18mo. 2s. 6d.

*GOYEN.—HIGHER ARITHMETIC AND ELEMENTARY MENSURATION. By P. GOYEN, Inspector of Schools, Dunedin, New Zealand. Cr. 8vo. 5s. [KEY *in the Press.*

*HALL and KNIGHT.—ARITHMETICAL EXERCISES AND EXAMINATION PAPERS. With an Appendix containing Questions in LOGARITHMS and MENSURATION. By H. S. HALL, M.A., Master of the Military Side, Clifton College, and S. R. KNIGHT, B.A., M.B., Ch.B. Gl. 8vo. 2s. 6d.

LOCK.—Works by Rev. J. B. LOCK, M.A., Senior Fellow and Bursar of Gonville and Caius College, Cambridge.
*ARITHMETIC FOR SCHOOLS. With Answers and 1000 additional Examples for Exercise. 4th Ed., revised. Gl. 8vo. 4s. 6d. Or, Part I. 2s. Part II. 3s. KEY. Cr. 8vo. 10s. 6d.
*ARITHMETIC FOR BEGINNERS. A School Class-Book of Commercial Arithmetic. Gl. 8vo. 2s. 6d. KEY. Cr. 8vo. 8s. 6d.
*A SHILLING BOOK OF ARITHMETIC, FOR ELEMENTARY SCHOOLS. 18mo. 1s. With Answers. 1s. 6d.

LOCK and COLLAR.—ARITHMETIC FOR THE STANDARDS. By Rev. J. B. LOCK, M.A., and GEO. COLLAR, B.A., B.Sc. Standards I. II. and III., 2d. each ; Standards IV. V. and VI., 3d. each. Answers, 2d. each.

*PEDLEY.—EXERCISES IN ARITHMETIC for the Use of Schools. Containing more than 7000 original Examples. By SAMUEL PEDLEY. Cr. 8vo. 5s. Also in Two Parts, 2s. 6d. each.

SMITH.—Works by Rev. BARNARD SMITH, M.A.
ARITHMETIC AND ALGEBRA, in their Principles and Application; with Examples taken from the Cambridge Examination Papers for the Ordinary B.A. Degree. Cr. 8vo. 10s. 6d.
*ARITHMETIC FOR SCHOOLS. Cr. 8vo. 4s. 6d. KEY. Cr. 8vo. 8s. 6d. A New Edition, revised by W. H. HUDSON, Professor of Mathematics, King's College, London. [*In the Press.*
EXERCISES IN ARITHMETIC. Cr. 8vo. 2s. With Answers, 2s. 6d. Answers separately, 6d.
SCHOOL CLASS-BOOK OF ARITHMETIC. 18mo. 3s. Or separately, in Three Parts, 1s. each. KEYS. Parts I., II., and III., 2s. 6d. each.
SHILLING BOOK OF ARITHMETIC. 18mo. Or separately, Part I., 2d. ; Part II., 3d. ; Part III., 7d. Answers, 6d. KEY. 18mo. 4s. 6d.
*THE SAME, with Answers. 18mo, cloth. 1s. 6d.
EXAMINATION PAPERS IN ARITHMETIC. 18mo. 1s. 6d. The Same, with Answers. 18mo. 2s. Answers, 6d. KEY. 18mo. 4s. 6d.
THE METRIC SYSTEM OF ARITHMETIC, ITS PRINCIPLES AND APPLICATIONS, with Numerous Examples. 18mo. 3d.
A CHART OF THE METRIC SYSTEM, on a Sheet, size 42 in. by 34 in. on Roller. New Ed. Revised by GEO. COLLAR, B.A., B.Sc. 4s. 6d.
EASY LESSONS IN ARITHMETIC, combining Exercises in Reading, Writing, Spelling, and Dictation. Part I. Cr. 8vo. 9d.
EXAMINATION CARDS IN ARITHMETIC. With Answers and Hints. Standards I. and II., in box, 1s. Standards III., IV., and V., in boxes, 1s. each. Standard VI. in Two Parts, in boxes, 1s. each.

BOOK-KEEPING.

*THORNTON.—FIRST LESSONS IN BOOK-KEEPING. By J. THORNTON. Cr. 8vo. 2s. 6d. KEY. Oblong 4to. 10s. 6d.
*PRIMER OF BOOK-KEEPING. 18mo. 1s. KEY. Demy 8vo. 2s. 6d.
EASY EXERCISES IN BOOK-KEEPING. 18mo. 1s.

MATHEMATICS

ALGEBRA.

*DALTON.—RULES AND EXAMPLES IN ALGEBRA. By Rev. T. DALTON, Senior Mathematical Master at Eton. Part I. 18mo. 2s. KEY. Cr. 8vo. 7s. 6d. Part II. 18mo. 2s. 6d.
HALL and KNIGHT.—Works by H. S. HALL, M.A., Master of the Military Side, Clifton College, and S. R. KNIGHT, B.A., M.B., Ch.B.
*ELEMENTARY ALGEBRA FOR SCHOOLS. 6th Ed., revised **and corrected.** Gl. 8vo. **3s. 6d.** With Answers, 4s. 6d. KEY. Cr. 8vo. 8s. 6d.
ALGEBRAICAL EXERCISES AND EXAMINATION **PAPERS.** To accompany ELEMENTARY ALGEBRA. 2d Ed., revised. Gl. 8vo. 2s. 6d.
*HIGHER ALGEBRA. 4th Ed. Cr. 8vo. 7s. 6d. KEY. Cr. 8vo. 10s. 6d.
JARMAN.—ALGEBRAICAL FACTORS. By J. ABBOT JARMAN. Gl. 8vo.
[*In the Press.*
*JONES and CHEYNE.—ALGEBRAICAL EXERCISES. Progressively Arranged. By Rev. C. A. JONES and C. H. CHEYNE, M.A., late Mathematical Masters at Westminster School. 18mo. 2s. 6d.
KEY. By Rev. W. FAILES, M.A. Cr. 8vo. 7s. 6d.
SMITH (Rev. BARNARD). *See* Arithmetic, p. 21.
SMITH.—Works by CHARLES SMITH, M.A., Master of Sidney Sussex College, Cambridge.
*ELEMENTARY **ALGEBRA.** 2d Ed., revised. Gl. 8vo. 4s. 6d. KEY. By A. G. CRACKNELL, **B.A. Cr. 8vo.** 10s. 6d.
*A TREATISE ON ALGEBRA. 2d Ed. Cr. 8vo. 7s. 6d. KEY. Cr. 8vo. 10s. 6d.
TODHUNTER.—Works by ISAAC TODHUNTER, F.R.S.
*ALGEBRA FOR BEGINNERS. 18mo. 2s. **6d.** KEY. Cr. 8vo. 6s. 6d.
***ALGEBRA** FOR COLLEGES AND SCHOOLS. By ISAAC TODHUNTER, F.R.S. **Cr. 8vo. 7s.** 6d. KEY. Cr. 8vo. 10s. 6d.

EUCLID AND PURE GEOMETRY.

COCKSHOTT and WALTERS.—A TREATISE ON GEOMETRICAL CONICS. By A. COCKSHOTT, M.A., Assistant Master at Eton, and Rev. F. B. WALTERS, M.A., Principal of King William's College, Isle of Man. Cr. 8vo. **5s.**
CONSTABLE.—GEOMETRICAL EXERCISES FOR BEGINNERS. By SAMUEL CONSTABLE. Cr. 8vo. 3s. 6d.
CUTHBERTSON.—EUCLIDIAN GEOMETRY. By FRANCIS CUTHBERTSON, M.A., LL.D. Ex. fcap. 8vo. 4s. 6d.
DAY.—PROPERTIES OF CONIC SECTIONS PROVED GEOMETRICALLY. By Rev. H. G. DAY, M.A. Part I. The Ellipse, with an ample collection of Problems. Cr. 8vo. 3s. 6d.
*DEAKIN.—RIDER PAPERS ON EUCLID. BOOKS I. AND II. By RUPERT DEAKIN, M.A. 18mo. 1s.
DODGSON.—Works by CHARLES L. DODGSON, M.A., Student and late Mathematical Lecturer, Christ Church, Oxford.
EUCLID, BOOKS I. AND II. 6th Ed., with words substituted for the Algebraical Symbols used in the 1st Ed. Cr. 8vo. 2s.
EUCLID AND HIS MODERN RIVALS. 2d Ed. Cr. 8vo. 6s.
CURIOSA MATHEMATICA. Part I. A New Theory of Parallels. 3d Ed. Cr. **8vo.** 2s.
DREW.—GEOMETRICAL TREATISE ON **CONIC SECTIONS.** By W. H. DREW, M.A. New Ed., enlarged. Cr. **8vo. 5s.**
DUPUIS.—ELEMENTARY SYNTHETIC GEOMETRY OF THE POINT, LINE AND **CIRCLE** IN THE PLANE. By N. F. DUPUIS, M.A., Professor of Mathematics, **University** of Queen's College, Kingston, Canada. Gl. 8vo. 4s. 6d.
***HALL and** STEVENS.—A TEXT-BOOK OF EUCLID'S ELEMENTS. Including Alternative Proofs, with additional Theorems and Exercises, classified and arranged. By H. S. HALL, M.A., and F. H. STEVENS, M.A., Masters of the Military Side, Clifton College. Gl. 8vo. Book I., 1s.; Books I. and II., 1s. 6d.; Books I.-IV., 3s.; Books III.-IV., 2s.; Books III.-VI., 3s.; Books V.-VI. and XI., 2s. 6d.; Books I.-VI. and XI., 4s. 6d.; Book XI., 1s. KEY to Books I.-IV., 6s. 6d.

GEOMETRICAL DRAWING—TRIGONOMETRY

HALSTED.—THE ELEMENTS OF GEOMETRY. By G. B. HALSTED, Professor of Pure and Applied Mathematics in the University of Texas. 8vo. 12s. 6d.

HAYWARD.—THE ELEMENTS OF SOLID GEOMETRY. By R. B. HAYWARD, M.A., F.R.S. Gl. 8vo. 3s.

LOCK.—THE FIRST BOOK OF EUCLID'S ELEMENTS ARRANGED FOR BEGINNERS. By Rev. J. B. LOCK, M.A. Gl. 8vo. 2s. 6d.

MILNE and DAVIS.—GEOMETRICAL CONICS. Part I. The Parabola. By Rev. J. J. MILNE, M.A., and R. F. DAVIS, M.A. Cr. 8vo. 2s.

*RICHARDSON.—THE PROGRESSIVE EUCLID. Books I. and II. With Notes, Exercises, and Deductions. Edited by A. T. RICHARDSON, M.A., Senior Mathematical Master at the Isle of Wight College. Gl. 8vo. 2s. 6d.

SYLLABUS OF PLANE GEOMETRY (corresponding to Euclid, Books I.-VI.)—Prepared by the Association for the Improvement of Geometrical Teaching. Cr. 8vo. Sewed. 1s.

SYLLABUS OF MODERN PLANE GEOMETRY.—Prepared by the Association for the Improvement of Geometrical Teaching. Cr. 8vo. Sewed. 1s.

*TODHUNTER.—THE ELEMENTS OF EUCLID. By I. TODHUNTER, F.R.S. 18mo. 3s. 6d. *Books I. and II. 1s. KEY. Cr. 8vo. 6s. 6d.

WILSON.—Works by Archdeacon WILSON, M.A., late Headmaster of Clifton College. ELEMENTARY GEOMETRY. BOOKS I.-V. (Corresponding to Euclid. Books I.-VI.) Following the Syllabus of the Geometrical Association. Ex. fcp. 8vo. 4s. 6d.
SOLID GEOMETRY AND CONIC SECTIONS. With Appendices on Transversals and Harmonic Division. Ex. fcap. 8vo. 3s. 6d.

GEOMETRICAL DRAWING.

EAGLES.—CONSTRUCTIVE GEOMETRY OF PLANE CURVES. By T. H. EAGLES, M.A., Instructor, Roy. Indian Engineering Coll. Cr. 8vo. 12s.

EDGAR and PRITCHARD.—NOTE-BOOK ON PRACTICAL SOLID OR DESCRIPTIVE GEOMETRY. Containing Problems with help for Solutions. By J. H. EDGAR and G. S. PRITCHARD. 4th Ed. Gl. 8vo. 4s. 6d.

*KITCHENER.—A GEOMETRICAL NOTE-BOOK. Containing Easy Problems in Geometrical Drawing. By F. E. KITCHENER, M.A., Headmaster of the High School, Newcastle-under-Lyme. 4to. 2s.

MILLAR.—ELEMENTS OF DESCRIPTIVE GEOMETRY. By J. B. MILLAR, Lecturer on Engineering in the Owens College, Manchester. Cr. 8vo. 6s.

PLANT.—PRACTICAL PLANE AND DESCRIPTIVE GEOMETRY. By E. C. PLANT. Globe 8vo. [In preparation.

MENSURATION.

STEVENS.—ELEMENTARY MENSURATION. With Exercises on the Mensuration of Plane and Solid Figures. By F. H. STEVENS, M.A. Gl. 8vo. [In prep.

TEBAY.—ELEMENTARY MENSURATION FOR SCHOOLS. By S. TEBAY. Ex. fcap. 8vo. 3s. 6d.

*TODHUNTER.—MENSURATION FOR BEGINNERS. By ISAAC TODHUNTER, F.R.S. 18mo. 2s. 6d. KEY. By Rev. FR. L. MCCARTHY. Cr. 8vo. 7s. 6d.

TRIGONOMETRY.

BEASLEY.—AN ELEMENTARY TREATISE ON PLANE TRIGONOMETRY. With Examples. By R. D. BEASLEY, M.A. 9th Ed. Cr. 8vo. 3s. 6d.

BOTTOMLEY.—FOUR-FIGURE MATHEMATICAL TABLES. Comprising Logarithmic and Trigonometrical Tables, and Tables of Squares, Square Roots, and Reciprocals. By J. T. BOTTOMLEY, M.A., Lecturer in Natural Philosophy in the University of Glasgow 8vo. **2s. 6d.**

HAYWARD.—THE ALGEBRA OF CO-PLANAR VECTORS AND TRIGONOMETRY By R. B. HAYWARD, M.A., F.R.S. [In preparation.

JOHNSON.—A TREATISE ON TRIGONOMETRY. By W. E. JOHNSON, M.A., late Mathematical Lecturer at King's College, Cambridge. Cr. 8vo. 8s. 6d.

24   MATHEMATICS

*LEVETT and DAVISON.—THE ELEMENTS OF PLANE TRIGONOMETRY.
    By RAWDON LEVETT, M.A., and C. DAVISON, M.A., Assistant Masters at King
    Edward's School, Birmingham. Gl. 8vo.   6s. 6d. ; or, in 2 parts, 3s. 6d. each.
LOCK.—Works by Rev. J. B. LOCK, M.A., Senior Fellow and Bursar of Gonville
    and Caius College, Cambridge.
    *THE TRIGONOMETRY OF ONE ANGLE. Gl. 8vo. 2s. 6d.
    *TRIGONOMETRY FOR BEGINNERS, as far as the Solution of Triangles. 3d
    Ed. Gl. 8vo. 2s. 6d. KEY. Cr. 8vo. 6s. 6d.
    *ELEMENTARY TRIGONOMETRY.   6th Ed. Gl. 8vo. 4s. 6d. KEY. Cr. 8vo.
    8s. 6d.
    HIGHER TRIGONOMETRY. 5th Ed. 4s. 6d. Both Parts complete in One
    Volume. 7s. 6d. KEY.   [In preparation.
M'CLELLAND and PRESTON.—A TREATISE ON SPHERICAL TRIGONO-
    METRY. By W. J. M'CLELLAND, M.A., Principal of the Incorporated Society's
    School, Santry, Dublin, and T. PRESTON, M.A. Cr. 8vo. 8s. 6d., or : Part I.
    To the End of Solution of Triangles, 4s. 6d. Part II., 5s.
MATTHEWS.—MANUAL OF LOGARITHMS. By G. F. MATTHEWS, B.A. 8vo.
    5s. net.
PALMER.—PRACTICAL LOGARITHMS AND TRIGONOMETRY. By J. H.
    PALMER, Headmaster, R.N., H.M.S. Cambridge, Devonport. Gl. 8vo. 4s. 6d.
SNOWBALL.—THE ELEMENTS OF PLANE AND SPHERICAL TRIGONO-
    METRY. By J. C. SNOWBALL. 14th Ed. Cr. 8vo. 7s. 6d.
TODHUNTER.—Works by ISAAC TODHUNTER, F.R.S.
    *TRIGONOMETRY FOR BEGINNERS. 18mo. 2s. 6d. KEY. Cr. 8vo. 8s. 6d.
    PLANE TRIGONOMETRY. Cr. 8vo. 5s. KEY. Cr. 8vo. 10s. 6d.
    A TREATISE ON SPHERICAL TRIGONOMETRY. Cr. 8vo. 4s. 6d.
TODHUNTER and HOGG.—Being a new edition of Dr. Todhunter's Plane Trigono-
    metry, revised by R. W. HOGG, M.A. Cr. 8vo. 5s.
WOLSTENHOLME.—EXAMPLES FOR PRACTICE IN THE USE OF SEVEN-
    FIGURE LOGARITHMS. By JOSEPH WOLSTENHOLME, D.Sc., late Professor
    of Mathematics, Royal Indian Engineering Coll., Cooper's Hill. 8vo. 5s.

ANALYTICAL GEOMETRY (Plane and Solid).

DYER.—EXERCISES IN ANALYTICAL GEOMETRY. By J. M. DYER, M.A.,
    Assistant Master at Eton. Illustrated. Cr. 8vo. 4s. 6d.
FERRERS.—AN ELEMENTARY TREATISE ON TRILINEAR CO-ORDIN-
    ATES, the Method of Reciprocal Polars, and the Theory of Projectors. By
    the Rev. N. M. FERRERS, D.D., F.R.S., Master of Gonville and Caius College,
    Cambridge. 4th Ed., revised. Cr. 8vo. 6s. 6d.
FROST.—Works by PERCIVAL FROST, D.Sc., F.R.S., Fellow and Mathematical
    Lecturer at King's College, Cambridge.
    AN ELEMENTARY TREATISE ON CURVE TRACING. 8vo. 12s.
    SOLID GEOMETRY. 3d Ed. Demy 8vo. 16s.
    HINTS FOR THE SOLUTION OF PROBLEMS in the above. 8vo. 8s. 6d.
JOHNSON.—CURVE TRACING IN CARTESIAN CO-ORDINATES. By W.
    WOOLSEY JOHNSON, Professor of Mathematics at the U.S. Naval Academy,
    Annapolis, Maryland. Cr. 8vo. 4s. 6d.
M'CLELLAND.—A TREATISE ON THE GEOMETRY OF THE CIRCLE, and
    some extensions to Conic Sections by the Method of Reciprocation. By W. J.
    M'CLELLAND, M.A. Cr. 8vo. 6s.
PUCKLE.—AN ELEMENTARY TREATISE ON CONIC SECTIONS AND AL-
    GEBRAIC GEOMETRY. By G. H. PUCKLE, M.A. 5th Ed. Cr. 8vo. 7s. 6d.
SMITH.—Works by CHARLES SMITH, M.A., Master of Sidney Sussex College.
    Cambridge.
    CONIC SECTIONS. 7th Ed. Cr. 8vo. 7s. 6d.
    SOLUTIONS TO CONIC SECTIONS. Cr. 8vo. 10s. 6d.
    AN ELEMENTARY TREATISE ON SOLID GEOMETRY. Cr. 8vo. 9s. 6d.

TODHUNTER.—Works by ISAAC TODHUNTER, F.R.S.
  PLANE CO-ORDINATE GEOMETRY, as applied to the Straight Line and the Conic Sections. Cr. 8vo. 7s. 6d. KEY. By C. W. BOURNE, M.A. Cr. 8vo. 10s. 6d.
  EXAMPLES OF ANALYTICAL GEOMETRY OF THREE DIMENSIONS. New Ed., revised. Cr. 8vo. 4s.

PROBLEMS AND QUESTIONS IN MATHEMATICS.

ARMY PRELIMINARY EXAMINATION, PAPERS 1882-Sept. 1891. With Answers to the Mathematical Questions. Cr. 8vo. 3s. 6d.
CAMBRIDGE SENATE-HOUSE PROBLEMS AND RIDERS, WITH SOLUTIONS:—
  1875—PROBLEMS AND RIDERS. By A. G. GREENHILL, F.R.S. Cr. 8vo. 8s. 6d.
  1878—SOLUTIONS OF SENATE-HOUSE PROBLEMS. Edited by J. W. L. GLAISHER, F.R.S., Fellow of Trinity College, Cambridge. Cr. 8vo. 12s.
CHRISTIE.—A COLLECTION OF ELEMENTARY TEST-QUESTIONS IN PURE AND MIXED MATHEMATICS. By J. R. CHRISTIE, F.R.S. Cr. 8vo. 8s. 6d.
CLIFFORD.—MATHEMATICAL PAPERS. By W. K. CLIFFORD. 8vo. 30s.
MILNE.—WEEKLY **PROBLEM PAPERS.** By Rev. JOHN J. MILNE, M.A. Pott 8vo. 4s. 6d.
  SOLUTIONS TO THE ABOVE. By the same. Cr. 8vo. 10s. 6d.
  COMPANION TO WEEKLY PROBLEM PAPERS. Cr. 8vo. 10s. 6d.
*****RICHARDSON.**—PROGRESSIVE MATHEMATICAL EXERCISES FOR HOME WORK. By A. T. RICHARDSON, M.A. First Series. Gl. 8vo. 2s. With Answers, 2s. 6d. Second Series. 3s. With Answers, 3s. 6d.
SANDHURST MATHEMATICAL PAPERS, for Admission into the Royal Military College, 1881-1889. Edited by E. J. BROOKSMITH, B.A. Cr. 8vo. 3s. 6d.
WOOLWICH MATHEMATICAL PAPERS, for Admission into the Royal Military Academy, Woolwich, 1880-1890 inclusive. By the same. Cr. 8vo. 6s.
WOLSTENHOLME.—MATHEMATICAL PROBLEMS, on Subjects included in the First and Second Divisions of Cambridge Mathematical Tripos. By JOSEPH WOLSTENHOLME, D.Sc. 3d Ed., greatly enlarged. 8vo. 18s.
  EXAMPLES FOR PRACTICE IN THE USE OF SEVEN-FIGURE LOGARITHMS. By the same. 8vo. 5s.

HIGHER PURE MATHEMATICS.

AIRY.—Works by Sir G. B. AIRY, K.C.B., formerly Astronomer-Royal.
  ELEMENTARY TREATISE ON PARTIAL DIFFERENTIAL EQUATIONS. With Diagrams. 2d Ed. Cr. 8vo. 5s. 6d.
  ON THE ALGEBRAICAL AND NUMERICAL THEORY OF ERRORS OF OBSERVATIONS AND THE COMBINATION OF OBSERVATIONS. 2d Ed., revised. Cr. 8vo. 6s. 6d.
BOOLE.—THE CALCULUS OF FINITE DIFFERENCES. By G. BOOLE. 3d Ed., revised by J. F. MOULTON, Q.C. Cr. 8vo. 10s. 6d.
EDWARDS.—THE DIFFERENTIAL CALCULUS. By JOSEPH EDWARDS, M.A. With Applications and numerous Examples. New Ed. 8vo. 14s.
FERRERS.—AN ELEMENTARY TREATISE ON SPHERICAL HARMONICS, and Subjects connected with them. By Rev. N. M. FERRERS. Cr. 8vo. 7s. 6d.
FORSYTH.—A TREATISE ON DIFFERENTIAL EQUATIONS. By ANDREW RUSSELL FORSYTH, F.R.S., Fellow and Assistant Tutor of Trinity College, Cambridge. 2d Ed. 8vo. 14s.
FROST.—AN ELEMENTARY TREATISE ON CURVE TRACING. By PERCIVAL FROST, M.A., D.Sc. 8vo. 12s.
GRAHAM.—GEOMETRY OF POSITION. By R. H. GRAHAM. Cr. 8vo. 7s. 6d.
GREENHILL.—DIFFERENTIAL AND INTEGRAL CALCULUS. By A. G. GREENHILL, Professor of Mathematics to the Senior Class of Artillery Officers, Woolwich. New Ed. Cr. 8vo. 10s. 6d.
  APPLICATIONS OF ELLIPTIC FUNCTIONS. By the same. [*In the Press.*

HEMMING.—AN ELEMENTARY TREATISE ON THE DIFFERENTIAL AND INTEGRAL CALCULUS. By G. W. HEMMING, M.A. 2d Ed. 8vo. 9s.

JOHNSON.—Works by W. W. JOHNSON, Professor of Mathematics at the U.S. Naval Academy.
INTEGRAL CALCULUS, an Elementary Treatise. Founded on the Method of Rates or Fluxions. 8vo. 9s.
CURVE TRACING IN CARTESIAN CO-ORDINATES. Cr. 8vo. 4s. 6d.
A TREATISE ON ORDINARY AND DIFFERENTIAL EQUATIONS. Ex. cr. 8vo. 15s.

KELLAND and TAIT.—INTRODUCTION TO QUATERNIONS, with numerous examples. By P. KELLAND and P. G. TAIT, Professors in the Department of Mathematics in the University of Edinburgh. 2d Ed. Cr. 8vo. 7s. 6d.

KEMPE.—HOW TO DRAW A STRAIGHT LINE: a Lecture on Linkages. By A. B. KEMPE. Illustrated. Cr. 8vo. 1s. 6d.

KNOX.—DIFFERENTIAL CALCULUS FOR BEGINNERS. By ALEXANDER KNOX, M.A. Fcap. 8vo. 3s. 6d.

MUIR.—THE THEORY OF DETERMINANTS IN THE HISTORICAL ORDER OF ITS DEVELOPMENT. Part I. Determinants in General, Leibnitz (1693) to Cayley (1841). By THOS. MUIR, F.R.S.E., Superintendent General of Education, Cape Colony. 8vo. 10s. 6d.

RICE and JOHNSON.—AN ELEMENTARY TREATISE ON THE DIFFERENTIAL CALCULUS. Founded on the Method of Rates or Fluxions. By J. M. RICE and W. W. JOHNSON. 3d Ed. 8vo. 18s. Abridged Ed. 9s.

TODHUNTER.—Works by ISAAC TODHUNTER, F.R.S.
AN ELEMENTARY TREATISE ON THE THEORY OF EQUATIONS. Cr. 8vo. 7s. 6d.
A TREATISE ON THE DIFFERENTIAL CALCULUS. Cr. 8vo. 10s. 6d. KEY. Cr. 8vo. 10s. 6d.
A TREATISE ON THE INTEGRAL CALCULUS AND ITS APPLICATIONS. Cr. 8vo. 10s. 6d. KEY. Cr. 8vo. 10s. 6d.
A HISTORY OF THE MATHEMATICAL THEORY OF PROBABILITY, from the time of Pascal to that of Laplace. 8vo. 18s.
AN ELEMENTARY TREATISE ON LAPLACE'S, LAME'S, AND BESSEL'S FUNCTIONS. Cr. 8vo. 10s. 6d.

MECHANICS: Statics, Dynamics, Hydrostatics, Hydrodynamics. (See also Physics.)

ALEXANDER and THOMSON.—ELEMENTARY APPLIED MECHANICS. By Prof. T. ALEXANDER and A. W. THOMSON. Part II. Transverse Stress. Cr. 8vo. 10s. 6d.

BALL.—EXPERIMENTAL MECHANICS. A Course of Lectures delivered at the Royal College of Science, Dublin. By Sir R. S. BALL, F.R.S. 2d Ed. Illustrated. Cr. 8vo. 6s.

CLIFFORD.—THE ELEMENTS OF DYNAMIC. An Introduction to the Study of Motion and Rest in Solid and Fluid Bodies. By W. K. CLIFFORD. Part I.—Kinematic. Cr. 8vo. Books I.-III. 7s. 6d.; Book IV. and Appendix, 6s.

COTTERILL.—APPLIED MECHANICS: An Elementary General Introduction to the Theory of Structures and Machines. By J. H. COTTERILL, F.R.S., Professor of Applied Mechanics in the Royal Naval College, Greenwich. 8vo. 18s.

COTTERILL and SLADE.—LESSONS IN APPLIED MECHANICS. By Prof. J. H. COTTERILL and J. H. SLADE. Fcap. 8vo. 5s. 6d.

GANGUILLET and KUTTER.—A GENERAL FORMULA FOR THE UNIFORM FLOW OF WATER IN RIVERS AND OTHER CHANNELS. By E. GANGUILLET and W. R. KUTTER. Translated by R. HERING and J. C. TRAUTWINE. 8vo. 17s.

GRAHAM.—GEOMETRY OF POSITION. By R. H. GRAHAM. Cr. 8vo. 7s. 6d.

*GREAVES.**—STATICS FOR BEGINNERS. By JOHN GREAVES, M.A., Fellow and Mathematical Lecturer at Christ's College, Cambridge. Gl. 8vo. 3s. 6d.
A TREATISE ON ELEMENTARY STATICS. By the same. Cr. 8vo. 6s. 6d.

MECHANICS—PHYSICS

GREENHILL.—HYDROSTATICS. By A. G. GREENHILL, Professor of Mathematics to the Senior Class of Artillery Officers, Woolwich. Cr. 8vo. [*In preparation.*

*****HICKS.**—ELEMENTARY DYNAMICS OF PARTICLES AND SOLIDS. By W. M. HICKS, D.Sc., Principal and Professor of Mathematics and Physics, Firth College, Sheffield. Cr. 8vo. 6s. 6d.

JELLETT.—A TREATISE ON THE THEORY OF FRICTION. By JOHN H. JELLETT, B.D., late Provost of Trinity College, Dublin. 8vo. 8s. 6d.

KENNEDY.—THE MECHANICS OF MACHINERY. By A. B. W. KENNEDY, F.R.S. Illustrated. Cr. 8vo. 12s. 6d.

LOCK.—Works by Rev J. B. LOCK, M.A.
*MECHANICS FOR BEGINNERS. Gl. 8vo. Part I. MECHANICS OF SOLIDS. 3s. 6d. [Part II. MECHANICS OF FLUIDS, *in preparation.*
*ELEMENTARY **STATICS.** 2d Ed. Gl. 8vo. 4s. 6d.
*ELEMENTARY DYNAMICS. 3d Ed. Gl. 8vo. 4s. 6d.
ELEMENTARY HYDROSTATICS. Gl. 8vo. [*In preparation.*

MACGREGOR.—KINEMATICS AND DYNAMICS. An Elementary Treatise. **By J.** G. MACGREGOR, D.Sc., Munro Professor of Physics in Dalhousie College, **Halifax,** Nova Scotia. Illustrated. Cr. 8vo. 10s. 6d.

PARKINSON.—AN ELEMENTARY TREATISE ON MECHANICS. By S. PARKINSON, D.D., F.R.S., late Tutor and Prælector of St. John's College, Cambridge. 6th Ed., revised. Cr. 8vo. 9s. 6d.

PIRIE.—LESSONS ON RIGID DYNAMICS. By Rev. G. PIRIE, M.A., Professor of Mathematics in the University of Aberdeen. Cr. 8vo. 6s.

ROUTH.—Works by EDWARD JOHN ROUTH, D.Sc., LL.D., F.R.S., Hon. Fellow of St. Peter's College, Cambridge.
A TREATISE ON THE DYNAMICS OF THE SYSTEM OF RIGID BODIES. With numerous Examples. Two Vols. 8vo. Vol. I.—Elementary Parts. 5th Ed. 14s. Vol. II.—The Advanced Parts. 4th Ed. 14s.
STABILITY OF A GIVEN STATE OF MOTION, PARTICULARLY STEADY MOTION. Adams Prize Essay for 1877. 8vo. 8s. 6d.

*****SANDERSON.**—HYDROSTATICS FOR BEGINNERS. By F. W. SANDERSON, M.A., Assistant Master at Dulwich College. Gl. 8vo. 4s. 6d.

SYLLABUS OF ELEMENTARY DYNAMICS. Part I. Linear Dynamics. **With** an Appendix on the Meanings of the Symbols in Physical Equations. Prepared by the Association for the Improvement of Geometrical Teaching. 4to. 1s.

TAIT and STEELE.—A TREATISE ON DYNAMICS OF A PARTICLE. By Professor TAIT, M.A., and W. J. STEELE, B.A. 6th Ed., revised. Cr. 8vo. 12s.

TODHUNTER.—Works by ISAAC TODHUNTER, F.R.S.
*MECHANICS FOR BEGINNERS. 18mo. 4s. 6d. KEY. Cr. 8vo. 6s. 6d.
A TREATISE ON ANALYTICAL STATICS. 5th Ed. Edited by Prof. J. D. EVERETT, F.R.S. Cr. 8vo. 10s. 6d.

PHYSICS: Sound, Light, Heat, Electricity, Elasticity, Attractions, etc. (See also Mechanics.)

AIRY.—ON SOUND AND ATMOSPHERIC VIBRATIONS. By Sir G. B. AIRY, K.C.B., formerly Astronomer-Royal. **With** the Mathematical Elements of Music. Cr. 8vo. 9s.

CUMMING.—AN INTRODUCTION TO THE THEORY OF ELECTRICITY. By LINNÆUS CUMMING, M.A., Assistant Master at Rugby. Illustrated. Cr. 8vo. 8s. 6d.

DANIELL.—A TEXT-BOOK OF THE PRINCIPLES OF PHYSICS. By ALFRED DANIELL, D.Sc. Illustrated. 2d Ed., revised and enlarged. 8vo. 21s.

DAY.—ELECTRIC LIGHT ARITHMETIC. By R. E. DAY. Pott 8vo. 2s.

EVERETT.—ILLUSTRATIONS OF THE C. G. S. SYSTEM OF UNITS WITH TABLES OF PHYSICAL CONSTANTS. By J. D. EVERETT, F.R.S., Professor of Natural Philosophy, Queen's College, Belfast. New Ed. Ex. fcap. 8vo. 5s.

FERRERS.—AN ELEMENTARY TREATISE ON SPHERICAL HARMONICS, and Subjects connected with them. By Rev. N. M. FERRERS, D.D., F.R.S., Master of Gonville and Caius College, Cambridge. Cr. 8vo. 7s. 6d.

MATHEMATICS

FESSENDEN.—PHYSICS FOR PUBLIC SCHOOLS. By C. FESSENDEN. Illustrated. Fcap. 8vo. [*In the Press.*

GRAY.—THE THEORY AND PRACTICE OF ABSOLUTE MEASUREMENTS IN ELECTRICITY AND MAGNETISM. By A. GRAY, F.R.S.E., Professor of Physics, University College, Bangor. Two Vols. Cr. 8vo. Vol. I. 12s. 6d. [Vol. II. *In the Press.*

ABSOLUTE MEASUREMENTS IN ELECTRICITY AND MAGNETISM. 2d Ed., revised and greatly enlarged. Fcap. 8vo. 5s. 6d.

IBBETSON.—THE MATHEMATICAL THEORY OF PERFECTLY ELASTIC SOLIDS, with a Short Account of Viscous Fluids. By W. J. IBBETSON, late Senior Scholar of Clare College, Cambridge. 8vo. 21s.

JOHNSON.—NATURE'S STORY BOOKS. I. Sunshine. By AMY JOHNSON, LL.A. Illustrated. [*In the Press.*

*JONES.—EXAMPLES IN PHYSICS. With Answers and Solutions. By D. E. JONES, B.Sc., late Professor of Physics, University College of Wales, Aberystwith. Fcap. 8vo. 3s. 6d.

*ELEMENTARY LESSONS IN HEAT, LIGHT, AND SOUND. By the same. Gl. 8vo. 2s. 6d.

HEAT AND LIGHT. By the same.

KELVIN.—Works by Lord KELVIN, P.R.S., Professor of Natural Philosophy in the University of Glasgow.

ELECTROSTATICS AND MAGNETISM, REPRINTS OF PAPERS ON. 2d Ed. 8vo. 18s.

POPULAR LECTURES AND ADDRESSES. 3 Vols. Illustrated. Cr. 8vo. Vol. I. CONSTITUTION OF MATTER. 7s. 6d. Vol. III. NAVIGATION. 7s. 6d.

LOCKYER.—CONTRIBUTIONS TO SOLAR PHYSICS. By J. NORMAN LOCKYER, F.R.S. With Illustrations. Royal 8vo. 31s. 6d.

LODGE.—MODERN VIEWS OF ELECTRICITY. By OLIVER J. LODGE, F.R.S., Professor of Physics, University College, Liverpool. Illus. Cr. 8vo. 6s. 6d.

LOEWY.—*QUESTIONS AND EXAMPLES ON EXPERIMENTAL PHYSICS: Sound, Light, Heat, Electricity, and Magnetism. By B. LOEWY, Examiner in Experimental Physics to the College of Preceptors. Fcap. 8vo. 2s.

*A GRADUATED COURSE OF NATURAL SCIENCE FOR ELEMENTARY AND TECHNICAL SCHOOLS AND COLLEGES. By the same. Part I. FIRST YEAR'S COURSE. Gl. 8vo. 2s. Part II. 2s. 6d.

LUPTON.—NUMERICAL TABLES AND CONSTANTS IN ELEMENTARY SCIENCE. By S. LUPTON, M.A. Ex. fcap. 8vo. 2s. 6d.

MACFARLANE.—PHYSICAL ARITHMETIC. By A. MACFARLANE, D.Sc., late Examiner in Mathematics at the University of Edinburgh. Cr. 8vo. 7s. 6d.

*MAYER.—SOUND: A Series of Simple Experiments. By A. M. MAYER, Prof. of Physics in the Stevens Institute of Technology. Illustrated. Cr. 8vo. 3s. 6d.

*MAYER and BARNARD.—LIGHT: A Series of Simple Experiments. By A. M. MAYER and C. BARNARD. Illustrated. Cr. 8vo. 2s. 6d.

MOLLOY.—GLEANINGS IN SCIENCE: Popular Lectures. By Rev. GERALD MOLLOY, D.Sc., Rector of the Catholic University of Ireland. 8vo. 7s. 6d.

NEWTON.—PRINCIPIA. Edited by Prof. Sir W. THOMSON, P.R.S., and Prof. BLACKBURNE. 4to. 31s. 6d.

THE FIRST THREE SECTIONS OF NEWTON'S PRINCIPIA. With Notes, Illustrations, and Problems. By P. FROST, M.A., D.Sc. 3d Ed. 8vo. 12s.

PARKINSON.—A TREATISE ON OPTICS. By S. PARKINSON, D.D., F.R.S., late Tutor of St. John's College, Cambridge. 4th Ed. Cr. 8vo. 10s. 6d.

PEABODY.—THERMODYNAMICS OF THE STEAM-ENGINE AND OTHER HEAT-ENGINES. By CECIL H. PEABODY. 8vo. 21s.

PERRY.—STEAM: An Elementary Treatise. By JOHN PERRY, Prof. of Applied Mechanics, Technical College, Finsbury. 18mo. 4s. 6d.

PICKERING.—ELEMENTS OF PHYSICAL MANIPULATION. By Prof. EDWARD C. PICKERING. Medium 8vo. Part I., 12s. 6d. Part II., 14s.

PRESTON.—THE THEORY OF LIGHT. By THOMAS PRESTON, M.A. Illustrated. 8vo. 15s. net.

THE THEORY OF HEAT. By the same. 8vo. [*In preparation.*

PHYSICS—ASTRONOMY

RAYLEIGH.—THE THEORY OF SOUND. By Lord Rayleigh, F.R.S. 8vo. Vol. I., 12s. 6d. Vol. II., 12s. 6d. [Vol. III. *In the Press.*

SHANN.—AN ELEMENTARY TREATISE ON HEAT, IN RELATION TO STEAM AND THE STEAM-ENGINE. By G. Shann, M.A. Cr. 8vo. 4s. 6d.

SPOTTISWOODE.—POLARISATION OF LIGHT. By the late W. Spottiswoode, F.R.S. Illustrated. Cr. 8vo. 3s. 6d.

STEWART.—Works by Balfour Stewart, F.R.S., late Langworthy Professor of Physics, Owens College, Manchester.
 *A PRIMER OF PHYSICS. Illustrated. **With Questions.** 18mo. 1s.
 *LESSONS IN ELEMENTARY PHYSICS. Illustrated. Fcap. 8vo. 4s. 6d.
 *QUESTIONS. By Prof. T. H. Core. Fcap. 8vo. 2s.

STEWART and GEE.—LESSONS IN ELEMENTARY PRACTICAL PHYSICS. By Balfour Stewart, F.R.S., and W. W. Haldane Gee, B.Sc. Cr. 8vo. Vol. I. General Physical Processes. 6s. Vol. II. Electricity and Magnetism. 7s. 6d. [Vol. III. Optics, Heat, and Sound. *In the Press.*
 *PRACTICAL PHYSICS FOR SCHOOLS AND THE JUNIOR STUDENTS OF COLLEGES. Gl. 8vo. Vol. I. Electricity and Magnetism. 2s. 6d. [Vol. II. Optics, Heat, and Sound. *In the Press.*

STOKES.—ON LIGHT. Burnett Lectures. By Sir G. G. Stokes, F.R.S., Lucasian Professor of Mathematics in the University of Cambridge. I. On the Nature of Light. II. On Light as a Means of Investigation. III. On the Beneficial Effects of Light. Cr. 8vo. 7s. 6d.

STONE.—AN ELEMENTARY TREATISE ON SOUND. **By W. H. Stone.** Illustrated. Fcap. 8vo. 3s. 6d.

TAIT.—HEAT. By P. G. Tait, Professor **of Natural** Philosophy in **the University** of Edinburgh. **Cr. 8vo. 6s.**
 LECTURES ON SOME RECENT ADVANCES IN PHYSICAL SCIENCE. By the same. 3d Edition. Crown 8vo. 9s.

TAYLOR.—SOUND AND MUSIC. An Elementary Treatise on the Physical Constitution of Musical Sounds and Harmony, including the Chief Acoustical Discoveries of Prof. Helmholtz. By S. Taylor, M.A. Ex. cr. 8vo. 8s. **6d.**

*THOMPSON.— ELEMENTARY LESSONS IN ELECTRICITY AND MAGNETISM. By Silvanus P. Thompson, Principal and Professor **of Physics in the Technical** College, Finsbury. Illustrated. Fcap. 8vo. **4s. 6d.**

THOMSON.—Works by J. J. Thomson, Professor of Experimental **Physics in the** University of Cambridge.
 A TREATISE ON THE MOTION OF VORTEX RINGS. 8vo. 6s.
 APPLICATIONS OF DYNAMICS TO PHYSICS AND CHEMISTRY. Cr. 8vo. 7s. 6d.

TODHUNTER.—Works by Isaac Todhunter, F.R.S.
 AN ELEMENTARY TREATISE ON LAPLACE'S, LAME'S, AND BESSEL'S FUNCTIONS. Crown 8vo. 10s. 6d.
 A HISTORY OF THE MATHEMATICAL THEORIES OF ATTRACTION, AND THE FIGURE OF THE EARTH, from the time of Newton to that of Laplace. 2 vols. 8vo. 24s.

TURNER.—A COLLECTION OF EXAMPLES ON HEAT AND ELECTRICITY. By H. H. Turner, Fellow of Trinity College, Cambridge. Cr. 8vo. 2s. 6d.

WRIGHT.—LIGHT: A Course of Experimental Optics, chiefly with the Lantern. By Lewis Wright. Illustrated. New Ed. Cr. 8vo. 7s. 6d.

ASTRONOMY.

AIRY.—Works by Sir G. B. Airy, K.C.B., formerly Astronomer-Royal.
 *POPULAR ASTRONOMY. Revised by H. H. Turner, M.A. 18mo. 4s. 6d.
 GRAVITATION: An Elementary Explanation of the Principal Perturbations in the Solar System. 2d Ed. Cr. 8vo. 7s. 6d.

CHEYNE.—AN ELEMENTARY TREATISE ON THE PLANETARY THEORY. By C. H. H. Cheyne. With Problems. 3d Ed., revised. Cr. 8vo. 7s. 6d.

CLARK and SADLER.—THE STAR GUIDE. By L. CLARK and H. SADLER. Roy. 8vo. 5s.

CROSSLEY, GLEDHILL, and WILSON.—A HANDBOOK OF DOUBLE STARS. By E. CROSSLEY, J. GLEDHILL, and J. M. WILSON. 8vo. 21s.
CORRECTIONS TO THE HANDBOOK OF DOUBLE STARS. 8vo. 1s.

FORBES.—TRANSIT OF VENUS. By G. FORBES, Professor of Natural Philosophy in the Andersonian University, Glasgow. Illustrated. Cr. 8vo. 3s. 6d.

GODFRAY.—Works by HUGH GODFRAY, M.A., Mathematical Lecturer at Pembroke College, Cambridge.
A TREATISE ON ASTRONOMY. 4th Ed. 8vo. 12s. 6d.
AN ELEMENTARY TREATISE ON THE LUNAR THEORY. Cr. 8vo. 5s. 6d.

LOCKYER.—Works by J. NORMAN LOCKYER, F.R.S.
*A PRIMER OF ASTRONOMY. Illustrated. 18mo. 1s.
*ELEMENTARY LESSONS IN ASTRONOMY. With Spectra of the Sun, Stars, and Nebulæ, and Illus. 36th Thousand. Revised throughout. Fcap. 8vo. 5s. 6d.
*QUESTIONS ON THE ABOVE. By J. FORBES ROBERTSON. 18mo. 1s. 6d.
THE CHEMISTRY OF THE SUN. Illustrated. 8vo. 14s.
THE METEORITIC HYPOTHESIS OF THE ORIGIN OF COSMICAL SYSTEMS. Illustrated. 8vo. 17s. net.
STAR-GAZING PAST AND PRESENT. Expanded from Notes with the assistance of G. M. SEABROKE, F.R.A.S. Roy. 8vo. 21s.

NEWCOMB.—POPULAR ASTRONOMY. By S. NEWCOMB, LL.D., Professor U.S. Naval Observatory. Illustrated. 2d Ed., revised. 8vo. 18s.

HISTORICAL.

BALL.—A SHORT ACCOUNT OF THE HISTORY OF MATHEMATICS. By W. W. ROUSE BALL, M.A. Cr. 8vo. 10s. 6d.
MATHEMATICAL RECREATIONS, AND PROBLEMS OF PAST AND PRESENT TIMES. By the same. Cr. 8vo. 7s. net.

NATURAL SCIENCES.

Chemistry ; Physical Geography, Geology, and Mineralogy ; Biology ; Medicine.

CHEMISTRY.

ARMSTRONG.—A MANUAL OF INORGANIC CHEMISTRY. By H. E. ARMSTRONG, F.R.S., Professor of Chemistry, City and Guilds Central Institute. [*In preparation.*

*COHEN.—THE OWENS COLLEGE COURSE OF PRACTICAL ORGANIC CHEMISTRY. By JULIUS B. COHEN, Ph.D., Assistant Lecturer on Chemistry, Owens College, Manchester. Fcap. 8vo. 2s. 6d.

COOKE.—ELEMENTS OF CHEMICAL PHYSICS. By JOSIAH P. COOKE, Professor of Chemistry and Mineralogy in Harvard University. 8vo. 21s.

FLEISCHER.—A SYSTEM OF VOLUMETRIC ANALYSIS. By EMIL FLEISCHER. Translated, with Additions, by M. M. P. MUIR, F.R.S.E. Cr. 8vo. 7s. 6d.

FRANKLAND.—AGRICULTURAL CHEMICAL ANALYSIS. (*See* Agriculture.)

HARTLEY.—A COURSE OF QUANTITATIVE ANALYSIS FOR STUDENTS. By W. N. HARTLEY, F.R.S., Professor of Chemistry, Royal College of Science, Dublin. Gl. 8vo. 5s.

HEMPEL.—METHODS OF GAS ANALYSIS. By Dr. WALTHER HEMPEL. Translated by Dr. L. M. DENNIS. Cr. 8vo. 7s. 6d.

CHEMISTRY

HIORNS.—Works by A. H. HIORNS, Principal of the School of Metallurgy, Birmingham and Midland Institute. Gl. 8vo.
  A TEXT-BOOK OF ELEMENTARY METALLURGY. 4s.
  PRACTICAL METALLURGY AND ASSAYING. 6s.
  IRON AND STEEL MANUFACTURE. For Beginners. 3s. 6d.
  MIXED METALS OR METALLIC ALLOYS. 6s.

JONES.—*THE OWENS COLLEGE JUNIOR COURSE OF PRACTICAL CHEMISTRY. By FRANCIS JONES, F.R.S.E., **Chemical Master at the** Grammar School, Manchester. Illustrated. Fcp. 8vo. 2s. 6d.
  *QUESTIONS ON CHEMISTRY. Inorganic and Organic. By the same. Fcap. 8vo. 3s.

LANDAUER.—BLOWPIPE ANALYSIS. By J. LANDAUER. **Translated** by J. TAYLOR and W. E. KAY, of Owens College, Manchester.

LOCKYER.—THE CHEMISTRY OF THE SUN. By J. NORMAN LOCKYER, F.R.S. Illustrated. 8vo. 14s.

LUPTON.—CHEMICAL ARITHMETIC. With 1200 Problems. By S. LUPTON, M.A. 2d Ed., revised. Fcap. 8vo. 4s. 6d.

MELDOLA.—THE CHEMISTRY OF PHOTOGRAPHY. By RAPHAEL MELDOLA, F.R.S., Professor of Chemistry, Technical College, Finsbury. Cr. 8vo. 6s.

MEYER.—HISTORY OF CHEMISTRY FROM THE EARLIEST TIMES TO THE PRESENT DAY. By ERNST VON MEYER, Ph.D. Translated by GEORGE McGOWAN, Ph.D. 8vo. 14s. net.

MIXTER.—AN ELEMENTARY TEXT-BOOK OF CHEMISTRY By W.G. MIXTER, **Professor of** Chemistry, Yale College. 2d Ed. Cr. 8vo. 7s. 6d.

MUIR.—PRACTICAL CHEMISTRY FOR MEDICAL STUDENTS: First M.B. Course. By M. M. P. MUIR, F.R.S.E., Fellow and Prælector in Chemistry at Gonville and Caius College, Cambridge. Fcap. 8vo. 1s. 6d.

MUIR — WILSON.—THE ELEMENTS OF THERMAL CHEMISTRY. **By** M. M. P. MUIR, F.R.S.E.; assisted by D. M. WILSON. 8vo. 12s. 6d.

OSTWALD.—OUTLINES OF GENERAL CHEMISTRY: Physical and Theoretical. By Prof. W. OSTWALD. Trans. by JAS. WALKER, D.Sc. 8vo. 10s. net.

RAMSAY.—EXPERIMENTAL PROOFS OF CHEMICAL THEORY FOR BEGINNERS. By WILLIAM RAMSAY, F.R.S., Professor of Chemistry, University College, London. 18mo. 2s. 6d.

REMSEN.—Works by IRA REMSEN, Prof. of Chemistry, Johns Hopkins University.
  *THE ELEMENTS OF CHEMISTRY. For Beginners. Fcap. 8vo. 2s. 6d.
  AN INTRODUCTION TO THE STUDY OF CHEMISTRY (INORGANIC CHEMISTRY). **Cr. 8vo. 6s.** 6d.
  COMPOUNDS OF CARBON: an Introduction to the Study of Organic Chemistry. Cr. 8vo. 6s. 6d.
  A TEXT-BOOK OF INORGANIC CHEMISTRY. 8vo. 16s.

ROSCOE.—Works by Sir HENRY E. ROSCOE, F.R.S., formerly Professor of Chemistry, Owens College, Manchester.
  *A PRIMER OF CHEMISTRY. **Illustrated.** With Questions. 18mo. 1s.
  *LESSONS IN ELEMENTARY CHEMISTRY, INORGANIC **AND ORGANIC.** With Illustrations and Chromolitho of the Solar Spectrum, **and of the Alkalies** and Alkaline Earths. New Ed., 1892. Fcap. 8vo. 4s. 6d.

ROSCOE—SCHORLEMMER.—A TREATISE ON INORGANIC AND ORGANIC CHEMISTRY. By Sir HENRY ROSCOE, F.R.S., and Prof. C. SCHORLEMMER, F.R.S. 8vo.
  Vols. I. and II. INORGANIC CHEMISTRY. Vol. I.—The Non-Metallic Elements. 2d Ed. 21s. Vol. II. Two Parts, 18s. each.
  Vol. III.—ORGANIC CHEMISTRY. THE CHEMISTRY OF THE HYDROCARBONS and their Derivatives. Parts I., II., IV., and VI. 21s. each. Parts III. and V. 18s. each.

ROSCOE — SCHUSTER.—SPECTRUM ANALYSIS. By Sir HENRY ROSCOE, F.R.S. 4th Ed., revised by the Author and A. SCHUSTER, F.R.S., Professor of Applied Mathematics in the Owens College, Manchester. 8vo. 21s.

*THORPE.—A SERIES OF CHEMICAL PROBLEMS. With Key. By T. E. THORPE, F.R.S., Professor of Chemistry, Royal College of Science. New Ed. Fcap. 8vo. 2s.
THORPE—RÜCKER.—A TREATISE ON CHEMICAL PHYSICS. By Prof. T. E. THORPE and Prof. A. W. RÜCKER. 8vo. [In preparation.
WURTZ.—A HISTORY OF CHEMICAL THEORY. By AD. WURTZ. Translated by HENRY WATTS, F.R.S. Crown 8vo. 6s.

PHYSICAL GEOGRAPHY, GEOLOGY, AND MINERALOGY.

BLANFORD.—THE RUDIMENTS OF PHYSICAL GEOGRAPHY FOR INDIAN SCHOOLS; with Glossary. By H. F. BLANFORD, F.G.S. Cr. 8vo. 2s. 6d.
FERREL.—A POPULAR TREATISE ON THE WINDS. Comprising the General Motions of the Atmosphere, Monsoons, Cyclones, etc. By W. FERREL, M.A., Member of the American National Academy of Sciences. 8vo. 18s.
FISHER.—PHYSICS OF THE EARTH'S CRUST. By Rev. OSMOND FISHER, M.A., F.G.S., Hon. Fellow of King's College, London. 2d Ed., enlarged. 8vo. 12s.
GEIKIE.—Works by Sir ARCHIBALD GEIKIE, F.R.S., Director-General of the Geological Survey of the United Kingdom.
*A PRIMER OF PHYSICAL GEOGRAPHY. Illus. With Questions. 18mo. 1s.
*ELEMENTARY LESSONS IN PHYSICAL GEOGRAPHY. Illustrated. Fcap. 8vo. 4s. 6d. *QUESTIONS ON THE SAME. 1s. 6d.
*A PRIMER OF GEOLOGY. Illustrated. 18mo. 1s.
*CLASS-BOOK OF GEOLOGY. Illustrated. Cheaper Ed. Cr. 8vo. 4s. 6d.
TEXT-BOOK OF GEOLOGY. Illustrated. 3d Ed. 8vo. 28s.
OUTLINES OF FIELD GEOLOGY. Illustrated. New Ed. Gl. 8vo. 3s. 6d.
THE SCENERY AND GEOLOGY OF SCOTLAND, VIEWED IN CONNEXION WITH ITS PHYSICAL GEOLOGY. Illustrated. Cr. 8vo. 12s. 6d.
HUXLEY.—PHYSIOGRAPHY. An Introduction to the Study of Nature. By T. H. HUXLEY, F.R.S. Illustrated. Cr. 8vo. 6s.
LOCKYER.—OUTLINES OF PHYSIOGRAPHY—THE MOVEMENTS OF THE EARTH. By J. NORMAN LOCKYER, F.R.S., Examiner in Physiography for the Science and Art Department. Illustrated. Cr. 8vo. Sewed, 1s. 6d.
MIERS.—A TREATISE ON MINERALOGY. By H. A. MIERS, of the British Museum. 8vo. [In preparation.
PHILLIPS.—A TREATISE ON ORE DEPOSITS. By J.A. PHILLIPS, F.R.S. 8vo. 25s.
ROSENBUSCH—IDDINGS.—MICROSCOPICAL PHYSIOGRAPHY OF THE ROCK-MAKING MINERALS: AN AID TO THE MICROSCOPICAL STUDY OF ROCKS. By H. ROSENBUSCH. Translated by J. P. IDDINGS. 8vo. 24s.
WILLIAMS.—ELEMENTS OF CRYSTALLOGRAPHY, for students of Chemistry, Physics, and Mineralogy. By G. H. WILLIAMS, Ph.D. Cr. 8vo. 6s.

BIOLOGY.

ALLEN.—ON THE COLOURS OF FLOWERS, as Illustrated in the British Flora. By GRANT ALLEN. Illustrated. Cr. 8vo. 3s. 6d.
BALFOUR.—A TREATISE ON COMPARATIVE EMBRYOLOGY. By F. M. BALFOUR, F.R.S., late Fellow and Lecturer of Trinity College, Cambridge. Illustrated. 2 vols. 8vo. Vol. I. 18s. Vol. II. 21s.
BALFOUR—WARD.—A GENERAL TEXT-BOOK OF BOTANY. By I. B. BALFOUR, F.R.S., Prof. of Botany, University of Edinburgh, and H. MARSHALL WARD, F.R.S., Prof. of Botany, Roy. Indian Engineering Coll., Cooper's Hill. 8vo. [In preparation.
*BETTANY.—FIRST LESSONS IN PRACTICAL BOTANY. By G. T. BETTANY. 18mo. 1s.

BIOLOGY 33

*BOWER.—A COURSE OF PRACTICAL INSTRUCTION IN BOTANY. By F. O. BOWER, D.Sc., F.R.S., Regius Professor of Botany in the University of Glasgow. Cr. 8vo. 10s. 6d. [Abridged Ed. *in preparation.*

BUCKTON.—MONOGRAPH OF THE BRITISH CICADÆ, OR TETTIGIDÆ. By G. B. BUCKTON. 2 Vols. 8vo. 33s. 6d. each, net.

CHURCH—VINES.—MANUAL OF VEGETABLE PHYSIOLOGY. By Professor A. H. CHURCH, and Professor S. H. VINES, F.R.S. Illustrated. Cr. 8vo. [*In preparation.*

COUES.—HANDBOOK OF FIELD AND **GENERAL** ORNITHOLOGY. By Prof. ELLIOTT COUES, M.A. Illustrated. **8vo. 10s.** net.

EIMER.—ORGANIC **EVOLUTION** as the Result of the Inheritance of Acquired Characters **according to** the Laws of Organic Growth. By Dr. G. H. T. EIMER. Transl. by **J. T.** CUNNINGHAM, F.R.S.E. 8vo. 12s. 6d.

FEARNLEY.—A **MANUAL OF** ELEMENTARY PRACTICAL **HISTOLOGY.** By WILLIAM FEARNLEY. Illustrated. Cr. 8vo. 7s. 6d.

FLOWER — **GADOW.**—**AN** INTRODUCTION TO THE OSTEOLOGY OF THE **MAMMALIA.** By **W. H.** FLOWER, F.R.S., Director of the Natural History **Museum.** Illus. 3d Ed., revised with the assistance of HANS GADOW, Ph.D., Lecturer on the Advanced Morphology of Vertebrates in the University of Cambridge. Cr. 8vo. 10s. 6d.

FOSTER.—Works by MICHAEL FOSTER, M.D., F.R.S., Professor of Physiology in the University of Cambridge.
*A PRIMER OF PHYSIOLOGY. Illustrated. 18mo. 1s.
A TEXT-BOOK OF PHYSIOLOGY. Illustrated. 5th Ed., largely revised. **8vo.** Part I. Blood—The Tissues of Movement, The Vascular Mechanism. 10s. 6d. Part II. The Tissues of Chemical Action, with their Respective Mechanisms—Nutrition. 10s. 6d. Part III. The Central Nervous System. 7s. 6d. Part IV. The Senses and Some Special Muscular Mechanisms, The Tissues **and** Mechanisms of Reproduction. 10s. 6d.

FOSTER — **BALFOUR.** — THE ELEMENTS OF EMBRYOLOGY. By **Prof.** MICHAEL FOSTER, M.D., **F.R.S., and the** late F. M. BALFOUR, F.R.S., 2d Ed., revised, by A. SEDGWICK, **M.A., Fellow and** Assistant Lecturer of Trinity **College,** Cambridge, and W. **HEAPE, M.A.** Illustrated. **Cr. 8vo.** 10s. 6d.

FOSTER—LANGLEY.—A COURSE OF ELEMENTARY PRACTICAL PHYSIOLOGY AND HISTOLOGY. By Prof. MICHAEL FOSTER, and J. N LANGLEY, F.R.S., Fellow of Trinity College, Cambridge. 6th Ed. Cr. 8vo. 7s. 6d.

GAMGEE.—A TEXT-BOOK OF THE PHYSIOLOGICAL CHEMISTRY OF THE ANIMAL BODY. By A. GAMGEE, M.D., F.R.S. **8vo.** Vol. I. 18s.

GOODALE.—PHYSIOLOGICAL **BOTANY. I. Outlines of** the Histology of Phænogamous Plants. II. **Vegetable Physiology.** By GEORGE LINCOLN GOODALE, M.A., M.D., **Professor of Botany in Harvard** University. 8vo. 10s. 6d.

GRAY.—STRUCTURAL BOTANY, **OR ORGANOGRAPHY ON** THE BASIS OF MORPHOLOGY. By Prof. ASA GRAY, LL.D. 8vo. 10s. 6d.

HAMILTON.—A TEXT-BOOK OF PATHOLOGY. (*See* Medicine, p. 35.)

HARTIG.—TEXT-BOOK OF THE DISEASES OF TREES. (*See* Agriculture, p. 89.)

HOOKER.—Works by Sir JOSEPH HOOKER, F.R.S., &c.
*PRIMER OF BOTANY. Illustrated. 18mo. 1s.
THE **STUDENT'S FLORA OF THE BRITISH ISLANDS.** 3d Ed., revised. Gl. 8vo. 10s. 6d.

HOWES.—AN ATLAS **OF** PRACTICAL ELEMENTARY BIOLOGY. By G. B. HOWES, Assistant Professor of Zoology, Royal College of Science. 4to. 14s.

HUXLEY.—Works by Prof. T. H. HUXLEY, F.R.S.
*INTRODUCTORY PRIMER OF SCIENCE. 18mo. 1s.
*LESSONS IN ELEMENTARY PHYSIOLOGY. Illust. Fcap. 8vo. 4s. 6d.
*QUESTIONS ON THE ABOVE. By T. ALCOCK, M.D. 18mo. 1s. 6d.

C

HUXLEY — MARTIN.—A COURSE OF PRACTICAL INSTRUCTION IN ELEMENTARY BIOLOGY. By Prof. T. H. HUXLEY, F.R.S., assisted by H. N. MARTIN, F.R.S., Professor of Biology in the Johns Hopkins University. New Ed., revised by G. B. HOWES and D. H. SCOTT, D.Sc., Assistant Professors, Royal College of Science. Cr. 8vo. 10s. 6d.

KLEIN.—MICRO-ORGANISMS AND DISEASE. (*See* Medicine, p. 35.)
THE BACTERIA IN ASIATIC CHOLERA. (*See* Medicine, p. 35.)

LANG.—TEXT-BOOK OF COMPARATIVE ANATOMY. By Dr. ARNOLD LANG, Professor of Zoology in the University of Zurich. Transl. by H. M. and M. BERNARD. Introduction by Prof. HAECKEL. 2 vols. Illustrated. 8vo. Part I. 17s. net. [*Part II. in the Press.*

LANKESTER.—A TEXT-BOOK OF ZOOLOGY. By E. RAY LANKESTER, F.R.S., Linacre Professor of Human and Comparative Anatomy, University of Oxford. 8vo. [*In preparation.*

LUBBOCK.—Works by the Right Hon. Sir JOHN LUBBOCK, F.R.S., D.C.L.
THE ORIGIN AND METAMORPHOSES OF INSECTS. Illus. Cr. 8vo. 3s. 6d.
ON BRITISH WILD FLOWERS CONSIDERED IN RELATION TO INSECTS. Illustrated. Cr. 8vo. 4s. 6d.
FLOWERS, FRUITS, AND LEAVES. Illustrated. 2d Ed. Cr. 8vo. 4s. 6d.

MARTIN and MOALE.—ON THE DISSECTION OF VERTEBRATE ANIMALS. By Prof. H. N. MARTIN and W. A. MOALE. Cr. 8vo. [*In preparation.*

MIVART.—LESSONS IN ELEMENTARY ANATOMY. By ST. G. MIVART, F.R.S., Lecturer on Comparative Anatomy at St. Mary's Hospital. Fcap. 8vo. 6s. 6d.

MÜLLER.—THE FERTILISATION OF FLOWERS. By HERMANN MÜLLER. Translated by D'ARCY W. THOMPSON, B.A., Professor of Biology in University College, Dundee. Preface by C. DARWIN, F.R.S. Illustrated. 8vo. 21s.

*OLIVER.—LESSONS IN ELEMENTARY BOTANY. By DANIEL OLIVER, F.R.S., late Professor of Botany in University College, London. Fcap. 8vo. 4s. 6d.
FIRST BOOK OF INDIAN BOTANY. By the same. Ex. fcap. 8vo. 6s. 6d.

PARKER.—Works by T. JEFFERY PARKER, F.R.S., Professor of Biology in the University of Otago, New Zealand.
A COURSE OF INSTRUCTION IN ZOOTOMY (VERTEBRATA). Illustrated. Cr. 8vo. 8s. 6d.
LESSONS IN ELEMENTARY BIOLOGY. Illustrated. Cr. 8vo. 10s. 6d.

PARKER and BETTANY.—THE MORPHOLOGY OF THE SKULL. By Prof. W. K. PARKER, F.R.S., and G. T. BETTANY. Illustrated. Cr. 8vo. 10s. 6d.

SEDGWICK.—TREATISE ON EMBRYOLOGY. By ADAM SEDGWICK, F.R.S., Fellow and Lecturer of Trinity College, Cambridge. 8vo. [*In preparation.*

SHUFELDT.—THE MYOLOGY OF THE RAVEN (*Corvus corax sinuatus*). A Guide to the Study of the Muscular System in Birds. By R. W. SHUFELDT. Illustrated. 8vo. 13s. net.

SMITH.—DISEASES OF FIELD AND GARDEN CROPS. (*See* Agriculture, p. 39.)

WALLACE.—Works by ALFRED RUSSEL WALLACE, LL.D.
DARWINISM: An Exposition of the Theory of Natural Selection. Cr. 8vo. 9s.
NATURAL SELECTION: AND TROPICAL NATURE. New Ed. Cr. 8vo. 6s.
ISLAND LIFE. New Ed. Cr. 8vo. 6s.

WARD.—TIMBER AND SOME OF ITS DISEASES. (*See* Agriculture, p. 39.)

WIEDERSHEIM.—ELEMENTS OF THE COMPARATIVE ANATOMY OF VERTEBRATES. By Prof. R. WIEDERSHEIM. Adapted by W. NEWTON PARKER, Professor of Biology, University College, Cardiff. 8vo. 12s. 6d.

MEDICINE.

BLYTH.—A MANUAL OF PUBLIC HEALTH. By A. WYNTER BLYTH, M.R.C.S. 8vo. 17s. net.

BRUNTON.—Works by T. LAUDER BRUNTON, M.D., F.R.S., Examiner in Materia Medica in the University of London, in the Victoria University, and in the Royal College of Physicians, London.

MEDICINE

A TEXT-BOOK OF PHARMACOLOGY, THERAPEUTICS, AND MATERIA MEDICA. Adapted to the United States Pharmacopœia by F. H. WILLIAMS M.D., Boston, Mass. 3d Ed. Adapted to the New British Pharmacopœia, 1885, and additions, 1891. 8vo. 21s. Or in 2 Vols. 22s. 6d. Supplement. 1s.
TABLES OF MATERIA MEDICA: A Companion to the Materia Medica Museum. Illustrated. Cheaper Issue. 8vo. 5s.
GRIFFITHS.—LESSONS ON PRESCRIPTIONS AND THE ART OF PRESCRIBING. By W. H. GRIFFITHS. Adapted to the Pharmacopœia, 1885. 18mo. 3s. 6d.
HAMILTON.—A TEXT-BOOK OF PATHOLOGY, SYSTEMATIC AND PRACTICAL. By D. J. HAMILTON, F.R.S.E., Professor of Pathological Anatomy, University of Aberdeen. Illustrated. Vol. I. 8vo. 25s.
KLEIN.—Works by E. KLEIN, F.R.S., Lecturer on General Anatomy and Physiology in the Medical School of St. Bartholomew's Hospital, London.
MICRO-ORGANISMS AND DISEASE. An Introduction into the Study of Specific Micro-Organisms. Illustrated. 3d Ed., revised. Cr. 8vo. 6s.
THE BACTERIA IN ASIATIC CHOLERA. Cr. 8vo. 5s.
WHITE.—A TEXT-BOOK OF GENERAL THERAPEUTICS. By W. HALE WHITE, M.D., Senior Assistant Physician to and Lecturer in Materia Medica at Guy's Hospital. Illustrated. Cr. 8vo. 8s. 6d.
ZIEGLER—MACALISTER.—TEXT-BOOK OF PATHOLOGICAL ANATOMY AND PATHOGENESIS. By Prof. E. ZIEGLER. Translated and Edited by DONALD MACALISTER, M.A., M.D., Fellow and Medical Lecturer of St John's College, Cambridge. Illustrated. 8vo.
Part I.—GENERAL PATHOLOGICAL ANATOMY. 2d Ed. 12s. 6d.
Part II.—SPECIAL PATHOLOGICAL ANATOMY. Sections I.-VIII. 2d Ed. 12s. 6d. Sections IX.-XII. 12s. 6d.

HUMAN SCIENCES.

Mental and Moral Philosophy; Political Economy; Law and Politics; Anthropology; Education.

MENTAL AND MORAL PHILOSOPHY.

BALDWIN.—HANDBOOK OF PSYCHOLOGY: SENSES AND INTELLECT. By Prof. J. M. BALDWIN, M.A., LL.D. 2d Ed., revised. 8vo. 12s. 6d.
FEELING AND WILL. By the same. 8vo. 12s. 6d.
BOOLE.—THE MATHEMATICAL ANALYSIS OF LOGIC. Being an Essay towards a Calculus of Deductive Reasoning. By GEORGE BOOLE. 8vo. 5s.
CALDERWOOD.—HANDBOOK OF MORAL PHILOSOPHY. By Rev. HENRY CALDERWOOD, LL.D., Professor of Moral Philosophy in the University of Edinburgh. 14th Ed., largely rewritten. Cr. 8vo. 6s.
CLIFFORD.—SEEING AND THINKING. By the late Prof. W. K. CLIFFORD, F.R.S. With Diagrams. Cr. 8vo. 3s. 6d.
HÖFFDING.—OUTLINES OF PSYCHOLOGY. By Prof. H. HÖFFDING. Translated by M. E. LOWNDES. Cr. 8vo. 6s.
JAMES.—THE PRINCIPLES OF PSYCHOLOGY. By WM. JAMES, Professor of Psychology in Harvard University. 2 vols. 8vo. 25s. net.
A TEXT-BOOK OF PSYCHOLOGY. By the same. Cr. 8vo. 7s. net.
JARDINE.—THE ELEMENTS OF THE PSYCHOLOGY OF COGNITION. By Rev. ROBERT JARDINE, D.Sc. 3d Ed., revised. Cr. 8vo. 6s. 6d.
JEVONS.—Works by W. STANLEY JEVONS, F.R.S.
*A PRIMER OF LOGIC. 18mo. 1s.
*ELEMENTARY LESSONS IN LOGIC, Deductive and Inductive, with Copious Questions and Examples, and a Vocabulary. Fcap. 8vo. 3s. 6d.
THE PRINCIPLES OF SCIENCE. Cr. 8vo. 12s. 6d.

STUDIES IN DEDUCTIVE LOGIC. 2d Ed. Cr. 8vo. 6s.
PURE LOGIC: AND OTHER MINOR WORKS. Edited by R. ADAMSON, M.A., LL.D., Professor of Logic at Owens College, Manchester, and HARRIET A. JEVONS. With a Preface by Prof. ADAMSON. 8vo. 10s. 6d.

KANT—MAX MÜLLER.—CRITIQUE OF PURE REASON. By IMMANUEL KANT. 2 vols. 8vo. 16s. each. Vol. I. HISTORICAL INTRODUCTION, by LUDWIG NOIRÉ; Vol. II. CRITIQUE OF PURE REASON, translated by F. MAX MÜLLER.

KANT—MAHAFFY and BERNARD.—KANT'S CRITICAL PHILOSOPHY FOR ENGLISH READERS. By J. P. MAHAFFY, D.D., Professor of Ancient History in the University of Dublin, and JOHN H. BERNARD, B.D., Fellow of Trinity College, Dublin. A new and complete Edition in 2 vols. Cr. 8vo.
Vol. I. THE KRITIK OF PURE REASON EXPLAINED AND DEFENDED. 7s. 6d.
Vol. II. THE PROLEGOMENA. Translated with Notes and Appendices. 6s.

KEYNES.—FORMAL LOGIC, Studies and Exercises in. By J. N. KEYNES, D.Sc. 2d Ed., revised and enlarged. Cr. 8vo. 10s. 6d.

McCOSH.—Works by JAMES McCOSH, D.D., President of Princeton College.
PSYCHOLOGY. Cr. 8vo. I. THE COGNITIVE POWERS. 6s. 6d. II. THE MOTIVE POWERS. 6s. 6d.
FIRST AND FUNDAMENTAL TRUTHS: a Treatise on Metaphysics. 8vo. 9s.
THE PREVAILING TYPES OF PHILOSOPHY. CAN THEY LOGICALLY REACH REALITY? 8vo. 3s. 6d.

MAURICE.—MORAL AND METAPHYSICAL PHILOSOPHY. By F. D. MAURICE, M.A., late Professor of Moral Philosophy in the University of Cambridge. 4th Ed. 2 vols. 8vo. 16s.

*RAY.—A TEXT-BOOK OF DEDUCTIVE LOGIC FOR THE USE OF STUDENTS. By P. K. RAY, D.Sc., Professor of Logic and Philosophy, Presidency College, Calcutta. 4th Ed. Globe 8vo. 4s. 6d.

SIDGWICK.—Works by HENRY SIDGWICK, LL.D., D.C.L., Knightbridge Professor of Moral Philosophy in the University of Cambridge.
THE METHODS OF ETHICS. 4th Ed. 8vo. 14s.
OUTLINES OF THE HISTORY OF ETHICS. 2d Ed. Cr. 8vo. 3s. 6d.

VENN.—Works by JOHN VENN, F.R.S., Examiner in Moral Philosophy in the University of London.
THE LOGIC OF CHANCE. An Essay on the Foundations and Province of the Theory of Probability. 3d Ed., rewritten and enlarged. Cr. 8vo. 10s. 6d.
SYMBOLIC LOGIC. Cr. 8vo. 10s. 6d.
THE PRINCIPLES OF EMPIRICAL OR INDUCTIVE LOGIC. 8vo. 18s.

POLITICAL ECONOMY.

BASTABLE.—PUBLIC FINANCE. By C. F. BASTABLE, Professor of Political Economy in the University of Dublin. [In the Press.

BÖHM-BAWERK.—CAPITAL AND INTEREST. Translated by WILLIAM SMART, M.A. 8vo. 12s. net.
THE POSITIVE THEORY OF CAPITAL. By the same. 8vo. 12s. net.

CAIRNES.—THE CHARACTER AND LOGICAL METHOD OF POLITICAL ECONOMY. By J. E. CAIRNES. Cr. 8vo. 6s.
SOME LEADING PRINCIPLES OF POLITICAL ECONOMY NEWLY EXPOUNDED. By the same. 8vo. 14s.

COSSA.—GUIDE TO THE STUDY OF POLITICAL ECONOMY. By Dr. L. COSSA. Translated. [New Edition in the Press.

*FAWCETT.—POLITICAL ECONOMY FOR BEGINNERS, WITH QUESTIONS. By Mrs. HENRY FAWCETT. 7th Ed. 18mo. 2s. 6d.

FAWCETT.—A MANUAL OF POLITICAL ECONOMY. By the Right Hon. HENRY FAWCETT, F.R.S. 7th Ed., revised. Cr. 8vo. 12s. 6d.
AN EXPLANATORY DIGEST of above. By C. A. WATERS, B.A. Cr. 8vo. 2s. 6d.

POLITICAL ECONOMY—LAW AND POLITICS

GILMAN.—PROFIT-SHARING BETWEEN EMPLOYER AND EMPLOYEE. By N. P. Gilman. Cr. 8vo. 7s. 6d.

GUNTON.—WEALTH AND PROGRESS: An examination of the Wages Question and its Economic Relation to Social Reform. By George Gunton. Cr. 8vo. 6s.

HOWELL.—THE CONFLICTS OF CAPITAL AND LABOUR HISTORICALLY AND ECONOMICALLY CONSIDERED. Being a History and Review of the Trade Unions of Great Britain. By George Howell, M.P. 2d Ed., revised. Cr. 8vo. 7s. 6d.

JEVONS.—Works by W. Stanley Jevons, F.R.S.
*PRIMER OF POLITICAL ECONOMY. 18mo. 1s.
THE THEORY OF POLITICAL ECONOMY. 3d Ed., revised. 8vo. 10s. 6d.

KEYNES.—THE SCOPE AND METHOD OF POLITICAL ECONOMY. By J. N. Keynes, D.Sc. 7s. net.

MARSHALL.—PRINCIPLES OF ECONOMICS. By Alfred Marshall, M.A., Professor of Political Economy in the University of Cambridge. 2 vols. 8vo. Vol. I. 2d Ed. 12s. 6d. net.
ELEMENTS OF ECONOMICS OF INDUSTRY. By the same. New Ed., 1892. Cr. 8vo. 3s. 6d.

PALGRAVE.—A DICTIONARY OF POLITICAL ECONOMY. By various Writers. Edited by R. H. Inglis Palgrave, F.R.S. 3s. 6d. each, net. No. I. *July* 1891.

PANTALEONI.—MANUAL OF POLITICAL ECONOMY. By Prof. M. Pantaleoni. Translated by T. Boston Bruce. [*In preparation.*

SIDGWICK.—THE PRINCIPLES OF POLITICAL ECONOMY. By Henry Sidgwick, LL.D., D.C.L., Knightbridge Professor of Moral Philosophy in the University of Cambridge. 2d Ed., revised. 8vo. 16s.

SMART.—AN INTRODUCTION TO THE THEORY OF VALUE. By William Smart, M.A. Crown 8vo. 3s. net.

WALKER.—Works by Francis A. Walker, M.A.
FIRST LESSONS IN POLITICAL ECONOMY. Cr. 8vo. 5s.
A BRIEF TEXT-BOOK OF POLITICAL ECONOMY. Cr. 8vo. 6s. 6d.
POLITICAL ECONOMY. 2d Ed., revised and enlarged. 8vo. 12s. 6d.
THE WAGES QUESTION. Ex. Cr. 8vo. 8s. 6d. net.
MONEY. Ex. Cr. 8vo. 8s. 6d. net.

WICKSTEED.—ALPHABET OF ECONOMIC SCIENCE. By P. H. Wicksteed, M.A. Part I. Elements of the Theory of Value or Worth. Gl. 8vo. 2s. 6d.

LAW AND POLITICS.

BALL.—THE STUDENT'S GUIDE TO THE BAR. By W. W. Rouse Ball, M.A., Fellow of Trinity College, Cambridge. 4th Ed., revised. Cr. 8vo. 2s. 6d.

BOUTMY.—STUDIES IN CONSTITUTIONAL LAW. By Emile Boutmy. Translated by Mrs. Dicey, with Preface by Prof. A. V. Dicey. Cr. 8vo. 6s.
THE ENGLISH CONSTITUTION. By the same. Translated by Mrs. Eaden, with Introduction by Sir F. Pollock, Bart. Cr. 8vo. 6s.

*BUCKLAND.—OUR NATIONAL INSTITUTIONS. By A. Buckland. 18mo. 1s.

CHERRY.—LECTURES ON THE GROWTH OF CRIMINAL LAW IN ANCIENT COMMUNITIES. By R. R. Cherry, LL.D., Reid Professor of Constitutional and Criminal Law in the University of Dublin. 8vo. 5s. net.

DICEY.—INTRODUCTION TO THE STUDY OF THE LAW OF THE CONSTITUTION. By A. V. Dicey, B.C.L., Vinerian Professor of English Law in the University of Oxford. 3d Ed. 8vo. 12s. 6d.

HOLMES.—THE COMMON LAW. By O. W. Holmes, Jun. Demy 8vo. 12s.

JENKS.—THE GOVERNMENT OF VICTORIA. By Edward Jenks, B.A., LL.B., late Professor of Law in the University of Melbourne. 14s.

MUNRO.—COMMERCIAL LAW. (*See* Commerce, p. 40).

PHILLIMORE.—PRIVATE LAW AMONG THE ROMANS. From the Pandects. By J. G. Phillimore, Q.C. 8vo. 16s.

POLLOCK.—ESSAYS IN JURISPRUDENCE AND ETHICS. By Sir FREDERICK POLLOCK, Bart. 8vo. 10s. 6d.
INTRODUCTION TO THE HISTORY OF THE SCIENCE OF POLITICS. By the same. Cr. 8vo. 2s. 6d.
SIDGWICK.—THE ELEMENTS OF POLITICS. By HENRY SIDGWICK, LL.D. 8vo. 14s. net.
STEPHEN.—Works by Sir JAMES FITZJAMES STEPHEN, Bart.
A DIGEST OF THE LAW OF EVIDENCE. 5th Ed. Cr. 8vo. 6s.
A DIGEST OF THE CRIMINAL LAW: CRIMES AND PUNISHMENTS. 4th Ed., revised. 8vo. 16s.
A DIGEST OF THE LAW OF CRIMINAL PROCEDURE IN INDICTABLE OFFENCES. By Sir J. F. STEPHEN, Bart., and H. STEPHEN. 8vo. 12s. 6d.
A HISTORY OF THE CRIMINAL LAW OF ENGLAND. Three Vols. 8vo. 48s.
A GENERAL VIEW OF THE CRIMINAL LAW OF ENGLAND. 8vo. 14s.

ANTHROPOLOGY.

TYLOR.—ANTHROPOLOGY. By E. B. TYLOR, F.R.S., Reader in Anthropology in the University of Oxford. Illustrated. Cr. 8vo. **7s.** 6d.

EDUCATION.

ARNOLD.—REPORTS ON ELEMENTARY SCHOOLS. 1852-1882. By MATTHEW ARNOLD. Edited by LORD SANDFORD. Cr. 8vo. 3s. 6d.
HIGHER SCHOOLS AND UNIVERSITIES IN GERMANY. By the same. Crown 8vo. 6s.
BALL.—THE STUDENT'S GUIDE TO THE BAR. (*See* Law, p. 37.)
*****BLAKISTON.**—THE TEACHER. Hints on School Management. **By J. R.** BLAKISTON, H.M.I.S. Cr. 8vo. 2s. 6d.
CALDERWOOD.—ON TEACHING. By Prof. HENRY CALDERWOOD. New Ed. Ex. fcap. 8vo. 2s. 6d.
FEARON.—SCHOOL INSPECTION. By D. R. FEARON. 6th Ed. Cr. 8vo. 2s. 6d.
FITCH.—NOTES ON AMERICAN SCHOOLS AND TRAINING COLLEGES. By J. G. FITCH, M.A., LL.D. Gl. 8vo. 2s. 6d.
GEIKIE.—THE TEACHING OF GEOGRAPHY. (*See* Geography, p. 41.)
GLADSTONE.—SPELLING REFORM FROM A NATIONAL POINT OF VIEW. By J. H. GLADSTONE. Cr. 8vo. 1s. 6d.
HERTEL.—OVERPRESSURE IN HIGH SCHOOLS IN DENMARK. By Dr. HERTEL. Introd. by Sir J. CRICHTON-BROWNE, F.R.S. Cr. 8vo. 3s. 6d.
RECORD OF TECHNICAL AND SECONDARY EDUCATION. 8vo. Sewed 2s., net. Part I. Nov. 1891.
TODHUNTER.—THE CONFLICT OF STUDIES. By ISAAC TODHUNTER, F.R.S. 8vo. 10s. 6d.

TECHNICAL KNOWLEDGE.

Civil and Mechanical Engineering; Military and Naval Science; Agriculture; Domestic Economy; Book-Keeping; Commerce.

CIVIL AND MECHANICAL ENGINEERING.

ALEXANDER and THOMSON.—ELEMENTARY APPLIED MECHANICS. (*See* Mechanics, p. 26.)
CHALMERS.—GRAPHICAL DETERMINATION OF FORCES IN ENGINEERING STRUCTURES. By J. B. CHALMERS, C.E. Illustrated. 8vo. 24s.
COTTERILL.—APPLIED MECHANICS. (*See* Mechanics, p. 26.)

MILITARY AND NAVAL SCIENCE—AGRICULTURE

COTTERILL and SLADE.—LESSONS IN APPLIED MECHANICS. (See Mechanics, p. 26.)
GRAHAM.—GEOMETRY OF POSITION. (See Mechanics, 26.)
KENNEDY.—THE MECHANICS OF MACHINERY. (See Mechanics, 27.)
PEABODY.—THERMODYNAMICS OF THE STEAM-ENGINE AND OTHER HEAT-ENGINES. (See Physics, p. 28.)
SHANN.—AN ELEMENTARY TREATISE ON HEAT IN RELATION TO STEAM AND THE STEAM-ENGINE. (See Physics, p. 29.)
WHITHAM.—STEAM-ENGINE DESIGN. By J. M. WHITHAM. 8vo. 25s.
YOUNG.—SIMPLE PRACTICAL METHODS OF CALCULATING STRAINS ON GIRDERS, ARCHES, AND TRUSSES. By E. W. YOUNG, C.E. 8vo. 7s. 6d.

MILITARY AND NAVAL SCIENCE.

ARMY PRELIMINARY EXAMINATION PAPERS, 1882-1891. (See Mathematics.)
KELVIN.—POPULAR LECTURES AND ADDRESSES. By Lord KELVIN. 3 vols. Illustrated. Cr. 8vo. Vol. III. Navigation. 7s. 6d.
MATTHEWS.—MANUAL OF LOGARITHMS. (See Mathematics, p. 24.)
MAURICE.—WAR. By Col. G. F. MAURICE, C.B., R.A. 8vo. 5s. net.
MERCUR.—ELEMENTS OF THE ART OF WAR. Prepared for the use of Cadets of the United States Military Academy. By JAMES MERCUR. 8vo. 17s.
PALMER.—**TEXT-**BOOK OF PRACTICAL LOGARITHMS **AND TRIGONO-**METRY. (See Mathematics, p. 24.)
ROBINSON.—TREATISE ON MARINE SURVEYING. For younger Naval Officers. With Questions and Exercises. By Rev. J. L. ROBINSON. Cr. 8vo. 7s. 6d.
SANDHURST MATHEMATICAL PAPERS. (See Mathematics, p. 25.)
SHORTLAND.—NAUTICAL SURVEYING. By Vice-Adm. SHORTLAND. 8vo. 21s.
WOLSELEY.—Works by General Viscount WOLSELEY, G.C.M.G.
 THE SOLDIER'S POCKET-BOOK FOR FIELD SERVICE. 16mo. Roan. 5s.
 FIELD POCKET-BOOK FOR THE AUXILIARY FORCES. 16mo. 1s. 6d.
WOOLWICH MATHEMATICAL PAPERS. (See Mathematics, p. 25.)

AGRICULTURE AND FORESTRY.

FRANKLAND.—AGRICULTURAL CHEMICAL ANALYSIS. By P. F. FRANKLAND, F.R.S., Prof. of Chemistry, University College, Dundee. Cr. 8vo. 7s. 6d.
HARTIG.—TEXT-BOOK OF THE DISEASES OF TREES. By Dr. ROBERT HARTIG. Translated by WM. SOMERVILLE, B.S., **D.Œ.**, Professor of Agriculture **and** Forestry, Durham College of Science, Newcastle-on-Tyne. Edited, with Introduction, **by** Prof. H. MARSHALL WARD. 8vo. [*In preparation.*
LASLETT.—TIMBER AND TIMBER TREES, NATIVE **AND FOREIGN.** By THOMAS LASLETT. Cr. 8vo. 8s. 6d.
SMITH.—DISEASES OF FIELD AND GARDEN CROPS, chiefly such as are caused by Fungi. By WORTHINGTON G. SMITH, F.L.S. Fcap. 8vo. 4s. 6d.
TANNER.—*ELEMENTARY LESSONS IN THE SCIENCE OF AGRICULTURAL PRACTICE. By HENRY TANNER, F.C.S., M.R.A.C., Examiner in Agriculture under the Science and Art Department. Fcap. 8vo. 3s. 6d.
 *FIRST PRINCIPLES OF AGRICULTURE. By the same. 18mo. 1s.
 *THE PRINCIPLES OF AGRICULTURE. For use in Elementary Schools. By the same. Ex. fcap. 8vo.
  I. The Alphabet of the Principles of Agriculture. 6d.
  II. Further Steps in the Principles of Agriculture. 1s.
  III. Elementary School Readings on the Principles of Agriculture for the Third Stage. 1s.
WARD.—TIMBER AND SOME OF ITS DISEASES. By H. MARSHALL WARD, F.R.S., Prof. of Botany, Roy. Ind. Engin. Coll., Cooper's Hill. Cr. 8vo. 6s.

DOMESTIC ECONOMY.

*BARKER.—FIRST LESSONS IN THE PRINCIPLES OF COOKING. By LADY BARKER. 18mo. 1s.
*BERNERS.—FIRST LESSONS ON HEALTH. By J. BERNERS. 18mo. 1s.
*COOKERY BOOK.—THE MIDDLE CLASS COOKERY BOOK. Edited by the Manchester School of Domestic Cookery. Fcap. 8vo. 1s. 6d.
CRAVEN.—A GUIDE TO DISTRICT NURSES. By Mrs. CRAVEN. Cr. 8vo. 2s. 6d.
FREDERICK.—HINTS TO HOUSEWIVES on several points, particularly on the preparation of economical and tasteful dishes. By Mrs. FREDERICK. Cr. 8vo. 1s.
*GRAND'HOMME.—CUTTING-OUT AND DRESSMAKING. From the French of Mdlle. E. GRAND'HOMME. With Diagrams. 18mo. 1s.
GRENFELL.—DRESSMAKING. A Technical Manual for Teachers. By Mrs. HENRY GRENFELL. With Diagrams. 18mo. 1s.
JEX-BLAKE.—THE CARE OF INFANTS. A Manual for Mothers and Nurses. By SOPHIA JEX-BLAKE, M.D. 18mo. 1s.
*TEGETMEIER.—HOUSEHOLD MANAGEMENT AND COOKERY. Compiled for the London School Board. By W. B. TEGETMEIER. 18mo. 1s.
*WRIGHT.—THE SCHOOL COOKERY-BOOK. Compiled and Edited by C. E. GUTHRIE WRIGHT, Hon. Sec. to the Edinburgh School of Cookery. 18mo. 1s.

BOOK-KEEPING. (See p. 21.)

COMMERCE.

MACMILLAN'S ELEMENTARY COMMERCIAL CLASS BOOKS. Edited by JAMES GOW, Litt.D., Headmaster of the High School, Nottingham. Globe 8vo.
*THE HISTORY OF COMMERCE IN EUROPE. By H. DE B. GIBBINS, M.A. 3s. 6d. [Ready.
INTRODUCTION TO COMMERCIAL GERMAN. By F. C. SMITH, B.A., formerly scholar of Magdalene College, Cambridge. 2s. 6d. [Ready.
COMMERCIAL GEOGRAPHY. By E. C. K. GONNER, M.A., Professor of Political Economy in University College, Liverpool [In preparation.
COMMERCIAL FRENCH.
COMMERCIAL ARITHMETIC. By A. W. SUNDERLAND, M.A., late Scholar of Trinity College, Cambridge; Fellow of the Institute of Actuaries. [In prep.
COMMERCIAL LAW. By J. E. C. MUNRO, LL.D., Professor of Law and Political Economy in the Owens College, Manchester. [In preparation.

GEOGRAPHY.

(See also PHYSICAL GEOGRAPHY.)

BARTHOLOMEW.—*THE ELEMENTARY SCHOOL ATLAS. By JOHN BARTHOLOMEW, F.R.G.S. 4to. 1s.
*MACMILLAN'S SCHOOL ATLAS, PHYSICAL AND POLITICAL. 80 Maps and Index. By the same. Royal 4to. 8s. 6d. Half-morocco, 10s. 6d.
THE LIBRARY REFERENCE ATLAS OF THE WORLD. By the same. 84 Maps and Index to 100,000 places. Half-morocco. Gilt edges. Folio. £2:12:6 net. Also in parts, 5s. each, net. Index, 7s. 6d. net.
*CLARKE.—CLASS-BOOK OF GEOGRAPHY. By C. B. CLARKE, F.R.S. With 18 Maps. Fcap. 8vo. 3s.; sewed, 2s. 6d.
*GREEN.—A SHORT GEOGRAPHY OF THE BRITISH ISLANDS. By JOHN RICHARD GREEN, LL.D., and A. S. GREEN. With Maps. Fcap. 8vo. 3s. 6d.
*GROVE.—A PRIMER OF GEOGRAPHY. By Sir GEORGE GROVE. 18mo. 1s.
KIEPERT.—A MANUAL OF ANCIENT GEOGRAPHY. By Dr. H. KIEPERT. Cr. 8vo. 5s.

MACMILLAN'S GEOGRAPHICAL SERIES.—Edited by Sir ARCHIBALD GEIKIE, F.R.S., Director-General of the Geological Survey of the United Kingdom.
*THE TEACHING OF GEOGRAPHY. A Practical Handbook for the Use of Teachers. By Sir ARCHIBALD GEIKIE, F.R.S. Cr. 8vo. 2s.
*MAPS AND MAP-DRAWING. By W. A. ELDERTON. 18mo. 1s.
*GEOGRAPHY OF THE BRITISH ISLES. By Sir A. GEIKIE, F.R.S. 18mo. 1s.
*AN ELEMENTARY CLASS-BOOK OF GENERAL GEOGRAPHY. By H. R. MILL, D.Sc. Illustrated. Cr. 8vo. 3s. 6d.
*GEOGRAPHY OF EUROPE. By J. SIME, M.A. Illustrated. Gl. 8vo. 3s.
*ELEMENTARY GEOGRAPHY OF INDIA, BURMA, AND CEYLON. By H. F. BLANFORD, F.G.S. Gl. 8vo. 2s. 6d.
GEOGRAPHY OF NORTH AMERICA. By Prof. N. S. SHALER. [In preparation.
GEOGRAPHY OF THE BRITISH COLONIES. By G. M. DAWSON and A. SUTHERLAND.
STRACHEY.—LECTURES ON GEOGRAPHY. By General RICHARD STRACHEY, R.E. Cr. 8vo. 4s. 6d.
*TOZER.—A PRIMER OF CLASSICAL GEOGRAPHY. By H. F. TOZER, M.A. 18mo. 1s.

HISTORY.

ARNOLD.—THE SECOND PUNIC WAR. (See Antiquities, p. 12.)
ARNOLD.—A HISTORY OF THE EARLY ROMAN EMPIRE. (See p. 11.)
*BEESLY.—STORIES FROM THE HISTORY OF ROME. (See p. 12.)
BRYCE.—THE HOLY ROMAN EMPIRE. By JAMES BRYCE, M.P., D.C.L., Regius Professor of Civil Law in the University of Oxford. Cr. 8vo. 7s. 6d. Library Edition. 8vo. 14s.
*BUCKLEY.—A HISTORY OF ENGLAND FOR BEGINNERS. By ARABELLA B. BUCKLEY. With Maps and Tables. Gl. 8vo. 3s.
BURY.—A HISTORY OF THE LATER ROMAN EMPIRE FROM ARCADIUS TO IRENE. (See Antiquities, p. 12.)
CASSEL.—MANUAL OF JEWISH HISTORY AND LITERATURE. **By Dr. D.** CASSEL. Translated by Mrs. HENRY LUCAS. Fcap. 8vo. 2s. 6d.
ENGLISH STATESMEN, TWELVE. Cr. 8vo. 2s. 6d. each.
　WILLIAM THE CONQUEROR. By EDWARD A. FREEMAN, D.C.L., LL.D.
　HENRY II. By Mrs. J. R. GREEN.
　EDWARD I. By F. YORK POWELL. [In preparation.
　HENRY VII. By JAMES GAIRDNER.
　CARDINAL WOLSEY. By Bishop CREIGHTON
　ELIZABETH. By E. S. BEESLY.
　OLIVER CROMWELL. By FREDERIC HARRISON.
　WILLIAM III. By H. D. TRAILL.
　WALPOLE. By JOHN MORLEY.
　CHATHAM. By JOHN MORLEY. [In preparation.
　PITT. By LORD ROSEBERY.
　PEEL. By J. R. THURSFIELD.
FISKE.—Works by JOHN FISKE, formerly Lecturer on Philosophy at Harvard University.
　THE CRITICAL PERIOD IN AMERICAN HISTORY, 1783-1789. Ex. cr. 8vo. 10s. 6d.
　THE BEGINNINGS OF NEW ENGLAND. Cr. 8vo. 7s. 6d.
　THE AMERICAN REVOLUTION. 2 vols. Cr. 8vo. 18s.
FREEMAN.—Works by EDWARD A. FREEMAN, D.C.L., late Regius Professor of Modern History in the University of Oxford.
*OLD ENGLISH HISTORY. With Maps. Ex. fcap. 8vo. 6s.
　METHODS OF HISTORICAL STUDY. 8vo. 10s. 6d.

HISTORY

THE CHIEF PERIODS OF EUROPEAN HISTORY. Six Lectures. With an Essay on Greek Cities under Roman Rule. 8vo. 10s. 6d.

HISTORICAL ESSAYS. 8vo. First Series. 10s. 6d. Second Series. 10s. 6d. Third Series. 12s. Fourth Series. 12s. 6d.

THE GROWTH OF THE ENGLISH CONSTITUTION FROM THE EARLIEST TIMES. 5th Ed. Cr. 8vo. 5s.

GREEN.—Works by JOHN RICHARD GREEN, LL.D.

*A SHORT HISTORY OF THE ENGLISH PEOPLE. Cr. 8vo. 8s. 6d.

*Also in Four Parts. With Analysis. Crown 8vo. 3s. each. Part I. 607-1265. Part II. 1204-1553. Part III. 1540-1689. Part IV. 1660-1873. Illustrated Edition. 8vo. Monthly parts 1s. net. Part I. Oct. 1891.

HISTORY OF THE ENGLISH PEOPLE. In four vols. 8vo. 16s. each.
Vol. I.—Early England, 449-1071; Foreign Kings, 1071-1214; The Charter, 1214-1291; The Parliament, 1307-1461. 8 Maps.
Vol. II.—The Monarchy, 1461-1540; The Reformation, 1540-1603.
Vol. III.—Puritan England, 1603-1660; The Revolution, 1660-1688. 4 Maps.
Vol. IV.—The Revolution, 1688-1760; Modern England, 1760-1815.

THE MAKING OF ENGLAND, **449-829.** With Maps. 8vo. 16s.

THE CONQUEST OF ENGLAND, 758-1071. With Maps and Portrait. **8vo. 18s.**

*ANALYSIS OF ENGLISH HISTORY, based on Green's "Short History of the English People." By C. W. A. TAIT, M.A. Crown **8vo. 4s.** 6d.

*READINGS IN ENGLISH HISTORY. Selected by J. R. GREEN. Three Parts. Gl. 8vo. 1s. 6d. each. I. Hengist to Cressy. II. Cressy to Cromwell. III. Cromwell to Balaklava.

GUEST.—LECTURES ON THE HISTORY OF ENGLAND. By M. J. GUEST. With Maps. Cr. 8vo. 6s.

*HISTORICAL COURSE FOR SCHOOLS.—Edited by E. A. FREEMAN. 18mo.
GENERAL SKETCH OF EUROPEAN HISTORY. By E. A. FREEMAN. 3s. **6d.**
HISTORY OF ENGLAND. By EDITH THOMPSON. 2s. 6d.
HISTORY OF SCOTLAND. By MARGARET MACARTHUR. 2s.
HISTORY OF ITALY. By Rev. W. HUNT, M.A. 3s. 6d.
HISTORY OF GERMANY. By J. SIME, M.A. 3s.
HISTORY OF AMERICA. By JOHN A. DOYLE. 4s. 6d.
HISTORY OF EUROPEAN COLONIES. By E. J. PAYNE, M.A. 4s. 6d.
HISTORY OF FRANCE. By CHARLOTTE M. YONGE. 3s. 6d.

*HISTORY PRIMERS.—Edited by JOHN RICHARD GREEN, LL.D. 18mo. 1s. each.
ROME. By Bishop CREIGHTON.
GREECE. By C. A. FYFFE, M.A., late Fellow of University College, Oxford.
EUROPE. By E. A. FREEMAN, D.C.L.
FRANCE. By CHARLOTTE M. YONGE.
ROMAN ANTIQUITIES. By Prof. WILKINS, Litt.D. Illustrated.
GREEK ANTIQUITIES. By Rev. J. P. MAHAFFY, D.D. Illustrated.
GEOGRAPHY. By Sir G. GROVE, D.C.L. Maps.
CLASSICAL GEOGRAPHY. By H. F. TOZER, M.A.
ENGLAND. By ARABELLA B. BUCKLEY. [In preparation.
ANALYSIS OF ENGLISH HISTORY. By Prof. T. F. TOUT, M.A.
INDIAN HISTORY: ASIATIC AND EUROPEAN. By J. TALBOYS WHEELER.

HOLE.—A GENEALOGICAL STEMMA OF THE KINGS OF ENGLAND AND FRANCE. By Rev. C. HOLE. On Sheet. 1s.

JENNINGS.—CHRONOLOGICAL TABLES OF ANCIENT HISTORY. By Rev. A. C. JENNINGS. 8vo. 5s.

LABBERTON.—NEW HISTORICAL ATLAS AND GENERAL HISTORY. By R. H. LABBERTON. 4to. 15s.

LETHBRIDGE.—A SHORT MANUAL OF THE HISTORY OF INDIA. With an Account of INDIA AS IT IS. By Sir ROPER LETHBRIDGE. Cr. 8vo. 5s.

HISTORY—ART

MACMILLAN'S HISTORY READERS. Adapted to the New Code, 1891. Cr. 8vo. Standard III. 1s. Standard IV. 1s. 3d. Standard V. 1s. 6d. [Standard VI. 1s. 6d. *in preparation.*

MAHAFFY.—GREEK LIFE AND THOUGHT FROM THE AGE OF ALEXANDER TO THE ROMAN CONQUEST. (*See* Classics, p. 12.)
THE **GREEK WORLD** UNDER ROMAN SWAY. (*See* Classics, **p. 13.**)
PROBLEMS IN GREEK HISTORY. (*See* Classics, p. 13.)

MARRIOTT.—THE MAKERS OF MODERN ITALY: MAZZINI, CAVOUR, GARIBALDI. By J. A. R. MARRIOTT, M.A. Cr. 8vo. 1s. 6d.

MICHELET.—A SUMMARY OF MODERN HISTORY. By M. MICHELET. Translated by M. C. M. SIMPSON. Gl. 8vo. 4s. 6d.

NORGATE.—ENGLAND UNDER THE ANGEVIN KINGS. By KATE NORGATE. With Maps and Plans. 2 vols. 8vo. 32s.

OTTÉ.—SCANDINAVIAN HISTORY. By E. C OTTÉ. With Maps. Gl. 8vo. 6s.

SEELEY.—THE EXPANSION OF ENGLAND. By J. R. SEELEY, M.A., Regius Professor of Modern History in the University of Cambridge. Cr. 8vo. 4s. 6d.
OUR COLONIAL EXPANSION. Extracts from the above. Cr. 8vo. Sewed. 1s.

SEWELL and YONGE.—EUROPEAN HISTORY. Selections from the Best Authorities. Edited by E. M. SEWELL and C. M. YONGE. Cr. 8vo. First Series, 1003–1154. 6s. Second Series, 1088–1228. 6s.

*TAIT.—**ANALYSIS** OF ENGLISH HISTORY. (*See* under Green, p. 42.)

WHEELER.—Works by J. TALBOYS WHEELER.
*A PRIMER OF INDIAN HISTORY. 18mo. 1s.
*COLLEGE HISTORY OF INDIA. With Maps. Cr. 8vo. 3s.; sewed, 2s. 6d.
A SHORT HISTORY OF INDIA AND OF THE FRONTIER STATES OF AFGHANISTAN, NEPAUL, AND BURMA. With Maps. Cr. 8vo. 12s.

YONGE.—Works by CHARLOTTE M. YONGE.
CAMEOS FROM ENGLISH HISTORY. Ex. fcap. 8vo. 5s. each. (1) From Rollo to Edward II. (2) The Wars in France. (3) The Wars of the Roses. (4) Reformation Times. (5) England and Spain. (6) Forty Years of Stewart Rule (1603–1643). (7) Rebellion and Restoration (1642–1678).
THE VICTORIAN HALF CENTURY. Cr. 8vo. 1s. 6d.; sewed, 1s.

ART.

*ANDERSON.—LINEAR PERSPECTIVE AND MODEL DRAWING. With Questions and Exercises. By LAURENCE ANDERSON. Illustrated. 8vo. 2s.

COLLIER.—A PRIMER OF ART. By Hon. JOHN COLLIER. 18mo. 1s.

COOK.—THE NATIONAL GALLERY, A POPULAR HANDBOOK TO. By E. T. COOK, with preface by Mr. RUSKIN, and Selections from his Writings. 3d Ed. Cr. 8vo. Half-mor., 14s. Large Paper Edition. 2 vols. 8vo.

DELAMOTTE.—A BEGINNER'S DRAWING BOOK. By P. H. DELAMOTTE, F.S.A. Progressively **arranged.** Cr. **8vo. 3s.** 6d.

ELLIS.—SKETCHING FROM NATURE. A Handbook. By TRISTRAM J. ELLIS. Illustrated by H. STACY MARKS, R.A., and the Author. Cr. 8vo. 3s. 6d.

GROVE.—A DICTIONARY OF MUSIC AND MUSICIANS. 1450–1889. Edited by Sir GEORGE GROVE. Four vols. 8vo. 21s. each. INDEX. 7s. 6d.

HUNT.—TALKS ABOUT ART. By WILLIAM HUNT. Cr. 8vo. 3s. 6d.

MELDOLA.—THE CHEMISTRY OF PHOTOGRAPHY. By RAPHAEL MELDOLA, F.R.S., Professor of Chemistry in the Technical College, Finsbury. Cr. 8vo. 6s.

TAYLOR.—A PRIMER OF PIANOFORTE-PLAYING. By F. TAYLOR. 18mo. 1s.

TAYLOR.—A SYSTEM OF SIGHT-SINGING FROM THE ESTABLISHED MUSICAL NOTATION; based on the Principle of Tonic Relation. By SEDLEY TAYLOR, M.A. 8vo. 5s. net.

TYRWHITT.—OUR SKETCHING CLUB. Letters and Studies on Landscape Art. By Rev. R. St. John Tyrwhitt. With reproductions of the Lessons and Woodcuts in Mr. Ruskin's "Elements of Drawing." Cr. 8vo. 7s. 6d.

DIVINITY.

The Bible; History of the Christian Church; The Church of England; The Fathers; Hymnology.

THE BIBLE.

History of the Bible.—THE ENGLISH BIBLE; A Critical History of the various English Translations. By Prof. John Eadie. 2 vols. 8vo. 28s.
 THE BIBLE IN THE CHURCH. By Right Rev. B. F. Westcott, Bishop of Durham. 10th Ed. 18mo. 4s. 6d.

Biblical History.—BIBLE LESSONS. By Rev. E. A. Abbott. Cr. 8vo. 4s. 6d.
 SIDE-LIGHTS ON BIBLE HISTORY. By Mrs. Sydney Buxton. [*In the Press.*
 STORIES FROM THE BIBLE. By Rev. A. J. Church. Illustrated. Cr. 8vo. 2 parts. 3s. 6d. each.
 *BIBLE READINGS SELECTED FROM THE PENTATEUCH AND THE BOOK OF JOSHUA. By Rev. J. A. Cross. Gl. 8vo. 2s. 6d.
 *THE CHILDREN'S TREASURY OF BIBLE STORIES. By Mrs. H. Gaskoin. 18mo. 1s. each. Part I. Old Testament. Part II. New Testament. Part III. The Apostles.
 *A CLASS-BOOK OF OLD TESTAMENT HISTORY. By Rev. G. F. Maclear, D.D. 18mo. 4s. 6d.
 *A CLASS-BOOK OF NEW TESTAMENT HISTORY. 18mo. 5s. 6d.
 *A SHILLING BOOK OF OLD TESTAMENT HISTORY. 18mo. 1s.
 *A SHILLING BOOK OF NEW TESTAMENT HISTORY. 18mo. 1s.
 *SCRIPTURE READINGS FOR SCHOOLS AND FAMILIES. By C. M. Yonge. Globe 8vo. 1s. 6d. each; also with comments, 3s. 6d. each. Genesis to Deuteronomy. Joshua to Solomon. Kings and the Prophets. The Gospel Times. Apostolic Times.

The Old Testament.—THE PATRIARCHS AND LAWGIVERS OF THE OLD TESTAMENT. By F. D. Maurice. 7th Ed. Cr. 8vo. 4s. 6d.
 THE PROPHETS AND KINGS OF THE OLD TESTAMENT. By the same. Cr. 8vo. 6s.
 THE CANON OF THE OLD TESTAMENT. By Rev. H. E. Ryle, Hulsean Professor of Divinity in the University of Cambridge. Cr. 8vo. 6s.

The Pentateuch.—AN HISTORICO-CRITICAL INQUIRY INTO THE ORIGIN AND COMPOSITION OF THE HEXATEUCH (PENTATEUCH AND BOOK OF JOSHUA). By Prof. A. Kuenen. Trans. by P. H. Wicksteed, M.A. 8vo. 14s.

The Psalms.—THE PSALMS CHRONOLOGICALLY ARRANGED. By Four Friends. Cr. 8vo. 5s. net.
 GOLDEN TREASURY PSALTER. Student's Edition of above. 18mo. 3s. 6d.
 THE PSALMS, WITH INTRODUCTION AND NOTES. By A. C. Jennings, M.A., and W. H. Lowe, M.A. 2 vols. Cr. 8vo. 10s. 6d. each.
 INTRODUCTION TO THE STUDY AND USE OF THE PSALMS. By Rev. J. F. Thrupp. 2d Ed. 2 vols. 8vo. 21s.

Isaiah.—ISAIAH XL.-LXVI. With the Shorter Prophecies allied to it. Edited by Matthew Arnold. Cr. 8vo. 5s.
 ISAIAH OF JERUSALEM. In the Authorised English Version, with Introduction and Notes. By the same. Cr. 8vo. 4s. 6d.

BIBLE

A BIBLE-READING FOR SCHOOLS,—THE GREAT PROPHECY OF ISRAEL'S RESTORATION (Isaiah, Chapters xl.-lxvi.) Arranged and Edited for Young Learners. By the same. 18mo. 1s.

COMMENTARY ON THE BOOK OF ISAIAH: CRITICAL, HISTORICAL, AND PROPHETICAL; including a Revised English Translation. By T. R. BIRKS. 2d Ed. 8vo. 12s. 6d.

THE BOOK OF ISAIAH CHRONOLOGICALLY ARRANGED. By T. K. CHEYNE. Cr. 8vo. 7s. 6d.

Zechariah.—THE **HEBREW** STUDENT'S **COMMENTARY ON ZECHARIAH**, HEBREW AND LXX. By W. H. LOWE, M.A. 8vo. 10s. 6d.

The New Testament.—THE NEW TESTAMENT. Essay on the Right Estimation of MS. Evidence in the Text of the New Testament. By T. R. BIRKS. Cr. 8vo. 3s. 6d.

THE MESSAGES OF THE BOOKS. Discourses and Notes on the Books of the New Testament. By Archd. FARRAR. 8vo. 14s.

THE CLASSICAL ELEMENT IN THE NEW TESTAMENT. Considered as a proof of its Genuineness, with an Appendix on the Oldest Authorities used in the Formation of the Canon. By C. H. HOOLE. 8vo. 10s. 6d.

ON A FRESH REVISION OF THE ENGLISH NEW TESTAMENT. With an Appendix on the Last Petition of the Lord's Prayer. By Bishop LIGHTFOOT. Cr. 8vo. 7s. 6d.

THE UNITY OF THE NEW TESTAMENT. By F. D. MAURICE. 2 vols. Cr. 8vo. 12s.

A COMPANION TO THE GREEK TESTAMENT AND THE ENGLISH VERSION. By PHILIP SCHAFF, D.D. Cr. 8vo. 12s.

A GENERAL SURVEY OF THE HISTORY OF THE CANON OF THE NEW TESTAMENT DURING THE FIRST FOUR CENTURIES. By Bishop WESTCOTT. Cr. 8vo. 10s. 6d.

THE NEW TESTAMENT IN THE ORIGINAL GREEK. The Text revised by Bishop WESTCOTT, D.D., and Prof. F. J. A. HORT, D.D. 2 vols. Cr. 8vo. 10s. 6d. each. Vol. I. Text. Vol. II. Introduction and Appendix.

SCHOOL EDITION OF THE ABOVE. 18mo, 4s. 6d.; 18mo, roan, 5s. 6d.; morocco, gilt edges, 6s. 6d.

The Gospels.—THE COMMON TRADITION OF THE SYNOPTIC GOSPELS, in the Text of the Revised Version. By Rev. E. A. ABBOTT and W. G. RUSHBROOKE. Cr. 8vo. 3s. 6d.

SYNOPTICON: AN EXPOSITION OF THE COMMON MATTER OF THE SYNOPTIC GOSPELS. By W. G. RUSHBROOKE. Printed in Colours. In six Parts, and Appendix. 4to. Part I. 3s. 6d. Parts II. and III. 7s. Parts IV. V. and VI., with Indices, 10s. 6d. Appendices, 10s. 6d. Complete in 1 vol. 35s. *Indispensable to a Theological Student.*

INTRODUCTION TO THE STUDY OF THE FOUR GOSPELS. By Bishop WESTCOTT. Cr. 8vo. 10s. 6d.

THE COMPOSITION OF THE FOUR GOSPELS. By Rev. ARTHUR WRIGHT. Cr. 8vo. 5s.

The Gospel according to St. Matthew.—THE GREEK TEXT. With Introduction and Notes by Rev. A. SLOMAN. Fcap. 8vo. 2s. 6d.

CHOICE NOTES ON ST. MATTHEW. Drawn from Old and New Sources. Cr. 8vo. 4s. 6d. (St. Matthew and St. Mark in 1 vol. 9s.)

The Gospel according to St. Mark.—*SCHOOL READINGS IN THE GREEK TESTAMENT. Being the Outlines of the Life of our Lord as given by St. Mark, with additions from the Text of the other Evangelists. Edited, with Notes and Vocabulary, by Rev. A. CALVERT, M.A. Fcap. 8vo. 2s. 6d.

CHOICE NOTES ON ST. MARK. Drawn from Old and New Sources. Cr. 8vo. 4s. 6d. (St. Matthew and St. Mark in 1 vol. 9s.)

DIVINITY

The Gospel according to St. Luke.—THE GREEK TEXT, with Introduction and Notes by Rev. J. BOND, M.A. Fcap. 8vo. 2s. 6d.

CHOICE NOTES ON ST. LUKE. Drawn from Old and New Sources. Cr. 8vo. 4s. 6d.

THE GOSPEL OF THE KINGDOM OF HEAVEN. A Course of Lectures on the Gospel of St. Luke. By F. D. MAURICE. Cr. 8vo. 6s.

The Gospel according to St. John.—THE GOSPEL OF ST. JOHN. By F. D. MAURICE. 8th Ed. Cr. 8vo. 6s.

CHOICE NOTES ON ST. JOHN. Drawn from Old and New Sources. Cr. 8vo. 4s. 6d.

The Acts of the Apostles.—*THE GREEK TEXT, with Notes by T. E. PAGE, M.A. Fcap. 8vo. 3s. 6d.

THE CHURCH OF THE FIRST DAYS. THE CHURCH OF JERUSALEM, THE CHURCH OF THE GENTILES, THE CHURCH OF THE WORLD. Lectures on the Acts of the Apostles. By Very Rev. C. J. VAUGHAN. Cr. 8vo. 10s. 6d.

The Epistles of St. Paul.—THE EPISTLE TO THE ROMANS. The Greek Text, with English Notes. By the Very Rev. C. J. VAUGHAN. 7th Ed. Cr. 8vo. 7s. 6d.

THE EPISTLES TO THE CORINTHIANS. Greek Text, with Commentary. By Rev. W. KAY. 8vo. 9s.

THE EPISTLE TO THE GALATIANS. A Revised Text, with Introduction, Notes, and Dissertations. By Bishop LIGHTFOOT. 10th Ed. 8vo. 12s.

THE EPISTLE TO THE PHILIPPIANS. A Revised Text, with Introduction, Notes, and Dissertations. By the same. 8vo. 12s.

THE EPISTLE TO THE PHILIPPIANS. With Translation, Paraphrase, and Notes for English Readers. By Very Rev. C. J. VAUGHAN. Cr. 8vo. 5s.

THE EPISTLE TO THE COLOSSIANS AND TO PHILEMON. A Revised Text, with Introductions, etc. By Bishop LIGHTFOOT. 9th Ed. 8vo. 12s.

THE EPISTLES TO THE EPHESIANS, THE COLOSSIANS, AND PHILEMON. With Introduction and Notes. By Rev. J. LL. DAVIES. 8vo. 7s. 6d.

THE FIRST EPISTLE TO THE THESSALONIANS. By Very Rev. C. J. VAUGHAN. 8vo. Sewed, 1s. 6d.

THE EPISTLES TO THE THESSALONIANS. Commentary on the Greek Text. By Prof. JOHN EADIE. 8vo. 12s.

The Epistle of St. James.—THE GREEK TEXT, with Introduction and Notes. By Rev. JOSEPH MAYOR. 8vo. [*In the Press.*

The Epistles of St. John.—THE EPISTLES OF ST. JOHN. By F. D. MAURICE. 4th Ed. Cr. 8vo. 6s.

THE GREEK TEXT, with Notes. By Bishop WESTCOTT. 2d Ed. 8vo. 12s. 6d.

The Epistle to the Hebrews.—GREEK AND ENGLISH. Edited by Rev. F. RENDALL. Cr. 8vo. 6s.

ENGLISH TEXT, with Commentary. By the same. Cr. 8vo. 7s. 6d.

THE GREEK TEXT, with Notes. By Very Rev. C. J. VAUGHAN. Cr. 8vo. 7s. 6d.

THE GREEK TEXT, with Notes and Essays. By Bishop WESTCOTT. 8vo. 14s.

Revelation.—LECTURES ON THE APOCALYPSE. By F. D. MAURICE. 2d Ed. Cr. 8vo. 6s.

THE REVELATION OF ST. JOHN. By Prof. W. MILLIGAN. Cr. 8vo. 7s. 6d.

LECTURES ON THE APOCALYPSE. By the same. Cr. 8vo. 5s.

LECTURES ON THE REVELATION OF ST. JOHN. By Very Rev. C. J. VAUGHAN. 5th Ed. Cr. 8vo. 10s. 6d.

WRIGHT.—THE BIBLE WORD-BOOK. By W. ALDIS WRIGHT. Cr. 8vo. 7s. 6d.

HISTORY OF THE CHRISTIAN CHURCH.

CUNNINGHAM.—THE GROWTH OF THE CHURCH IN ITS ORGANISATION AND INSTITUTIONS. By Rev. JOHN CUNNINGHAM. 8vo. 9s.

CUNNINGHAM.—THE CHURCHES OF ASIA: A METHODICAL SKETCH OF THE SECOND CENTURY. By Rev. WILLIAM CUNNINGHAM. Cr. 8vo. 6s.

DALE.—THE SYNOD OF ELVIRA, AND CHRISTIAN LIFE IN THE FOURTH CENTURY. By A. W. W. DALE. Cr. 8vo. 10s. 6d.

HARDWICK.—Works by Archdeacon HARDWICK.
  A HISTORY OF THE CHRISTIAN CHURCH: MIDDLE AGE. Edited by Bishop STUBBS. Cr. 8vo. 10s. 6d.
  A HISTORY OF THE CHRISTIAN CHURCH DURING THE REFORMATION. 9th Ed., revised by Bishop STUBBS. Cr. 8vo. 10s. 6d.

HORT.—TWO DISSERTATIONS. 1. ON ΜΟΝΟΓΕΝΗΣ ΘΕΟΣ IN SCRIPTURE AND TRADITION. II. ON THE "CONSTANTINOPOLITAN" CREED AND OTHER CREEDS OF THE FOURTH CENTURY. 8vo. 7s. 6d.

KILLEN.—ECCLESIASTICAL HISTORY OF IRELAND, from the earliest date to the present time. By W. D. KILLEN. 2 vols. 8vo. 25s.

SIMPSON.—AN EPITOME OF THE HISTORY OF THE CHRISTIAN CHURCH. By Rev. W. SIMPSON. 7th Ed. Fcap. 8vo. 3s. 6d.

VAUGHAN.—THE CHURCH OF THE FIRST DAYS: THE CHURCH OF JERUSALEM, THE CHURCH OF THE GENTILES, THE CHURCH OF THE WORLD.' By Very Rev. C. J. VAUGHAN. Cr. 8vo. 10s. 6d.

THE CHURCH OF ENGLAND.

BENHAM.—A COMPANION TO THE LECTIONARY. By Rev. W. BENHAM, B.D. Cr. 8vo. 4s. 6d.

COLENSO.—THE COMMUNION SERVICE FROM THE BOOK OF COMMON PRAYER. With Select Readings from the Writings of the Rev. F. D. MAURICE. Edited by Bishop COLENSO. 6th Ed. 16mo. 2s. 6d.

MACLEAR.—Works by Rev. G. F. MACLEAR, D.D.
  *A CLASS-BOOK OF THE CATECHISM OF THE CHURCH OF ENGLAND. 18mo. 1s. 6d.
  *A FIRST CLASS-BOOK OF THE CATECHISM OF THE CHURCH OF ENGLAND. 18mo. 6d.
  THE ORDER OF CONFIRMATION. With Prayers and Devotions. 32mo. 6d.
  FIRST COMMUNION. With Prayers and Devotions for the newly Confirmed. 32mo. 6d.
  *A MANUAL OF INSTRUCTION FOR CONFIRMATION AND FIRST COMMUNION. With Prayers and Devotions. 32mo. 2s.
  *AN INTRODUCTION TO THE CREEDS. 18mo. 3s. 6d.
  AN INTRODUCTION TO THE THIRTY-NINE ARTICLES. [In the Press.

PROCTER.—A HISTORY OF THE BOOK OF COMMON PRAYER. By Rev. F. PROCTER. 18th Ed. Cr. 8vo. 10s. 6d.

*PROCTER—MACLEAR.—AN ELEMENTARY INTRODUCTION TO THE BOOK OF COMMON PRAYER. By Rev. F. PROCTER and Rev. G. F. MACLEAR, D.D. 18mo. 2s. 6d.

VAUGHAN.—TWELVE DISCOURSES ON SUBJECTS CONNECTED WITH THE LITURGY AND WORSHIP OF THE CHURCH OF ENGLAND. By Very Rev. C. J. VAUGHAN. Fcap. 8vo. 6s.

THE FATHERS.

CUNNINGHAM.—THE EPISTLE OF ST. BARNABAS. Its Date and Authorship. With Greek Text, Latin Version, Translation, and Commentary. By Rev. W. CUNNINGHAM. Cr. 8vo. 7s. 6d.

DIVINITY

DONALDSON.—THE APOSTOLIC FATHERS. A Critical Account of **their Genuine Writings**, and of their Doctrines. By Prof. JAMES DONALDSON. 2d Ed. Cr. 8vo. 7s. 6d.

LIGHTFOOT.—THE APOSTOLIC FATHERS. Revised Texts, with Introductions, Notes, Dissertations, and Translations. By Bishop LIGHTFOOT. Part I. ST. CLEMENT OF ROME. 2 vols. 8vo. 32s. Part II. ST. IGNATIUS TO ST. POLYCARP. 2d Ed. 3 vols. 8vo. 48s.

THE APOSTOLIC FATHERS. Abridged Edition. **With short Introductions, Greek Text,** and English Translation. **By** the same. **8vo. 16s.**

HYMNOLOGY.

PALGRAVE.—ORIGINAL HYMNS. By Prof. F. T. PALGRAVE. 18mo. 1s. 6d.

SELBORNE.—THE BOOK OF PRAISE. By ROUNDELL, EARL OF SELBORNE. 18mo. 2s. 6d. net.

A HYMNAL. Chiefly from "The Book of Praise." A. Royal 32mo, limp. **6d.** B. 18mo, larger type. 1s. C. Fine Paper. 1s. 6d. With Music, Selected, Harmonised, and Composed by JOHN HULLAH. 18mo. 3s. 6d.

WOODS.—HYMNS FOR SCHOOL WORSHIP. By M. A. WOODS. 18mo. 1s. 6d.

www.ingramcontent.com/pod-product-compliance
Lightning Source LLC
Chambersburg PA
CBHW032027220426
43664CB00006B/392